Reading David Hume's "Of the Standard of Taste"

Reading David Hume's "Of the Standard of Taste"

Edited by
Babette Babich

DE GRUYTER

ISBN 978-3-11-058564-3
e-ISBN (PDF) 978-3-11-058557-5
e-ISBN (EPUB) 978-3-11-058550-6

Library of Congress Control Number: 2018962692

Bibliographic information published by the Deutsche Nationalbibliothek
The Deutsche Nationalbibliothek lists this publication in the Deutsche Nationalbibliografie;
detailed bibliographic data are available on the Internet at http://dnb.dnb.de.

© 2020 Walter de Gruyter GmbH, Berlin/Boston
This volume is text- and page-identical with the hardback published in 2019.
Printing and binding: CPI books GmbH, Leck
Cover image: Jan Vermeer van Delft (1632-1675), The Glass of Wine. WikimediaCommons, Public Domain.

www.degruyter.com

Acknowledgments

There are as many, if not more debts accumulated in the course of editing a collective volume than in the writing of a monograph. Many of these debts are elliptical ones which makes them no less urgent or real, even debts to what is, apparently, absent: in this case, referring to missing chapters both with respect to Hume's original plans to publish Five Dissertations (reduced in the end to four) and with respect to the missing chapters in this volume. The current volume was conceived to address concerns related to this absence and that also means that it is dedicated not to settling questions, as in many book collections that mean to be definitive or ultimate but rather to inspiring further discussion.

Hume is a key name in aesthetics and philosophy of art, especially in university courses. Here, I am grateful to my students on every level at Fordham University, undergraduate and graduate, as well as the students at Fordham's College at 60 – Fordham's Lincoln Center campus being located at the intersection of 60th Street and Columbus Avenue in New York City – as well as to my students at the School of Visual Arts and at Juilliard where I have also had productive discussions with faculty, including Tom Huhn. I am especially grateful to the late Peter Kivy who corresponded with me about this project in addition to the late Annette Baier. I thank Emilio Mazza and Roger Scruton in very different ways for correspondence and personal engagement. There were other scholars I had hoped to have on board as contributors to this book which technical issues prevented. I thank them for their inspiration.

I thank Christoph Schirmer and I am also grateful to Anett Rehner and to Tim Vogel at de Gruyter.

Thanks to the British Museum for providing the image used in Babette Babich's "Editor's Introduction" of the illuminated version of Albrecht Dürer, *Allegorie der Beredsamkeit*.

Thanks are due to the *British Journal of Aesthetics* for permission to reprint Peter Kivy's "Hume's Standard of Taste: Breaking the Circle."

The editors of *Hume Studies* graciously allowed the reprinting of Christopher MacLachlan: "Hume and the Standard of Taste," *Hume Studies*.

Oxford University Press granted permission to reprint a selection from Roger Scruton's *Beauty* (Oxford: Oxford University Press, 2012).

Permission from the editors of *The Journal of Aesthetics and Art Criticism* is gratefully acknowledged to reprint Roger Shiner's chapter, "Hume and the Causal Theory of Taste."

Thanks to Penn State University Press for permission to reprint Carolyn Korsmeyer's chapter, "Gendered Concepts and Hume's Standard of Taste," from

Peggy Zeglin Brand and Carolyn Korsmeyer (Eds.) *Feminism and Tradition in Aesthetics* (State College: Penn State University Press, 1994).

Taylor and Francis Group granted permission to use the final chapter from Dabney Townsend, *Taste and Sentiment* (London: Routledge, 2001).

Wiley granted permission to reprint selections of a chapter, "Taste and Civil Society" from Howard Caygill's *Art of Judgment* (Oxford: Blackwell, 1989).

SUNY Press generously granted permission to reprint a chapter from Bernard Freydberg's book, *David Hume: Platonic Philosopher, Continental Ancestor* (Albany: State University of New York Press, 2012).

Table of Contents

I Editor's Introduction

Babette Babich
Signatures and Taste: Hume's Mortal Leavings and Lucian —— 3

II "Of the Standard of Taste"

David Hume
Of the Standard of Taste —— 25

III Of Taste and Standards

Peter Kivy
Hume's Standard of Taste: Breaking the Circle —— 43

Christopher MacLachlan
Hume and the Standard of Taste —— 53

Roger Scruton
Taste and Order —— 67

Timothy M. Costelloe
General Rules and Hume's "Of the Standard of Taste" —— 77

Carolyn Korsmeyer
Gendered Concepts and Hume's Standard of Taste —— 97

IV Causal Theory and the Problem, Dispositional Critique and the Classic

Roger A. Shiner
Hume and the Causal Theory of Taste —— 117

Dabney Townsend
The Problem of a Standard of Taste —— 133

Howard Caygill
Taste and Civil Society —— 177

Babette Babich
Nietzsche's Aesthetic Science and Hume's Standard of Taste —— 213

V Comparisons, Art, Anatomies

Andrej Démuth and Slávka Démuthová
The Comparison as the Standardization of Aesthetic Norms —— 249

Bernard Freydberg
Plato and Hume's Philosophy of Art —— 263

Emilio Mazza
"Cloathing the Parts again": The Ghost of the Treatise in the Standard of Taste —— 281

Notes on Contributors —— 301

Research and Citation Bibliography —— 305

Subject Index —— 323

Name Index —— 329

Editor's Introduction

Babette Babich
Signatures and Taste: Hume's Mortal Leavings and Lucian

> Νᾶφε καὶ μέμνασο ἀπιστεῖν
> [Stay sober and remember not to believe.]
> — Epicharmus / David Hume[1]

Of Books and Signatures

In his introduction to his collection of David Hume's essays, Alasdair MacIntyre writes what surely wins the palm for an introductory first sentence to a book collection: "An introduction should introduce."[2] The point is elegant and MacIntyre is compelled to explain: "It should not be an attempt at a substitute for the book it is introducing."

In the essayistic case of David Hume's essays, and collections of the same, of which there are a number, Hume's essays speak for themselves, that is to say, apart from an 'advertisement,' without an editor's introduction. Additionally, there is a tradition of scholarly reflection on Hume's essays as such. The current collection adds to this and hopes to inspire reflection on what is arguably the most exceptional of Hume's essays.

"Of the Standard of Taste" was written to avoid damages threatened in response to the planned publication of Hume's *Five Dissertations* (a book including: "The Natural History of Religion," "Of the Passions," "Of Tragedy," "Of Suicide," and "Of the Immortality of the Soul"). The threats were promised by William Warburton (1698–1779), the influential theologian who subsequently

---

[1] Written by David Hume on the back of his memoranda, and cited from Mossner, "Hume's Early Memoranda, 1729–40: The Complete Text," see here p. 503. Usually translated to the benefit of the tradition linking Hume and skepticism as "Keep sober and remember to be skeptical" but which translation sacrifices the injunction's negative force. Peter S. Fosl also features this epigraph in his "The Bibliographic Bases of Hume's Understanding of Sextus Empiricus and Pyrrhonism," pp. 261–278. Fosl's essay begins by claiming that the use of the hermeneutic method in understanding modern philosophy ought to be traced to Richard Popkin. Fosl's claim is not accurate and although a student of Hans-Georg Gadamer's I might wish to favor Gadamer, Martin Heidegger or, given his priority, Heinrich Rickert or even just Leo Strauss, would seemingly be more likely candidates for the title of those "first to articulate a hermeneutical approach." To be sure, Fosl's focus is analytic history of philosophy which at times misses other approaches.
[2] Alasdair MacIntyre, *Hume's Ethical Writings: Selections from David Hume*, p. 9.

went on to become Bishop of Gloucester (and dedicated Shakespeare aficionado), who guaranteed a suit for excommunication of Hume *and* his cousin (the clergyman and playwright, John Home, author of *Douglas*),³ *as well as* Hume's publisher Andrew Millar (1706–1768) were Hume's *Five Dissertations* to be published as originally designed. Millar duly urged Hume to revise the first essay and cut "Of Suicide" and "Of the Immortality of the Soul," literally slicing the final two sections from the already printed book. The three remaining essays were insufficient to make the book a book and Hume quickly composed "Of the Standard of Taste" to fill out the missing signatures, permitting the book to be published, with a new title, *Four Dissertations*.

The version of "Of the Standard of Taste" included here follows that same first publication, including punctuation, and spelling, if not to the letter – *ſ*'s and all —indicating in brackets the pagination of the original printing.⁴ But if today's extant facsimile edition claims that it brings together, in the words of James Fieser: "the long-separated essays ... united as Hume intended," this would not be entirely precise. To such an end, one would need the original five essays, in accord with Hume's original design, *less* "Of the Standard of Taste" substituted in place of the elided essays. The socio-political and theological (and legal) reasons that compelled Hume to revise "The Natural History of Religion," i.e., the first offending essay, and to exclude his final two essays were thus quite different from his reasons for including "Of the Standard of Taste," although one might well read the essay itself as a commentary on the judgment, such as it was, that necessitated the exclusions.

To retrace this history, the first volume of the doubly initialed (T.H. Green and T.H. Grose) edition of Hume's *Essays Moral, Political, and Literary*,⁵ begins with Hume's autobiographical essay⁶ together with Adam Smith's letter to William Strahan,⁷ painting a detailed account of these same complexities, represent-

---

3 The essay by Jacob Sider Jost & John Immerwahr, "Hume the Sociable Iconoclast: The Case of the Four Dissertations," is valuable on the topic of *Douglas*. See too for a more comprehensive, contextual background and for an understanding of Hume, of John Home, along with Henry Home or Lord Kames (1696–1762), Howard Caygill's comprehensive discussion in *The Art of Judgment*, a selection of which is included in his chapter below.
4 See David Hume, *Four Dissertations and Essays on Suicide & the Immortality of the Soul*. Cf. *Essays Literary, Moral, and Political by David Hume, Esq., The Historian*, beginning with "Of the Delicacy of Taste and Passion". pp. 9–11 and "Of the Standard of Taste," pp. 134–149.
5 David Hume, *Essays Moral, Political, and Literary*.
6 Hume, "On My Own Life," in: *Essays Moral, Political, and Literary*, pp. 1–8.
7 Letter from Adam Smith, LL.D., to William Strahan, Esq., in *Essays Moral, Political, and Literary*, pp. 9–14.

ed in the editors' preface, itself a piecing together of further letters, yielding "The History of the Editions." It is important to underscore that cutting the offending essays was simple. More delicate was the need to produce an exact range of additional pages – 40 pages having been cut with the loss of the two essays (38 pages) and the preface (2 pages) – such that "Of the Standard of Taste" 203–240, in addition to its own title page (L1–2), kept the book at its necessary length of 240 pages.

Here, the signatures are key (the missing signature of the essays cut corresponding to the section letter K, the replacement signature L, ending on 224, as one can still see this in the facsimile edition),[8] and if the only thing that one needs to know is that "Of the Standard of Taste" was written to order – and to printer's length – it is also essential to underline that only certain multiples of signatures make a book.

Why that should be so requires something of the contextual sensibility Hume tended to foreground in his own discussion of taste: a matter of delicacy, refined but not less scientific,[9] and not less dependent on the culture of polite society but also technical precision and convention, as the "standards" for the same. "Of the Standard of Taste" would prove to be Hume's very last philosophical essay.[10] And a relation to final things, including a philosopher's reflection on his philosophical legacy, including his contemporary reception, requires both convention and the optic of distance.

Final Essays and Last Things, or Hume and Lucian

A similarly relevant sensibility is needed for the question concerning which dialogue of Lucian's several "Dialogues of the Dead" Hume references in his final conversations with Adam Smith. The question is perhaps more esoteric than might have been necessary had one been able to assume a certain classically philological acquaintance than is in fact common among Hume scholars (or mainstream professional philosophers). But one cannot make such assumptions

---

8 Hume, *Four Dissertations and Essays on Suicide & the Immortality of the Soul*, 201. The 'L' is centered in the bottom quarter of the page. The signature runs to p. 224, with the next signature 'M' beginning on p. 225.
9 See Hume, "Of the Delicacy of Taste and Passion." For a broad thematization beyond the framework of the current discussion, see Roger L. Emerson, *Essays on David Hume, Medical Men and the Scottish Enlightenment: 'Industry, Knowledge and Humanity.'*
10 See again, as cited above, Jost and Immerwahr, "Hume the Sociable Iconoclast."

not only because of the state of professional philosophy (now nearly utterly 'analytic' which means more rather than less innocent of history) but also because Lucian, a 2nd Century C.E. Syrian satirist who was once common coin among scholars when learning Greek was standard, has become less and less well-known, an object illustration of changes in taste over time that Hume foregrounds. If taste and its deficits also correspond to "a lack of philology," as Nietzsche was fond of describing what Aristotle characterizes as "a want of learning," it is significant that the reference to Lucian was once so very standard it did not require disambiguation.

I corresponded about this with Annette Baier (1929–2012) before her own death – in the wake of her publications in both essay and book form on Hume on the question of 'last things,' including deathbed readings.[11] I also made acquaintance in the same way, via email, of the Milan Hume scholar Emilio Mazza whom Baier invokes in the same constellation.[12]

The mysteries of analytic and continental philosophy collide in this one strange node, on this one curious detail. Baier recounts her difficulties and not less her bafflement at even being asked the question, *which dialogue?* The easy solution, looking it up, sheds little light on the passage in question, as one then finds only those dialogues editors publish under the title: *Dialogues of the Dead*, such that Baier could only regard it as a puzzle that became more problematic the more she investigated it.[13] In the end, Baier would resolve the question on the side of received convention, along the way carefully exploring the ambiguous reference to the dialogue. But, from a hermeneutic perspective, the puzzle evaporates if one has read Lucian *and* if one is not hoping, as Baier seemed to be hoping, to prefer one witness (Adam Smith's account) over another (one of Hume's attending doctors, William Cullen who names the dialogue). In addition, Baier adds a bit of biographical fancy – thus I understand some of the terms of her argument – by insisting that what is at issue must correspond to Hume's own life rather than to what is recounted in the dialogue itself, as Hume details this.

Baier doubts Hume's doctor, William Cullen's, direct account in a letter written at the time of Hume's death, identifying the dialogue by name, as Lucian's

---

11 Annette Baier, "Hume's Deathbed Reading: A Tale of Three Letters," pp. 347–356 and included, in revised form in: Baier, *Death and Character: Further Reflections on Hume*.
12 Baier, "Hume's Deathbed Reading," p. 349.
13 See, again, Baier (2006), "Hume's Deathbed Reading" and *Death and Character*, pp. 100–110.

Kataplous,¹⁴ In the course of her hunt as instigated by Mazza's query, she tells us his name and later refers to Mazza again, namelessly, identifying his city of residence (Milan). A contribution by Mazza is included in this collection, albeit not directly on this theme, but which repays reading in this same connection.¹⁵ In order to preserve her interpretive scheme, and given her initial unfamiliarity with Lucian as she herself tells us, Baier makes the allusion more of a mystery than it is. On this point, we may recall Hume,

> A thousand men may have a thousand different opinions about some one thing; but just exactly one of the opinions is true, and the only difficulty is to find out which one that is.¹⁶

Smith's account gives a generic title to Lucian's quintessentially sardonic Κατάπλους ἢ Τύραννος, usually translated *The Downward Journey or The Tyrant* (in other translations the title is given as the *Journey to Hell* or *Journey into Port*), an all-purpose assault on religious persuasions, including the Greek, the Roman, the Jewish, the Christian and so on.¹⁷

As historian, Hume knew Lucian because of his aphoristic reflections on 'History.' In addition, Lucian is also the author of the tongue in cheek, Ἀληθῶν Διηγημάτων, *A True Story* or *True History*, which is also the first science-fiction story and one of the first tall tales or lying tales, – one of Lucian's epithets is 'friend of lies' corresponding to his claim that where all other authors lie when they claim the truth, he, by contrast, quite by telling the reader in advance that he is lying, is the only author who tells the truth. Hume would likely also have read Lucian's dialogues for their elegant and amusing Greek in order to recoup, as he tells us he recoups¹⁸ his knowledge of Greek. Now the present editor knows Lucian's *Kataplous* not only for the same reasons – it is great fun to read in Greek – but not less, in the context of Nietzsche scholarship, because

---

14 William Cullen to John Hunter, 17 September 1776, in James Fieser, *Early Responses to Hume, Life, and Reputations*, p. 292 and cited in Baier, *Death and Character*, p. 103.
15 As Baier underscored again, in an email communication with the editor, she likewise acknowledges in a footnote: "This essay began as an e-conversation with Emilio Mazza, initiated by him" *Death and Character*, p. 110.
16 Hume, "Of the Standard of Taste," p. 208.
17 Lucian, Volumes 1–8. Cf. Lucian, *Selected Satires of Lucian*, and see too the contributions to Martin Ebner, Holger Gzella, Heinz-Günther Nesselrath, and Ernst Ribbat (Eds.), *Philopseudeis è Apiston. Die Lügenfreunde oder: Der Ungläubige* as well as for a discussion of Lucian although the topic of the essay is Menippus, Joel C. Relihan, "Menippus in Antiquity and the Renaissance" along with Christopher Robinson, *Lucian and His Influence in Europe*.
18 Hume, "On My Own Life," where, to be sure, he does not specifically refer to Lucian but just where the great ubiquity of Lucian had everything to do with both the purity of this Syrian's Greek and its pedagogic value.

Nietzsche draws on this dialogue for his very complex conception of his *Übermensch*, echoing both Lucian's parodic sense of the term as it also recalls Goethe's ironic invocation at the start of *Faust* as expressed in the mouth of the *Erdgeist*.[19] Nietzsche plays on this parodic sense fairly in the way Adam Smith celebrates David Hume's goodness as a human being by contrast with more churchly sensibilities.[20]

To consider this, an illustration can be helpful of another of Lucian's dialogues, *Heracles*. Dürer's allegory of eloquence features the central character, Hermes, dressed as Ogmios, the *Celtic* Hercules, ordinarily represented as an elderly figure.

Dürer opts for a less feeble and more youthful Hermes, representing the go-between between the human and the divine, the world of the living and the realm of the dead, complete with thickly feathered winged boots, but outfitted with the rest of the attributes of Ogmios/Heracles, not only the dress of "lion's skin"[21], following Lucian's description, but also dragging after him

> a great crowd of men who are all tethered by the ears! His leashes are delicate chains fashioned of gold and amber, resembling the prettiest of necklaces. Yet though led by bonds so weak they do not pull back at all or brace their feet … But let me tell you the strangest thing of all … the ends of the chains … [are pierced through] the tip of his tongue and [whereby the painter] represented him as drawing the men by that means. Moreover, he has his face turned towards his captives, and is smiling.[22]

Lucian continues, underscoring the source of his account as taken directly from the mouth of "a Celt at my elbow": for the Celts, we are told, the old Ogmios is a better candidate for eloquence than the youthful and fit Hermes, as eloquence is mightier than muscular force, moving its objects to comply willingly and represented by an old man, as age increases persuasive prowess where it withers other youthful capacities.[23]

---

19 Johann Wolfgang von Goethe, *Faust, Volume 1 and 2*, p. 19. See further, Babich, "Heidegger and Hölderlin on Aether and Life," p. 116.
20 Babich, "Nietzsche's Zarathustra and Parodic Style: On Lucian's *Hyperanthropos* and Nietzsche's *Übermensch*," pp. 58–74 and via Empedocles (and Hölderlin's recognition of political modernity and the still present dangers of tyranny), "Nietzsche's Zarathustra, Nietzsche's Empedocles: The Time of Kings" pp. 157–174.
21 Lucian, "Heracles," Volume 1, p. 63.
22 Lucian, "Heracles," Volume 1, p. 65.
23 Instructively this is a syncretistic – very fitting in the case of Lucian – representation of Hermes as Ogmios in Lucian's dialogue: *Hercules*. See for a summary of Lucian's description in addition to further references of which there are many, even beyond the listing provided here, and including patent connections with Hume, Jaś Elsner's chapter "Discourses of Style:

Figure 1: Albrecht Dürer, *Allegorie auf die Beredsamkeit (Hermes mit vier irdischen Gestalten: Frau, Krieger, Gelehrter und Bürger)* [*Allegory of Eloquence (Hermes with four earthly figures: woman, knight, scholar, citizen)*]. (1514) Wien Kunsthistorisches Museum. Color version courtesy of the British Museum. Public domain.

Dürer's allegory of rhetoric depicts Lucian's Hermes not only as leading his captives by the ear, chained with amber and gold chains piercing his own tongue, but as psychogogue: leading or guiding souls on their journey in this world and beyond it.²⁴ It is as *pychopompos*, that Hermes appears in several of

---

Pausanias and Lucian," in his *Roman Eyes: Visuality & Subjectivity in Art & Text*, pp. 49–66. The tradition is a long standing one, see in French, F. Le Roux, "Les dieux celtiques aux liens: de l'Ogmios de Lucien à l'Ogmios de Dürer," pp. 209–234 as well as for discussion and further references, also Anne-Marie Favreau-Lindner, "Lucien et le mythe de 'Ηρακλῆς ὁ λόγος" in: Malika Bastin-Hammou, ed., *Kaina pragmata: mélanges offerts à Jean-Claude Carrière*, pp. 155–168. See too with respect to the artist's own image, Moritz Thausing, *Dürer: Geschichte seines Lebens und seiner Kunst, mit Illustrationen und Titelkupfer*, Vol. 1 on the cult of Mercury/Hermes, p. 297.
24 Additional studies connect Hume and Lucian with a death cult, not via the *Kataplous* and one analytically minded author strangely dismisses Annette Baier's argument but then proceeds to argue the same conclusion as she does (combining both *Kataplous* and the *Dialogues of the Dead*) albeit under a darker conventionality, see George Couvalis, "Hume's Lucianic Thanato-

Lucian's dialogues, particularly the *Kataplous*, where we may recall a key vignette, recounting the supposed 'excuses' offered to avoid being carried off to judgment, excuses contradicted by the marks left on the soul by misdeeds in life, as Rhadamanthus explains,[25] excuses given by the tyrant, the man of this-wordly power and wealth. Just these delimited protests correspond to Hume's words as Smith recounts them to us, offered to "Charon for not entering readily into his boat, [as for Hume it is not the case that] he could not find one that fitted him; he [Hume] had no house to finish, he had no daughter to provide for, he had no enemies upon whom he wished to revenge himself."[26]

Thus, the excuses instantiated are not generic: they are the excuses offered by the tyrant Megapenthes. Still what was key for Baier's puzzlement is the fact, as she observes, that the complaints are not indeed offered to Hermes [Mercury]. The point is duly repeated in the literature on the theme (including unattributed appropriations of Baier's argument)[27] but, hermeneutically speaking, as it were, any communication prior to entering the boat would perforce be via Hermes for whomsoever one might be meaning to address hoping for intercession, given Hermes as ψυχοπομπός but also just because the *Kataplous* is a Lucianic dialogue. Addresses to "lady Clotho," one of the three sisters of destiny, are in this sense and just in this particular context not less addressed to Hermes *and* Charon. Nor are these the only personages in the dialogue which is why Mycillus can chime in on just the same points as Hermes is the collector of souls, and it is this that Dürer's 1514 *Allegory of Eloquence* no less illustrates as his Hermes leads his band of souls, representing the Ogmios of Lucian's *Heracles* drawing an updated cast of personages, here depicted and as likewise variously detailed in the *Kataplous*.

The *Kataplous* is ultimately a dialogue of complaints, specifically being a litany of the laments accompanying the downward journey into that port that is the afterlife, the underworld. The tyrant, Megapenthes, has to address Hermes (even as his claim is addressed to Clotho to intercede on his behalf) as he hopes to avoid being taken on board, persuaded as he is of his importance (the shoemaker, Mycillus confirms that the tyrant had all the appearances in life of superiority,

---

therapy," pp. 327–344 as well in connection with esoteric literature and economics and including Adam Smith in addition to Arthurian studies. See also Mazza's section "Lifelong Lucian and the Irish Skyths" in his "Hume's Life, Intellectual Context and Reception" in: Alan Bailey and Dan O'Brien (Eds.), *The Continuum Companion to Hume*, pp. 20–37, here pp. 28–30.

25 "For every wicked deed that each of you has done in his life, he bears an invisible mark on his soul." Lucian, *The Downward Journey*, 47.
26 Letter from Adam Smith, LL.D., to William Strahan, 11.
27 See Couvalis, "Hume's Lucianic Thanatotherapy."

virtually superhuman [ὑπεράνθρωπος] as he seemed to him then to be), and who accordingly extensively protests being carried off, alternating bribes with threats, as he is not ready and hence ought not die.[28]

Hume's point, as Smith tells us, is that he himself could not be tempted to offer any of these excuses, as in his own case none apply. The one concern he mentions has to do with the fortunes of his writings, not less with his hopes to address important and ultimate things, specifically relevant to the fate of *Five Dissertations* (thence to the *Four Dissertations* as ultimately published), including what he might have in all probability intended among his last essays on the theme of last things: "Of the Immortality of the Soul." By contrast, the very last philosophical essay he would happen to write was less by design as the above essays would have been, than happenstance, an essay on taste, a cut that weighed on his mind, as an author concerned as he was throughout his life with his editions. In just this measure, Hume tells Smith that his only reserves are with ensuring that certain of his essays might finally see the light.

For Baier's part, just to go back to her hunt to identify the Lucianic dialogue of the dead in question, while assuming more precision than may have been justified by consulting the Loeb editions (eight volumes of them are at hand), Baier also elides a complex account of ancient Menippean satire, condensing it into Fielding *and* Swift, and so opting for overdetermination in order finally to settle the matter while insisting that the dialogues carrying the specific title of *Dialogues of the Dead* be exclusively identifiable as such. For Baier, the dialogical short arrays assembled under this title[29] (many of Lucian's dialogues, as Baier duly notes, are generically dialogues between the dead) must be the referent (and contra Cullen's designation, merely present as he was at Hume's bedside, as the *Kataplous*), whereby Smith's unnamed and generic reference is accorded higher value. Baier summarizes that Hume "may have been reading more than one downward journey as spiritual preparation for his own,"[30] a point which is perhaps true but not when it comes to the particular dialogue as she extends

---

28 Lucian, "The Downward Journey" in: *Lucian*, Vol. II, pp. 16–19.
29 Lucian's so-titled "Dialogues of the Dead" are short dialogues which Hume may well have been reading in addition to the above noted *Kataplous*, which are editorial compilations and arrangements bound together in the new Loeb edition, following Harmon's earlier version, with similar short forms under the titles "Dialogues of the Sea Gods," "Dialogues of the Gods," and, apparently, to round things out: "Dialogues of the Courtesans." *Lucian Volume VII*. See for a recent discussion attesting to the challenges of just these dialogues (formal and otherwise), Rafael Guimarães Tavares da Silva, "The Laughter Within the Dialogues of the Dead."
30 Baier, *Death and Character*, p. 104.

the claim.³¹ Nor indeed can the matter be settled as already detailed above simply by noting as Baier does "that the excuses are offered to Mercury rather than Charon" as, of course the excuses are offered in dialogue itself mediatedly, i.e., to "good lady Clotho."³² One of the advantages of classically hermeneutic philosophy informed no less by Gadamer than by Nietzsche³³ is the recognition of the role played by Hermes/Mercury as go-between among gods and humans. At the end of the day, only Charon will matter when it comes to that journey.

Hence it is just as relevant, as this too informs Smith's reflection and not less Hume's own irony, that when it comes to religion Lucian's *Kataplous* is less a dialogue about the famous man Megapenthes than it is a dialogue about the 'good man,' *good* inasmuch as he is conscious of and at terms with his mortality. This is Mycillus, the shoemaker who, like Hume, having no attachments had no reasons for wishing to remain and no illusions about excuses that might spare him and thus comes running, literally so – no hesitation at all. At the outset of the dialogue we meet Mycillus identified not by name but as laughing and protesting to Clotho at having to be made to wait to board, by contrast with the others who seek any delay, however minor. When Charon chides this eager soul for his hurry, pointing out that the bark is full and that he can wait for the next ferry, Mycillus insists on coming aboard. This takes some persuasion and, when he is brought on board, as there is no space, he has to be told, on Hermes' orders and to Clotho's applause, to stand "on the tyrant's neck."³⁴ The *communal* signifier and reference of laughter is one Bracht Branham rightly emphasizes,³⁵ but here this shoemaker's laughter functions to singularize him. Thus, Hermes has to remonstrate "Nobody may cross without a tear": "Do cry, however, even if only a little, for custom's sake."³⁶ Despite the parody of regret ('Alas my old shoes') duly uttered (more laughter), Mycillus' laughter is ongoing as the dialogue proceeds contra the *Übermensch* himself (the tyrant Megapenthes), ostensibly at the shoemaker's own expense as he laughs at himself for having been so taken in by the

---

31 Baier, *Death and Character*, p. 103–104.
32 Lucian, "The Downward Journey," p. 16. *Clotho* is one of the fates who spins as we may recall Milton's words as the dialogue invokes the agency of *Atropos,* who cuts the thread of life. In the poem Milton writes on the drowning death of his friend, his *Lycidas*, "Comes the blind Fury with th' abhorred shears, / And slits the thin-spun life."
33 See for a discussion of hermeneutics in broader this context the contributions to Niall Keane (Ed.), *Blackwell Companion to Hermeneutics*, including, more specifically, Babich, "Friedrich Nietzsche," pp. 366–377.
34 Lucian, "The Downward Journey," p. 39.
35 R. Bracht Branham, *Unruly Eloquence: Lucian and the Comedy of Traditions*.
36 Lucian, "The Downward Journey," p. 42.

accoutrements, smells and tastes associated with the man who in life seemed a *hyperanthropos*, a higher human being:

> I held him happy when I saw the splendour of his purple, the number of his attendants, his plate, his jewelled goblets, and his couches with legs of silver; besides the savour of the dishes prepared for his dinner drove me to distraction. Therefore he appeared to me a superman, thrice blessed, better looking and a full royal cubit taller than almost anyone else; for he was uplifted by his good fortune, walked with a majestic gait, carried his head high and dazzled all he met.[37]

Mycillus, the 'good man' does not merely come 'readily' – as Epictetus suggested that one always should be at the ready,[38] – but gladly, laughing. Thus on an utterly different level, Hume showed himself, on Smith's parallel, to be good.

De gustibus non disputandum est

It is assumed that we know what classics are valued and that is why we call them 'classics.' We admire Milton and Shakespeare, Goethe and Schiller, Homer and Aristotle and Plato and so on. As a historian, David Hume raised another question, as historical sensibilities are liable to change such that some things that appear in their day to be sure classics, things that have until then withstood the test of time, can undergo a shift in value for another era. Hence the Lucian who was popular in Hume's own day and even through to the beginning of the 20th century, has today so diminished in 'classical' value that he is sufficiently esoteric that Hume scholars like Baier have trouble tracking him down. The same is true for Homer and Archilochus, to cite the fathers of genres of epic and lyric poetry respectively, esteemed in equal measure by the Greeks, as Nietzsche will tell us, but which, just where Homer shines brilliantly as a classic to the current day (if John's Ogilby's translation as Hume mentions him has dimmed for us today and newer (re)translations of Homer's *Odyssey* excite attention instead),[39] *Archilochus* remains sufficiently obscure that scholars insist that Nietzsche must be

---

37 Lucian, *Downward Journey*, 33.
38 Epictetus, *Enchiridion*, § 7. Cf. *The Works of Epictetus A Translation from the Greek based on that of Elizabeth Carter*, and *Discourses of Epictetus*.
39 See the literary scholar, Emily Wilson's new, "contemporary" translation of Homer's *Odyssey* now out with Norton a translation that has gotten significant attention less owing to its freedom than because she is the first woman to translate the *Odyssey* into English. By contrast, the *Iliad* exists already in a translation by Caroline Alexander.

wrong in setting him equal to Homer.⁴⁰ Scholarly claims that judgments made by other scholars are "wrong" (we see these in abundance in the essays below, notably in Shiner and Townsend among most of the others included here to a greater and lesser degree) may well be the only thing to endure (to use one of Nietzsche's phrases) "beyond the day after tomorrow."

The entire concern of this volume is all about the critical basis for such claims. How can we determine a standard for estimating tomorrow's likely classic, whether in the literary domain or other areas where taste plays a role? Hume's own example, ironically underlined as borrowed "not to draw our philosophy from too profound a source" (ST 216) from Cervantes' tale of Don Quixote's companion, cites Sancho Panza's account of a rustic sensibility, outing posh presumptions of supposed taste, underscoring the problematic tensions between social conventions – as nearly every chapter below discusses this example. Attesting to this ability is Hume's 'delicacy': judging, by subjective taste alone, the objective fact of the physical presence of an old leathern thong and a rusted iron key that had fallen into a cask of clichéd costly Malmsey wine. It is a yet further detail that this permitted Hume to cite a then wildly popular book, newly retranslated in English by Smollett and published by Hume's own printer, Andrew Millar (helpful pitches worked the same for books in Hume's day as they do on a television talk show or Twitter today).⁴¹ Hume's point in giving us such an example is that taste does not always follow expectations: more expensive wines are not necessarily better, and one generation's enthusiasm often fades with the shifts of fashion in the next generation – not to speak of the course of centuries. There are, as Roger Scruton emphasizes in his contribution below, cultural issues at work, questions of the contemporary or of the latest trends, as Giorgio Agamben, speaking of the couture culture of Milan reminds us, are often constant concomitants at all levels of supposed "delicacy."⁴² And there are gendered issues, as Hume suggests, he argues that the

---

40 I discuss this in Babich, "Nietzsches Lyrik. Archilochos, Musik, Metrik." See for an English version, Babich, "Nietzsche's Archilochus."

41 Miguel de Cervantes, *The Adventures of Don Quixote de la Mancha*. Cervantes, novel was originally published in 1605 and 1615, Smollet's was not the first translation, which was Thomas Shelton's version which appeared very quickly, the first volume in 1612, the second in 1620. For some estimations, the most popular version of Cervantes was Charles Jarvas (or Jarvis) 1842 translation on which to be sure Smollett's translation was based. MacLachlan's chapter below makes reference to this translation.

42 Giorgio Agamben, "What is the Contemporary," pp. 40–41.

"fairer sex" is often gifted with more refined discrimination, as Carolyn Korsmeyer's classic chapter below likewise argues.[43]

Thus, although as is routinely conceded: "there is no disputing concerning taste," Hume's point was that precisely such is – or better said, *ought to be* – a matter of keen disputation. Indeed, nothing would be more valuable in matters of investment or speculation. Thus, as Hume pointed out, rather a great deal rides on this, especially in the business of wine where he first made his acquaintance with "taste" and "delicacy" (cf. ST 216) and, by extension, wine futures – and, *ceteris paribus*, art futures.

In this sense, although the young David Hume wished to do nothing but pursue a life of letters, his lack of fortune compelled him to work for a living, which he pursued fortuitously as assistant to a Scots importer in France whose business included wine. This, among other reasons, including family connections and thrift (few decisions in life are settled upon for just one reason), was how Hume found himself in the company of the Jesuits of La Flèche. Working where needed, and conserving his resources by turn, Hume was able to write, which means that he also hoped for an alternative career, and thus published *A Treatise of Human Nature*. But the book was judged 'unintelligible' by its first critics – complicated works often demanding more of a readership than a readership is prepared to offer – such that Hume himself repudiated it as having fallen "*dead-born from the press.*"

In hindsight, as we know (and it is precisely Hume's point that this knowledge comes too late), his critics were wrong. But what is at stake here with respect to Hume's "Of the Standard of Taste" is far more than a matter of judging what philosophic text is likely to have a future. There is also ironic counterpoise in offering an essay on just this topic in just this circumstance in order to fill out the missing signatures for a book.

More generally, just where, with relatively few exceptions, most writers on Hume flatten questions concerning irony, the more earnest question of determining a "standard" of taste would be invaluable for[44] improving judgments concerning colleagues and friends on social occasions. What wine do they order?

---

43 For a discussion mixing additional cultural and gendered concerns see Monique Roelofs, *The Cultural Promise of the Aesthetic*, esp. pp. 57 ff.

44 See however Carolyn Korsmeyer's chapter here below, including a reference to John V. Price's 1965 usefully taxonomic, *The Ironic Hume*. See too and likewise, MachLachlan's chapter below in addition, though focusing more on play, Freydberg. I do not mean here to imply that Hume scholars fail to reference irony with respect to religion. See, including further references, Ton Vink, "David Hume: Sceptical Atheist or Religious Conservative?" For a historically contextualized discussion, see M.A. Box's 1990 *The Suasive Art of David Hume*.

What taste do they show themselves to have? And why, how justifiably, do we take ourselves to set the standard?

To keep to Hume's original examples in the business of literature, i.e., in publishing especially given the peer review that determines the future of a text in advance, the question looms today with different names: Tolstoy or Flaubert? Jane Austen or Ernest Hemingway – or why not J.K. Rowling? The question is by no means unrelated to the literary imagination itself, including the rise and fall of certain characters in the popular mind. Thus, if *Sister Carrie* is no longer much read unless assigned at university, *Harry Potter and the Sorcerer's Stone* would, by contrast, seem to be going great guns if Rowling's book is, one might argue, just as likely to be encountered in a literature as in a film or media studies course.

The point concerns what Kant named common sense, and it is the point Hume raised against nothing other the literary critic's judgment of literature as such, that is, for or against a work and whether a given text can be expected to be likely to become a classic or not, something Hume had already noted in the 18th century. Literary fame is a matter of fashion and fad. Thus Hume's examples today will be less a matter of esteeming superior "elegance and genius" than a matter of names we recognize – the issue of recognition undergirding Theodor Adorno's point concerning contemporary musical tastes on the radio – and those we do not when it comes to distinguishing between "Ogilby and Milton or Bunyan and Addison." (ST 210)

If fashions and fads fade, Hume's worry about literary "futures" induced him to use the parallel example of wine in order to reflect on the "standard of taste."[8] The alcohol allusion has an even broader history, as Simone de Beauvoir, who first tells us in her memoir *La force de l'âge* of the youthful rue Montparnasse evening together with comrades in philosophical arms at the time, recalling Jean-Paul Sartre, listening to Raymond Aron extol the benefits of phenomenology, using as illustration, the challenge of philosophizing about an apricot cocktail or – as Hume does, – a glass of wine. To this account can be added estimations of art more broadly: painting, architecture, sculpture, – and perhaps science and perhaps the market itself.

The Volume

The essays in the present volume accompanying "Of the Standard of Taste" offer a varying range of interpretations of this one text and reading between these different assessments can enhance an understanding of the breadth and complexity of Hume's essay.

Regarded more comprehensively – and beyond the specific theme of "Of the Standard of Taste," – there has been sustained scholarly engagement with Hume's essays, complex as this history is, including a tumultuous focus, beginning in Hume's own lifetime of the falling out, on the one hand, between Hume and Rousseau.[45] Added to this is a complicated aesthetic "contest," at least as art historians assess these contests as "philosophical" disputes[46] – this point being not rendered more perspicuous by considering the analytic-continental divide (and vigorous analytic denial of the very idea of any such distinction) that today haunts professional, disciplinary discussion[47] apart from the historical complications added by the 18th century articulation of what can seem to have been a parallel divide. To this must be added a more Brexit-minded focus on Hume and Smith (and the Scottish Enlightenment beginning by foregrounding the routinely not often-noted James Dunbar),[48] but more recently still focussing on the same Adam Smith already discussed above with reference to Lucian (and Hume's deathbed reading).[49]

Where the lion's share of Hume scholarship continues to look to his political and moral theory, or to his work as a historian, or indeed and at the heart of philosophy proper, at his epistemology, specifically on the nature of causation (here represented in Shiner and, in connection with continental philosophy of science,

---

45 One might regard this is as the oldest instantiation of the Anglophone-Continental divide. See Robert Zaretsky and John T. Scott, *The Philosophers' Quarrel: Rousseau, Hume, and the Limits of Human Understanding*. An intriguing take on this is offered via the German language compilation, Sabine Schulz (Ed.), *"Leben Sie wohl für immer"*: *Die Affäre Hume-Rousseau in Briefen und Zeitdokumenten*. And cf. Hume's own *Exposé succinct de la contestation qui s'est élevée entre M. Hume et M. Rousseau avec les pieces justificatives*.
46 I am grateful to Nigel Warburton for reminding me, on the most academically relevant social media platform (Twitter), of this debate. See further, David Fordham, "Allan Ramsay's Enlightenment: Or, Hume and the Patronizing Portrait," pp. 508–524.
47 For a discussion indicating some of these complexities, see a dialogue series between the editor and the philosopher and gaming and AI theorist, Chris Bateman, beginning with "The Last Continental Philosopher."
48 Christopher J. Berry, *Essays on Hume, Smith and the Scottish Enlightenment*.
49 Dennis C. Rasmussen, *The Infidel and the Professor: David Hume, Adam Smith, and the Friendship That Shaped Modern Thought,* and see too his earlier (and more comprehensively articulated: *The Pragmatic Enlightenment: Recovering the Liberalism of Hume, Smith, Montesquieu, and Voltaire*. This is, to be sure, hardly limited to a recent concern, as some of the contributors to the current collection also make plain, see for example, W.L. Taylor, *Francis Hutcheson and David Hume as Predecessors of Adam Smith*.

Babich),⁵⁰ Hume's reflections on taste, are as central to aesthetics as to the philosophy of art and beauty (Scruton), including delicacy (Costelloe) – and not coincidentally juridical and critical reflection (Caygill), but also to art and as much to speculative or economic investment, as to 'standards,' (Kivy, MacLachlan, Costelloe, Townsend, Démuth/Démuthová), these including historical philosophical reflections (Caygill, Mazza), involving antiquity with Plato (Freydberg) as well as moving forward to Nietzsche (Babich), while also including questions of gender (Korsmeyer, but also referenced in Townsend, Démuth/Démuthová, and Mazza).

Significantly, as this is a volume dedicated to an essay written to take the place of excluded essays, this volume also and alas has its own excluded essays – chapters the editor had originally hoped to include but which could not be included owing to prohibitive publisher's fees.⁵¹ The one comfort to be taken here is that these particular texts are published, if not as easily accessible as one might wish for fruitful scholarship in the best sense of Nietzsche's *"la gaya scienza"* – *Die fröhliche Wissenschaft*.

By contrast, Hume's essays, at least initially, were suppressed: excluded from his *Five Dissertations* as already seen and quite for reasons of literary style or judgment (and parallels on such judgments of taste corresponding to Warburton on Shakespeare, versus Hume on John Home).⁵² To this extent, one might sidestep the kind of exaggerated claim sometimes made in writing about the virtues of a monograph or collective volume. It is not that Hume's essay "Of the Standard of Taste" has been neglected as it has been read in the extensive literature (see, for an overview, for a start, Costelloe's chapter

---

50 There are many discussions of causation and taste, including some of the contributions to the present volume. Noteworthy too is Mary Mothersill, "In Defence of Hume and the Causal Theory of Taste."

51 These missing contributions are available in print which is a comfort that did not apply, hence Hume's end of life regrets for his suppressed/excluded essays and to which I refer the reader to, here listed alphabetically Jonathan Friday, "Hume's Sceptical Standard of Taste"; Theodore Gracyk, "Delicacy in Hume's Theory of Taste"; Jacob Sider Jost & John Immerwahr, "Hume the Sociable Iconoclast: The Case of the Four Dissertations"; Jens Kulenkampff, "The Objectivity of Taste: Hume and Kant"; and Denise Gigante, "Purging Mist: On Hume, Humors, and Taste." An additional essay germane to the discussion of David Hume and taste (and wine) is featured in a collection I published in 2016, Steven Shapin, "The Sciences of Subjectivity." See also, if more peripherally, Paul Guyer's discussion of Hume's influence on Kant in the last chapter of Guyer, *Knowledge, Reason, and Taste: Kant's Response to Hume*.

52 See again Jost and Immerwahr, "Hume the Sociable Iconoclast," and see too, for a sense of the original debate the letters on the topic in James Fieser, *Early Responses to Hume's Life and Reputation: Volumes 9 and 10*, pp. 75–76, in addition to Ernest Campbell Mossner, "Hume and the Scottish Shakespeare."

below) with respect to classical and aesthetic judgment, as well as with respect to calculative evaluation or estimation. But Hume's essay on taste and the standard by which one might evaulate claims of the same all too often functions as a mere mention and there are no *collective* studies that have made this essay and its related concerns a central theme. The current collection offers a range of reflections for scholars of aesthetics, art and beauty, together with questions of disputations, addressed to students and to philosophers, both analytic and continental, not to mention the occasional oenophile, in addition to issues of diet, physiology, and anatomy, slightly contra Hume's own ambitions to establish a standard but for the sake of further thinking. Hume's essay is key to this undertaking and thus we begin with it below.[53]

Bibliography

Agamben, Giorgio (2009) "What is the Contemporary." In: Agamben, *What is an Apparatus and Other Essays*. David Kishik and Stefan Pedatella, trans. Stanford: University of Stanford Press. 39–54

Babich, Babette (2018) "Heidegger and Hölderlin on Aether and Life." *Études Phénoménologique, Phenomenological Studies*. 2. 111–133.

Babich, Babette (2017) "Nietzsches Lyrik. Archilochos, Musik, Metrik." In: Christian Benne and Claus Zittel (Eds.) *Nietzsche und die Lyrik. Ein Kompendium*. Frankfurt am Main: Springer/Metzler. 405–429.

Babich, Babette (2016) "Nietzsche's Archilochus." *New Nietzsche Studies*. Vol 10, Nos. 1/2 (2016): 133–170.

Babich, Babette (2015) "Friedrich Nietzsche." In: Niall Keane, (Ed.) *Blackwell Companion to Hermeneutics*. Oxford: Wiley, 2015. 366–377.

Babich, Babette (2012) "Nietzsche's Zarathustra and Parodic Style: On Lucian's Hyperanthropos and Nietzsche's Übermensch." *Diogenes*. 58(4): 58–74.

Babich, Babette (2013) "Nietzsche's Zarathustra, Nietzsche's Empedocles: The Time of Kings." In: Horst Hutter and Eli Friedlander, (Eds.) *Nietzsche's Therapeutic Teaching: For Individuals and Culture*. London: Continuum. 157–174.

---

[53] At the time of this printing, there is only an 'art' edition of Hume's essay as a stand-alone edition, an "indie" paperback, published by the online art journal, *Post-Modern Times*, David Hume, "Of the Standard of Taste: Post-Modern Times Aesthetic Classics." Previously, there had been an edition (now out of print) by John W. Lenz in the Library of Liberal Arts series, *Of the Standard of Taste and Other Essays*. To be sure, the essay is also available under the title of one of the other four dissertations (the four that were meant to have been originally published), *On Suicide*. In addition, it can be found among a wider selection of other essays in MacIntyre's collection, already cited above, *Hume's Ethical Writings*, as well as in Stephen Copley and Andrew Edgard (Eds.), *Selected Essays*.

Baier, Annette C. (2008) *Death and Character: Further Reflections on Hume*. Cambridge: Harvard University Press.

Baier, Annette C. (2006) "Hume's Deathbed Reading: A Tale of Three Letters." *Hume Studies*. Vol. 32, No. 2: 347–356.

Bailey, Alan and Dan O'Brien (Eds.), (2012) *The Continuum Companion to Hume* (London: Bloomsbury).

Bastin-Hammou, Malika (Ed.) (2009) *Kaina pragmata: mélanges offerts à Jean-Claude Carrière* (Toulouse: Presses Univ. du Mirail).

Bateman, Chris (with Babette Babich) (2016) "The Last Continental Philosopher." http://onlyagame.typepad.com/only_a_game/2016/11/babich-and-bateman-1.html. Last accessed 24 March 2018.

Berry, Christopher J. (2018) *Essays on Hume, Smith and the Scottish Enlightenment*. Edinborough: Edinborough University Press.

Box, M. A. (1990) *The Suasive Art of David Hume*. Princeton: Princeton University Press.

Branham, R. Bracht (1989) *Unruly Eloquence: Lucian and the Comedy of Traditions*. Cambridge: Cambridge University Press.

Caygill, Howard (1989) *The Art of Judgment*. Oxford: Blackwell.

Cervantes, Miguel de (1755) *The Adventures of Don Quixote de la Mancha*. Tobias Smollet, trans. London: Millar.

Copley, Stephen and Andrew Edgard (Eds.) (1993) *Selected Essays*. Oxford: Oxford University Press.

Couvalis, George (2013–2014) "Hume's Lucianic Thanatotherapy." *Modern Greek Studies. Australia and New Zealand*, 16–17, B: 327–344.

Cullen, William (1999) Letter to John Hunter, 17 September 1776. In: James Fieser (Ed.), *Early Responses to Hume, Life, and Reputations*. London: Thoemes. Vol. 1. 292.

da Silva, Rafael Guimarães Tavares (2015) "The Laughter Within the Dialogues of the Dead." *Revele*. Nr. 8, (May): 232–246.

Ebner, Martin, Holger Gzella, Heinz-Günther Nesselrath, and Ernst Ribbat (Eds.) (2011) *Philopseudeis è Apiston. Die Lügenfreunde oder: Der Ungläubige*. Darmstadt: Wissenschaftliche Buchgesellschaft.

Elsner, Jaś (2007) "Discourses of Style: Pausanias and Lucian." In: *Roman Eyes: Visuality & Subjectivity in Art & Text*. Princeton: Princeton University Press. 49–66.

Epictetus (1758) *Enchiridion*, § 7. In: *All the Works of Epictetus, Which are Now Extant*. Elizabeth Carter, trans. London: Printed by S. Richardson

Epictetus (1865) *The Works of Epictetus. Consisting of His Discourses, in Four Books, The Enchiridion, and Fragments. A Translation from the Greek based on that of Elizabeth Carter*. Thomas Wentworth Higginson, trans. Boston: Little, Brown, and Co.

Epictetus (1904) *Discourses of Epictetus*. George Long, trans. New York: D. Appleton and Company.

Favreau-Lindner, Anne-Marie (2009) "Lucien et le mythe de Ἡρακλῆς ὁ λόγος." In: Malika Bastin-Hammou (Ed.), *Kaina pragmata: mélanges offerts à Jean-Claude Carrière*. Toulouse: Presses Univ. du Mirail. 155–168.

Emerson, Roger L. (2016) *Essays on David Hume, Medical Men and the Scottish Enlightenment: 'Industry, Knowledge and Humanity.'* London: Routledge.

Fieser, James (2003) *Early Responses to Hume's Life and Reputation: Volumes 9 and 10*. London: Bloomsbury Publishing.

Friday, Jonathan (1998) "Hume's Sceptical Standard of Taste." *Journal of the History of Philosophy.* 36: 545–566.

Fordham, David (2006) "Allan Ramsay's Enlightenment: Or, Hume and the Patronizing Portrait." *Art Bulletin.* Volume 88, Issue 3: 508–524.

Fosl, Peter S. (1998) "The Bibliographic Bases of Hume's Understanding of Sextus Empiricus and Pyrrhonism." *Journal of the History of Philosophy.* 36:9 (April): 261–278.

Gigante, Denise (2008) "Purging Mist: On Hume, Humors, and Taste." In: *Taste: A Literary History.* New Haven: Yale University Press. 54–66.

Goethe, Johann Wolfgang von (2012) *Faust, Volume 1 and 2.* Bayard Taylor, trans. New York: Modern Library.

Gracyk, Theodore (2011) "Delicacy in Hume's Theory of Taste." *The Journal of Scottish Philosophy,* 9/1: 1–16.

Guyer, Paul (2013) *Knowledge, Reason, and Taste: Kant's Response to Hume.* Princeton: Princeton University Press, 2013.

Hume, David (2013) *Of the Standard of Taste: Post-Modern Times Aesthetic Classics.* Birmingham: The Birmingham Free Press.

Hume, David (2005) *On Suicide.* London: Penguin.

Hume, David (2000) *Four Dissertations and Essays on Suicide & the Immortality of the Soul.* South Bend Indiana: Saint Augustine.

Hume, David (1875) *Essays Moral, Political, and Literary.* London: Longmans, Green, and Company.

Hume, David (1870) "Of the Standard of Taste." In: *Essays Literary, Moral, and Political by David Hume, Esq., The Historian.* London: Ward, Lock, and Tyler, Warwick House, Paternoster Row. 134–149.

Hume, David "On My Own Life." In: *Essays Moral, Political, and Literary.* 1–8.

Hume, David (1757) *Four Dissertations.* London: Printed for A. MILLAR, in the Strand, MDCCLVII.

Keane, Niall (Ed.) (2015) *Blackwell Companion to Hermeneutics.* Oxford: Wiley.

Le Roux, Françoise (1960) "Les dieux celtiques aux liens: de l'Ogmios de Lucien à l'Ogmios de Dürer." *Orgam* 12: 209–234.

Lucian (1913–1967) *Volumes 1–8.* A. M. Harmon, trans. Cambridge, MA: Harvard University Press, Loeb Classical Library.

Lucian (1996) "Heracles." In: *Volume 1.* Harmon, trans. Cambridge: Harvard University Press, Loeb Classical Library 14. 1996 [1913]. 62–71.

Lucian (1968) *Selected Satires of Lucian.* Lionel Casson, trans. New York: Norton.

Lucian (1961) *Lucian Volume VII*, M.D. Macleod, trans. Cambridge: Harvard University Press, Loeb Library 431.

Lucian (1915) "The Downward Journey." In: *Volume II*, Harmon, trans. Cambridge: Harvard University Press, Loeb Classical Library 54, Vol. II. 16–19.

Jost, Jacob Sider and John Immerwahr (2013) "Hume the Sociable Iconoclast: The Case of the Four Dissertations." *The European Legacy.* Volume 18, Issue 5: 603–618.

Keane, Niall (Ed.) (2015), *Blackwell Companion to Hermeneutics* (Oxford: Wiley)

Kulenkampff, Jens (1990) "The Objectivity of Taste: Hume and Kant." *Noûs.* Vol. 24, No. 1: *On the Bicentenary of Immanuel Kant's Critique of Judgement.* (Mar.): 93–110.

MacIntyre, Alasdair (1965) "Introduction." In: MacIntyre, (Ed.) *Hume's Ethical Writings: Selections from David Hume.* Notre Dame: University of Notre Dame Press. 9–17.

Mazza, Emilio (2012) "Hume's Life, Intellectual Context and Reception." In: Alan Bailey and Dan O'Brien (Eds.), *The Continuum Companion to Hume*. London: Bloomsbury. 20–37.

Mossner, Ernest Campbell (1948) "Hume's Early Memoranda, 1729–40: The Complete Text." *Journal of the History of Ideas*. 9/4 (October): 492–518.

Mossner, Ernest Campbell (Jul., 1940) "Hume and the Scottish Shakespeare." *Huntington Library Quarterly*. Vol. 3, No. 4: 419–441.

Mothersill, Mary (1997) "In Defence of Hume and the Causal Theory of Taste." *The Journal of Aesthetics and Art Criticism*. Vol. 55, No. 3: 312–317.

Price, John Valdimir (1965) *The Ironic Hume*. Austin: University of Texas Press.

Rasmussen, Dennis C. (2017) *The Infidel and the Professor: David Hume, Adam Smith, and the Friendship That Shaped Modern Thought*. Princeton: Princeton University Press.

Rasmussen, Dennis C. (2013) *The Pragmatic Enlightenment: Recovering the Liberalism of Hume, Smith, Montesquieu, and Voltaire*. Cambridge: Cambridge University Press.

Roelofs, Monique (2014) *The Cultural Promise of the Aesthetic*. London: Bloomsbury.

Schulz, Sabine (Ed.) (2012) *"Leben Sie wohl für immer": Die Affäre Hume-Rousseau in Briefen und Zeitdokumenten*. Zürich: Diaphanes Verlag.

Sider, Jacob & John Immerwahr (2013), "Hume the Sociable Iconoclast: The Case of the Four Dissertations," *The European Legacy*, Volume 18, Issue 5, pp. 603–618

Shapin, Steven (2017) "The Sciences of Subjectivity." In: Babich (Ed.), *Hermeneutic Philosophies of Social Science*. Berlin: de Gruyter, 2017. 123–142.

Smith, Adam, LL.D. (1875) Letter to William Strahan, Esq. In: Hume, *Essays Moral, Political, and Literary*. 9–14.

Taylor, William Leslie (1965) *Francis Hutcheson and David Hume as Predecessors of Adam Smith*. North Carolina: Duke University Press.

Thausing, Moritz (1884) *Dürer: Geschichte seines Lebens und seiner Kunst, mit Illustrationen und Titelkupfer*. Vol. 1. Leipzig: E. A. Seemann.

Vink, Ton (2013) "David Hume: Sceptical Atheist or Religious Conservative?" In: Stanley Tweyman (Ed.) *David Hume. A Tercentenary Tribute*. Ann Arbor, Michigan: Caravan Books. 107–123.

Zaretsky, Robert and John T. Scott (2009) *The Philosophers' Quarrel: Rousseau, Hume, and the Limits of Human Understanding*. New Haven: Yale University Press.

II **"Of the Standard of Taste"**

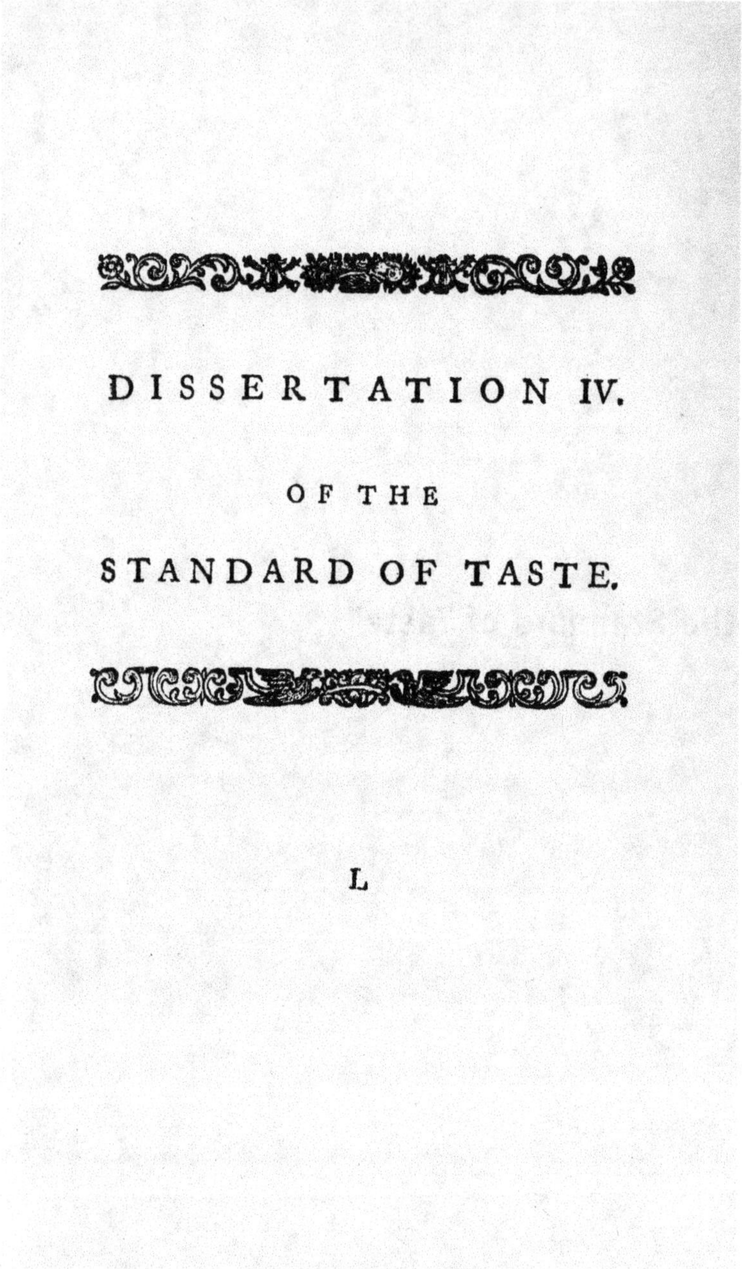

DISSERTATION IV.

OF THE
STANDARD OF TASTE.

L

Figure 2: Hume, *Four Dissertations*, (London: Millar, in the Strand, 1757), title page L1–2. Public Domain.

David Hume
Of the Standard of Taste[1]

[203] THE great variety of Tastes, as well as of opinions, which prevail in the world, is too obvious not to have fallen under every one's observation. Men of the most confined knowledge are able to remark a difference of taste in the narrow circle of their acquaintance, even where the persons have been educated under the same government, and have early imbibed the same prejudices. But those, who can enlarge their view to contemplate distant nations and remote ages, are still more surprised at the great inconsistence and contrariety. We are apt to call *barbarous* whatever departs widely from our own taste and apprehension: but soon find the epithet of reproach retorted on us. And the highest arrogance and self-conceit is at last startled, on observing an equal assurance on all sides, and scruples, amidst such a contest of sentiment, to pronounce positively in its own favour.

As this variety of taste is obvious to the most careless inquirer; so will it be found, on examination, [204] to be still greater in reality than in appearance. The sentiments of men often differ with regard to beauty and deformity of all kinds, even while their general discourse is the same. There are certain terms in every language, which import blame, and others praise; and all men, who use the same tongue, must agree in their application of them. Every voice is united in applauding elegance, propriety, simplicity, spirit in writing; and in blaming fustian, affectation, coldness, and a false brilliant: But when critics come to particulars, this seeming unanimity vanishes; and it is found, that they had affixed a very different meaning to their expressions. In all matters of opinion and science, the case is opposite: The difference among men is there oftener found to lie in generals than in particulars; and to be less in reality than in appearance. An explication of the terms commonly ends the controversy; and the disputants are surprised to find, that they had been quarrelling, while at bottom they agreed in their judgment.

Those who found morality on sentiment, more than on reason, are inclined to comprehend ethics under the former observation, and to suppose, that in all questions, which regard conduct [205] and manners, the difference among men

---

1 Numbers in brackets here correspond to the original pagination. David Hume, "Of the Standard of Taste" in: Hume, *Four Dissertations* (London: Millar, in the Strand, MDCCLVII). Facsimile reprint: Hume, *Four Dissertations and Essays on Suicide & the Immortality of the Soul* (South Bend, Indiana: Saint Augustine, 2000), 201–240. The text can also be found online: http://www.davidhume.org/texts/fd.html.

is really greater than at first sight it appears. It is indeed obvious, that writers of all nations and all ages concur in applauding justice, humanity, magnanimity, prudence, veracity; and in blaming the opposite qualities. Even poets and other authors, whose compositions are chiefly calculated to please the imagination, are yet found, from *Homer* down to *Fenelon*, to inculcate the same moral precepts, and to bestow their applause and blame on the same virtues and vices. This great unanimity is usually ascribed to the influence of plain reason; which, in all these cases, maintains similar sentiments in all men, and prevents those controversies, to which the abstract sciences are so much exposed. So far as the unanimity is real, this account may be admitted as satisfactory: But we must also allow, that some part of the seeming harmony in morals may be accounted for from the very nature of language. The word *virtue*, with its equivalent in every tongue, implies praise; as that of *vice* does blame: And no one, without the most obvious and grossest impropriety, could affix reproach to a term, which in general use is understood in a good sense; or bestow applause, where the idiom requires disapprobation. *Homer's* [206] general precepts, where he delivers any such, will never be controverted; but it is very obvious, that when he draws particular pictures of manners, and represents heroism in *Achilles* and prudence in *Ulysses*, he intermixes a much greater degree of ferocity in the former, and of cunning and fraud in the latter, than *Fenelon* would admit of. The sage *Ulysses* in the *Greek* poet seems to delight in lies and fictions, and often employs them without any necessity or even advantage: But his more scrupulous son, in the *French* epic writer, exposes himself to the most imminent perils, rather than depart from the most exact line of truth and veracity.

The admirers and followers of the *Alcoran* insist on the excellent moral precepts, which are interspersed through that wild performance. But it is to be supposed, that the *Arabic* words, which correspond to the *English*, equity, justice, temperance, meekness, charity were such as, from the constant use of that tongue, must always be taken in a good sense; and it would have argued the greatest ignorance, not of morals, but of language, to have mentioned them with any epithets, besides those of applause and approbation. But would we know, [207] whether the pretended prophet had really attained a just sentiment of morals? Let us attend to his narration; and we shall soon find, that he bestows praise on such instances of treachery, inhumanity, cruelty, revenge, bigotry, as are utterly incompatible with civilized society. No steady rule of right seems there to be attended to; and every action is blamed or praised, so far only as it is beneficial or hurtful to the true believers.

The merit of delivering true general precepts in ethics is indeed very small. Whoever recommends any moral virtues, really does no more than is implied in the terms themselves. That people, who invented the word *modesty*, and used it in a good sense, inculcated more clearly and much more efficaciously, the precept, be modest, than any pretended legislator or prophet, who should insert such a *maxim* in his writings. Of all expressions, those, which, together with their other meaning, imply a degree either of blame or approbation, are the least liable to be perverted or mistaken.

It is very natural for us to seek a *Standard of Taste*; a rule, by which the various sentiments of men may be reconciled; or at least, a decision [208] afforded, confirming one sentiment, and condemning another.

There is a species of philosophy, which cuts off all hopes of success in such an attempt, and represents the impossibility of ever attaining any standard of taste. The difference, it is said, is very wide between judgment and sentiment. All sentiment is right; because sentiment has a reference to nothing beyond itself, and is always real, wherever a man is conscious of it. But all determinations of the understanding are not right; because they have a reference to something beyond themselves, to wit, real matter of fact; and are not always conformable to that standard. Among a thousand different opinions which different men may entertain of the same subject, there is one, and but one, that is just and true; and the only difficulty is to fix and ascertain it. On the contrary, a thousand different sentiments, excited by the same object, are all right: Because no sentiment represents what is really in the object. It only marks a certain conformity or relation between the object and the organs or faculties of the mind; and if that conformity did not really exist, the sentiment could never possibly have a being. Beauty is no [209] quality in things themselves: It exists merely in the mind which contemplates them; and each mind perceives a different beauty. One person may even perceive deformity, where another is sensible of beauty; and every individual ought to acquiesce in his own sentiment, without pretending to regulate those of others. To seek the real beauty, or real deformity is as fruitless an enquiry, as to pretend to ascertain the real sweet or real bitter. According to the disposition of the organs, the same object may be both sweet and bitter; and the proverb has justly determined it to be fruitless to dispute concerning tastes. It is very natural, and even quite necessary, to extend this axiom to mental, as well as bodily taste; and thus common sense, which is so often at variance with philosophy, especially with the sceptical kind, is found, in one instance at least, to agree in pronouncing the same decision.

But though this axiom, by passing into a proverb, seems to have attained the sanction of common sense; there is certainly a species of common sense, which opposes it, or at least serves to modify and restrain it. Whoever would assert an equality of genius and elegance between [210] *Ogilby* and *Milton*, or *Bunyan* and *Addison*, would be thought to defend no less an extravagance, than if he had maintained a mole-hill to be as high as *Teneriffe*, or a pond as extensive as the ocean. Though there may be found persons, who give the preference to the former authors; no one pays attention to such a taste; and we pronounce, without scruple, the sentiment of these pretended critics to be absurd and ridiculous. The principle of the natural equality of tastes is then totally forgot, and while we admit it on some occasions, where the objects seem near an equality, it appears an extravagant paradox, or rather a palpable absurdity, where objects so disproportioned are compared together.

It is evident that none of the rules of composition are fixed by reasonings *a priori*, or can be esteemed abstract conclusions of the understanding, from comparing those habitudes and relations of ideas, which are eternal and immutable. Their foundation is the same with that of all the practical sciences, experience; nor are they any thing but general observations, concerning what has been universally found to please in all countries and in all ages. Many of the beauties of poetry, and even of eloquence, [211] are founded on falsehood and fiction, on hyperboles, metaphors, and an abuse or perversion of expressions from their natural meaning. To check the sallies of the imagination, and to reduce every expression to geometrical truth and exactness, would be the most contrary to the laws of criticism; because it would produce a work, which, by universal experience, has been found the most insipid and disagreeable. But though poetry can never submit to exact truth, it must be confined by rules of art, discovered to the author either by genius or observation. If some negligent or irregular writers have pleased, they have not pleased by their transgressions of rule or order, but in spite of these transgressions: They have possessed other beauties, which were conformable to just criticism; and the force of these beauties has been able to overpower censure, and give the mind a satisfaction superior to the disgust arising from the blemishes. *Ariosto* pleases; but not by his monstrous and improbable fictions, by his bizarre mixture of the serious and comic styles, by the want of coherence in his stories, or by the continual interruptions of his narration. He charms by the force and clearness of his expression, by the readiness and variety of his inventions, and by his natural [212] pictures of the passions, especially those of the gay and amorous kind: And however his faults may diminish our satisfaction, they are not able entirely to destroy it. Did our pleasure really arise from those parts of his poem, which we denominate faults, this would be no objection to criticism in general: It would only be an objection to those particular rules of criticism, which would establish such circumstances to be faults, and would represent them as universally blameable. If they are found to please, they cannot be faults; let the pleasure, which they produce, be ever so unexpected and unaccountable.

But though all the general rules of art are founded only on experience, and on the observation of the common sentiments of human nature, we must not imagine, that, on every occasion, the feelings of men will be conformable to these rules. Those finer emotions of the mind are of a very tender and delicate nature, and require the concurrence of many favourable circumstances to make them play with facility and exactness, according to their general and established principles. The least exterior hindrance to such small springs, or the least internal disorder, [213] disturbs their motion, and confounds the operation of the whole machine. When we would make an experiment of this nature, and would try the force of any beauty or deformity, we must choose with care a proper time and place, and bring the fancy to a suitable situation and disposition. A perfect serenity of mind, a recollection of thought, a due attention to the object; if any of these circumstances be wanting, our experiment will be fallacious, and we shall be unable to judge of the catholic and universal beauty. The relation, which nature has placed between the form and the sentiment, will at least be more obscure; and it will require greater accuracy to trace and discern it. We shall be able to ascertain its influence, not so much from the operation of each particular beauty, as from the durable admiration, which attends those works, that have survived all the caprices of mode and fashion, all the mistakes of ignorance and envy.

The same *Homer*, who pleased at *Athens* and *Rome* two thousand years ago, is still admired at *Paris* and at *London*. All the changes of climate, government, religion, and language, have not been able to obscure his glory. [214] Authority or prejudice may give a temporary vogue to a bad poet or orator; but his reputation will never be durable or general. When his compositions are examined by posterity or by foreigners, the enchantment is dissipated, and his faults appear in their true colours. On the contrary, a real genius, the longer his works endure, and the more wide they are spread, the more sincere is the admiration which he meets with. Envy and jealousy have too much place in a narrow circle; and even familiar acquaintance with his person may diminished the applause due to his performances: But when these obstructions are removed, the beauties, which are naturally fitted to excite agreeable sentiments, immediately display their energy; and while the world endures, they maintain their authority over the minds of men.

It appears then, that amidst all the variety and caprice of taste, there are certain general principles of approbation or blame, whose influence a careful eye may trace in all operations of the mind. Some particular forms or qualities, from the original structure of the internal fabric, are calculated to please, and others to displease; and if they fail of their effect in any particular [215] instance, it is from some apparent defect or imperfection in the organ. A man in a fever would not insist on his palate as able to decide concerning flavours; nor would one, affected with the jaundice, pretend to give a verdict with regard to colours. In each creature, there is a sound and a defective state; and the former alone can be supposed to afford us a true standard of taste and sentiment. If, in the sound state of the organ, there be an entire or a considerable uniformity of sentiment among men, we may thence derive an idea of the perfect and universal beauty; in like manner as the appearance of objects in day-light to the eye of a man in health is denominated their true and real colour, even while colour is allowed to be merely a phantasm of the senses.

Many and frequent are the defects in the internal organs, which prevent or weaken the influence of those general principles, on which depends our sentiment of beauty or deformity. Though some objects, by the structure of the mind, be naturally calculated to give pleasure, it is not to be expected, that in every individual the pleasure will be equally felt. Particular incidents and situations occur, which either throw [216] a false light on the objects, or hinder the true from conveying to the imagination the proper sentiment and perception.

One obvious cause, why many feel not the proper sentiment of beauty, is the want of that *delicacy* of imagination, which is requisite to convey a sensibility of those finer emotions. This delicacy every one pretends to: Every one talks of it; and would reduce every kind of taste or sentiment to its standard. But as our intention in this dissertation is to mingle some light of the understanding with the feelings of sentiment, it will be proper to give a more accurate definition of delicacy than has hitherto been attempted. And not to draw our philosophy from too profound a source, we shall have recourse to a noted story in *Don Quixote*.

> 'Tis with good reason, says *Sancho* to the squire with the great nose, that I pretend to have a judgment in wine: This is a quality hereditary in our family. Two of my kinsmen were once called to give their opinion of a hogshead, which was supposed to be excellent, being old and of a good vintage. One of them tastes it; considers it, and after mature reflection, pronounces [217] the wine to be good, were it not for a small taste of leather, which he perceived in it. The other, after using the same precautions, gives also his verdict in favor of the wine; but with the reserve of a taste of iron, which he could easily distinguish. You cannot imagine how much they were both ridiculed for their judgment. But who laughed in the end? On emptying the hogshead, there was found at the bottom, an old key with a leathern thong tied to it.

The great resemblance between mental and bodily taste will easily teach us to apply this story. Though it be certain, that beauty and deformity, more than sweet and bitter, are not qualities in objects, but belong entirely to the sentiment, internal or external; it must be allowed, that there are certain qualities in objects, which are fitted by nature to produce those particular feelings. Now as these qualities may be found in a small degree or may be mixed and confounded with each other, it often happens, that the taste is not affected with such minute qualities, or is not able to distinguish all the particular flavours, amidst the disorder, in which they are presented. Where the organs are so fine, as to allow nothing [218] to escape them; and at the same time so exact as to perceive every ingredient in the composition: This we call delicacy of taste, whether we employ these terms in the natural or metaphorical sense. Here then the general rules of beauty are of use, being drawn from established models, and from the observation of what pleases or displeases, when presented singly and in a high degree: And if the same qualities, in a continued composition and in a smaller degree, affect not the organs with a sensible delight or uneasiness, we exclude the person from all pretensions to this delicacy. To produce these general rules or avowed patterns of composition is like finding the key with the leathern thong; which justified the verdict of *Sancho's* kinsmen, and confounded those pretended judges who had condemned them. Though the hogshead had never been emptied, the taste of the one was still equally delicate, and that of the other equally dull and languid: But it would have been more difficult to have proved the superiority of the former, to the conviction of every by-stander. In like manner, though the beauties of writing had never been methodized, or reduced to general principles; though no excellent models had ever been acknowledged; the different degrees [219] of taste would still have subsisted, and the judgment of one man been preferable to that of another; but it would not have been so easy to silence the bad critic, who might always insist upon his particular sentiment, and refuse to submit to his antagonist. But when we show him an avowed principle of art; when we illustrate this principle by examples, whose operation, from his own particular taste, he acknowledges to be conformable to the principle; when we prove that the same principle may be applied to the present case, where he did not perceive nor feel its influence: He must conclude, upon the whole, that the fault lies in himself, and that he wants the delicacy, which is requisite to make him sensible of every beauty and every blemish, in any composition or discourse.

'Tis acknowledged to be the perfection of every sense or faculty, to perceive with exactness its most minute objects, and allow nothing to escape its notice and observation. The smaller the objects are, which become sensible to the eye, the finer is that organ, and the more elaborate its make and composition. A good palate is not tried by strong flavours, but by a mixture of small ingredients, where we are still sensible [220] of each part, notwithstanding its minuteness and its confusion with the rest. In like manner, a quick and acute perception of beauty and deformity must be the perfection of our mental taste; nor can a man be satisfied with himself while he suspects that any excellence or blemish in a discourse has passed him unobserved. In this case, the perfection of the man, and the perfection of the sense or feeling, are found to be united. A very delicate palate, on many occasions, may be a great inconvenience both to a man himself and to his friends: But a delicate taste of wit or beauty must always be a desirable quality, because it is the source of all the finest and most innocent enjoyments, of which human nature is susceptible. In this decision the sentiments of all mankind are agreed. Wherever you can ascertain a delicacy of taste, it is sure to be approved of; and the best way of fixing it is to appeal to those models and principles, which have been established by the uniform approbation and experience of nations and ages.

But though there be naturally a very wide difference in point of delicacy between one person and another, nothing tends further to encrease and improve this talent, than *practice* in a particular [221] art, and the frequent survey or contemplation of a particular species of beauty. When objects of any kind are first presented to the eye or imagination, the sentiment, which attends them is obscure and confused: and the mind is, in a great measure, incapable of pronouncing concerning their merits or defects. The taste cannot perceive the several excellencies of the performance, much less distinguish the particular character of each excellency, and ascertain its quality and degree. If it pronounce the whole in general to be beautiful or deformed, 'tis the utmost that can be expected; and even this judgment a person, so unpractised, will be apt to deliver with great hesitation and reserve. But allow him to acquire experience in those objects, his feeling becomes more exact and nice: He not only perceives the beauties and defects of each part, but marks the distinguishing species of each quality, and assigns it suitable praise or blame. A clear and distinct sentiment attends him through the whole survey of the objects; and he discerns that very degree and kind of approbation or displeasure which each part is naturally fitted to produce. The mist dissipates which seemed formerly to hang over the object: The organ acquires [222] greater perfection in its operations; and can pronounce, without danger of mistake, concerning the merits of each performance. In a word, the same address and dexterity, which practice gives to the execution of any work, is also acquired, by the same means, in the judging of it.

So advantageous is practice to the discernment of beauty, that, before we can pronounce judgment on any work of importance, it will even be requisite that that very individual performance be more than once perused by us, and be surveyed in different lights with attention and deliberation. There is a flutter or hurry of thought which attends the first perusal of any piece, and which confounds the genuine sentiment of beauty. The relation of the parts is not discerned: The true characters of style are little distinguished. The several perfections and defects seem wrapped up in a species of confusion, and present themselves indistinctly to the imagination. Not to mention, that there is a species of beauty, which, as it is florid and superficial, pleases at first; but being found incompatible with a just expression either of reason or passion, soon palls upon the taste, and is then rejected with disdain, at least rated at a much lower value.

[223] It is impossible to continue in the practice of contemplating any order of beauty, without being frequently obliged to form *comparisons* between the several species and degrees of excellence, and estimating their proportion to each other. A man, who had had no opportunity of comparing the different kinds of beauty, is indeed totally unqualified to pronounce an opinion with regard to any object presented to him. By comparison alone we fix the epithets of praise or blame, and learn how to assign the due degree of each. The coarsest daubing contains a certain lustre of colours and exactness of imitation, which are so far beauties, and would affect the mind of a peasant or Indian with the highest admiration. The most vulgar ballads are not entirely destitute of harmony or nature; and none but a person familiarised to superior beauties would pronounce their numbers harsh, or narration uninteresting. A great inferiority of beauty gives pain to a person conversant in the highest excellence of the kind, and is for that reason pronounced a deformity: As the most finished object with which we are acquainted is naturally supposed to have reached the pinnacle of perfection, and to be entitled to the highest [224] applause. One accustomed to see, and examine, and weigh the several performances, admired in different ages and nations, can alone rate the merits of a work exhibited to his view, and assign its proper rank among the productions of genius.

But to enable a critic the more fully to execute this undertaking, he must preserve his mind free from all prejudice, and allow nothing to enter into his consideration but the very object which is submitted to his examination. We may observe, that every work of art, in order to produce its due effect on the mind, must be surveyed in a certain point of view, and cannot be fully relished by persons, whose situation, real or imaginary, is not conformable to that which is required by the performance. An orator addresses himself to a particular audience, and must have a regard to their particular genius, interests, opinions, passions, and prejudices; otherwise he hopes in vain to govern their resolutions, and inflame their affections. Should they even have entertained some prepossessions against him, however unreasonable, he must not overlook this disadvantage; but, before he enters upon the subject, must endeavour to conciliate their affection, and acquire [225] their good graces. A critic of a different age or nation, who should peruse this discourse, must have all these circumstances in his eye, and must place himself in the same situation as the audience, in order to form a true judgment of the oration. In like manner, when any work is addressed to the public, though I should have a friendship or enmity with the author, I must depart from this situation; and considering myself as a man in general, forget, if possible, my individual being, and my peculiar circumstances. A person influenced by prejudice, complies not with this condition, but obstinately maintains his natural position, without placing himself in that point of view which the performance supposes. If the work be addressed to persons of a different age or nation, he makes no allowance for their peculiar views and prejudices; but, full of the manners of his own age and country, rashly condemns what seemed admirable in the eyes of those for whom alone the discourse was calculated. If the work be executed for the public, he never sufficiently enlarges his comprehension, or forgets his interest as a friend or enemy, as a rival or commentator. By this means, his sentiments are perverted; nor have the same beauties and blemishes the same influence upon him, as if he had imposed a proper [226] violence on his imagination, and had forgotten himself for a moment. So far his taste evidently departs from the true standard, and of consequence loses all credit and authority.

It is well known, that in all questions submitted to the understanding, prejudice is destructive of sound judgment, and perverts all operations of the intellectual faculties: It is no less contrary to good taste: nor has it less influence to corrupt our sentiment of beauty. It belongs to *good sense* to check its influence in both cases; and in this respect, as well as in many others, reason, if not an essential part of taste, is at least requisite to the operations of this latter faculty. In all the nobler productions of genius, there is a mutual relation and correspondence of parts; nor can either the beauties or blemishes be perceived by him, whose thought is not capacious enough to comprehend all those parts, and compare them with each other, in order to perceive the consistence and uniformity of the whole. Every work of art has also a certain end or purpose for which it is calculated; and is to be deemed more or less perfect, as it is more or less fitted to attain this end. The object of eloquence is to persuade, of history to instruct, of poetry to [227] please, by means of the passions and the imagination. These ends we must carry constantly in our view when we peruse any performance; and we must be able to judge how far the means employed are adapted to their respective purposes. Besides, every kind of composition, even the most poetical, is nothing but a chain of propositions and reasonings; not always indeed, the justest and most exact, but still plausible and specious, however disguised by the colouring of the imagination. The persons introduced in tragedy and epic poetry, must be represented as reasoning, and thinking, and concluding, and acting, suitably to their character and circumstances; and without judgment, as well as taste and invention, a poet can never hope to succeed in so delicate an undertaking. Not to mention, that the same excellence of faculties which contributes to the improvement of reason, the same clearness of conception, the same exactness of distinction, the same vivacity of apprehension, are essential to the operations of true taste, and are its infallible concomitants. It seldom or never happens, that a man of sense, who has experience in any art, cannot judge of its beauty; and it is no less rare to meet with a man who has a just taste without a sound understanding [228].

Thus, though the principles of taste be universal, and nearly, if not entirely, the same in all men; yet few are qualified to give judgment on any work of art, or establish their own sentiment as the standard of beauty. The organs of internal sensation are seldom so perfect as to allow the general principles their full play, and produce a feeling correspondent to those principles. They either labour under some defect, or are vitiated by some disorder; and by that means, excite a sentiment, which may be pronounced erroneous. When the critic has no delicacy, he judges without any distinction, and is only affected by the grosser and more palpable qualities of the object: The finer touches pass unnoticed and disregarded. Where he is not aided by practice, his verdict is attended with confusion and hesitation. Where no comparison has been employed, the most frivolous beauties, such as rather merit the name of defects, are the object of his admiration. Where he lies under the influence of prejudice, all his natural sentiments are perverted. Where good sense is wanting, he is not qualified to discern the beauties of design and reasoning, which are the highest and most excellent. Under some or other of these [229] imperfections, the generality of men labour; and hence a true judge in the finer arts is observed, even during the most polished ages, to be so rare a character: Strong sense, united to delicate sentiment, improved by practice, perfected by comparison, and cleared of all prejudice, can alone entitle critics to this valuable character; and the joint verdict of such, wherever they are to be found, is the true standard of taste and beauty.

But where are such critics to be found? By what marks are they to be known? How distinguish them from pretenders? These questions are embarrassing; and seem to throw us back into the same uncertainty, from which, during the course of this essay, we have endeavoured to extricate ourselves.

But if we consider the matter aright, these are questions of fact, not of sentiment. Whether any particular person be endowed with good sense and a delicate imagination, free from prejudice, may often be the subject of dispute, and be liable to great discussion and inquiry: But that such a character is valuable and estimable, will be agreed in by all mankind. Where these [230] doubts occur, men can do no more than in other disputable questions which are submitted to the understanding: They must produce the best arguments, that their invention suggests to them; they must acknowledge, a true and decisive standard to exist somewhere, to wit, real existence and matter of fact; and they must have indulgence to such as differ from them in their appeals to this standard. It is sufficient for our present purpose, if we have proved, that the taste of all individuals is not upon an equal footing, and that some men in general, however difficult to be particularly pitched upon, will be acknowledged by universal sentiment to have a preference above others.

But in reality, the difficulty of finding, even in particulars, the standard of taste, is not so great as it is represented. Though in speculation, we may readily avow a certain criterion in science, and deny it in sentiment, the matter is found in practice to be much more hard to ascertain in the former case than in the latter. Theories of abstract philosophy, systems of profound theology, have prevailed during one age: In a successive period, these have been universally exploded: Their absurdity has been detected: Other [231] theories and systems have supplied their place, which again gave place to their successors: And nothing has been experienced more liable to the revolutions of chance and fashion than these pretended decisions of science. The case is not the same with the beauties of eloquence and poetry. Just expressions of passion and nature are sure, after a little time, to gain public applause, which they maintain for ever. *Aristotle*, and *Plato*, and *Epicurus*, and *Descartes*, may successively yield to each other: But *Terence* and *Virgil* maintain an universal, undisputed empire over the minds of men. The abstract philosophy of *Cicero* has lost its credit: The vehemence of his oratory is still the object of our admiration.

Though men of delicate taste be rare, they are easily to be distinguished in society by the soundness of their understanding, and the superiority of their faculties above the rest of mankind. The ascendant, which they acquire, gives a prevalence to that lively approbation, with which they receive any productions of genius, and renders it generally predominant. Many men, when left to themselves, have but a faint and dubious perception of beauty, who yet are capable of relishing any fine stroke which is pointed out to them. Every convert to the [232] admiration of the real poet or orator is the cause of some new conversion. And though prejudices may prevail for a time, they never unite in celebrating any rival to the true genius, but yield at last to the force of nature and just sentiment. Thus, though a civilized nation may easily be mistaken in the choice of their admired philosopher, they never have been found long to err, in their affection for a favourite epic or tragic author.

But notwithstanding all our endeavours to fix a standard of taste, and reconcile the discordant apprehensions of men, there still remain two sources of variation, which are not sufficient indeed to confound all the boundaries of beauty and deformity, but will often serve to produce a difference in the degrees of our approbation or blame. The one is the different humours of particular men; the other, the particular manners and opinions of our age and country. The general principles of taste are uniform in human nature: Where men vary in their judgments, some defect or perversion in the faculties may commonly be remarked; proceeding either from prejudice, from want of practice, or want of delicacy: and there is just reason for approving one taste, and condemning another. But where there is such a diversity in the internal frame or external situation as is entirely [233] blameless on both sides, and leaves no room to give one the preference above the other; in that case a certain degree of diversity in judgment is unavoidable, and we seek in vain for a standard, by which we can reconcile the contrary sentiments.

A young man, whose passions are warm, will be more sensibly touched with amorous and tender images, than a man more advanced in years, who takes pleasure in wise, philosophical reflections, concerning the conduct of life and moderation of the passions. At twenty, *Ovid* may be the favourite author; *Horace* at forty; and perhaps *Tacitus* at fifty. Vainly would we, in such cases, endeavour to enter into the sentiments of others, and divest ourselves of those propensities which are natural to us. We choose our favourite author as we do our friend, from a conformity of humour and disposition. Mirth or passion, sentiment or reflection; which ever of these most predominates in our temper, it gives us a peculiar sympathy with the writer who resembles us.

One person is more pleased with the sublime; another with the tender; a third with raillery. One has a strong sensibility to blemishes, and is extremely studious of correctness: Another has [234] a more lively feeling of beauties, and pardons twenty absurdities and defects for one elevated or pathetic stroke. The ear of this man is entirely turned towards conciseness and energy; that man is delighted with a copious, rich, and harmonious expression. Simplicity is affected by one; ornament by another. Comedy, tragedy, satire, odes, have each its partizans, who prefer that particular species of writing to all others. It is plainly an error in a critic, to confine his approbation to one species or style of writing, and condemn all the rest. But it is almost impossible not to feel a predilection for that which suits our particular turn and disposition. Such preferences are innocent and unavoidable, and can never reasonably be the object of dispute, because there is no standard by which they can be decided.

For a like reason, we are more pleased, in the course of our reading, with pictures and characters that resemble objects which are found in our own age or country, than with those which describe a different set of customs. It is not without some effort, that we reconcile ourselves to the simplicity of ancient manners, and behold princesses carrying water from the spring, and kings and heroes dressing their own victuals. We may allow in general, that the representation of such manners is no fault in the author, nor deformity in the piece; but we are [235] not so sensibly touched with them. For this reason, comedy is not easily transferred from one age or nation to another. A *Frenchman* or *Englishman* is not pleased with the *Andria* of *Terence*, or *Clitia* of *Machiavel*; where the fine lady, upon whom all the play turns, never once appears to the spectators, but is always kept behind the scenes, suitably to the reserved humour of the ancient *Greeks* and modern *Italians*. A man of learning and reflection can make allowance for these peculiarities of manners; but a common audience can never divest themselves so far of their usual ideas and sentiments, as to relish pictures which nowise resemble them.

But here there occurs a reflection, which may, perhaps, be useful in examining the celebrated controversy concerning ancient and modern learning; where we often find the one side excusing any seeming absurdity in the ancients from the manners of the age, and the other refusing to admit this excuse, or at least admitting it only as an apology for the author, not for the performance. In my opinion, the proper boundaries in this subject have seldom been fixed between the contending parties. Where any innocent peculiarities of manners are represented, such as those above mentioned, they ought [236] certainly to be admitted; and a man, who is shocked with them, gives an evident proof of false delicacy and refinement. The poet's *monument more durable than brass*, must fall to the ground like common brick or clay, were men to make no allowance for the continual revolutions of manners and customs, and would admit of nothing but what was suitable to the prevailing fashion. Must we throw aside the pictures of our ancestors, because of their ruffs and fardingales? But where the ideas of morality and decency alter from one age to another, and where vicious manners are described, without being marked with the proper characters of blame and disapprobation, this must be allowed to disfigure the poem, and to be a real deformity. I cannot, nor is it proper I should, enter into such sentiments; and however I may excuse the poet, on account of the manners of his age, I never can relish the composition. The want of humanity and of decency, so conspicuous in the characters drawn by several of the ancient poets, even sometimes by *Homer* and the *Greek* tragedians, diminishes considerably the merit of their noble performances, and gives modern authors an advantage over them. We are not interested in the fortunes and sentiments of such rough heroes; We are displeased to find the limits of vice and virtue so much [237] confounded; and whatever indulgence we may give to the writer on account of his prejudices, we cannot prevail on ourselves to enter into his sentiments, or bear an affection to characters, which we plainly discover to be blameable.

The case is not the same with moral principles as with speculative opinions of any kind. These are in continual flux and revolution. The son embraces a different system from the father. Nay there scarcely is any man, who can boast of great constancy and uniformity in this particular. Whatever speculative errors may be found in the polite writings of any age or country, they detract but little from the value of those compositions. There needs but a certain turn of thought or imagination to make us enter into all the opinions, which then prevail, and relish the sentiments or conclusions derived from them. But a very violent effort is requisite to change our judgment of manners, and excite sentiments of approbation or blame, love or hatred, different from those to which the mind, from long custom, has been familiarized. And where a man is confident of the rectitude of that moral standard, by which he judges, he is justly jealous of it, and will not pervert the sentiments of his heart for a moment, in complaisance to any writer whatsoever.

[238] Of all speculative errors, those which regard religion are the most excusable in compositions of genius; nor is it ever permitted to judge of the civility or wisdom of any people, or even of single persons, by the grossness or refinement of their theological principles. The same good sense, that directs men in the ordinary occurrences of life, is not hearkened to in religious matters, which are supposed to be placed altogether above the cognisance of human reason. On this account, all the absurdities of the pagan system of theology must be overlooked by every critic, who would pretend to form a just notion of ancient poetry; and our posterity, in their turn, must have the same indulgence to their forefathers. No religious principles can ever be imputed as a fault to any poet, while they remain merely principles, and take not such strong possession of his heart, as to lay him under the imputation of *bigotry* or *superstition*. Where that happens, they confound the sentiments of morality, and alter the natural boundaries of vice and virtue. They are therefore eternal blemishes, according to the principle above mentioned; nor are the prejudices and false opinions of the age sufficient to justify them.

[239] 'Tis essential to the Roman Catholic religion to inspire a violent hatred of every other worship, and to represent all pagans, mahometans, and heretics, as the objects of Divine wrath and vengeance. Such sentiments, though they are in reality very blameable, are considered as virtues by the zealots of that communion, and are represented in their tragedies and epic poems as a kind of divine heroism. This bigotry has disfigured two very fine tragedies of the *French* theatre, *Polieucte* and *Athalia*; where an intemperate zeal for particular modes of worship is set off with all the pomp imaginable, and forms the predominant character of the heroes. "What is this," says the sublime *Joad* to Josabet, finding her in discourse with *Mathan* the priest of *Baal*,

> "Does the daughter of *David* speak to this traitor? Are you not afraid, lest the earth should open and pour forth flames to devour you both? Or lest these holy walls should fall and crush you together? What is his purpose? Why comes that enemy of God hither to poison the air, which we breathe, with his horrid presence?"

Such sentiments are received with great applause on the theatre of *Paris*; but at *London* the spectators would be full as much pleased to hear *Achilles* tell *Agamemnon*, that he [240] was a dog in his forehead, and a deer in his heart; or *Jupiter* threaten *Juno* with a sound drubbing, if she will not be quiet.

Religious principles are also a blemish in any polite composition, when they rise up to superstition, and intrude themselves into every sentiment, however remote from any connection with religion. It is no excuse for the poet, that the customs of his country had burthened life with so many religious ceremonies and observances, that no part of it was exempt from that yoke. It must for ever be ridiculous in *Petrarch* to compare his mistress, *Laura*, to *Jesus Christ*. Nor is it less ridiculous in that agreeable libertine, *Boccace* [Boccacio], very seriously to give thanks to God Almighty and the ladies, for their assistance in defending him against his enemies.

Finis

Acknowledgements

Originally published in 1757 as the last of *Four Dissertations* issued after the (withdrawn) collection of *Five Dissertations* was truncated by the removal of two dissertations, "Of Suicide" and "Of the Immortality of the Soul." This version follows, including punctuation and bracketed indication [of page numbers] corresponding to, the original printing. Hume, "Of the Standard of Taste" in: Hume, Four *Dissertations* (London: Printed for A. MILLAR, in the Strand, MDCCLVII), pp. 201–240. See for a facsimile reproduction of the original version(s), Hume, *Four Dissertations and Essays on Suicide & the Immortality of the Soul* (South Bend Indiana: Saint Augustine, 2000). Cf., *Essays Literary, Moral, and Political* by David Hume, Esq., The Historian (London: Ward, Lock, and Tyler, Warwick House, Paternoster Row, 1870), pp. 134–149.

III Of Taste and Standards

Peter Kivy
Hume's Standard of Taste: Breaking the Circle

I

There can be no doubt but that Hume's moral theory had roots in the writings of Francis Hutcheson. An examination of the respective positions reveals it clearly enough; but Hume has left us even more substantial historical evidence in the form of letters to Hutcheson written between 1739 and 1741 – the period which saw publication of the *Treatise of Human Nature*. Hume was explicit with regard to what he obviously considered a meeting of minds in ethics. "Morality according to your Opinion as well as mine," he wrote to Hutcheson, "is determin'd merely by Sentiment ..."[1] An analogous agreement existed in the realm of aesthetic theory, as Hume made manifest throughout his writings and particularly in the essay "Of the Standard of Taste" (1757). There are two premises fundamental to Hutcheson's moral and aesthetic theory: (1) the value terms 'good' and 'beautiful' are applied to moral and aesthetic objects which occasion in the perceiver particular kinds of Lockean 'ideas'; and (2) these ideas are perceived by 'internal senses'.

Hume accepts the first of these premises, although he substitutes 'sentiment', 'pleasure' and the like for the more general term 'idea'. The second premise, for Hume, coalesces with the first: all that can be said about the moral sense and sense of beauty is contained in the contention that 'good' and 'beautiful' are applied in virtue of our having moral and aesthetic 'sentiments'. The position is summarized in the *Treatise*:

> An action, or sentiment, or character, is virtuous or vicious; why? because its view causes a pleasure or uneasiness of a particular kind. In giving a reason, therefore, for the pleasure or uneasiness, we sufficiently explain the vice or virtue. To have the sense of virtue, is nothing but to feel a satisfaction of a particular kind from the contemplation of a character. The very *feeling* constitutes our praise or admiration ... We do not infer a character to be virtuous, because it pleases; but in feeling that it pleases after such a particular manner, we in effect feel that it is virtuous. The case is the same as in our judgements concerning all kinds of beauty, and tastes, and sensations. Our approbation is implied in the immediate pleasure they convey to us.[2]

---

[1] *The Letters of David Hume*, Vol. I, p. 40.
[2] David Hume, *A Treatise of Human Nature*, III, i, 2.

For a thoroughgoing empiricist the moral sense and sense of beauty are extra philosophical baggage. We are aware of the *sentiments,* not the *senses;* to say that we have a moral sense or sense of beauty can only be an elliptical way of saying that we have moral and aesthetic feelings. Having chosen the path of 'sentiment' in aesthetics Hume was faced, as were others before him, with the spectre of a subjective relativism. But no previous thinker had perceived the possible consequences of the 'new aesthetic' more acutely or expressed them more forthrightly than the 'dispassionate' sceptic who, in Kant's words, was "so peculiarly fitted for balanced judgement."[3] Yet Hume recognized that if relativism in taste seems an unimpeachable fact, so too does the existence of critical standards.

> Beauty is no quality in things themselves: it exists merely in the mind which contemplates them; and each mind perceives a different beauty. One person may even perceive deformity, where another is sensible of beauty; and every individual ought to acquiesce in his own sentiment, without pretending to regulate those of others .... But though this axiom, by passing into a proverb, seems to have attained the sanction of common sense; there is certainly a species of common sense, which opposes it, at least serves to modify and restrain it. Whoever would assert an equality of genius and elegance between Ogilby and Milton, or Bunyan and Addison, would be thought to defend no less an extravagance, than if he had maintained a mole-hill to be as high as Teneriffe, or a pond as extensive as the ocean. (ST 210)

The resolution of this paradox, this 'antinomy' of taste, was Hume's task as it is ours; and the resolution he essayed merits the most serious consideration.

II

Hume believed that a standard of taste could be saved only by a strong commitment to the rational. And the Enlightenment did not look upon feeling and reason as necessarily incompatible. Hume was echoing a host of eighteenth-century moralists and critics when he wrote in the *Enquiry Concerning the Principles of Morals* (1757): "*reason* and *sentiment* concur in almost all moral determinations and conclusions," and specifically with regard to the problem of taste he tells us that "in many orders of beauty, particularly those of the finer arts, it is requisite to employ much reasoning, in order to feel the proper sentiment; and a false relish may frequently be corrected by argument and reflection."[4] Thus the principal

---

[3] Immanuel Kant, *Critique of Pure Reason*, p. 597.
[4] Hume, *Enquiry Concerning the Principles of Morals*.

goal of criticism, Hume believed, must be "to mingle some light of the understanding with the feelings of sentiment ..." (ST 216).

If I make an empirical statement, it is judged true or false on the basis of whether what I assert is or is not the case. This judgment is the province of reason. The touchstone of any such reasoning process is some external state of affairs; the 'standard' of reason here consists in correspondence to the facts of the case. "In the operation of reasoning," Hume tells us,

> the mind does nothing but run over its objects, as they are supposed to stand in reality, without adding any thing to them or diminishing any thing from them .... To this operation of the mind, therefore, there seems to be always a real, though often unknown, standard, in the nature of things; nor is truth or falsehood variable by the various apprehensions of mankind.[5]

But aesthetic judgments are not of this kind according to Hume. We do not, when we pronounce the judgment 'beautiful' or the reverse, merely 'run over' the 'objects' of thought "as they are supposed to stand in reality, without adding any thing to them." We do add something; we add our feelings – our emotional reactions to the objects we perceive:

> the case is not the same with the qualities of *beautiful and deformed, desirable and odious,* as with truth and falsehood. In the former case, the mind is not content with merely surveying its objects, as they stand in themselves: it also feels a sentiment of delight or uneasiness, approbation or blame, consequent to that survey; and this sentiment determines it to affix the epithet *beautiful or deformed, desirable or odious.*[6]

Now our feelings vary with our subjective natures: "nor can the same object, presented to a mind totally different, produce the same sentiment." We lack, in our aesthetic judgments, the 'external standard' which our factual judgments possess. The quest for a standard of taste, then, is a quest for such an external standard. The Humean program in aesthetics is the translation of value judgments into factual judgments – judgments of sentiment into judgements of reason. This is what Hume intends when he speaks of mingling "some light of the understanding with the feelings of sentiment." The standard of taste is determined by judgments based on sentiment.

But not all men are equal in their fitness to judge by sentiment: "few are qualified to give judgement on any work of art, or establish their own sentiment as the standard of beauty." [ST 228] The standard of taste, then, is set by those

---

5 Hume, "The Sceptic," *Essays.*
6 Hume, "The Sceptic."

qualified to give judgment on the basis of sentiment. And thus, the question "What is good art?" is easily answered. Good art is the art which good critics – those who are fit to judge by sentiment – approve.

But now a new series of questions arises involving the nature of good critics. "Where are such critics to be found?" queries Hume. "By what marks are they to be known? How distinguish them from pretenders? These questions are embarrassing; and seem to throw us back into the same uncertainty from which ... we have endeavoured to extricate ourselves." Yet we have made some progress. For, Hume maintains, questions concerning good critics "are questions of fact, not of sentiment"; and such questions, "submitted to the understanding," are susceptible, at least in principle, of a rational determination.

If, however, a rational judgment is to distinguish good critics from bad, it must find its criteria, its 'standard,' in the *facts* of the case; there must be some enumerable set of characteristics whereby the sheep may be separated from the goats. Hume provides five such distinguishing qualities:

> [1] When the critic has no *delicacy* he judges without distinction and is only affected by the grosser and more palpable qualities of the object: the finer touches pass unnoticed and disregarded. [2] Where he is not aided by *practice* his verdict is attended with confusion and hesitation. [3] Where no *comparison* [between different kinds of beauty] has been employed the most frivolous beauties, such as rather merit the name of defects, are the object of his admiration. [4] Where he lies under the influence of *prejudice* all his natural sentiments are perverted. [5] Where *good sense* is wanting he is not qualified to discern the beauties of design and reasoning [i.e. the mutual relation of the parts of the work of art, and the purpose of the work], which are the highest and most excellent (ST 228).

III

Now it has often been maintained that Hume is involved here in a vicious circle whereby good art is defined in terms of the good critic and the good critic in terms of good art.[7] And it is in fact easy enough to generate just such a circular definition simply by asking ourselves how it is to be determined whether or not an individual possesses the five qualities of the good critic enumerated above. If the answer is that we know a good critic to possess these qualities because he approves of good art, then we have certainly moved in a circle, to wit: (1) good works of art are works of art approved by good critics; (2) good critics

---

7 See, for example, Stuart Gerry Brown, "Observations on Hume's Theory of Taste" and James Noxon, "Hume's Opinion of Critics."

are critics possessing five requisite qualities; and (3) critics possessing the five requisite qualities are critics who approve good works of art.

Is this a fair representation of what Hume has to say concerning aesthetic judgment? In part, I am afraid, it is – but only in part. For there are, after all, *five* qualities that, according to Hume, distinguish the good critic; and they are not all of a piece. Some land us in a circular definition; others, I believe, do not. Thus, we must examine these qualities more closely if we wish to do Hume justice in this matter.

Hume conceives *practice* as "the frequent survey or contemplation of a particular species of beauty." (ST 221) *Use of comparisons* requires juxtaposing "the several species and degrees of excellence." (ST 223) But we must be able to recognize the beautiful before we are able to determine whether a critic has or has not been engaged in "the frequent survey or contemplation of a particular species of beauty." We must know what is excellent before we are able to determine whether or not a critic has compared "the several species and degrees of excellence." Thus, (1) the beautiful (or excellent) is defined in terms of the good critic; (2) the good critic is defined in terms of *practice* and *use of comparisons;* and (3) *practice* and *use of comparisons* are defined in terms of the beautiful (or excellent). Obviously in these two cases the definition of beauty is circular.

If, however, we examine the remaining three *qualities – delicacy, lack of prejudice, good sense* – we find quite another situation obtaining. What I wish to argue is that these qualities have, for Hume, certain crucial features in common: all are qualities not limited to critics alone; all are qualities requisite not only for aesthetic judgment but for other activities as well; hence all are identifiable by marks other than the critic's approval of good art. This being the case, the circle is broken; having defined good art in terms of good critics, Hume need not, with respect to these qualities, ultimately define good critics in terms of good art.

Hume describes *delicacy* in the following way: "Where the organs are so fine as to allow nothing to escape them, and at the same time so exact as to perceive every ingredient in the composition, this we call delicacy of taste, whether we employ these terms in the literal or metaphorical sense" (ST 217–218). How are we to determine whether or not a critic possesses *delicacy of taste* in the aesthetic sense? In "Of the Standard of Taste" the implication seems to be that such *delicacy* is determined on the basis of the critic's ability to distinguish aesthetic qualities in *good art*. And this of course leads us again to a circular definition: (1) good art is art approved by good critics; (2) good critics are critics possessing *delicacy;* and (3) *delicacy* is the ability to distinguish the aesthetic qualities of good art. But in an earlier essay, "Of the Delicacy of Taste and Passion" (1741), Hume relates aesthetic sensibility to emotive sensibility in general, implying in one place that those individuals characterized by the latter are likely to possess the former as well. He writes:

> How far the delicacy of taste, and that of passion are connected together in the original frame of the mind, is hard to determine. To me there appears to be a very considerable connexion betwixt them. For we may observe that women, who have more delicate passions than men, have also a more delicate taste of the ornaments of life, of dress, equipage, and the ordinary decencies of behaviour. Any excellency in these hits their taste much sooner than ours; and when you please their taste, you soon engage their affections.[8]

Thus, *delicacy of taste* can be identified (although not perhaps in all cases) by a non-aesthetic quality, namely, *delicacy of passion*. One could reasonably suppose an individual to possess *delicacy of taste* not on the basis of his critical judgments but rather on the basis of his general emotional reactions to non-aesthetic situations. With this qualification in view, we can define good art in terms of *delicacy* and yet avoid the previous circularity. Our revised definition will be: (1) good art is art approved by good critics; (2) good critics are critics possessing *delicacy of taste;* and (3) *delicacy of taste* is a concomitant of *delicacy of passion*.

As for Hume's requirement that the critic be free from bias, its relevance seems obvious enough; we expect fairness in judgments, whether they be aesthetic, moral or any other kind. "It is well known, that, in all questions submitted to the understanding, prejudice is destructive of sound judgement, and perverts all operations of the intellectual faculties: it is no less contrary to good taste; nor has it less influence to corrupt our sentiment of beauty." (ST 226) There is a special sense, however, in which an aesthetic judgment must be free from bias. Hume makes this demand of himself as a critic: "considering myself as a man in general, [I must] forget, if possible, my individual being, and my peculiar circumstances." (ST 225) In passing critical judgments we must shed our private skins. By means of a mental exercise we take the point of view of "a man in general" and disregard our "individual being" and "peculiar circumstances." This is essentially an aesthetic version of what in Hume's moral philosophy has come to be known as the "disinterested spectator theory." Hume writes in the *Treatise,* for example:

> Nor is every sentiment of pleasure or pain which arises from characters and actions, of that *peculiar* kind which makes us praise or condemn.... It is only when a character is considered in general, without reference to our particular interest, that it causes such a feeling or sentiment as denominates it morally good or evil.[9]

---

8 Hume, "Of the Delicacy of Taste and Passion," *Essays* (1903).
9 Hume, *A Treatise of Human Nature,* III, i, 2.

We attempt, in both our moral and our aesthetic judgments, to separate in thought that which varies with our own personalities and times and attend only to the common element in all human sentiment. Only thus

> ... free
> From taint of personality,
> can we hope to make judgements on the basis of sentiment that are not merely expressions of personal preference but universal judgements.[10]

As in the case of *delicacy*, the crucial point here for our purposes is that *lack of prejudice*, even in its special application to aesthetic judgments, is not a quality unique in the critic. It is, therefore, a quality that need not be determined solely on the basis of the critic's approving or recognizing good art. An individual who is generally fair-minded or able to take the point of view of the 'disinterested spectator' in moral situations would likewise be able, one supposes, to take the point of view of 'a man in general' when exercising critical judgment. Here again is a quality of good critics that can be recognized prior to any knowledge of the critic's aesthetic performance. So, having defined good art in terms of approval by good critics, and good critics in terms of *lack of prejudice*, there is no need to close the circle and define *lack of prejudice* in terms of good art.

Finally, it seems abundantly clear that *good sense*, the last of Hume's critical qualities, can hardly be considered solely an attribute of critics. Indeed, it is precisely Hume's point here that intelligence is as much a part of criticism as it is of rational inquiry: "the same excellence of faculties which contributes to the improvement of reason, the same clearness of conception, the same exactness of distinction, the same vivacity of apprehension, are essential to the operation of true taste, and are its infallible concomitants." (ST 227) Fools seldom make good critics, and clever people usually do – nor need we make any reference to critical ability in separating the two. Again, good art can be defined in terms of approval by good critics, and good critics in terms of *good sense*; but

---

10 Cf. Kant, *Critique of Aesthetic Judgement*, p. 151: "by the name *sensus communis* is to be understood the idea of a public sense, i.e. a critical faculty which in its reflective act takes account (*a priori*) of the mode of representation of everyone else, in order, as it were, to weigh its judgement with the collective reason of mankind, and thereby avoid the illusion arising from subjective and personal conditions which could readily be taken for objective, an illusion that would exert prejudicial influence upon its judgement. This is accomplished by weighing the judgement, not so much with actual, as rather with the merely possible, judgements of others, and by putting ourselves in the position of everyone else, as the result of a mere abstraction from the limitations which contingently affect our own estimate"

good sense, having wider application than merely to good critics, need not be defined in terms of good art.

IV

Hume's definition of good art, or beauty, then, although circular in some instances, is not so in all. Good art, or the beautiful, is that approved by good critics; and good critics are characterized by five qualities: *delicacy, practice, use of comparisons, lack of prejudice, good sense. Practice* and *use of comparisons* lead, as we have seen, to the vicious circle of which Hume has often been accused, for both are defined in terms of the beautiful. But *delicacy, lack of prejudice,* and *good sense,* being qualities not unique to critics, are free from this circularity. They are identifiable by marks other than the critic's approval of aesthetic objects and need not be defined in terms of good art.

But if Hume's definition of good art is free from the charge of circularity, the general argument of the essay on taste is not totally unblemished. Hume seems in fact to be involved in (among other things) an infinite regress.

Let us imagine that Smith and Jones disagree about a poem: Smith approves and Jones does not. Smith supports his judgment by reference to the favourable verdict of a critic, to which Jones replies that the critic in question lacks *good sense.* This might at least be one sort of dispute in aesthetics envisaged by Hume; and he would claim here, as he apparently did at times with regard to ethical disputes, that (to use Professor Stevenson's ethical terminology) disagreements in evaluation are to a large extent "rooted in disagreement in belief." This is what Hume means in maintaining that a critical judgment based on "sentiment" can be reduced to a rational judgment involving 'facts'. If Smith and Jones are thoroughly apprised of the facts, they will agree with regard to the now disputed poem – the facts, in this instance, being the credentials of the critic whom Smith invokes as his authority.

But suppose we scrutinize the facts (so called) of the case, the *good sense,* for example, which the critic is said to possess. The phrase *good sense* describes; it also *approves.* What has happened is that in his attempt to reduce disagreements about aesthetic values to disagreements about facts, Hume has simply pushed the value judgment a step back: the question "Is *x* a good poem?" has become: "Does *y* have *good sense?"* And both are evaluative questions, questions of 'sentiment,' not (solely) questions of fact. Smith and Jones do not (to use Stevenson's ethical terminology again) merely disagree in "belief' about the critic, as Hume would have us think, but in "attitude" towards the critic. Thus, we are now faced with the task of reducing *good sense* to matters of fact; and the result of that reduction will doubtless require a reduction of its own.

Many would claim that the Humean attempt to reduce matters of aesthetic sentiment to matters of fact is doomed from the start: there just is no guarantee to be had that agreement about facts will result in agreement about what is beautiful. And Hume himself seems in the last analysis to have been of the same mind. For although Hume did maintain that *some* aesthetic disputes are rooted in disagreement about facts, he did not, it appears, believe that all are. Very near the conclusion of the essay on taste he wrote:

> The general principles of taste are uniform in human nature: where men vary in their judgements, some defect or perversion in the faculties [a matter of fact] may commonly be remarked; proceeding either from prejudice, from want of practice, or want of delicacy: and there is just reason for approving one taste, and condemning another. But where there is such diversity in the internal frame or external situation as is entirely blameless on both sides, and leaves no room to give one the preference above the other [where, in other words, there is substantial agreement with regard to the facts]; in that case a certain degree of diversity in judgement [disagreement in attitudes] is unavoidable, and we seek in vain for a standard, by which we can reconcile the contrary sentiments (ST 223).

When an aesthetic dispute arises the facts of the case, which for Hume are the credentials of the critic, are relevant; and *may* lead to a resolution of the dispute. This will occur when the facts either clearly condemn or clearly authorize the critic in the eyes of the disputants. But when the critic's credentials have been examined, or when two rival critics present equally authoritative credentials and yet still disagree in their judgment, the facts of the case have been exhausted. If the dispute continues, it is now one of sentiment, not reason; it is a disagreement in attitudes, not beliefs, and "no *reasoned* solution of any sort is possible."[11] We have done all we can *rationally* do when we have laid bare the facts of the case. If disagreement remains – and, for Hume, we have no assurance that it will not – it is a disagreement not susceptible of resolution by rational methods.

Hume, then, held out no absolute guarantees of resolution in aesthetic questions; and for an age that pursued such guarantees with the tenacity of a Grail Quest, this was a disappointment. As an anonymous reviewer of the essay on taste sadly remarked shortly after its publication, "instead of fixing and ascertaining the standard of taste, as we expected, our author only leaves us in the same uncertainty as he found us: and concludes with the philosopher of old,

---

11 C. L. Stevenson, *Ethics and Language*, p. 138. Stevenson's remark has reference to ethical disputes and I have appropriated it for this analysis of Hume's aesthetic theory.

that all we know is, that we know nothing."[12] Hume might well have replied with the words of another 'philosopher of old': "it is the mark of an educated mind to seek only so much exactness in each type of inquiry as may be allowed by the nature of the subject matter."[13]

Acknowledgements

This essay was originally published as "Hume's Standard of Taste: Breaking the Circle," *British Journal of Aesthetics*, 7:1 (Jan. 1967): 57–66. The editor gratefully acknowledges the late Peter Kivy's contribution of this chapter as part of the original inspiration for the current collection of essays.

Bibliography

Anonymous (1757) "Mr. Hume's Dissertations." *Critical Review*. Vol. 3 (March): 209–216.
Aristotle (1935) *Nicomachean Ethics*. Philip Wheelwright, trans. New York: The Odyssey Press.
Brown, Stuart Gerry (1938) "Observations on Hume's Theory of Taste." *English Studies*. XX: 93–98.
Grieg, J. Y. T. (Ed.) (1932) *The Letters of David Hume*. Oxford: Oxford University Press.
Hume, David (1978) *A Treatise of Human Nature*, L.A. Selby-Bigge, (Ed.) P.H. Nidditch, (Ed.) Oxford: Clarendon Press. [1739]
Hume, David (1903) *Essays Moral, Political and Literary*. London: Grant Richards.
Hume, David (1903) "Of the Standard of Taste." *Essays*.
Hume, David (1903) "The Sceptic," *Essays*.
Hume, David (1903) "Of the Delicacy of Taste and Passion," *Essays*.
Hume, David (1751) *Enquiry Concerning the Principles of Morals*. London: A. Millar.
Hume, David (1757) *Four Dissertations*. London: Millar, in the Strand.
Kant, Immanuel (1950) *Critique of Pure Reason*. Norman Kemp Smith, trans. New York: The Humanities Press.
Kant, Immanuel (1911) *Critique of Aesthetic Judgement*. J. C. Meredith, trans. Oxford: Oxford University Press.
Noxon, James (1961) "Hume's Opinion of Critics." *Journal of Aesthetics and Art Criticism*. 20 (2): 157–162.
Stevenson, C.L. (1953) *Ethics and Language*. New Haven: Yale University Press.

---

12 Anonymous.
13 Aristotle, *Nicomachean Ethics*, 1094b.

Christopher MacLachlan
Hume and the Standard of Taste

I

David Hume's critical theories, although fragmentary, have drawn increasingly serious attention in the twentieth century, yet even in 1976 Peter Jones, in reassessing Hume's aesthetics,[1] can describe one of the most substantial of his critical essays, "Of the Standard of Taste," as underrated. Jones praises it as "subtle and highly complex," but while I agree with that judgment I also find the essay quite puzzling. I am struck by certain features which look like structural weaknesses and by what seem to be inconsistencies, even contradictions, in Hume's argument. But perhaps the gravest difficulty facing interpretation of this essay is the irony which Hume seems to use, for this raises the question of just how seriously we are to take some of the more conventional views contained in "Of the Standard of Taste."

I can begin to illustrate my uneasiness by considering Hume's use of a tall tale from *Don Quixote*, Part II, Chapter xiii. Hume introduces this in a light-hearted way as part of his definition of delicacy of taste. It is the story of Sancho Panza's two kinsmen, who are such sensitive judges of wine that they can detect the taint of iron and leather imparted to a hogshead by the presence in it of a key on a thong. Now there are some interesting differences between Hume's version of this tale and the original. For example, where Hume has the two tasters deliberate over their wine before pronouncing it good, except for the slight taste of leather or iron, Cervantes says the first merely tried it with the tip of his tongue and the second just sniffed it, without tasting any at all. Further, Hume says "both were ridiculed for their judgment"[2] but there is no such reaction mentioned in the original. Lastly, Hume calls the cause of the taint of iron "an old key," where Cervantes describes it as "little."[3]

In short, while in the original interest is in the sensitivity of the taste of Sancho's kinsmen for its own sake, Hume's emphasis is more on the relation of their

---
[1] Peter Jones, "Hume's Aesthetics Reassessed."
[2] David Hume, "Of the Standard of Taste" in *Essays Moral, Political, and Literary*, ed. T.H. Green and T.H. Grose, London, 1875, Vol. I, 272. Subsequent references to this edition are given in parentheses in the text.
[3] As far as I can establish, eighteenth-century translators of *Don Quixote* into English, for example, Motteux (1700) and Jarvis (1742), give the correct rendering, "little."

taste to that of other people. He makes the procedure of tasting the wine as normal as possible and he gives prominence to the reactions of other people. Hume both tones down the more fabulous aspects of the story, making it less extraordinary and hence a better starting-point for a generalization about taste, and makes more explicit the conflict of opinion about the wine. He is using the story not just to define delicacy of taste but also to relate it to the problem of aesthetic judgment and the standard of taste.

This is confirmed by the application Hume makes of his example. First, he uses the analogy between physical and aesthetic taste to claim that delicacy in both consists of the ability to detect minute effects and make fine discriminations. But the crucial question is what serves, like the key on the thong in the story, to confirm to outsiders that a man's aesthetic judgment is in fact more delicate than his neighbours'. Hume's answer is "the general rules of beauty ... to produce these general rules or avowed patterns of composition is like finding the key with the leathern thong; which justified the verdict of Sancho's kinsmen, and confounded those pretended judges who had condemned them" (273).

But of course producing a general rule is not exactly like finding a physical key on a thong, and Hume's use of the word "avowed" here, which he repeats later, raises the difficulty of how the principles of art become accepted, and by whom. But, that apart, there is something odd about the discussion since the avowed principle is used, with support from examples, to convince a bad critic that he is wrong on the grounds that his judgment does not accord with the general judgment. This is the opposite of Sancho's story, in which his kinsmen were in a minority, derided, adds Hume, by the dull majority, and only vindicated by the discovery of the tainting key and thong. The aesthetic equivalent of the key and thong is being used not to confirm a particularly discerning criticism but to uphold a well-established opinion. Although it is possible to imagine a positive use of the rules of art, in which the critic appealed to a general principle to support his own view, the part played by the rules would be the same and would mean the subordination of individual to general response. Hume's actual case, the suppression of a deviant view, perhaps shows this more clearly. The so-called bad critic is guilty of nothing but idiosyncrasy, but when this becomes known he is forced to recant his divergence from the general rule. Thus the general rules operate against refinement or delicacy of taste, in so far as these mean individual variation of sensibility, and seek to impose uniformity.

Hume's attempt to define delicacy of taste has led to a restriction of its effectiveness by the very thing which is meant to confirm its existence. Nowhere, however, is this consequence expressed directly by Hume. One is left to wonder how far he was aware of it, or, in other words, whether the passage is to be read ironically, its real meaning unstated. There are perhaps clues, in the word "avowed," which begs the question, or in the rather bald way the general rules are equated with the key on the thong. But perhaps more convincing are signs of irony in other parts of the essay.

The next section consists of a rather conventional expansion of the definition of a good critic. He must have delicacy of taste, he must be well-practised, he must be adept in making comparisons, he must be free from prejudice and he must have good sense. If there is any irony here, it lies in the accumulation of these demands, so that Hume concludes that "though the principles of taste be universal, and, nearly, if not entirely the same in all men; yet few are qualified to give judgment on any work of art, or establish their own sentiment as the standard of beauty" (278).[4] One's confidence in the general rules of art is seriously undermined by the statement that "a true judge in the finer arts is observed, even during the most polished ages, to be so rare a character" (278). Yet Hume ends the paragraph by asserting that "the joint verdict of such, wherever they are to be found, is the true standard of taste and beauty."

It is most significant that the paragraph immediately following this sentence should begin with the obvious question it raises: "but where are such critics to be found?" (279). Two similar questions follow. Such piling up of questions has a marked rhetorical effect. The prose becomes excited and the reader expects some revelation to be made. Hume describes the three questions as embarrassing. He admits that they seem to jeopardize whatever progress his essay has made so far. This extraordinary paragraph, therefore, seems designed to mark a crisis in the essay; the reader is led to wonder how Hume, to use his own word, will extricate himself.

The answer is that he simply abandons the argument. He makes no effort to tell us where to find the true critic, but anticlimactically retreats into generalities: "It is sufficient for our present purpose," he writes, "if we have proved, that the taste of all individuals is not upon an equal footing, and that some men in general, however difficult to be particularly pitched upon, will be acknowledged by universal sentiment to have a preference above others" (279). Having raised the reader's expectations by elaborate means, Hume blatantly disappoints them. The inelegance and lack of subtlety here are striking, but much more so is the fact that this escape into generalities is not just a disappointment but is also a near-contradiction. To see this one has to look at the beginning of the essay.

---

4 There seems to be a discrepancy here between the claim that the judgments of especially sensitive critics form the standard of taste and earlier statements that the general rules of art are the basis for a standard.

The work begins conventionally enough, commenting on the variety of taste, but then a comparison with moral debate is introduced and this leads to two or three paragraphs of digression on morality. That this is a digression is signalled by the abrupt beginning of the single sentence of the sixth paragraph: "It is natural for us to seek a Standard of Taste..." (ST 268). This seems to bring us back sharply to the subject of the essay and to mark its real beginning. The crudeness of this arrangement seems a literary blemish on the essay. One is inclined to ask why Hume did not effect this transition with more dexterity, or indeed make it unnecessary by omitting the digression. But the function of this inelegant sixth paragraph may be to direct our attention to the digression preceding it and thus to why Hume included it. The starting point is the observation that in moral as in critical discussion men will agree in general terms but disagree in particular applications. Just as "every voice is united in applauding elegance, propriety, simplicity, spirit in writing; and in blaming fustian, affectation, coldness, and a false brilliancy" (266), so "writers of all nations and all ages concur in applauding justice, humanity, magnanimity, prudence, veracity; and in blaming the opposite qualities" (267). Disagreement begins when these generalizations are applied in particular instances and we find that one man's elegance is another man's fustian, and, to take Hume's example, that what Homer calls heroism Fénelon would call ferocity. Slyly, Hume extends the discussion to the Koran, pointing out that though the Arabic equivalents of the English words for equity, justice, charity and so on must be taken in a good sense, examination of their particular applications suggests that in practice the ethics of the Koran are not at all compatible with those of England; this is sly because one suspects that here the Koran is being used as a stalking horse for the Bible and that Hume's condemnation of its treachery, inhumanity, cruelty, revenge and bigotry is not directed at only one religious work.

What the digression leads to, then, is the statement that "the merit of delivering true general precepts in ethics is indeed very small" (268) because the terms themselves imply blame or approbation. Furthermore, given that the argument began by noting something similar about the language of criticism, inherent in Hume's conclusion is a parallel statement about the small merit of delivering true general precepts in aesthetics, too. And this brings us back to Hume's evasion of the question of how to identify truly good critics, for in contenting himself with nothing more than a general description of the qualities of a good critic, avoiding particulars, Hume commits the very fault he condemns in this introductory digression, albeit in aesthetics rather than ethics. Again the reader is left to ask whether Hume was aware of this inconsistency. There is no direct evidence that he was, but, on the other hand, what is the point of the digression on moral generalizations, so abruptly broken off, unless intended for the ironic purpose of undermining the appeal to general agreement later in the essay?

The form and function of the first six paragraphs of the essay seem evidence of a technique of ironic contrast in the work. Because of this, the reader has to be prepared to make comparisons between statements and arguments is often separated by several pages. For example, in discussing the need for the good critic to free himself from prejudice, Hume writes that

> when any work is addressed to the public, though I should have a friendship or enmity with the author, I must depart from this situation; and considering myself as a man in general, forget, if possible, my individual being and my peculiar circumstances (276).

This seems fair enough, although we might ask how strong the phrase "if possible" is here. But later in the essay Hume discusses personal preferences in literature: "at twenty, Ovid may be the favourite author; Horace at forty; and perhaps Tacitus at fifty" (281). He goes on to say that "vainly would we, in such cases, endeavour to enter into the sentiments of others, and divest ourselves of those propensities, which are natural to us." If it is so difficult to divest ourselves of our natural propensities in the second case, how is it easier in the earlier one? Hume's language here suggests difficulty, not ease; he writes of how the prejudiced critic fails to respond "as if he had imposed a proper violence on his imagination, and had forgotten himself for a moment" (277). The oxymoron "proper violence" implies more than a dilemma in the mind of the critic but a conflict of values, for he must, it seems, violate his own feelings for the sake of a higher, selfless end.

It might be argued that the contexts significantly alter Hume's meaning in these two cases; that in the first he is, reasonably enough, warning against a particular kind of prejudice for or against an author with whom one is personally acquainted, and in the second he is merely noting a natural and acceptable tendency which it would be absurd to oppose. We do expect critics to be disinterested in certain obvious ways, for instance, financially, but we make allowances for, and sometimes prize, youthful enthusiasm, mature wisdom and national, political or religious sympathy with an author. But against this line of argument can be set the presence in "Of the Standard of Taste" of other ironic contrasts, especially between its last few pages and the middle section of remarks on the ideal critic, and these also focus on the question of the point of view the critic should adopt.

If we return to the paragraph discussing the critic's need to be free from prejudice, we find Hume asserting that every work of art, in order to produce its due effect on the mind, must be surveyed in a certain point of view, and cannot be fully relished by persons, whose situation, real or imaginary, is not conformable to that which is required by the performance (276).

Now there are obvious problems here concerning what the "due effect" of a work of art is and how we discover the situation of the spectator required by that work, but let us ignore these and turn to the general point that the critic must put himself into the correct point of view before passing judgment. Otherwise, says Hume,

> if the work be addressed to persons of a different age or nation, he makes no allowance for their peculiar views and prejudices; but, full of the manners of his own age and country, rashly condemns what seemed admirable in the eyes of those for whom alone the discourse was calculated (277).

Towards the end of the essay, however, Hume returns to this matter to quite a different effect. Perhaps it is significant that here he considers it in more particular detail and instead of talking generally of "a different age or nation" he mentions specifically the controversy about ancient and modern learning and the rival arts of England and France.

He begins by remarking that "we are more pleased ... with pictures and characters, that resemble objects which are found in our own age or country, than with those which describe a different set of customs" (281) and instances modern dislike of the rustic behavior of aristocrats in ancient literature and the difficulty of transferring comedy from one age or country to another. True, he allows that "a man of learning and reflection can make allowance for these peculiarities of manners" (282), which seems like a reference back to the ideal, detached critic of the earlier passage. But the next paragraph develops a different point. Hume offers a reflection on "the celebrated controversy concerning ancient and modern learning." He proposes a distinction between what is and is not a legitimate allowance for the changes in civilization since ancient times:

> where any innocent peculiarities of manners are represented ... they ought certainly to be admitted; and a man, who is shocked with them, gives an evident proof of false delicacy and refinement.... But where the ideas of morality and decency alter from one age to another, and where vicious manners are described, without being marked with the proper characters of blame and disapprobation; this must be allowed to disfigure the poem, and to be a real deformity. I cannot, nor is it proper I should, enter into such sentiments; and however I may excuse the poet, on account of the manners of his age, I never can relish the composition (282).

To draw the line at condoning what you regard as immorality must make it impossible to adopt the correct point of view required of the ideal judge earlier in the essay. Further, if we follow Hume's suggestion and make allowances for "innocent peculiarities of manners" but not for moral differences, then we open ourselves to the more trivial aspects of alien culture and close our minds to its more serious side, or at any rate as much of it as we disapprove of. Hume seems to be advocating the exercise, not the abolition, of prejudice, except in unimportant matters of customs and manners.

Yet over this paragraph, as over many in these last pages of the essay, hangs an ironic air of paradox. The paragraph ends with sharp criticism of the morals of Homer and Greek tragedians, as though Hume relishes the opportunity to snipe at these cultural monuments. I suspect that it is not so much the case that he disapproves of their morality as that he is showing the "unco quid"[5] that the Greek classics they profess to admire are morally dubious.[6] At the same time he raises again the problem of the critic's point of view and whether or not he could or should divest himself of his own beliefs in order to accommodate those of the work in question. Hume articulates an extreme attitude: "where a man is confident of the rectitude of that moral standard, by which he judges, he is justly jealous of it, and will not pervert the sentiments of his heart for a moment, in complaisance to any writer whatsoever" (283). This is a far cry from "placing himself in that point of view, which the performance supposes" (277). It seems that either the ideal critic has to deny his own morality or the moral critic has to succumb to the prejudice under which "all his natural sentiments are perverted" (278).

Hume carries the irony a stage further by carefully separating morality and religion; where the first admits no compromise, the second may be excused. As he impishly puts it, "all the absurdities of the pagan system of theology must be overlooked by every critic, who would pretend to form a just notion of ancient poetry; and our posterity, in their turn, must have the same indulgence to their forefathers" (283); that is to say, future readers must excuse the Christianity of Hume's contemporaries as a transient cultural aberration. The effect of this is

---

5 This is a reference to Robert Burns's poem *Address to the Unco Guid, or Rigidly Righteous* (1786).
6 Hume indulges in a similar trick in the "Dialogue" appended to his *Enquiry concerning the Principles of Morals* (1751), in which Palamedes, using unrecognizable names, describes what seems to be an immoral and corrupt society, only to reveal that he has in fact been talking about the ancient Greeks. His aim is to show "that fashion, vogue, custom, and law, were the chief foundation of all moral determination." This seems to me not dissimilar to Hume's purpose in "Of the Standard of Taste."

to drain much of the significance from Christian literature. If, for the sake of argument, we call the moderns Christian, as opposed to the pagan ancients, Hume might be said to have argued two things: first, that ancient literature cannot now be seriously considered because it does not conform to modern, Christian morality and, second, that modern literature is equally vitiated by its conformity to a religious cult.

The only exception to Hume's rule of religious tolerance is when religious principles lay a poet under the imputation of bigotry or superstition, since these offend against morality and hence cannot be excused. Religious principles become bigotry or superstition when they take strong possession of the poet's heart, that is to say, when he takes them seriously enough to believe in them. Thus it seems that any work of art with a serious religious purpose alien to the critic must be rejected by him. Hume disguises the scope of this conclusion by using the conventional eighteenth-century whipping-post, Roman Catholicism, as his example of religious bigotry and superstition, and thus seems to conform to the British bigotry and superstition of his day. We might defend him against this charge by saying that his attack on Catholicism displays just that prejudice which he has been ironically describing as a laudable refusal to compromise in moral judgments. Indeed, what develops in the penultimate paragraph of the essay is not so much a diatribe against Popery as a reminder of the cultural differences, and prejudices, dividing France from England, with Hume, as a Scot and a philosopher, playing the impartial observer. Here again he seems to be showing that when we come down to particular examples in specified cultural contexts, what we find is variety, even incommensurability, of taste rather than a universal standard.

II

Now if "Of the Standard of Taste" does indeed have the inconsistencies and contradictions I have pointed out, one is left wondering how coherent it is, whether indeed it was meant to be coherent, and therefore if it is a serious work at all. One might argue that it is a muddle, a series of unrelated and unrelatable arguments of different tendencies, Hume's random thoughts on the subject. It might be said that, being only an essay, such lack of rigor is to be expected. Hume's excuse is that he is writing in a leisurely way for leisure readers. But a far more interesting speculation is that although the essay may appear to lack rigor Hume in fact exploits this patchiness to ironic effect by blandly confronting conventional arguments with their contradictions, leaving it to the percipient reader to see his serious meaning. This meaning must be sought in the combined effects of the ironies I have noted. The next stage is to see what tendencies these ironies have and upon what presuppositions they are based.

The treatment of the story from *Don Quixote* has certain implications. It suggests, for instance, the outlandishness of delicacy of taste, making it seem not only rare but also abnormal. Related to this is the acrimony Hume introduces into the story, which later passes into the aesthetic parallel, in which a deviant critic is made to see the error of his ways. In this competitive situation power seems to lie with the big battalions, especially after Hume has made the shift from the physical key and thong as vindication of the tasters to the much more abstract general rules of art. Tradition, convention, "what oft was thought" seem to rule in matters of artistic taste. But perhaps the reader ought to be struck by the disparity of the equivalence Hume asserts. For the obvious equivalent to the key and thong is surely some physical feature of a work of art, the evidence of what it is like, the cause of the sentiments felt in the critic. Instead, Hume ostentatiously avoids this possibility, thus ironically suggesting the lack of such conclusive verification of a critic's view. As he says, if the key and thong had not been found, it would have been very difficult for Sancho's kinsmen to prove their superior taste. The implication is that since critics cannot really produce anything so conclusive, their judgments are correspondingly open to dispute. The story as a whole suggests the crucial difference between physical tasting and aesthetic taste, while purporting to use this analogy conventionally.[7]

Hume's treatment of the definition of the ideal critic similarly undermines a conventional view, for his stress on the difficulties facing the critic and the consequent rarity of the good critic make the possibility of a standard of taste based on the views of several such critics seem more and more remote. Although it seems at first acceptable that good taste should be determined by the judgments of the best critics, by the time Hume has finished describing the qualifications of those critics he has made them seem, like Sancho's kinsmen, over-refined creatures, hardly human at all in their freedom from prejudice and individual propensities. The later passages, in which Hume restores preference and prejudice to importance, seem more realistic about human nature. The ironic effect is that the theory that ideal critics make the standard of taste is shown to be unworkable because it does not match reality. This is confirmed by the escape into generalization at the crucial point where the argument demands that some particular definition of the good critic and his principles be given.

---

7 For an uncritical use of the analogy between physical taste and aesthetic taste, see *The Spectator* 409, by Joseph Addison.

Yet there is perhaps a deeper irony in that the presentation of this line of argument seems so conventional and familiar, as though Hume is saying that although it is inconclusive and cannot proceed beyond generalization, nevertheless this is the best argument of its kind for the standard of taste, and is often used.[8] And if in fact the standard of taste has no more secure basis than this, its application must owe its success not to any reasoned acceptance of it by critics and people of taste but to some kind of habitual acquiescence, never very thoroughly questioned. That there are critics who strongly influence the opinions of others is indubitable; that they conform to the ideal demanded by the theorists of the standard of taste is less certain. Perhaps the unfounded generalizations of the theorists merely add respectability to the eminence of those who occupy the commanding heights of culture.

The last few pages of the essay reintroduce prejudices and personal beliefs as influences on taste. The effect is to bring the debate about a standard back into relation with other topics, especially morality and religion. It is noticeable that this comes about as soon as the discussion becomes particular enough to mention actual writers, the Greeks, and actual publics, the French and the English. The standard of taste is brought down from an ideal, detached level of lofty debate and found to be at the mercy of other sets of beliefs. Indeed, Hume ironically makes a purely aesthetic approach seem trivial by restricting it to those aspects of art which are not morally serious. If art and criticism are to be really valuable, they will have to enmesh with the moral values of their time and place, and that will inevitably affect their status in relation to any supposed general rules. In such a conflict Hume seems clearly to see that success lies with the demands of the here and now, hence the cultural relativism of these concluding remarks in his essay.

Throughout there is vagueness about the constancy of the art-object and its value. Of course, an essay about the standard of taste is bound to concentrate on the mechanics of critical debate rather than on the precise nature of the aesthetic experience, but the impression remains that, for Hume, the contribution from the nature of the works of art themselves seems remarkably slight. They initiate the debate, but do not control it. The influences which seem more important are the personal and cultural variables, and these are quite fluid. Appeal may be made to general rules, or to the supposed excellence of a critic or to moral standards to

---

[8] Very similar lines of argument are taken by Alexander Gerard in his *Essay on Taste*, 1759, by Henry Home, Lord Kames, in his *Elements of Criticism*, 1762, and in the seventh of Sir Joshua Reynolds's *Discourses*, 1776.

establish the quality of a work, but these are essentially temporary. They are open to variations and manipulation.

It is because of the significant influence of individual prejudices in judgments of taste that a major centre of interest in Hume's essay is the point of view of the critic. In his first, negative discussion of this Hume makes the idealistic demand that the critic renounce his own individual point of view and adopt one which is correct for the work in question and free from personal bias. This is very much a conventional approach and goes with the notion that the good critic bases his judgments on general rules of taste, which by definition are free from individual prejudice. But Hume seems to realise that such freedom is impossible. The point of view of a general rule is itself a generalization and need not, perhaps cannot, coincide with any individual's actual viewpoint. If a critic claims to occupy exactly the point of view demanded by a general rule, based on generalization of several different critics' opinions, then he has either succeeded in depersonalizing himself or hopes to convince others that he has. In other words, the neo-classical appeal to general rules of taste can in practice amount to either of two things: an unattainable ideal, to which critics strive genuinely but without expectation of full success, or an empty gesture intended to lend spurious authority to what is really personal opinion. In the latter case the appeal to general rules appears only as a social convention which disguises the real state of affairs, the struggle by critics to establish and maintain their authority. Thus there may be another layer of irony in Hume's conclusion that "it is sufficient for our present purpose, if we have proved, that ... some men ... will be acknowledged by universal sentiment to have a preference above others" (279) in that this minimal statement may be all there is to say about the actual behaviour usually described as the operation of a standard of taste. The implication is that an established critic has put himself in a position to exercise a self-perpetuating influence on critical opinion.

Some plausibility is given to this reading by a slightly later paragraph in the essay that describes the operation of a system of taste in which a few leaders generate opinions that are then propagated to become acknowledged verdicts:

> Though men of delicate taste be rare, they are easily to be distinguished in society, by the soundness of their understanding and the superiority of their faculties above the rest of mankind. The ascendent, which they acquire, gives a prevalence to that lively approbation, with which they receive any productions of genius, and renders it generally predominant. Many men, when left to themselves, have but a faint and dubious perception of beauty, who yet are capable of relishing any fine stroke, which is pointed out to them. Every convert to the admiration of the real poet or orator is the cause of some new conversion. And though prejudices may prevail for a time, they never unite in celebrating any rival to the true genius, but yield at last to the force of nature and just sentiment ... (280).

What is noticeable here is that the ascendent critic alone has the responses to the work of art, which he then teaches the dull majority to appreciate. This process is likened, in the use of the words "convert" and "conversion," to the spread of religious belief, whose opposite is easily labelled "prejudice." The critic acts like a missionary, interpreting the truth of the work of art to a benighted public who seem incapable of finding it out for themselves. Once persuaded, however, the public hold fast to their opinion and will not readily change; hence the lasting reputations of classical authors. Hume contrasts their long popularity with the revolutions in philosophy and theology, ironically omitting the point that philosophers and, one supposes, theologians are attempting to make statements of fact which may be true or false and judged accordingly. The claims of critics, however, are justified by general acceptance and their errors are forms of social deviance. Thus it is hardly surprising that "though a civilized nation may easily be mistaken in the choice of their admired philosopher, they never have been found long to err, in their affection for a favourite epic or tragic author" (280). Hume's essay, then, ironically undermines the neo-classical beliefs it seems to support and reduces them to a disguise of the social machinery by which tastes are in fact created and changed.[9] Central to this is the acknowledged critic, who can, by virtue of his social position, mold opinion and create reputations. From the historical point of view, the interesting thing is that Hume himself seems to have attempted to do this. Having acquired a certain literary reputation, he tried to use his influence to promote several Scottish writers, Blacklock, Wilkie and his cousin John Home.[10] His motive seems to have been patriotism; he seems to have felt the need for a Scottish literary achievement. His method conformed closely to the outline quoted above. He wrote letters to friends both in Scotland and England asking, almost badgering, them to read the latest Scottish masterpiece, assuring them of its worth in encomia which make pointed comparisons with classical literature. In addition, he urges them to bring the work to the notice of their friends, especially those of some prominence in English letters, and tries to encourage all concerned by repeatedly mentioning respected critics and their re-

---

[9] Mary Carman Rose, in "The Importance of Hume in the History of Western Aesthetics," claims that Hume was innovatory in treating aesthetic questions without metaphysical preconceptions and that his views are "drawn from his study of what he takes to be *de facto* human responses to art objects" (p. 220). She concludes that "Hume's suggestion that in seeking understanding of the nature and mode of being of beauty we turn from the object to the person who responds to it aesthetically informs much twentieth-century analysis of the status of being and of the meaning of the linguistic expressions in which we talk about aesthetic experience and aesthetic objects" (p. 222).
[10] See E.C. Mossner, *The Life of David Hume*, Chapter 27.

marks on the work, as though to create the required influential body of opinion needed to lift the work into public attention.

All Hume's attempts were failures, although John Home's play *Douglas* did enjoy a vogue. His grasp of the public relations aspect of literary success, however, was prescient, for within a few years of his death was to come the astonishing rise of a provincial Scottish poet to national, indeed international, fame. The rise of Robert Burns's reputation, transmitted through the Edinburgh *literati* to London and beyond, is almost a model of Hume's conception of the critical process. So too is the rise to fame of Sir Walter Scott. Perhaps this suggests that "Of the Standard of Taste" is really an account of what is now known as the best-seller.

Finally, let me stress two important aspects of Hume's notion of taste. The first, upon which Peter Jones lays much emphasis, is the public nature of critical debate, the need for the critic to have his judgments accepted by others. In "Of the Standard of Taste" Hume inclines to a social view of his subject. Sancho's kinsmen are involved in a social activity in trying to convince others of their wine-tasting ability. Similarly, the great critic will have his delicacy all to himself unless he can persuade others to accept his expertise. The qualities of the good critic which Hume describes are publicly observable. The community can see for itself whether a critic is well-practised, whether he can make comparisons, whether he is free from prejudice and whether he has good sense (the only exception is delicacy of taste itself, and this, Hume suggests, goes naturally with good sense). There is, of course, nothing here about untutored genius, natural sensibility, or good taste as opposed to popular opinion. The good critic is synonymous with his reputation, and the standard of taste he promotes reflects his society's cultural values.

For this reason, there is a second aspect to Hume's theory of taste which is worth bringing out. Implicit in his cultural relativism is the plurality of taste. Historically and geographically there is not one taste but many. These tastes are, as it were, assessments of prevailing critical opinion and preferences in particular times and places. Hume's awareness of the differences between ancient and modern taste, and between English and French taste in his own time (perhaps sharpened by his awareness of the differences between English and Scottish taste), leads him away from the conventional eighteenth-century view of taste as a mental faculty towards taste as an ordering concept, what Eva Schaper calls

> one among the concepts by which we bring order into the social and aesthetic history of art, design and culture.... The taste concept is used and needed by art history to make

the mere catalogue of artistic achievements 'history,' and to make the mere assortment of past and present group phenomena amenable as ordered patterns ....[11]

She goes on to say that "if on such a view we want to talk of 'standards of taste,' we must see them as derivative from and created by art works as they form a historical order" (66). Hume would disagree; it is not the artworks but the critics who create standards of taste, by imposing an order on them, and thus the crucial point is not the nature of the artwork but the nature of the critic and the society he reflects.

Acknowledgements

This essay was originally published in *Hume Studies*, Vol 12/1 (1986): 18–38. The editor is grateful to Doctor MacLachlan for contributing this essay as well as to the collegial kindness of the editors of *Hume Studies* for their permission to reprint this essay here.

Bibliography

Addison, Joseph (1712) "Taste." *The Spectator*. 409. June 19.
Cervantes, Miguel de [Saavedra] (1700) *Don Quixote*. Peter Anthony Motteux, trans. London: Printed for Sam. Buckley.
Cervantes, Miguel de [Saavedra] (1742) *Don Quixote*. Charles Jarvis, trans. London: J. & R. Tonson & R. Dodsley.
Gerard, Alexander (1759) *Essay on Taste*. London: Printed for A. Millar, A. Kincaid and J. Bell.
Home, Henry, Lord Kames, (1762) *Elements of Criticism*. Edinburgh: A. Kincaid & J. Bell, Edinburgh, 1762.
Reynolds, Sir Joshua (1776) *Discourses*. i.
Hume, David (1875) "Of the Standard of Taste." In: *Essays Moral, Political, and Literary*, T.H. Green and T.H. Grose (Eds.), Vol. 1. London: Longmans, Green, and Company.
Hume, David (1751) *Enquiry concerning the Principles of Morals*. London: A. Millar.
Jones, Peter (1976) "Hume's Aesthetics Reassessed." *Philosophical Quarterly*. 26: 48–62.
Mossner, E.C. (1954) *The Life of David Hume*. Oxford: Oxford University Press.
Rose, Mary Carman (1976) "The Importance of Hume in the History of Western Aesthetics." *British Journal of Aesthetics*. 16: 218–229.
Schaper, Eva (1966) "Symposium: About Taste 1." *British Journal of Aesthetics*. 6: 55–67.

---

11 Eva Schaper, "Symposium: About Taste 1."

Roger Scruton
Taste and Order

In a democratic culture people are inclined to believe that it is presumptuous to claim to have better taste than your neighbour. By doing so you are implicitly denying his right to be the thing that he is. You like Bach, she likes U2; you like Leonardo, he likes Mucha; she likes Jane Austen, you like Danielle Steele. Each of you exists in his own enclosed aesthetic world, and so long as neither harms the other, and each says good morning over the fence, there is nothing further to be said.

The Common Pursuit

But things are not so simple, as the democratic argument already implies. If it is so offensive to look down on another's taste, it is, as the democrat recognizes, because taste is intimately bound up with our personal life and moral identity. It is part of our rational nature to strive for a community of judgement, a shared conception of value, since that is what reason and the moral life require. And this desire for a reasoned consensus spills over into the sense of beauty.

This we discover as soon as we take into account the public impact of private tastes. Your neighbor fills her garden with kitsch mermaids and Disneyland gnomes, polluting the view from your window; she designs her house in a ludicrous Costa Brava style, in loud primary colors that utterly ruin the tranquil atmosphere of the street, and so on. Now her taste has ceased to be a private matter and inflicted itself on the public realm. We begin to dispute the matter: you appeal to the town council, arguing that her house and garden are not in keeping with the street, that this particular part of town is scheduled to retain a Georgian serenity, that her house clashes with the classical facades of adjacent buildings. (In a recent British case a house-owner, influenced by art school fashions, erected a plastic sculpture of a shark on his roof, to give the appearance of a great fish that had crashed through the tiles into the attic. Protests from neighbours and the local planning officer led to a prolonged legal battle, which the house-owner – an American, who no longer lives in the house – eventually won.)

We know from experience that there is much to argue about here, and that argument does not aim to win by whatever means, but rather to generate a *consensus*. Implicit in our sense of beauty is the thought of community – of the agreement in judgments that makes social life possible and worthwhile. That is one of the reasons why we have planning laws – which, in the great days of Western civilization, have been extremely strict, controlling the heights of buildings (nineteenth-century Helsinki), the materials to be used in construction (eighteenth-century Paris), the tiles to be used in roofing (twentieth-century Provence), even the crenelations on buildings that face the thoroughfares (Venice, from the fifteenth century onwards).

Nor is this desire for consensus confined to the public realm of architecture and garden design. Think of clothes, interior decor, and bodily ornaments: here too we can be put on edge, excluded or included, made to feel inside or outside the implied community, and we strive by comparison and discussion to achieve a consensus within which we can feel at home. Many of the clothes we wear have the character of uniforms, designed to express and confirm our inoffensive membership of the community (the office suit, the tuxedo, the baseball cap, the school uniform), or perhaps our solidarity with a community of offenders (the 'convict' style of black American 'gangstas') Others, like women's party clothes, are designed to draw attention to our individuality, though without offending the proprieties. Fashion is integral to our nature as social beings: it arises from, and also amplifies, the aesthetic signals with which we make our social identity apparent to the world. We begin to see why concepts like decorum and propriety are integral to the sense of beauty, but they are concepts that range equally across the aesthetic and the moral spheres.

Yet there are also private arts like music and literature.

Why are we so concerned that our children should learn to like the things that *we* regard as beautiful? Why do we worry when children are drawn to literature that is, in our eyes, ugly, stupefying, sentimental or obscene? Plato believed that the various modes of music are connected with specific moral characteristics of those who dance or march to them, and that in a well-ordered city only those modes would be permitted which are in some way fitted to the virtuous soul. This is a striking and in its own way plausible claim, though the concept of 'fit' is explained by Plato through a theory of imitation (*mimēsis*) that is no longer plausible.

Subjectivity and Reasons

Someone might respond that there is no real argument here – consensus, if it is achieved, arises in some other way, by emotional infection, rather than by reasoning. You like Brahms, say, and I detest him. So you invite me to listen to your favourite pieces, and after a while they 'work on me'. Maybe I am influenced by my friendship for you and make a special effort on your behalf. How it happens, I do not know – but if it happens that I come to like Brahms, then this is not a rational decision, nor a rational conclusion of mine: it is a change comparable to that undergone by children when, having begun life by hating greens, they learn at last to relish them. An experience that repelled them now attracts them; but it was not an argument that persuaded them. While a change of taste is not a 'change of mind,' in the way that a change of belief or even of moral posture is a change of mind, this does not mean that there are no extraneous reasons that might justify the change in taste. After all, there are extraneous reasons that justify the child's graduation from burgers to broccoli. Greens are far more healthy, maybe part of a superior lifestyle, maybe even a spiritual improvement, as Vegans argue. But those reasons are not internal to the change in taste: they rationalize the change, but do not produce it – since it is not the kind of change that could be produced by rational argument.

We are in deep water here. But it is worth meditating on what actually happens when you argue about matters of aesthetic taste. We have been listening to Brahms's Fourth Symphony, say, and you ask me how I like it. "Heavy, lugubrious, oily, gross," I say. You play me the first subject of the first movement on the piano. "Listen," you say. And you invert the sixths so that they become thirds and I hear how the theme goes down one ladder of thirds and up another. You show me how the harmonies are also organized by third progressions and how the ensuing themes unfold from the same melodic and harmonic cells that generate the opening melody. After a while I understand that there is a kind of minimalism at work here – everything emerges from a concentrated seed of musical material, and after a while I hear this happening and then – suddenly – it all sounds right to me. The heaviness and oiliness vanish in a moment, and instead I hear a kind of breaking into leaf and flower of a beautiful plant.

Figure 3: James Whistler (1834–1903) *Nocturne in Grey and Silver* (1873–1875). Public Domain.

Surface Shadow, or a Deeper Darkness?

Or take another example: we are looking at a Whistler 'Nocturne'. You find it vapid, maybe (following a famous judgment of Ruskin's) reprehensible in its focus on momentary effects, and in its refusal to explore the deeper realities. This painting, you say, draws a veil over the toil and trouble of modern life; it sees as charm and evocation what is in fact labor and exploitation. And all this is summarized in the title: *Nocturne in Grey and Silver,* as though you could abstract the human energy that made this effect and judge it as a play of lighted colors.

Yes, I respond, you can see it that way. But the painting is not just an impression: its very shadowy quality indicates the extent to which people and their projects have darkened the world. There is no denial, here, of labor and its exploitation, but on the contrary, an attempt to see in the shadow-filled moment the extent of man's trespass on the natural order. The title opens our minds to this, in fact: a 'nocturne' is a human creation, and a recent one, not known before the industrial revolution and the retreat of the property-owning classes into their drawing rooms, to be entertained at the piano by willowy aesthetes. Silver and grey are the colours of widowhood, and the atmosphere of the painting is one of melancholy recognition that, thanks to human industry, the sheen of the world is henceforth to be an artificial one. To justify this judgment, I will refer to the shades of color, to the prominent shapes in the canvas, which are the shapes of man-made things, and to the points of light which are man-made lights.

As our discussion proceeds, unfolding the two rival interpretations of the painting, as pure impression and as social comment, the aspect of the picture will perhaps shift from one to the other – so that the painting seems to contain a lesson, reminding us that we can to some extent choose how the new world of industry should be seen.

We can find simpler, and logically more transparent cases of this kind of change in aspect – like the celebrated duck-rabbit discussed by Wittgenstein. There may be a right and wrong way to see such figures – and I can reason you out of seeing a duck, where you ought to be seeing a rabbit. (Say the figure appears on a packet of rabbit food.) Such cases are not exceptional. On the contrary, in every perspective picture there are choices to make, concerning what size to attribute to which figure, and what distance to see between the various grounds. And the reasoning here will be like that which I gave in connection with the Whistler, i.e., reasoning concerning the meaning of the picture, and how you should see the picture if the meaning is, as it were, properly to *inhabit* it.

The criticism of poetry, too, follows this pattern. When you describe Blake's "Oh rose, thou art sick | The invisible worm | That flies in the night" as an evocation of sexual desire and the worm of jealousy, and I reply with a theory of its Christian iconology, and interpret the worm and the bed of crimson joy as lust and the soul respectively, you begin to hear the words differently – that "dark secret love" has a new resonance, and one that is filled with ominous meaning for your own life. Such criticism is not just saying: here is what the poem means, as though you could now discard the poem and make do with my superior translation. The poetry is not a means to its meaning, as though a translation would do just as well. I want you to experience the poem differently, and my critical argument is aimed precisely at a change in your perception.

The argument can be mounted for architecture, for sculpture, for novels and plays; it can be mounted for natural objects too, such as landscapes and flowers. In every case we recognize that there is such a thing as reasoning which has a changed perception as its goal. Moreover, any argument that did not aim at a changed perception could not be considered as a critical argument: it would not be a relevant reflection on its object, as an object of aesthetic judgement. You can confirm this by considering how you might answer questions like the following: "Is the Grand Canyon breathtaking or corny?" "Is *Bambi* moving or kitsch?" "Is *Madame Bovary* tragic or cruel?" "Is *The Magic Flute* childish or sublime?" These are real questions, and hotly disputed too. But to argue them is to present an experience and to present it as appropriate or right.

The Search for Objectivity

Suppose you accept, in broad outline, what I have just argued for – namely, that there is a kind of reasoning that has aesthetic judgment as its goal, and that this judgment is bound up with the experience of the one who makes it. You might still question whether this kind of reasoning is objective, in the sense of being based in and invoking standards that are persuasive to all rational beings. Indeed, there are important considerations to the contrary.

First, taste is rooted in a broader cultural context, and cultures (at least in the sense that we here have in mind) are not universal. The whole point of the concept of culture is to mark out the significant *differences* between the forms of human life, and the satisfactions that people take in them. Consider the ragas of Indian classical music: these belong to a long-standing tradition of listening and performance, and this tradition is dependent on the discipline associated with religious rituals and a devout way of life. Conventions, allusions and applications resonate in the minds and ears of those who play and enjoy this music, and the difference between a good and a bad performance cannot be established in terms that might equally be used to evaluate a Mozart symphony or a work of jazz.

Secondly, as noted in the first chapter of my book, *Beauty*,[1] there is no deductive relation between premises and conclusion when the conclusion is a judgment of taste. I am always free to reject a critical argument in a way that I am not free to reject a valid scientific inference or a valid moral claim.

Finally, we must recognize that any attempt to lay down objective standards threatens the very enterprise that it purports to judge. Rules and precepts are there to be transcended, and because originality and the challenging of orthodoxies are fundamental to the aesthetic enterprise, an element of freedom is built into the pursuit of beauty, whether the minimal beauty of everyday arrangements, or the higher beauties of art.

How might we respond to such arguments? First, it is important to recognize that cultural variation does not imply the absence of cross-cultural universals. Nor does it imply that those universals, if they exist, are not rooted in our nature, or that they do not feed into our rational interests at a very fundamental level. Symmetry and order, proportion, closure, convention, harmony, and also novelty and excitement: all these seem to have a permanent hold on the human psyche. Now of course those words are all vague and multiply ambiguous, and you might well object that they are themselves likely to fragment along the fracture lines that divide culture from culture in the human lot. The early medieval regarded the fourth as harmonious, the third as dissonant: for us, if anything, it is the other way around. *Harmonia* for the Greeks consisted in the relation between successive sounds in a melody and not the consonance of simultaneous notes. And so on.

Objectivity and Universality

But that brings me to a more important observation, which is that, in the matter of aesthetic judgement, objectivity and universality come apart. In science and morality, the search for objectivity is the search for universally valid results – results that must be accepted by every rational being. In the judgement of beauty, the search for objectivity is for valid and heightened forms of human experience

---

1 Scruton, *Beauty: A Very Short Introduction*.

– forms in which human life can flower according to its inner need and achieve the kind of fruition that we witness in the Sistine Chapel ceiling, in *Parsifal*, or in *Hamlet*. Criticism is not aiming to show that you *must* like *Hamlet*, for example: it is aiming to expose the vision of human life which the play contains, the forms of belonging which it endorses, and to persuade you of their value. It is not claiming that this vision of human life is universally available. This does not mean that no cross-cultural comparisons can be made. It is certainly possible to compare a play like *Hamlet* with a puppet play by Chikamatsu, for example: indeed, it has been done. There are works of Japanese theatre that satirize human life (the Kabuki comedy *Hokaibo*, for example), and works which exalt it, and the question whether Beaumarchais's *Le Mariage de Figaro* is a profounder treatment of human sexuality than *Hokaibo* is a perfectly meaningful one.

The objection that aesthetic reasons are purely persuasive simply reiterates the point, that aesthetic judgment is rooted in subjective experience. So is the judgment of color. And is it not an objective fact that red things are red, blue things blue?

Figure 4: *Staircase, Laurentian Library, Florence, Italy.* Sailko Creative Commons, GNU General Public License. Public Domain.

Rules and Originality

The final objection is, however, more serious. There may be rules of taste, but they do not guarantee beauty, and the beauty of a work of art may reside precisely in the act of transgressing them. Bach's *Forty-Eight Fugues* illustrate all the rules of fugal composition: but they do so by obeying them *creatively,* by showing how they can be used as a platform from which to rise to a higher realm of freedom. *Merely* obeying them would be a recipe for dullness, as in all the exercises from which we begin our lessons in counterpoint. Likewise, in architecture there may be buildings which we understand as entirely rule-governed, like the Parthenon, but this does not explain their perfection. The serenity and solidity of the Parthenon come about through that extra creative something: the scale, proportions, detailing that arise from the thinking that begins when the rule-following stops. And again, there are beauties that arise from the overt defiance of rules, as in Michelangelo's Laurentian library.

It is fairly obvious that there is no 'rule-following' or 'rule defying' in nature. Yet there are symmetries, harmonies, proportions, and also the aesthetically challenging lack of those things. Eighteenth-century thinkers, who wished to take natural beauty as their paradigm of the object of taste, were therefore quick to adopt Burke s contrast between the sublime and the beautiful. So too in art, we might usefully distinguish those works that please us on account of the order, harmony, and rule-governed perfection which they display, like the fugues of Bach, the Holy Virgins of Bellini, or the lyrics of Verlaine, and those which, on the contrary, please us by challenging and disturbing our routines, by throwing off the shackles of conformity and by standing out from the traditions to which they belong, like *King Lear* or Tchaikovsky's *Sixth Symphony.* But as soon as we make this distinction, we realize that even in the most orderly and rule-governed work there is no way of fixing a 'standard of taste' by appeal to the rules. It is not the rules but the use of them that appeals in a Bach fugue or a Bellini Virgin. Those who seek a standard in the rules open themselves to refutation, when it is pointed out that obedience to the rules is neither necessary nor sufficient for beauty. For if it were sufficient then once again we could acquire taste at second hand; and if it were necessary, then originality would cease to be a mark of success.

The Standard of Taste

Where then should we look for standards in the judgement of beauty? Or is our search destined to be vain? In a celebrated essay Hume tried to shift the focus of the discussion, arguing roughly as follows: taste is a form of preference, and this preference is the premise, not the conclusion of the judgement of beauty. To fix the standard, therefore, we must discover the *reliable judge,* the one whose taste and discriminations are the best guide to.... Guide to what? There is a potential circle here: beauty is what the reliable critic discerns, and the reliable critic is the one who discerns beauty. But such a circle is what we must expect: for Hume, seeing an object as beautiful is a matter of 'gilding or staining it with the colors borrowed from internal sentiment'. The standard, if it exists, does not lie in the qualities of the object but in the sentiments of the judge. So, Hume suggests, let us get away from the fruitless discussion of beauty and simply concentrate on the qualities we admire, and ought to admire, in a critic – qualities such as delicacy and discernment.

However, this opens us to another kind of scepticism: why should it be *those* qualities that we admire? Even if it seemed natural in the Scotland of Hume's day to admire delicacy and discernment, it seems less natural today when facetiousness and ignorance, so unfairly left out by the austere sages of the Enlightenment, are demanding, and receiving, their share of attention.

Is this where we should leave the topic? I think not, for Hume's argument suggests that the judgement of taste reflects the character of the one who makes it, and character matters. The characteristics of the good critic, as Hume envisaged them, point to virtues which, in Hume's thinking, are vital to the good conduct of life and not just to the discrimination of aesthetic qualities. In the last analysis there is as much objectivity in our judgments of beauty as there is in our judgments of virtue and vice. Beauty is therefore as firmly rooted in the scheme of things as is goodness. It speaks to us as virtue speaks to us, of human fulfilment: not of things that we want, but of things that we ought to want because human nature requires them.

Acknowledgements

This chapter first appeared in Roger Scruton, *Beauty: A Very Short Introduction* (Oxford, Oxford University Press, 2011), pp. 1–28.

Bibliography

Scruton, Roger (2011) *Beauty: A Very Short Introduction.* Oxford: Oxford University Press. 1–28.

Timothy M. Costelloe
General Rules and Hume's "Of the Standard of Taste"

Introduction

Hume's "Of the Standard of Taste" occupies a singular place in the history of aesthetics and has become important for interpreting elements of Hume's thought more broadly.[1] In the essay, Hume characterizes the "standard" in question as "a *rule*, by which the various sentiments of men may be reconciled" (ST 229, emphasis added). Elsewhere he speaks of "rules of art" (ST 231), "general rules of beauty," and "general rules or avowed patterns" (ST 235), which are founded on experience and "fix" what "has been universally found to please in all countries and in all ages" (ST 231).[2] While Hume himself describes the standard in these terms, however, interpreters of the essay have generally failed to ask what Hume *means* by "general rules," and my contention is that doing so illuminates the "standard" he seeks as well as revealing its function in "regulating" aesthetic judgment, and the role of the critic or "true judge."

"Of the Standard of Taste"

The outlines of Hume's "Of the Standard of Taste" are well known. The essay begins with the observation that ordinary language implies a general standard, which the philosophical mind naturally seeks out (ST 228–9). Hume then raises the objection that "beauty is not a quality in things themselves: It exists merely

---

[1] For an overview of the literature up to 2004 at least, see Timothy M. Costelloe, "Hume's Aesthetics: The Literature and Directions for Future Research."

[2] References to Hume's work are given as follows: *A Treatise of Human Nature*, ed. David Fate Norton and Mary Norton (Oxford: Oxford University Press, 2000) (T); *Enquiry Concerning Human Understanding*, ed. Tom L. Beauchamp (Oxford: Oxford University Press, 1999) (EHU); *Enquiry Concerning the Principle of Morals*, ed. Tom L. Beauchamp (Oxford: Oxford University Press, 1998) (EPM); "Of the Standard of Taste," in *Essays: Moral, Political, and Literary*, ed. Eugene F. Miller (Indianapolis: Liberty Classics, 1985) (ST); and *The History of England, From the Invasion of Julius Ceasar to the Revolution of 1688*, with the authors' last corrections and improvements, 6 vols. (Indianapolis: Liberty Classics, 1983) (H). References to the *Treatise* are to book, part, section, and paragraph, and to the *Enquiries* to section and paragraph, followed by page numbers of the Selby-Bigge editions.

in the mind which contemplates them." From this observation he draws the relativist conclusion that "each mind perceives a different beauty" (ST 230), a philosophical prejudice he then confounds by suggesting that there are "general rules" (ST 235) that govern the appropriateness of aesthetic judgments. These rules, he says, are to be met with most clearly in the person of the critic or true judge (ST 241). This conclusion is immediately challenged as premature, however, with Hume himself raising a series of "embarrassing" questions that threaten to throw the whole endeavor "back into the same uncertainty, from which ... we have endeavoured to extricate ourselves" (ST 241). Hume responds by acknowledging the co-existence of both "peculiarities of manners" and uniformity of sentiments, an impossible juxtaposition that is eased as the essay comes to a close. Hume thus reaches his conclusion having generated and overcome a series of contradictions in an explication of the standard of taste, the proposed existence of which motivated the essay in the first place.

There is disagreement over how to interpret both the form and content of Hume's essay, but apparent consensus on two basic issues. First, commentators generally regard the rule, and thus the standard, which Hume seeks, as an inductive generalization, inferred from empirical observation about what has pleased and displeased across time and place.[3] The text of the essay provides prima facie evidence for this view. Hume says, for example, that "rules of composition" are not "fixed by reasonings *a priori*," but are "general observations, concerning what has been universally found to please in all countries and in all ages," and are "discovered to the author either by genius or observation" (ST 231). The "same Homer, who pleased at ATHENS and ROME two thousand years ago," Hume observes later, "is still admired at PARIS and at LONDON. All the changes of climate, government, religion, and language, have not been able to obscure his glory" (ST 233). If principles governing our sentiment of beauty cannot be derived a priori, then the standard, it is reasonable to conclude, must arise from the "common sentiments of human nature" (ST 231).

Second, many interpret the standard of taste as having practical value, Hume's aim being to discover a normative criterion for guiding judgment and settling disputes when they arise.[4] Again, Hume appears to make such a claim in

---

[3] See, most recently, Jeffrey Wieand, "Hume's Two Standards of Taste"; Richard Shusterman, "The Scandal of Taste: Social Privilege as Nature in the Aesthetic Theories of Hume and Kant"; Jens Kulenkampff, "The Objectivity of Taste: Kant and Hume"; and Tina Baceski, "Hume on Art Critics, Wise Men, and the Virtues of Taste."

[4] Examples, from a large literature, include Christopher MacLachlan, "Hume and the Standard of Taste"; Steven Sverdlik, "Hume's Key and Aesthetic Rationality"; Mary Mothersill, "Hume and the Paradox of Taste"; and Paul Guyer, "The Standard of Taste and the 'Most Ardent Desire of

the course of the essay. In the case of the "bad critic," for example, who refuses to "submit to his antagonist," the standard can be "applied to the present case," Hume writes, such that the critic "must conclude ... that the fault lies in himself" (ST 236); "general rules of beauty are of use [and] ... drawn from established models, and from the observation of what pleases and displeases" (ST 235). These rules can also be "produced," as Hume says when discussing Sancho's kinsmen at the hogshead of wine, "like finding the key with the leather thong" (ST 235). Commentators tend to make both these claims—one concerning the empirical nature of the standard, the other regarding its practical use—without asking whether or not it is significant that Hume characterizes this standard in terms of a general rule.[5] Since he does this explicitly, it seems prudent to ask what he means by the term before drawing any conclusions about the nature of the standard he aims to discover. As I demonstrate in what follows, doing so obliges one to reevaluate the sense in which the standard is empirical and the degree to which it has normative value.

General Rules

Hume's most detailed discussion of general rules occurs in the *Treatise*, where he characterizes them as the source of an "unphilosophical species of probability." These rules are "unphilosophical" because they give rise to false judgments. "We rashly form [general rules] to ourselves," Hume writes, and they become "the source of what we properly call PREJUDICE"; that, for example, "an *Irishman* cannot have wit, and a *Frenchman* cannot have solidity." Such judgments are "errors," since they go against "sense and reason" and are persistently made despite evidence to the contrary (T 1.3.13.7/SBN 146–7). Why are such judgments made if they are clearly mistakes with no basis in matter of fact? Hume answers this question by distinguishing between two "influences" of general rules, which have their origin in the imagination and judgment, respectively. He begins by observing that unphilosophical judgments are one kind of reason-

---

Society.'" For the view that Hume is only to providing descriptions of certain phenomena, rather than attempting a normative reconciliation of divergent tastes, see (among others) Jonathan Friday, "Hume's Sceptical Standard of Taste."
5 Intimations of the view I develop here are to be found in John Passmore, *Hume's Intentions*; Bennett W. Helm, "Why We Believe in Induction: Standards of Taste and Hume's Two Definitions of Causation"; and Dabney Townsend, *Hume's Aesthetic Theory: Taste and Sentiment*. See also Christopher Williams, "Some Questions in Hume's Aesthetics," and Backeski, "Hume on Art Critics," esp. pp. 237–8.

ing from cause and effect, and like all such reasonings, are subject to the tendency that "when we have been accustom'd to see one object united to another, our imagination passes from the first to the second, by a natural transition, which precedes reflection, and which cannot be prevented by it." Custom operates with "full force" when the object presented is the *same* as that experienced in the past, but still "operates to an inferior degree" when the object is merely *similar* or "resembling," as in the case (to use Hume's examples) of a man who moves from peaches to melons or from red wine to white when his favored fruit and liquor is no longer available. As the resemblance grows weaker, Hume emphasizes, "the probability diminishes; but still has some force as long as there remains any traces of the resemblance" (T 1.3.13.8/SBN 147).

Were it always possible to distinguish sameness from similarity our ideas would be without error, since they could be traced back to experience and the genuine operations of the understanding. Sometimes, however, the imagination is influenced by "superfluous" circumstances so that we arrive at the "conception of the usual effect" even though features "essential" to the relationship are wanting. The force of habit and custom "gives a biass [sic] to the imagination," and we are led to the corresponding idea as if the requiste circumstances existed (T 1.3.13.9/SBN 148). Thus, a man in a cage suspended from a high tower fears for his safety though he knows himself to be securely fastened; the "circumstances of depth and descent strike so strongly upon him," Hume writes, "that their influence cannot be destroy'd by the contrary circumstances of support and solidity, which ought to give him a perfect security." Customary "ideas of fall and descent, and harm and death" therefore lead the man to conclude that his life is at risk (T 1.3.13.10/SBN 148).

This is what Hume calls the "first influence" of general rules. Such rules arise from the natural proclivity of the imagination to associate an effect with a cause even though the latter provides insufficient grounds for doing so. The "imagination naturally carries us to a lively conception of the usual effect," Hume observes, "tho' the object be different in the most material and most efficacious circumstances from that cause" (T 1.3.13.12/SBN 150). While the tendency to follow general rules of this kind is natural and often unavoidable, Hume also points to a "second influence" of general rules, formed not upon the imagination, but on "the more general and authentic operations of the understanding." When we thus "review" the act of mind based on the imagination, and compare it to rules of the latter, "we find it to be of an irregular nature," Hume says, "and destructive of all the most establish'd principles of reasonings; which is the cause of our rejecting it" (T 1.3.13.12/SBN 150). Individuals can thus reflect upon judgments and conduct, and by discovering their source in rules of the first influence, correct mistakes they have made. The man in the cage can then replace "imaginary danger" of falling with cognizance of his "real safety." Once the two influences of general rules are "set in opposition to each other," the second, being based on understanding, always implies the "condemnation" of the first. This does not mean that correction always takes place. "Sometimes the one, sometimes the other prevails," Hume observes, "according to the disposition and character of the person. The vulgar are commonly guided by the first, and wise men by the second" (T 1.3.13.12/SBN 149–50).

The main difference, then, between the two influences of general rules is that the first involves erroneous judgments arising from the imagination, while the second, as Thomas Hearn puts it, is "corrective, reflective and directive." Rules in their second influence correct the "generalizing propensity of the imagination," and indicate how, if judgments are to be justified, one ought to behave.[6] Hume himself offers an example in the form of "some general rules, by which we ought to regulate our judgment concerning causes and effects." Since these rules (eight in number) are "form'd on the nature of our understanding, and on our experience of its operations in the judgments we form concerning objects," reflection reveals them to be "more extensive and constant," and thus the correct way to regulate our behavior. Any inference that contradicts these rules is a general rule in its first influence, which the wise recognize as an "exception" arising from the "more capricious and uncertain" nature of the imagination (T 1.3.13.11/SBN 149). In this way, Hume maintains, it is possible to "fix some general rules" by which we may know that a given objects "really are" causes or effects to each other (T 1.3.15.2/SBN 173).

What, then, is the status of "fixing" rules in this manner? What *sort* of rules are they, and what relationship do they have to judgments about cause and effect that they "ought to regulate"? One way to articulate what Hume might have in mind is to compare his notion of general rules to Michael Oakeshott's discussion of "concrete" activity and the rules that "abridge" it. There is a tendency, Oakeshott observes, to think of knowledge as propositional and, consequently, to see rules as determining an "end for activity in advance of the activity itself." In actuality, however, rules are "abridgments" or "abstracts of some concrete activity," derived through reflection on the activity in question. Conduct itself requires know-how, which is given not in the propositional content of rules, but only in the activity itself. "A cook is not a man who first has a vision of a pie and then tries to make it," Oakeshott writes by way of example, "he is a man skilled

---

[6] Thomas K. Hearn, "'General Rules' in Hume's *Treatise*"; the quotes are taken from p. 411 and p. 421. See also Rudolph V. Vanterpool, "Hume's Account of General Rules," and Marie A. Martin, "The Rational Warrant for Hume's General Rules."

in cookery, and both his projects and his achievements spring from that skill. ... 'Good' English is not something that exists in advance of how English is written (that is to say, English literature); and the knowledge that such and such is sloppy, ambiguous construction, or is 'bad grammar,' is not something that can be known independently and in advance of knowing how to write the language."[7]

It is always possible to convert such skills into propositions and present them formally as a body of rules or principles and, since the rules are distilled from practices themselves, they present that practice in its pure or *ideal* form: recipes in cookery books depict perfect dishes, as an English grammar presents the key for flawless composition. Rules thus represent how one *ought* to behave in order to pursue an activity successfully—to cook or write well—and, as such, they can function as a "guide" to conduct. At the same time, they are always post hoc summaries of the activity in question, and knowledge of them will never substitute for the practice itself: one does not become a skilled chef through reading cookery books, or a great writer by studying grammar, but in and through the practice of cooking and writing, respectively. Rules are rarely if ever instantiated in their ideal form, both because they represent a vision of perfection that is largely unobtainable, and, more importantly, because the skill that constitutes fine cookery or producing great literature is not given in the rules themselves, but in the practice of cooking and writing well. This is why simply following recipes often terminates in unpalatable dishes, as the mechanical application of a grammar produces mediocre prose. The artistry and creativity that distinguish greatness cannot be captured in propositional knowledge, because it is part of knowing how to do something, which is in the activity itself.

Hume's rules by which to judge of causes and effects exhibit precisely this abridged character. General rules reflect customary ways of doing things and are transparent because they are always inseparable from the activities they organize and govern. They constitute the know-how or skill embodied in concrete activities. On the one hand, in common life, rules are "so implicit and obscure," Hume says, "that they often escape our strictest attention, and are not only unaccountable in their causes, but even unknown in their existence" (T 1.3.15.11/ SBN 175). On the other hand, while implicit and inseparable from the activities they govern, they can be made explicit by reflecting or, to use Hume's phrase, "reasoning upon," them. Such reasoning enables an individual to recognize the "exceptions" produced by general rules in their first influence and correct errors of judgment by following general rules in their second.

---

[7] Michael Oakeshott, *Rationalism in Politics and Other Essays*, p. 111.

Since everybody has the capacity to reflect and correct in this manner, it is appropriate to think of it as *ordinary* reflection: the process of attending to and assuaging a groundless fear is a routine part of common life. At the same time, Hume also suggests that those with a "tincture of philosophy" can cultivate a reflection of a peculiarly *philosophical* sort. Philosophy aims at "ordering and distinguishing ... the operations of the mind" through "a superior penetration, derived from nature, and improved by habit and reflexion" (EHU 1.13/SBN 13). For those "who have a propensity to philosophy," Hume writes later in the second *Enquiry*, recognize that "philosophical decisions are nothing but the *reflections of common life*, methodized and corrected" (EHU 12.25/SBN 162, emphasis added). Thus when Hume delineates the eight rules by which we ought to judge cause and effect, he is reflecting upon and making explicit what people do implicitly and as a matter of course when they make correct judgments about causal connection. This set of rules or "logic," as Hume also describes it, is already supplied "by the natural principles of our understanding" (T 1.3.15.11/SBN 175), but it is given expression as a set of *philosophical rules in their second influence:* these follow on philosophical reflection and present in propositional form directions for how one ought to behave if one is to judge correctly about cause and effect. These rules are at once, in Oakshotte's sense, abridgments of or abstracts from a concrete activity (making judgments about cause and effect) since they contain, in abbreviated form, the know-how that can only be exhibited in the activity itself.

Two things follow from this. First, producing philosophical general rules that abridge an activity means to have understood that activity. Articulating the eight rules of cause and effect constitutes a philosophical *explanation* of causal reasoning, since it represents the successful "ordering and distinguishing" of those implicit principles that govern the everyday practice of causal judgment. The rules reflect "our experience of the reality" of principles that order common life, but without going beyond experience and "imposing conjectures and hypotheses on the world" (T Intro.9/SBN xviii). Second, since philosophical general rules are abridgments, they are by definition post hoc *summaries* of the activity they abridge, which they present in ideal form. This means, in turn, that knowing the rules does not guarantee that mistakes will not be made, and simply learning and applying the rules is not sufficient for mastering the activity in question. In the case of regulating judgments about cause and effect, then, knowing Hume's eight rules will be of some use, but that can never substitute for the *experience* of judging, reflecting upon mistakes, and making appropriate corrections, which provides the know-how or wisdom that constitutes good judgment.

General Rules and "Of the Standard of Taste"

Having clarified what Hume means by "general rules," we can now turn to "Of the Standard of Taste," where Hume follows the same logic of explanation as he employs in discussing rules of cause and effect. In the aesthetic realm, general rules of the first influence may lead individuals to make incorrect judgments; those who take lesser poets like Ogilby over Milton or Bunyan over Addison (ST 230–31) reveal a lack of taste because they are ignoring what sense and reason should tell them to do. Hume writes:

> It is well known that, in all questions, submitted to the understanding, prejudice is destructive of sound judgment, and perverts all operations of the intellectual faculties: It is no less contrary to good taste; nor has it less influence to corrupt our sentiment of beauty. It belongs to *good sense* to check its influence in both cases; and in this respect ... reason, if not an essential part of taste, is at least requisite to the operations of this latter faculty (ST 240).

"Delicacy of taste" is analogous to correct judgment in relations of cause and effect. Correct aesthetic judgment—rules by which one ought to judge of beauty and deformity—are formed not on the faculty of understanding, however, but on that of *taste:*

> In all the nobler productions of genius, there is a mutual relation and correspondence of parts; nor can either the beauties or blemishes be perceived by him, whose thought is not capricious enough to comprehend all those parts, and compare them with each other, in order to perceive the consistence and uniformity of the whole. Every work of art has also a certain end or purpose, for which it is calculated; and is to be deemed more or less perfect, as it is more or less fitted to attain this end (ST 240).

The two influences of general rules here stand opposed to one another and produce contradictory judgments; like the wise man who judges correctly of cause and effect, however, *good* taste consists in overcoming the natural weakness of the faculties and the "faint and dubious perception of beauty" that prevails in pre-reflective life (ST 243). It involves following general rules in their second influence that have their basis in experience, and which, grasped through reflection, correct the first influence of general rules that otherwise produces errors of judgment or *bad* taste. The second influence of general rules implies the condemnation of rules formed rashly and prior to reflection. Following such rules consistently would make one's judgment unassailable, a picture of perfection Hume captures in the figure of the critic or true judge, one in whom judgment is always marked by "Strong sense, united to delicate sentiment, improved by practice, perfected by comparison, and cleared of all prejudice" (ST 241). Such characters are rare, Hume observes, because most people labor under one imperfection or another, and because they represent an ideal, perfection, towards which one should aim to achieve good taste.

What, then, does Hume's "standard" amount to and how does treating the standard as a general rule illuminate what Hume aims to discover in "Of the Standard of Taste"? Clearly, since the true judge is "so rare a character," the standard cannot be reduced to actual judgments: generalizing from imperfect judgments could never yield the "true standard" that Hume seeks to discover. The standard, rather, is an abstraction from actual practice that articulates how one ought to judge if one is to judge correctly in matters of beauty. Hume frames a principle that abridges and gives formal expression to the implicit rules that order the activity of judging things beautiful. The standard is thus a philosophical rule in its second influence that shows how a person of good taste is one who grasps the relation of parts to whole and understands the end of the artwork in question, though what constitutes good judgment will vary depending upon the work and the details of the activity: an eloquent speech will differ from a fine historical narrative, as a good poem will differ from both again. Since human beings share a common nature, in Hume's view, the "general principles of taste are uniform," and variations in judgment arise due to one or more of the imperfections that make the true judge so rare, but the standard governing any particular art can always be discovered, by abstracting from the practice and expressing it in the form of a "standard of taste."

Hume makes this point in his well-known recounting of the episode from *Don Quixote*, when Sancho tells a story of his two kinsmen who could each detect either the taste of either (but not both) leather or iron in the hogshead of wine:

> It is with good reason, says SANCHO to the squire with the great nose, that I pretend to have a judgment in wine: This is a quality hereditary in our family. Two of my kinsmen were once called to give their opinion of a hogshead, which was supposed to be excellent, being old and of a good vintage. One of them tastes it; considers it; and after mature reflection pronounces the wine to be good, were it not for a small taste of leather, which he perceived in it. The other, after using the same precautions, gives also his verdict in favour of the wine; but with the reserve of a taste of iron, which he could easily distinguish...On emptying the hogshead, there was found at the bottom, an old key with a leathern thong tied to it (ST 234–35).

The kinsmen have become people of good taste with respect to wine, a fact shown in their detection of leather and iron. They have achieved their expertise, in turn, through experience and practice, engaging in oenological criticism, reflecting upon their judgments and correcting mistakes, thus gaining skill or delicacy of taste in their chosen endeavor. The conduct that constitutes good taste is thus organized by rules in their second influence that correct errors and overcome prejudice to which we incline through the first influence of general rules. While these rules are implicit and inseparable from the activity they govern, they can, however, be formulated explicitly, abstracted from the activity they govern, and held as the standard against which any judgment in wine criticism must be held. Thus, as Hume says, "to produce...general rules or avowed patterns of comparison is *like* finding the key with the leather thong" (ST 235, emphasis added); formulating the rules of good taste with respect to wine is analogous to the philosophical task of showing what constitutes good taste in general. The former consists in the detection of leather and iron, the latter in grasping the relation of parts to whole and understanding the end of the artwork in question.

As with the rules of cause and effect, two things follow from discovering a standard in this sense. First, Hume *explains* the activity of aesthetic judgment; expressing the standard represents the successful "ordering and distinguishing" of those implicit principles that govern aesthetic life by showing in what good taste consists. The rules also reflect "our experience of the reality" of principles that order common life, and do so without going beyond experience and "imposing conjectures and hypotheses on the world." It also means, second, that since philosophical general rules are abridgments expressing an *ideal*, the rules will rarely if ever be instantiated and, moreover, are not themselves sufficient for acquiring taste – realizing the standard —in making aesthetic judgments. Again, as with regulating judgments about cause and effect, propositional knowledge of the standard will be of some use, but can never substitute for the *experience* of judging, reflecting upon mistakes, and making the appropriate corrections that provide the know-how or wisdom that constitutes good judgment. As Hume remarks, "nothing tends further to encrease and improve this talent [of delicacy], than practice in a particular art, and the frequent survey or contemplation of a particular species of beauty" (ST 237). It would be a mistake then to think of propositional knowledge as the source of aesthetic reasoning, which is to be found only in the activity of judging things beautiful.

With these observations in mind, we can return to the two claims noted at the outset, and upon which interpreters of Hume's essay generally agree, i.e., that the standard is empirical and that it has normative value. First, it should be clear that the standard *is* empirical in so far as it is derived from and does not go beyond experience. Given that the standard is a general rule, however, it cannot be an inductive principle drawn from actual judgments, since these are, as emphasized above, largely imperfect, and perfect judgment is rarely, if ever, met with in experience. The standard, rather, is an abstraction from the activity itself and presents in propositional form what good taste would consist in were individuals free of the imperfections in their natures. The standard is thus derived from experience but cannot be reduced to it and, for this reason, the critic remains ideal in the sense already urged. Second, in so far as it articulates how one ought to behave, the rules *do* have normative content. Following them has pedagogic value and, as such, they guide conduct; taste can, in some degree, be learned and taught. At the same time, it is important to realize that, since general rules express in ideal propositional form the concrete activities of common life, they are rarely, if ever, instantiated and can never substitute for engaging in the activities themselves. One becomes a person of eloquence, or an accomplished historian, poet, or wine critic, by practicing the respective craft and striving to achieve perfection according to the standards that govern it. Philosophy and the general rules it articulates, then, can be a partial and provisional guide to conduct, but never its source. Its primary purpose, on Hume's view, is to explain in what good judgment and taste consists.

The Role of Hume's Critic

In this latter part of the paper, I want to show how the above treatment of general rules clarifies Hume's notion of the "true judge" and the role he assigns this figure in "Of the Standard of Taste." Much of the interpretive focus on this aspect of the essay stems from Hume's apparently perplexing strategy of characterizing the standard as a rule, but discovering it finally in the conclusion that the "*joint verdict* of such [true judges], wherever they are to be found, is the true standard of taste and beauty" (ST 241, emphasis added). Broadly speaking, there are two schools of thought on this issue, both of which attempt to reconcile what Jeffrey Wieand has aptly called Hume's "two standards of taste."[8] In the first and most widespread interpretation, commentators side with Hume's emphasis on the critic and *identify* the standard with the joint verdict of true judges.[9] On the face of

---

[8] Jeffrey Wieand, "Hume's Two Standards of Taste," who argues the standard of taste is both a rule *and* a joint verdict. See also James Shelley, "Hume's Double Standard of Taste," who suggests that Hume switches from rules to a joint verdict because criteria for the latter (the five characteristics of the true judge) are easier to specify.
[9] The most recent contributions in a large literature include David Marshall, "Arguing by Analogy: Hume's Standard of Taste"; Christopher Perricone, "The Body and Hume's Standard of Taste"; Roger A. Shiner, "Hume and the Causal Theory of Taste"; Rochelle Gurstein, "Taste and 'the Conversible World' in the Eighteenth Century"; and Claudia Schmidt, *David Hume: Reason in History*.

it, this seems the most plausible way of understanding the essay, explaining as it does Hume's own shift from rule to joint verdict. The critic, after all, is somebody "*practice[d]* in a particular art" (ST 237), as Hume says, an advisor in aesthetic matters, so that it would be reasonable to take the joint verdict of such people as "the true standard of taste and beauty."

"So rare a character"

The clarification of general rules, however, speaks in favor of the second way of reconciling Hume's two standards, by focusing, that is, on Hume's initial characterization of the standard as a rule, but seeing it not as identical with, but *manifest* in the joint verdict of true judges who employ it to settle disputes over beauty when they arise. If the standard is a philosophical rule in its second influence that abridges concrete activity, then the judgments of critics cannot constitute the standard in question; it is not created by particular judges, but *presupposed* and *expressed* in their activity of judging things beautiful. The true judge thus personifies general rules that express know-how contained in concrete activities and, because the standard itself represents perfection that few attain, this figure must be *ideal* in the sense proposed above.[10]

Hume himself comes close to expressing this view in his observation that "a true judge in the finer arts is observed, even during the most polished ages, to be so rare a character" (ST 241). There is, of course, a practical problem of how the judgments of such individuals become so widely and uniformly disseminated such that they could become the standard, a concern Hume express in his "embarrassing" questions: "But where are such critics to be found?" he asks, "By what marks are they to be known? How distinguish them from pretenders?" (ST 241). The more important point, however, is that the actual judgments of critics are not tied *conceptually* to the standard the essay seeks; the questions are only "embarrassing" if the standard is identified with actual judgments. Hume does not deny that some individuals do achieve excellence, and Sancho's kins-

---

10 Harold Osborne, "Some Theories of Aesthetic Judgment," p. 136, comes closest to articulating the view I have in mind. I am not suggesting, as some have, that Hume's true judge is an "ideal observer" who express the "general point of view." For this emphasis, see Sverdlik, "Hume's Key and Aesthetic Rationality," p. 69; Gurstein, "Taste and the 'Conversible World,'" p. 210 and p. 214; Ted Cohen, "Partial Enchantments of the *Quixote* Story in Hume's Essay on Taste," pp. 148–9; Geoffrey Sayre-McCord, "On Why Hume's 'General Point of View Isn't Ideal—And Shouldn't Be"; Helm, "Why We Believe in Induction"; and Claude MacMillan, "Hume, Points of View and Aesthetic Judgments."

men and presumably Hume's own attempts at criticism are cases in point, though even here they *approximate* the ideal without achieving it: no kinsman detects *both* leather and iron, and Hume's own critical judgments of writers and literature is sometimes less delicate than it could be.[11]

It is thus possible that nobody will *actually* conform to the standard, but that does not mean that standards do not exist and govern what excellence, albeit imperfectly realized, consists. As Hume says, "though the beauties of writing had *never* been methodized, or reduced to general principles; though *no excellent models had ever been acknowledged*; the different degrees of taste would still have subsisted, and the judgment of one man been preferable to another" (ST 236, emphasis added). Good judges do not create or constitute standards, but presuppose and conform to them. As James Shelley puts it succinctly, the verdicts of true judges are "nothing but the verdicts of our perceptually better selves."[12]

"Questions of fact" and "questions of sentiment"

In addition to the rarity of actual true judges, Hume also points to their ideal nature through the distinction he draws between "questions of fact" and "questions of sentiment." There is often dispute, Hume observes, over whether particular persons have the characteristics of the true judge and whether, subsequently, they deserve the epithet. When such disputes arise, however, people acknowledge that there is indeed a standard while also accepting that others have tastes that departs from it. Indeed, Hume begins the essay by noting "the great variety of Taste, as well as of opinion, which prevails in the world" (ST 226). Individuals vary with respect to the degree of taste they have achieved,

---

11 See, for example, H IV 381–386; V 149–55, and VI, 150–154 and 540–545, and for some evaluation of Hume's views, John Laird, *Hume's Philosophy of Human Nature*, p. 273, and John B. Stewart, *The Moral and Political Philosophy of David Hume*, p. 263. A more sympathetic account of them is to be found in Teddy Brunius, *David Hume on Criticism*, Chapter 6.
12 James Shelley, "Hume and the Nature of Taste," p. 35. Cf. Elisa Galgut, "Hume's Aesthetic Standard," who argues (by analogy with judges who set legal precedents in common law) that Hume's critics "establish" the standard (p. 184), and Stephanie Ross, "Humean Critics: Real or Ideal?," who proposes that since criticism require practice and experience, those who practice it must be real. Paul Guyer, in "Humean Critics, Imaginative Fluency, and Emotional Responsiveness: A Follow-up to Stephanie Ross," defends Ross, whose view coincides with his earlier "The Standard of Taste and the 'Most Ardent Desire of Society.'"

and Hume suggests a number of reasons why this might be the case: dearth of necessary practice, inability to shake prejudice, the effects of age (ST 244) and cultural attachments (ST 245), or "some defect or perversion in the faculties" (ST 243). As a result, individuals or peoples are distinguished by "peculiarities of manner" (ST 245) and "humour and disposition," from which come preferences for one author above another or taking one person over another as a friend (ST 244).

All this undeniable diversity of taste, it is important to realize, falls under the heading "matters of fact." The variation is explicable as the many features that distinguish one person from another. That one person takes wine and another beer, reads German literature over French, prefers large dogs to small, and the like, are all facts explicable, in turn, by reference to other facts: that the man in question is English, has an aversion to affectation, is prone to take long solitary walks, and so on. Indeed, not only do individuals differ widely in their likes and dislikes, but they disagree about what counts as a "good" explanation for a given behavior. Is a category of race more relevant than one of gender, nationality than class, class than upbringing? As Hume explains elsewhere (T 1.3.1–2), matters of fact are characterized by the logical possibility of contradiction; people can and do disagree in their judgments and this is what constitutes the diversity of everyday life. Whereas matters of fact are *defined* by diversity, and disagreement does not give rise to any logical contradiction, disagreement of the same sort in sentiments involves denying standards that everyone accepts, which results in what Hume calls "palpable absurdities." The man who puts Ogilby over Milton or Bunyan over Addison "would be thought to defend no less an extravagance, than if he had maintained a mole-hill to be as high as TENERIFE, or a pond as extensive as the ocean" (ST 230–31). As Peter Kivy puts the point, "there are bounds of rationality to be trespassed" such that "someone who finds Rembrandt garish or Van Gogh subdued is slightly 'off the rails,' not merely of a different opinion."[13] There might well be people who take Ogilby over Milton as there are those who take molehills for mountains but, as Hume says, "no one pays attention to such a taste; and we pronounce without scruple the sentiment of these pretended critics to be absurd or ridiculous" (ST 231). Such people are in error: they are either defective in some measure or do not understand what they are saying.

The upshot of Hume's distinction, then, is that there is a logical difference between the two orders of phenomena. Whereas sentiments are universally

---

13 Peter Kivy, "Aesthetics and Rationality," p. 52. See also Gurstein, "Taste and 'the Conversible World," p. 204.

accepted and a "standard" can be sought out for them, in matters of fact there *is no standard to be discovered*; there is no right and wrong when it comes to preferring beer over wine, German literature over French, or large dogs over small. For "vainly, would we, in such cases," Hume says, "endeavour to enter the sentiments of others, and divest ourselves of those propensities, which are natural to us" (ST 244). In such matters, of course, disagreements are sometimes reconciled, but more often than not people (as we say) agree to disagree and the matter ends there. Agreement does not come about and, moreover, there is *no need* for it to come about. Judgments in matters of fact represent personal expressions of what gratifies: they fall under what Kant later calls *das Angenehme*, the "agreeable"; they do not make universal claims that command the assent of everybody else, but present an individual liking which, without risk of self-contradiction, can be juxtaposed to likings of a completely different sort.[14]

Exactly the same point applies to Hume's true judge. That a critic exists is an empirical question and, as argued above, standards do not disappear even though people of such character are rarely if ever found. The reason for this is that any actual judge who expresses a view about a work of art is expressing a judgment that falls under the *agreeable*; the judgment is not an "aesthetic judgment of taste" in Kant's sense because it does not command universal assent.[15] This is readily confirmed by noting that disputes occur among critics themselves, not to mention the fact that disagreements arise between non-experts who are often ignorant or disdainful of the experts in any given case. Hume's critic is not found among such actual personages because an ideal figure who personifies the universal sentiments that critics themselves presuppose, which can be expressed as a philosophical general rule or standard. Thus, the "embarrassing" questions Hume raises as unwelcome objections to his own argument are nugatory because *the answers they demand are matters of fact*. The attempt to distinguish the critic from his uncultivated counterpart mistakenly assumes that there is a standard to be discovered where none exists. The standard is of a different sort, an ideal that is presupposed by and expressed in judgments of critic and non-critic alike. People, of course, can disagree over whether a particular person

---

14 Kant, *Kritik der Urteilskraft*, pp. 205–7 *passim*. On this point, see Timothy M. Costelloe, "Hume, Kant, and the 'Antinomy of Taste.'" James Shelley, in "Hume and the Joint Verdict of True Judges," appears to make the same point more recently when he finds in Hume a distinction between variation in feeling and variation in judgments such that when we emphasize the latter, "true judges will never disagree" (p. 146). Cf. Budd, *Values of Art*, pp. 16–25; Alan H. Goldman, *Aesthetic Value*, Chapter 2; and Matthew Kieran, *Revealing Art*, pp. 226–30, the immediate interlocutors against whom Shelley develops his proposal.
15 See the "Second Moment of a Judgment of Taste," in Kant, *Kritik der Urteilskraft*, pp. 211ff.

in fact has the "good sense and delicate imagination" to qualify as a true judge, but this only shows, again, that aesthetic judgments do not depend upon such people or the judgments they make.

Conclusion

My argument in this paper has been motivated by the fact that Hume himself characterizes the standard of taste in terms of a general rule, and that clarifying this concept might shed light on the kind of standard Hume aims to discover. Hume's distinction between general rules in their first and second influence reflects the important difference between true judgments that conform to the understanding, and errors that follow from the nature of the imagination. Through reflection, the second influence of general rules can correct the first and, in making this explicit – by "fixing" the rules of cause and effect, or "discovering" a standard of taste – Hume produces philosophical rules in their second influence that both abridge concrete activity and explain in what true judgment consists. Having understood Hume's search for a standard in this sense, it becomes clear how the true judge is ideal in the sense of personifying general rules, which, if followed, would always render a judgment correct. Critics themselves conform to the standard in question and their judgments are manifestations or expressions of standards presupposed by everybody and accepted by those with sufficient experience and the educated taste that comes with it.

While the current paper has been concerned with general rules primarily as a way of understanding Hume's search for a standard in aesthetics, it also speaks to the larger question of Hume's view of philosophical inquiry more generally; as such, the conclusions drawn from concentrating on "Of the Standard of Taste" are potentially useful for shedding light on other parts of his thought. If the task of criticism is to frame general rules that abridge and explain human conduct, that is, why should the same form of inquiry not organize Hume's overall approach to epistemology (as in the eight rules of cause and effect), or his writing on history, politics, or morals? Hume's moral philosophy is of particular interest in this regard, since, as a number of commentators have pointed out, his search for a "principle of morals" has much in common with the search for a standard of taste. Hume's writing on morals is replete with aesthetic language, and there are clear parallels to be drawn between beauty, taste, and a true judge in nature and art, and the same phenomena in the sphere of morals. Thus, while gaining a clear understanding of any particular text is worthwhile in and of itself, at least part of the value in clarifying "Of the Standard of

Taste" is the interpretive inroads it opens up into the heart of Hume's philosophical system more generally.

Acknowledgements

This chapter first appeared in Timothy M. Costelloe, *Aesthetics and Morals in the Philosophy of David Hume* (New York: Routledge, 2008), pp. 1–22. It has been revised and updated for the current volume.

Bibliography

Baceski, Tina. (2013) "Hume on Art Critics, Wise Men, and the Virtues of Taste." *Hume Studies*. 39, 2: 233–256.
Brunius, Teddy (1952) *David Hume on Criticism*. Figura 2. Studies Edited by the Institute of Art History, University of Uppsala. Stockholm: Almquist & Wiksell.
Budd, Malcom (1996) *Values of Art: Pictures, Poetry, and Music*. Hassocks: Penguin.
Cohen, Ted (1994) "Partial Enchantments of the *Quixote* Story in Hume's Essay on Taste." In: Robert J. Yanal, (Ed.) *Institutions of Art: Reconsiderations of George Dickie's Philosophy*. University Park, Pennsylvania: The Pennsylvania State University Press. 145–156.
Costelloe, Timothy (2004) "Hume's Aesthetics: The Literature and Directions for Future Research." *Hume Studies* 30, 1: 87–126.
Costelloe, Timothy (2003) "Hume, Kant, and the 'Antinomy of Taste.'"*Journal of the History of Philosophy*. 41, 2: 165–185.
Friday, Jonathan (1998) "Hume's Sceptical Standard of Taste." *Journal for the History of Philosophy*. 36, 4 (October): 545–566.
Galgut, Elisa (2012) "Hume's Aesthetic Standard." *Hume Studies*. 38, 2: 183–200.
Goldman, Alan H. (1995) *Aesthetic Value*. Boulder, CO: Westview Press.
Gurstein, Rochelle (2000) "Taste and 'the Conversible World' in the Eighteenth Century." *Journal of the History of Ideas*. 61, 2: 203–221.
Guyer, Paul (1993) "The Standard of Taste and the 'Most Ardent Desire of Society.'" In: Ted Cohen, Paul Guyer, and Hilary Putnam, (Eds.) *Pursuits of Reason: Essays in Honor of Stanley Cavell*. Lubbock, Texas: Texas Tech University Press. 37–66.
Guyer, Paul (2008) "Humean Critics, Imaginative Fluency, and Emotional Responsiveness: A Follow-up to Stephanie Ross." *British Journal of Aesthetics*. 48, 4: 445–456.
Hearn, Thomas K. (1970) "'General Rules' in Hume's *Treatise*." *Journal of the History of Philosophy* 8, 4: 405–22.
Helm, Bennett W. (1993) "Why We Believe in Induction: Standards of Taste and Hume's Two Definitions of Causation." *Hume Studies*. 19, 1: 117–140.
Hume, David (2000) *A Treatise of Human Nature*, David Fate Norton and Mary Norton, (Eds.) Oxford: Oxford University Press.
Hume, David (1999) *Enquiry Concerning Human Understanding*, Tom L. Beauchamp (Ed.) Oxford: Oxford University Press.

Hume, David (1998) *Enquiry Concerning the Principle of Morals*, Tom L. Beauchamp (Ed.) Oxford: Oxford University Press.

Hume, David (1985) "Of the Standard of Taste." In: Hume, *Essays: Moral, Political, and Literary*, Eugene F. Miller (Ed.) Indianapolis: Liberty Classics.

Hume, David (1983) *The History of England, From the Invasion of Julius Ceasar to the Revolution of 1688, with the author's last corrections and improvements*, 6 vols. Indianapolis: Liberty Classics.

Hume, David (1978) *A Treatise of Human Nature*. L.A. Selby-Bigge (Ed.) 2nd edition with text revised and variant readings by P.H. Nidditch (Ed.) Oxford: Clarendon Press.

Hume, David (1975) *Enquiries Concerning Human Understanding and Concerning the Principles of Morals*. L.A. Selby-Bigge (Ed.) 3rd edition revised, P.H. Nidditch (Ed.) Oxford: Clarendon Press.

Kant, Immanuel (1902) *Kritik der Urteilskraft*. Königlich Preussischen Akademie der Wissenschaften, Berlin: Walter de Gruyter (and predecessors). Vol. 5.

Kieran, Matthew (2005) *Revealing Art*. London: Routledge.

Kivy, Peter (1975) "Aesthetics and Rationality." *Journal of Aesthetics and Art Criticism*. 34, 1, 51–57.

Kulenkampff, Jens (1990) "The Objectivity of Taste: Kant and Hume." *Noûs*. 24, 1: 93–110.

Laird, John (1932) *Hume's Philosophy of Human Nature*. London: Methuen & Co.

MacLachlan, Christopher (1986) "Hume and the Standard of Taste." *Hume Studies*. 12, 1: 18–38.

MacMillan, Claude (1986) "Hume, Points of View and Aesthetic Judgments." *Journal of Value Inquiry*. 20, 1: 109–123.

Marshall, David (1995) "Arguing by Analogy: Hume's Standard of Taste." *Eighteenth Century Studies*. 28, 3: 323–343.

Martin, Marie A. (1993) "The Rational Warrant for Hume's General Rules." *Journal of the History of Philosophy*. 31, 2: 245–57.

Mothersill, Mary (1989) "Hume and the Paradox of Taste." In: George Dickie, Richard Scalfani, and Ronald Roblin (Eds.) *Aesthetics: A Critical Anthology*. New York: St. Martin's Press. [2nd edition 1977] 269–86.

Oakeshott, Michael (1991) *Rationalism in Politics and Other Essays*. New and expanded edition. Indianapolis, Indiana: Liberty Classics [1962].

Osborne, Harold (1978) "Some Theories of Aesthetic Judgment." *Journal of Aesthetics and Art Criticism*. 38, 2: 135–144.

Passmore, John (1952) *Hume's Intentions*. Cambridge: Cambridge University Press.

Perricone, Christopher (1995) "The Body and Hume's Standard of Taste." *Journal of Aesthetics and Art Criticism*. 53, 4 (Fall): 371–378.

Ross, Stephanie (2008) "Humean Critics: Real or Ideal?" *British Journal of Aesthetics*. 48, 1: 20–28.

Sayre-McCord, Geoffrey (1994) "On Why Hume's 'General Point of View Isn't Ideal—And Shouldn't Be." In: Ellen Frankel Paul, Fred D. Miller, Jr., and Jeffrey Paul, (Eds.) *Cultural Pluralism and Moral Knowledge*. Cambridge: Cambridge University Press. 202–228.

Schmidt, Claudia (2003) *David Hume: Reason in History*. University Park, Pennsylvania: The University of Pennsylvania Press. 329–37.

Shelley, James (2013) "Hume and the Joint Verdict of True Judges." *Journal of Aesthetics and Art Criticism*. 71, 2: 145–153.

Shelley, James (1998) "Hume and the Nature of Taste." *Journal of Aesthetics and Art Criticism.* 56, 1: 29–38.

Shelley, James (1994) "Hume's Double Standard of Taste." *Journal of Aesthetics and Art Criticism.* 52, 4: 437–45.

Shiner, Roger A. (1996) "Hume and the Causal Theory of Taste." *Journal of Aesthetics and Art Criticism.* 54, 3: 237–249.

Shusterman, Richard (1989) "The Scandal of Taste: Social Privilege as Nature in the Aesthetic Theories of Hume and Kant." *The Philosophical Forum.* 20, 3 : 211–229.

Stewart, John B. (1963) *The Moral and Political Philosophy of David Hume.* New York: Columbia University Press.

Sverdlik, Steven (1986) "Hume's Key and Aesthetic Rationality." *Journal of Aesthetics and Art Criticism.* 45, 1: 69–76.

Townsend, Dabney (2001) *Hume's Aesthetic Theory: Taste and Sentiment.* New York: Routledge.

Vanterpool, Rudolph V. (1974) "Hume's Account of General Rules." *Southern Journal of Philosophy.* 12, 4: 481–492.

Wieand, Jeffrey (1984) "Hume's Two Standards of Taste." *The Philosophical Quarterly.* 34, 135: 129–142.

Williams, Christopher (2007) "Some Questions in Hume's Aesthetics." *Philosophy Compass.* 2, 2: 157–69.

Carolyn Korsmeyer
Gendered Concepts and Hume's Standard of Taste

Hume introduces his *Treatise of Human Nature* with a remark that summarizes his entire approach to philosophical investigation: "'Tis evident, that all the sciences have a relation, greater or less, to human nature; and that however wide any of them may seem to run from it, they still return back by one passage or another."[1] Thus his examinations of knowledge, of ethics, of politics, and – of particular interest for this essay – of art and taste, are all grounded on an understanding of human nature. Indeed, a trust in the common constitution of human nature permits Hume to admit considerable degrees of disagreement on matters of taste, without worrying that he has forfeited the grounds for a common standard of critical judgments.

Feminist scholarship has awakened us to the suspicion that such reliance on "common human nature" renders philosophical concepts not neutral and universal, as Hume believed, but heavily inflected by models of ideal masculinity that inform discussions of human nature. One purpose of this essay is to extend this line of thought by elucidating the idea of gendered concepts. By this phrase I refer to concepts that, lacking any obvious reference to males or females, or to masculinity or femininity, nevertheless are formulated in such a way that their neutral quality and universal applicability are questionable. Here I pursue this suspicion by examining Hume's famous standard of taste. Examination of gendered concepts not only casts doubt on the scope and operation of such a standard; it reveals the peculiarly unstable position of the idea of "female" in concepts of the "human."

The so-called problem of taste was a thorny issue for eighteenth-century theoreticians. Most granted the premise that "beauty" and like terms of aesthetic value signify, not qualities in beautiful objects, but pleasures aroused in perceivers. Since the experience of pleasure appears to be relative to the perceiver, this subjectivist analysis of beauty made the search for a standard of taste both difficult and urgent. On the one hand, good taste appeared to be very unevenly distributed; on the other, it was held to be a universal value with shared standards for quality. Reconciling these apparent contraries was the task of philosophers, who recognized two routes open for stabilizing taste disparities: (1) they could argue that human nature is so similarly formed in all that our pleasure reactions

---

1 David Hume, *Treatise of Human Nature*, p. xv.

are also basically the same, in spite of some apparent diversity, and (2) they could discover a common denominator in all the objects of beauty, thus finding some objective property that could be identified as the correlate of aesthetic pleasure. Many thinkers of the time pursued both courses. Hume chose only the former route and, since he puts all his faith in common human nature, his theory is ideal for analyzing presumptions of universality in the operations of aesthetic judgment and the extent to which this enterprise contains biases of both gender and culture.

Hume's most famous writing on taste appears in the essay "Of the Standard of Taste" (1757). The essay opens with the observation that every voice is united in praising basic aesthetic principles, a fact confirming the presence of a universal standard for taste. Yet immediately Hume notes that when we come to particular judgments, agreement is displaced by diversity of opinion as to how general principles apply.[2] On the one hand, he continues, it is clear that wherever there is pleasure there is beauty; yet it is equally obvious that some judgments are superior to others. As he puts it, "To seek the real beauty, or real deformity, is as limitless an enquiry, as to pretend to ascertain the real sweet or real bitter... and the proverb has justly determined it to be fruitless to dispute concerning tastes." Yet at the same time, "Whoever would assert an equality of genius and elegance between Olgilby and Milton, or Bunyan and Addison, would be thought to defend no less an extravagance, than if he had maintained a molehill to be as high as Teneriffe, or a pond as extensive as the ocean."[3]

How to resolve this apparent conundrum? Hume's answer is to bypass examination of the objects of aesthetic judgment and concentrate on the judge and the process by which judgments of taste are made. The result is the endorsement of the judgment of good critics throughout the ages, whose opinions converge as art passes the test of time and remains appreciated throughout history. He recommends that we should emulate the taste of persons whose good judgment is already recognized since, by following their example, we shall refine and develop our own tastes according to tested criteria of artistic judgment.

Though he has been castigated by critics and sympathizers alike for a conservative endorsement of canons of art (surprising from a philosopher labeled in his own day as a dangerous skeptic), this reliance on consensus of informed critics is, philosophically, a wily move. Being convinced that not all aesthetic pleas-

---

[2] Typically, Hume sets up a philosophical problem by calling to the reader's attention opposing propositions, both of which have some commonsense credibility. Donald W. Livingston gives extended consideration to this approach in *Hume's Philosophy of Common Life*; see especially Chapter 2.

[3] Hume, "Of the Standard of Taste," in *Essays*, 1, p. 269.

ures are equally worthy, and also skeptical that the objective world provides any discoverable property causally related to pleasure, Hume concludes that the only way to explain a standard of taste is to refer it to those who, as a matter of fact, are the taste-setters.[4]

The taste of a good critic, though founded on natural dispositions, must be cultivated, and the means of cultivation are – in theory – available to any person of sufficient leisure to pursue them. The foundation for critical judgment is a natural delicacy of taste. Hume describes this as a condition where "the organs are so fine, as to allow nothing to escape them; and at the same time so exact as to perceive every ingredient in the composition." (ST 217–218) In addition, critical acuity requires experience and practice; initial exposure to art is inevitably confusing. In order to learn to rank objects as to their beauty and artistry, the critic must learn to make comparisons of objects and, in so doing, should endeavor to form judgments with a mind free from prejudice. This ability is particularly important if judgments are to form a standard of taste valid for different times and different cultures, and not just reflect the conventional preferences of a particular society.[5] The generally useful characteristic of good sense regulates the interference of prejudice and other factors that skew judgments of artistic quality. Pursuit of these five routes to taste – delicacy of sentiment, practice; comparative judgment, freedom from prejudice, and good sense – produces a person who readily and reliably perceives the qualities in objects that all of us have a basic natural disposition to enjoy.

At the same time that he relies upon common human nature to defend universal values and standards, Hume recognizes that there is considerable variety in the ways in which those values are manifest. Preferences for one poetic form over another, for a particular style of music, even for variant codes of conduct, may be accommodated within the general standards for taste and good living that Hume believed obtain for all human creatures. Because Hume permits a degree of variety and disagreement among equally sound judgments, if any ap-

---

[4] I have argued that the best candidate for a correlative objective property is the relational property of utility in Korsmeyer, "Hume and the Standard of Taste."

[5] Hume and many others of his time saw in historical and social differences the sources of disruption for naturally uniform taste. But it is doubtful that social privilege was regarded as an actual prerequisite to taste. Instructive here is the highly popular novel *Pamela*, published in 1740, whose virtuous heroine moves from the position of servant girl to aristocrat's wife, but whose natural taste shines through even in her days of service, and additionally provides a signal of her inviolable virtue. Samuel Richardson, *Pamela*; see especially Lady Davers's letter, 2:33–34. However, see below and note 32 for further consideration of class and taste.

proaches to taste are successfully universalist without being arbitrary, his should be among them.

The standard of taste thus developed is not a set of criteria or principles, but a kind of person or group of people; it is a pragmatic standard that focuses upon the process of discerning aesthetic merit. How successful is this approach as a standard of taste? Is Hume really invoking commonalities of human nature, such that the standard of taste functions universally? Or is he mistaking culturally specific properties such as education, class, gender, and nationality for the properties ideally attributable to us all? I choose gender as the principal lens for exploring these questions because Hume made sufficiently complex remarks about gender to construct a pattern of his thought on the subject. In fact, I shall argue that gender has a particularly deep place in theories such as Hume's that employ arguments assuming universal human nature.

As is the case with many philosophers, Hume's direct comments about sex differences and women are scattered and apparently unsystematic. They are also complicated and open to divergent interpretations. Apparent inconsistency, as we shall see, is less a symptom of bad reasoning in the case of gendered concepts than of the complexity of the philosophical role of the concept "female" and its kin. We must reconstruct Hume's analysis of gender before sorting through its relevance for the establishment of standards of taste.

Hume enjoys a small reputation for being accommodating to the idea of sex equality.[6] To a certain extent, this is merited. Paging through Hume's writings on morals and manners, one can find a number of passages where women's equality is suggested or where their qualities are particularly praised. His personal sociability emerges in much of this writing, and he praises societies that foster *friendship* among men and women. Hume was alert to the distortions that society contributes to our understanding not only of what is right and proper, but also what is "natural." (One of his objections to social contract theory, for example, is that it focuses exclusively on adult males in the notional state of nature.)[7] He was aware that we have often mistaken customary relations between the sexes for the dictates of nature, and insofar as he incorporates observations like this into his writing he anticipates the liberal feminism of Wollstonecraft and Mill. However,

---

6 The most articulate feminist defender of Hume is Annette Baier. See her "Hume: The Reflective Women's Epistemologist?"; "Hume, the Women's Moral Theorist?"; and "Good Men's Women: Hume on Chastity and "Whist." See also John V. Price, *The Ironic Hume*. For a contrasting view see Christine Battersby, "An Enquiry Concerning the Humean Woman," and the brief but interesting comments of Michele Le Doeuff, in *Hypparchias Choice*.

7 See Hume, *Essays*, Volume 1, "Of the Origin of Government," esp. p. 113; and "Of the Original Social Contract," esp. p. 451. See also *Treatise* HI, ii, esp. p. 493.

at the same time that Hume evinces progressive sentiments about women, males and females play very different roles in the formulation of the basic concept of human nature, and these differences undermine the very foundation of his philosophical goals.

Because Hume denies that moral virtues are founded on any objective relations, he frees his philosophy from the task of explaining any stable, unchanging codes of behavior that would fix present social disparities in the roles of men and women. Hume discovers two distinct foundations for moral behavior: natural sentiments and social utility. As he proceeds through analyses of commonly named virtues, he argues that if there were no *social use* for certain "artificial" virtues, there would be no reason to recommend them at all.[8] Such is the context in which he discusses chastity.

While sexual self-discipline is commendable for both men and women, Hume considers chastity primarily a female virtue. (In fact, sexual abstinence in men counts as one of the "monkish virtues" Hume scorns.)[9] There is, however, no pretence that women's innate nature requires any particular kind of sexual conduct. If chastity is a moral trait, it is so only because it describes behaviour that fits into a social pattern that maximizes utility. This discussion of female chastity is, however, both iconoclastic and conservative; after puncturing the idea that there is any intrinsic merit to chastity, Hume repeats the bromide that the reason chastity is important for social utility is that children promiscuously conceived would be deprived of known paternity and stable families. He goes on to acknowledge that, logically, chastity ought only to apply to women who can bear children. This logic is overridden, however, by the worry that the evident fun of older women would be dangerous for the younger, who might unduly advance the time of their own release from the constraints of this virtue.[10] Thus, chastity for all females remains socially desirable. Although much of this discussion takes an ironic tone that mocks the gravity that often attends discussions of chastity, later in the *Enquiry* Hume betrays an interesting anxiety about the difficulty of keeping track of a woman s virtue. "A female has so many opportunities of secretly indulging these appetites, that nothing can give us security but her absolute modesty and reserve; and where a breach is

---

[8] Hume does not draw a firm line dividing natural from artificial virtues, since appreciation of social utility also comes to us naturally in the confirmation of useful actions by sentiments. "Mankind is an inventive species; and where an invention is obvious and absolutely necessary, it may as properly be said to be natural as any thing that proceeds immediately from original principles, without the intervention of thought or reflexion" (*Treatise*, p. 484).
[9] Hume, *An Enquiry Concerning the Principles of Morals*, p. 246.
[10] Hume, *An Enquiry Concerning the Principles of Morals*, p. 199.

once made, it can scarcely ever be fully repaired."[11] Thus, having briefly opened the possibility that women's sexual behavior is not governed by laws that limit their freedom any more than men's, Hume quickly closes it by finding sufficient social utility in preserving norms of chastity.

Hume's considerable interest in the relations of the sexes is also pursued in his discussions of manners and marriage customs. His judgments about exotic sexual customs and moral development are often presented with a tone of address that complicates their meaning. Thus, not only the substance but also the style of Hume's discussion of relations between the sexes pertains to the way that gender permeates his work. Hume famously revelled in the company of ladies, engaging with them in intellectual conversation and friendship. Some were aristocrats, some were friends of humbler background; all were "modest," having good manners and a sense of propriety. (Of course, what was deemed proper varied hugely in Hume's own experience. His friend Mme de Boufflers could have lovers both for her own entertainment and for sustaining and improving her social rank; a servant fallen into sexual labor became a prostitute, a situation for which Hume evidently had scant sympathy.)[12] Though Hume personally did not seem to think women lacked intellectual capacity – and his company in the salons of France and the drawing rooms of England would have borne this out – the fact was that no matter how accomplished, women remained for him in a different social category from men. As a result, Hume adopts a pervasive tone of gallantry when addressing women or even sometimes when discussing gender in his essays. Gallantry in fact is both a style and a natural virtue, and as such provides an illuminating angle on human nature and gender.

For example, gallantry is a social corrective for what Hume refers to now and again as the "natural" superiority of men over women. Just what constitutes this superiority is never explored very thoroughly, but it seems to stem from commonplace and vague observations about greater physical strength. In a just society, Hume remarks, natural male superiority must be *corrected* to bring the sexes into more equal status. "As nature has given *man* the superiority above *woman,* by endowing him with greater strength both of mind and body; it is his part to alleviate that superiority, as much as possible, by the generosity of his behaviour, and by a studied deference and complaisance for all her inclinations and opinions."[13] There is nothing of particular social utility to be preserved

---

11 Hume, *An Enquiry Concerning the Principles of Morals*, p. 222.
12 See Letter 104 in *New Letters of David Hume,* Raymond Klibansky and Ernest Mossner (Eds.), p. 191.
13 Hume, "Of the Rise and Progress of the Arts and Sciences," *Essays*, p. 193.

in the subordination of women, so social practices ought to equalize gender roles.

While barbarian nations make slaves of their women, Hume observes, those of civilized Europe have gentler means: "But the male sex, among a polite people, discover their authority in a more generous, though not a less evident manner; by civility, by respect, by complaisance, and, in a word, by gallantry."[14] Pursuing the implications of this statement, we may define gallantry as the gentle art of consolidating authority by treating with tactful solicitude one's gender inferiors.

Despite the fact that this disposition emerges among "polite" peoples, Hume stresses that gallantry is a "natural" sentiment. The term "natural" is, as ever, fraught with multiple meanings; but labelling gallantry "natural" places this conduct in the company of that fundamental natural virtue that makes Hume's ethics so warm-hearted and kindly, i.e., benevolence. As a natural sentiment, gallantry is refined but not created by civilization. A central agent in that refinement, moreover, is the softening influence of a woman.

"What better school for manners, than the company of virtuous women; where the mutual endeavor to please must insensibly polish the mind, where the example of the female softness and modesty must communicate itself to their admirers, and where the delicacy of that sex puts every one on his guard, lest he give offense by any breach of decency."[15]

Thus, women are both the object of gallant good manners and the fund of development for those manners. (Similarly, as we shall see, they are both the object of taste and its judgments, and a source of development of good taste.) Natural gallantry leads men to relinquish their position of superiority to allow women an honored social place; and women, cultivated and refined because of that deference (for only *modest* and *virtuous* women can serve in this way), foster still further the development and honing of fine manners.

Gallantry is sufficiently out of fashion now as to appear simply obnoxious in many circles, though of course nothing could have been further from the effect of this style or this sentiment in Hume's time.[16] However, no matter how it is appreciated, when gallantry is a norm of conduct, it not only puts its object on a dif-

---

14 Hume, "Of the Rise and Progress of the Arts and Sciences," *Essays*, p. 193.
15 Hume, "Of the Rise and Progress of the Arts and Sciences," *Essays*, p. 194.
16 It is a mark of how complicated it is to evaluate the manners of another time that "condescension" formerly could describe a good character trait, indicating the generous attention of one of superior rank to an inferior. See Mr. Collins's references to Lady Catherine de Burgh in *Pride and Prejudice*. Jerome Christensen discusses Hume's gallantry in his *Practicing Enlightenment: Hume and the Formation of a Literary Career*, Chap. 4.

ferent standing from the bestower of gallant behavior, but, because its purpose is amelioratory, it blinds one to the effects of this practice. This partially accounts for the fact that Hume, ordinarily careful to guard against inconsistency, could assert the equality of the sexes in certain contexts, call it into question in others, and treat females as actually outside the realm of general humanity in still others.

For in spite of an often inclusive use of the term "man," Hume on several occasions alludes to females as though they stand outside the domain of interest he investigates: human nature. Much of the time this is implicit: the social roles and activities that he discusses (with the obvious exception of love and marriage) – eloquence, politics, etc. – are public affairs that in his time excluded women so thoroughly that their absence was unremarkable. But sometimes the exclusion is dramatically explicit, as when women are considered the objects of an attention that reveals some truth of the human nature of the subject attending. Frequently this emerges when women are considered the objects of judgments of taste. Women are ranked alongside works of art in this passage from the *Treatise* discussing the conversion of pleasure into pain through repetition: "But when the fair sex, or music, or good cheer, or any thing, that naturally ought to be agreeable, becomes indifferent, it easily produces the opposite affection."[17]

Women play a similar role as the objects of some passion of "human" nature, as when Hume speculates on the effects of climate on national character. Temperate climate is the most conducive to accomplishment, he surmises, because passion is high enough to fuel ambition, yet not so high as to keep one in a frenzy of sexual desire: "the people, in very temperate climates, are the most likely to attain all sorts of improvement; their blood not being so inflamed as to render them jealous, and yet being warm enough to make them set a due value on the charms and endowments of the fair sex."[18]

The antecedents of "they" in this passage oscillate wildly. "People" sounds generic, and certainly all people of particular areas live in the same climates. Yet the objects of "their" passion turn out to be some portion of "them" whose own objects of passion are unnamed. Similar confusion of referents is evident in scattered passages *passim*, as for example in the essay "Of Dignity or Meanness in Human Nature," where in the space of only two lines *"our sex,"* referring quite obviously to men (to whose good looks is contrasted the beauty of women),

---

17 Hume, *Treatise*, p. 424. See also remarks on Fontenelle in "The Sceptic."
18 Hume, "Of National Characters," *Essays*, 1, p. 258. See also "A Dissertation on the Passions," *Essays*, 2, p. 163, concerning "a person" and "his mistress."

gives way to a mention of *"our species."*[19] Women flicker in and out of inclusion in the first-person plural, and since the discussion is human nature itself, women are from time to time thrust to the very rim of that category. Like virtually all writers, Hume used the term "man" loosely and uncritically, and while sometimes he clearly construes it inclusively, the intended scope of much of this usage is simply unclear. I suspect that most of the time Hume intended its use generically in a vague sort of way, while having as his model a man rather like himself. This is the most typical use of the generic masculine, and I shall have more to say about it later. But Hume was not merely unthinking about the implications of this language, and from time to time he finds it necessary to stipulate that he indeed does mean *everybody*. The contexts for such emphases are those where he might have anticipated that his readers would exempt women from the general assertion. The most remarkable instance concerns sexual drives, where Hume is led to insist, "there is in all men, both male and female, a desire and power of generation, more active than is ever universally exerted."[20] In a long footnote to the essay that contains this passage, Hume explores the relationship between pairs of terms he calls "correlatives." Consideration of correlative concepts illuminates the problems of generalization in which Hume welters. He writes: "It is an universal observation, which we may form upon language, that where two related parts of a whole bear any proportion to each other, in numbers, rank or consideration, there are always correlative terms invented, which answer to both the pairs, and express their mutual relation.... Thus *man* and *woman, master* and *servant, father* and *son, prince* and *subject, stranger* and *citizen*, are correlative terms."[21] But lest we presume such relations are fixed, he continues: "Languages differ very much with regard to the particular words where this distinction obtains; and may thence afford very strong inferences, concerning the manners and customs of different nations." It would be nice to discover here the idea that any imbalance in gender correlates is attributable merely to culture. However, not only does Hume not pursue this possibility, he elsewhere asserts the superiority of the male correlate in such a way that it appears virtually impossible to challenge. The locus is the long "Dissertation on the Passions," where Hume engages in an analytical catalogue of human characteristics and feelings, explaining them all according to the fact that they afford pleasure. The subject is pride – a good trait in Hume's view when it stops short of conceit – and the objects of which we are proud or even vain. "We" (says Hume, brother

---

[19] Hume, "On the Dignity or Meanness of Human Nature," *Essays*, 1, p. 154.
[20] Hume, "Of the Populousness of Ancient Nations," *Essays*, 1, p. 383–84.
[21] Hume, "Of the Populousness of Ancient Nations," *Essays*, 1, p. 389.

of Lord Home of Ninewells) are proud of ancient families, and particularly proud if our line of descent proceeds unbroken through the male line.[22] He explains the source of this sentiment:

> It is an obvious quality of human nature, that the imagination naturally turns to whatever is important and considerable; and where two objects are presented, a small and a great, it usually leaves the former, and dwells entirely on the latter. This is the reason, why children commonly bear their father's name, and are esteemed to be of a nobler or meaner birth, according to *his* family.[23]

Hume is clear that this habit of evaluation has nothing to do with the merits of the individuals in question: "And though the mother should be possessed of superior qualities to the father, as often happens, the *general rule* prevails, notwithstanding the exception."[24]

When the exception proves the rule so stubbornly, it is clear that it is principally the conceptual framework itself that holds the masculine correlate superior. That is, the abstract category "male" remains dominant, even when most members of that class are inferior to the members of the correlative female class. This rigidity of systemic thinking imports gendered concepts into seemingly neutral terrain. Indeed, the material for this very point is present in Hume's own analysis of abstract ideas. Hume notes in the *Treatise* that an "abstract" idea is always experienced as an idea of an *individual* thing. "Abstract ideas are therefore in themselves individual, however they may become general in their representation. The image in the mind is only that of a particular object, tho' the application of it in our reasoning be the same, as if it were universal."[25] No matter how wide our experience, and how carefully we collect diverse qualities of real individuals to represent their class, the abstract ideas we form to represent *all* are always manifest in an image of a representative *individual*. Individual differences are blurred as the mind relates particulars according to their relations of *resemblance*. Hume himself trusts the similar constitution of human nature and does not anticipate the dangers lurking in the observation: "If ideas be particular in their nature, and at the same time finite in their number, 'tis only by custom they can become general in their representation, and

---

22 Hume, "A Dissertation on the Passions," *Essays*, 2, p. 150. This section elaborates the argument presented in *Treatise* II, part I, section k.
23 Hume, "A Dissertation on the Passions," *Essays*, 2, p. 150–51. Cf. Pamela's husband's argument to Lady Davers, that in marrying a servant girl, he has the power to elevate her rank; whereas an aristocratic woman marrying a common man descends to his rank.
24 Hume, "A Dissertation on the Passions," *Essays*, 2, p. 151.
25 Hume, *Treatise*, p. 20.

contain an infinite number of other ideas under them."²⁶ These cautions he asserts about the formation of abstract ideas go far to explain the difficulties a reader has in determining the scope of the vexing generic term "man." There is an abiding tension in his discussions of gender between basic common nature and the channels societies impose on manners. At the same time that Hume analyzes sex inequality as inutile cultural distortion of natural relations, he also retains disparity between male and female in his treatment of fundamental human nature.

How do these observations regarding women bear upon Hume's general philosophy of human nature and on his attempt to establish the foundations for uniform normative standards? It is now pretty clear that Hume's philosophy viewed women in a way that, however amiable and graceful, ranked them in one way or another secondary or adjunct to men. Can we, however, uproot eighteenth-century prejudices and retain Hume's standard of taste, in much the way that essentially democratic legislation can extend rights to a larger population? To anticipate my conclusion, there is a degree to which I think we, in rather obvious ways, *can* do so. But this will turn out to be the least philosophically interesting discovery about uniform standards and gendered concepts. For to do so would be to look at gender only as it refers to individuals who use a standard, and not also as it penetrates the concept of the standards themselves.

As we have seen, the establishment of criteria for artistic merit proceeds according to the accumulation of the judgments of good critics whose conclusions are reaffirmed by generations over time. One of the requirements of the good critic is *delicacy* of taste. And Hume notes repeatedly that females excel in this dimension.²⁷ It is a dangerous trait to overindulge, however, because of its closeness to delicacy of passions (at which females also excel), which is not a good moral characteristic, being more histrionic than sensible. The other characteristics of a good critic – good sense, lack of prejudice, discernment in comparisons, and practice – are even more cultivable than delicacy. Theoretically, nothing at all rules out anyone from participating in the standard of taste so far.²⁸

Furthermore, the standard of taste accommodates a wide variety of irreconcilable preferences. The grounds Hume notes for these are "the different humours of particular men" and

> the particular manners and opinions of our age and country. The general principles of taste are uniform in human nature.... But where there is such a diversity in the internal frame or

---

26 Hume, *Treatise*, p. 24, see also p. 34.
27 Hume, "Of the Delicacy of Taste and Passion."
28 Hume, "Of Eloquence."

external situation as is entirely blameless on both sides, and leaves no room to give one the preference above the other; in that case a certain degree of diversity in judgment is unavoidable, and we seek in vain for a standard, by which we can reconcile the contrary sentiments (ST 232–233).

Differences of taste that emerge from such contingencies neither undermine the existence of standards nor require a ranking of preferences. Since Hume explicitly allows diversity of taste within the operation of a universal standard of taste, might we add gender to factors like age and nationality, to account without prejudice for differences of taste, when they occur? This issue is not addressed, though collateral comments raise serious doubts that this can be done, raising again the unstable position that females have within the idea of mankind.

When Hume respects difference, he does so not with terms he elsewhere calls "correlatives," but with examples where no superiority may be presumed: the young man who prefers Ovid over Tacitus is neither inferior nor superior to the man of mature taste. But "male" and "female" are correlative pairs, as we have seen, and the disparity of quality assigned them is evident in the language of criticism. "Feminine" might correlate with "masculine" when describing tastes or artistic styles, but in point of fact the correlative term Hume almost always uses with "masculine" is the pejorative *"effeminate."*[29]

Could the standard of taste be established in part through contributions of "feminine" judgments? The question opens up a gap in the text. Good critics have basic points of agreement, all of which satisfy traditional standards of style. Good female critics concur in these judgments – as a matter of fact they often do. But can they as women be the *arbiters* of the standard of taste? That is, are they included in that body of good critics that constitutes the standard of taste itself? There are two reasons to be doubtful that this is the case. There is first of all a powerful social disparity to be reckoned with in women's abilities to cultivate taste. Hume is high in his praise of modest and virtuous women, who are the civilizing influences that promote taste generally. But such women face a problem in launching their careers as good critics, for retaining one's modesty and virtue requires a certain *limitation* on experience, and breadth of experience is another necessary prerequisite for the development of good taste. (Even if the requirement of experience is interpreted to refer only to experience of art, there are limits of decency in the worlds of art that prevent a virtuous woman's adventures into immodest taste. Perhaps this is another instance, like chastity, where the overriding utility of limited feminine experience argues for lesser freedom for

---

[29] Hume, "Of the Rise and Progress of the Arts and Sciences," *Essays*, 1, p. 183; and "Of Refinement in the Arts," *Essays*, 1, p. 304.

women.) Moreover, were women to lose these feminine virtues, they would also lose what limited standing they have as taste-setters. Once this is noticed, it is also evident why a tone of leisure and class privilege pervades discussions of writings on taste. Modesty and virtue also suggest limitations on the activities, both domestic and public, that one can engage in to earn a wage. Taking a male perspective, we can see that the refining influence of modest and virtuous women is going to be reaped only by those men who are in a position to fraternize with such women.[30]

It may be argued that this consideration is an artefact of eighteenth-century bourgeois manners, expungable from Hume's basic philosophy. However, let me offer further support for the claim that women of good taste are those who find amenable a standard set outside of their own distinctive participation. It is straying from the standard of taste, but I think into relevant territory, to note two passages where Hume does address the union of male and female and the cancellation of their differences, i.e., the subject of marriage.

The fascinating essay "Of Polygamy and Divorces" opens with observations about the various forms of marriage, referring to them all as contracts between equals. The equality is more asserted than demonstrated, however, as wives are invariably spoken of as commodities to be parcelled out to available husbands, no matter which sex is in the majority because of warfare, shipwreck, or whatever circumstance renders a shortage of partners. Despite an initial liberality about forms of marriage, Hume goes on to argue against polygamy for reasons that are a combination of a preference for European monogamy over the exotic practices of the Turkish seraglio, and egalitarian arguments concluding that utilitarian good is never served by social practices that do not foster friendship between the sexes. The sovereignty of the male, states Hume, "is a real usurpation, and destroys that nearness of rank, not to say equality, which nature has established between the sexes."[31]

Monogamy having been defended, the subject turns to divorce. Human nature loves liberty, effuses Hume, and any permanent constraint in its way leads not to increased conjugal loyalty, but to aversion and deceit. In fact, Hume outlines reasons to approve the possibility of divorce as a freedom from bondage and unhappiness with so much eloquence that one is surprised to discover he ends with thudding arguments *against* freedom from the ties of marriage. (As if in anticipation of this observation, he remarks: "But what is man

---

[30] See also Richard Shusterman, "Of the Scandal of Taste: Social Privilege as Nature in the Aesthetic Theories of Hume and Kant."
[31] Hume, "Of Polygamy and Divorces," *Essays*, 1, p. 234.

but a heap of contradictions!"[32]) Some of these reasons are familiar ones concerning the responsibility for children when a marriage ends, but the fervor of argument concentrates on a union of man and wife that is so thorough in a good marriage that there is no longer any dissension to prompt divorce. "Nothing is more dangerous than to unite two persons so closely in all their interests and concerns, as man and wife, without rendering the union entire and total."[33]

Here is another suggestive passage. The essay "Of Love and Marriage" concocts a variation on Aristophanes' myth of sexual attraction in the *Symposium*. In Hume's version of the story the restless search for one's missing counterpart explains not only desire but also marriage. He has Jupiter decreeing that marriage between male and female shall only take place where that union is utter and complete. As he puts it, in the reunited androgyne, "The seam is scarce perceived that joins the two beings; but both of them combine to form one perfect and happy creature." (Unlike Plato, Hume leaves no scope for the union of two halves of the same sex.)[34]

In this ideal union, it would be the female who discards whatever differences she has with her husband and adopts his preferences as her own. Supporting this extrapolation is Hume's own observation in the *Treatise* about the weakening of children's ties to their mother upon her second marriage.[35] So strong is a woman's identity with her husband, that when she marries again, her children's chain of associated ideas, formerly from themselves to her back to themselves again, is now drawn from themselves to her and to her husband, lingering there because of her new ties and obligations to him. Only with difficulty does the imagination return to the children; thus the relation of children to mother is actually weakened, since she has become a different social person with her new set of family ties.

What I import from these passages to an understanding of normative standards and the accommodation of difference is this: there is something systematic and dangerous for sexual difference in this philosophy, *if* that difference is to be given the kind of notice that other differences such as those of age, nationality, or even personal preference are accorded. And I speculate that this has to do with the conceptual depth of gender as well as the unstable position that the idea of femaleness occupies in the concept of human nature. This means that

---

32 Hume, "Of Polygamy and Divorces," *Essays*, 1, p. 238.
33 Hume, "Of Polygamy and Divorces," *Essays*, 1, p. 239.
34 Hume, "Of Love and Marriage," *Essays*, 2, p. 388. This is one of the essays Hume later withdrew from republication. See the comments by Green and Grose in *Essays*, 1, pp. 43–44.
35 Hume, *Treatise* II, ii, sect. iv. One can view these comments as a logical extension of the doctrine of coverture.

when attention to *differences* among people is directed to *gender* differences, honoring them undermines the project of analyzing human nature. When Hume countenances differences of taste, the model judges he considers are all appropriate *subjects* whose perceptions and judgments form part of the continuum from which standards of taste and comprehension of utilitarian values emerge. But females are frequently considered as the "objects" of perceptions and judgments – perceptions and judgments that are used to draw conclusions about human nature. So if we grant any important standing to judgments that issue from some "female point of view," we shift out of the normal subject position and risk the loss of confidence that there are general standards or norms left at all.

That is one part of the picture. We also have to remember that Hume frequently refers to women as the catalysts of refinement in taste and morals. This puts females (though still not in a subject position) in the center of the spectrum of judgments from which standards emerge. I hypothesize that in such cases, Hume is positing the *union* of minds and values that he rather hyperbolically stresses when he discusses marriage. Male and female are ideal critics when they do *not* diverge in taste. Whatever diversity they systematically manifest sunders his foundation for universal human nature, if that diversity is treated as philosophically significant.

If this is the case, then the diversity that Hume does countenance is of necessity a superficial sort. Hume appears to embrace much variation and disagreement on normative matters without undermining the discovery of basic standards for judgment. The sorts of differences he mentions, however, are typically of three sorts: age, culture, and personal preference. The first is something we all pass through, and thus differences in age are ones that any individual might experience in the course of a lifetime. The standard remains steady, since we ("we") all go through these various stages. The second, culture, is an explanation for variety of taste that does not founder on the idea of uniform human nature, because differences in education and culture are major and obvious ways to *account* for difference. These differences are variations on a theme, and the basic theme is still stable. The third source of disagreement in taste, idiosyncratic personal preference, is not one that Hume dwells on, nor is it one he apparently took very seriously, philosophically speaking. I see it as a residue category that acknowledges the mysteries of pleasures when their sources cannot be accounted for. Gender differences pose a deeper problem.

If Hume were both to acknowledge philosophically the gender differences he subscribes to, and rely as heavily on uniform human nature as he does to stabilize differences of taste and valuation, the result would be a concept of human nature that is so obviously riven with difference as to recommend abandonment of the pretense to any uniform constitution in human nature at all. With a philosophy like Hume's, gender differences cannot be brought into the light and pursued systematically without sacrificing the basis for the root philosophical enterprise. Gendered concepts depend for their operation on the subtle shifts possible from their hidden positions.

In this philosophy, gendered concepts like the standard of taste are a symptom of ideas of femaleness that oscillate in their proximity to and distance from the paradigmatic human. Thus, it is not correct to say that women are ignored by Hume's philosophy, such that his conclusions apply only to males, indeed, only to eighteenth-century, genteel, male Europeans. It is clear that women are not only intentionally included within the scope of his ideas of human nature, but also that in some respects female presence is accommodated as easily as male. On the other hand, *and* at the same time, the concept of human nature proceeds from a point of view that shifts women from the position of participating subject to that of objects to be considered in philosophical deliberations about "human nature," so frequently arrived at by a combination of introspection and social analysis. It is in doing the former that the female reader undergoes the split of consciousness that simultaneously makes her a participant in the analysis and an object of the analysis, puts her with the other humans in the center of things, and with other females at the edge. I have used the metaphor of *oscillation* to capture this phenomenon because it connotes a continuous, repeating movement from one point to another. Gendered concepts are oscillating concepts in that the ideas of the female and the feminine that they covertly employ move back and forth from center to periphery in relation to the focus of analysis, occupying unstable and therefore ceaselessly moving positions.

Philosophies like Hume's are probably no more riven with the complexities of identity and unstable subject positions than our own current ways of thinking; indeed, the various places assigned women in this theory are familiar. Moreover, the oscillating position of ideas of the female in philosophical concepts also complicates the discovery of a stable perspective from which to pursue feminist analyses. The standard of taste cannot be dismissed as a masculinist artefact. Nor, as we have seen, is it easily patched up. I prefer to view it as one more proving ground for discovering how tangled is the concept of human nature, as well as how complex is the whole discussion of uniformity in standards and norms. For if concepts like taste are gendered, they are also the operational tools that drive philosophizing. As such, they have to be repaired while in use as we explore how many of the presumptions of universality we wish to discard or retain, and what is gained and sacrificed along the way.

Acknowledgments

This essay was first published in a special issue of the *Journal of Aesthetics and Art Criticism*, 48:4 (Fall, 1990): 181–94 and later in a book collection edited by Peggy Zeglin Brand and Carolyn Korsmeyer, *Feminism and Tradition in Aesthetics* (State College: Penn State University Press, 1994), pp. 49–65.

Bibliography

Baier, Annette (1993) "Hume: The Reflective Women's Epistemologist?" In: Louise M. Anthony and Charlotte Witt (Eds.) (2002) *A Mind of One's Own*. Boulder, CO.: Westview, 39–48.
Baier, Annette (1987) "Hume, the Women's Moral Theorist?" In: *Women and Moral Theory*. Eva Feder Kittay and Diana T. Meyers (Eds.) Totowa, N.J.: Rowman and Littlefield, 37–57.
Baier, Annette (1979) "Good Men's Women: Hume on Chastity and 'Whist.'" *Hume Studies* 5, no. 1: 1–19.
Battersby, Christine (1981) "An Enquiry Concerning the Humean Woman." *Philosophy* 56, no. 217 (July): 303–12.
Christensen, Jerome (1987) *Practicing Enlightenment: Hume and the Formation of a Literary Career*. Madison: University of Wisconsin Press.
Hume, David (1978) *A Treatise of Human Nature*. L.A. Selby-Bigge (Ed.) Oxford: Oxford University Press, 1973 reprinted from the 1888 edition.
Hume, David (1898) Oxford: Oxford University Press, 1973 reprinted from the 1888 edition. *Essays Moral, Political, and Literary*. 2 vols. T. H. Green and T. H. Grose (Eds.) London: Longmans, Green.
Hume, David (1898) *An Enquiry Concerning the Principles of Morals*. In: *Essays*, Vol 2, Green and Grose (Eds.)
Klibansky, Raymond and Ernest Mossner (Eds.) (1954) *New Letters of David Hume*. Oxford: Clarendon Press.
Korsmeyer, Carolyn (1976) "Hume and the Standard of Taste." JAAC 35, no. 2 (Winter): 201–215.
Le Doeuff, Michele (1991) *Hypparchias Choice*. Trista Selous, trans. Oxford: Blackwell.
Livingston Donald W. (1984) *Hume's Philosophy of Common Life*. Chicago: University of Chicago Press.
Price, John V. (1965) *The Ironic Hume*. Austin: University of Texas Press.
Richardson, Samuel (1962) *Pamela*. New York: Everyman's Library.
Shusterman, Richard (1989) "Of the Scandal of Taste: Social Privilege as Nature in the Aesthetic Theories of Hume and Kant." *Philosophical Forum,* 20: 211–29.

IV Causal Theory and the Problem, Dispositional Critique and the Classic

Roger A. Shiner
Hume and the Causal Theory of Taste

Consider the following two lines of thought which might occur in philosophical reflection about aesthetic taste. First, in thinking about judgments of taste, one may be struck by the elusiveness of the properties which are the targets of judgments of taste, in comparison with the steadfastness of many other kinds of property and objects. This elusiveness is well expressed thus: "no sentiment of taste represents what is really in the object ... beauty is no quality in things in themselves: it exists merely in the mind which contemplates them."[1] We might think that the impression we have of elegance – that slice of our mental life – reveals to us the property of an object. But, this first line of thought says, we would be wrong in so thinking. There is no such property; there is only our impression. Second, in thinking about judgments of taste, one may also be struck both by the fact that persons seem to differ in the degree to which they possess the capacity to make judgments of taste, and moreover that among those who seemingly are more experienced and skilled at judgments of taste there is some convergence at a fairly general level in such judgments. For instance, if at first I do not see the elegance my friend sees in a sculpture or a dance, my friend can say, "Look at this line; see how these lines complement each other; see how the piece would be different if this curve were more concave or more convex. Look at how this variation in the arm or leg movement would change the character of the dance altogether." And thus I come to see that the sculpture or the dance is indeed elegant. These thoughts are well summarized thus: "amidst all the variety and caprice of taste, there are certain general principles of approbation or blame.... Persons of taste may be distinguished by the soundness of their understanding" (ST 214).

Much of philosophical interest in judgments of taste has to do with a tension between these two lines of thought and with possibilities for its resolution. Let us first investigate the tension. The first line of thought seems to locate the ground of judgments of taste, not in some object which is the target of the judgment, but in the maker of the judgment. If someone says that he finds a dance elegant and powerful, or a soloist's musical interpretation fractured, this first line of thought implies that ground for the judgment of elegance is to be found, not in the

---

[1] Unless otherwise specified, the source of the quotations in this chapter is the edition of David Hume's essay "On the Standard of Taste" in *Essays Moral, Political and Literary*, Eugene F. Miller (Ed.), (Indianapolis: Liberty Classics, 1967). For the words in this paragraph, cf. p. 230, p. 233.

dance, but in the speaker. As Hume puts it, in describing this line of thought, "sentiment has a reference to nothing beyond itself ... no sentiment represents what is really in the object" (ST 208). This line of thought Hume associates with the maxim *de gustibus non est disputandum*, and is his first "species of common sense" thinking about taste. Let us call it the Internalist Theory.

The second line of thought, Hume's second species of common sense about taste, is quite different. It affirms a genuine difference between "Ogilby and Milton, or Bunyan and Addison. ... The principle of the natural equality of tastes is totally forgot" (ST 210). Some judgments of taste are rejected out of hand as "absurd and ridiculous" (ST 210). Although in the next paragraph, Hume is at pains to point out that "none of the rules of composition are fixed by reasonings a priori, or can be esteemed abstract conclusions of the understanding" (ST 210), nonetheless, in discussing Ariosto, Hume displays the fact that his judgments do have a reference to Ariosto's oeuvre – "he charms by the force and clearness of his expression, by the readiness and variety of his inventions, and by his natural picture of the passions" (211). The inventions are in the oeuvre, not in Hume's mind; the same is true of the force and clarity of the expression, and of the picture of the passions. Let us call this line of thought, for reasons which will be clearer later, the Criterial Theory. It is clear that there is a tension between these two lines of thought. A judgment of taste cannot both make reference to something outside the mind *and* make no reference to something outside the mind. Yet the difficulties in resolving the tension seem deep. Both lines of thought have intuition on their side, as Hume is aware.

The Casual Theory of Taste

Causal theories of X, for different kinds of X, have been prominent in recent philosophy. Defenders exist of the causal theory of reference or of names; the causal theory of perception, and of knowledge; the causal theory of action; and the causal theory of expression. There are different versions of each theory. It is impossible to extract from all of them one single distinguishing characteristic of causal theories as a philosophical kind. There is, for instance,[2] a crucial difference between theories of *understanding* (e. g., the correct analysis of the concept of action) and theories of *explanation* (e. g., accounts of what will serve as an adequate explanation of an action). My focus here is on theories of understanding – the causal theorist of X is one who claims that the best way to understand the

---

[2] See Frederick Stoutland, "The Causal Theory of Action," p. 272.

nature of X or Xes or Xing is to see it/them essentially as an element in, or as consisting in, a causal process of some sort. Gareth Evans, for instance, characterizes Saul Kripke's Causal Theory of Names as maintaining that "a speaker, using a name 'NN' on a particular occasion will denote some item X if there is a causal chain of *reference-preserving links* leading back from his use on that occasion ultimately to the item X itself being involved in a name – acquiring transaction."[3] Exactly what it is to give the essential character of X for purposes of a philosophical appreciation of X I leave unspecified. Analytic philosophers of a traditional sort will say that one has to give the necessary and sufficient conditions for the application of the term "X." Other methodologies will give different answers. A causal theory of taste, therefore, will argue that the nature of taste, and of judgments expressing taste, are best understood as essentially parts of a causal process linking the artwork(s) or other object of taste with the critic or appreciator. In short, the causal theory of taste is reductionist. The artwork has some feature or combination of features which cause a certain feeling or combination of feelings to arise in the critic. The judgment that an artwork possesses a certain aesthetic property is grounded in the existence of this causal process. If in judging the sculpture to be elegant, I am genuinely displaying taste, then what it is for this to be so is just this: I contemplate the sculpture, and the sculpture causes to arise in me a particular sentiment of beauty. That is all.

I believe that the causal theory of taste gains much attractiveness from the fact that it seems to make an end run round the intractable conflict of intuition outlined just above. It seems to preserve the best of both kinds of naive theory while dispensing with what is most controversial. The supposed merging of the two intuitive theories into one sound theory seems to arise in the following way. What is counterintuitive about the first species of common sense, the internalist theory, is that it makes the referent or target of judgments of taste exactly what on the surface of the language it does not appear to be: a feeling inside the critic rather than a property of the artwork. The causal theory does not do that. It makes the target of judgments of taste not the critic, but the causal process in which the critic is an element. What is counterintuitive about the second species of common sense, the criterial theory, is that it seems to imply that artworks have the properties that they have independently of the reactions of persons to them. The causal theory does not do that either; it includes a reference to human reaction as part of the construal of judgments of taste. The strength of the first spe-

---

[3] Gareth Evans, "The Causal Theory of Names," p. 191, Evans's italics. He is referring to Kripke's "Naming and Necessity."

cies is to draw attention to the role of human reactions in the appreciation of art, and the strength of the second species is to draw attention to the role of features of the artwork in the appreciation of art. The causal theory gives both of these elements an indispensable role. Moreover, it seems just true, in the vast majority of cases, that but for a person reading a novel or poem, seeing a dance, movie, or painting, or hearing a piece of music, the person is in no legitimate position to appreciate the artwork in question. If there is no appreciation without sentiment, then the thought that the sentiment is causally related to the appreciation has a grip on reality. I shall try to show, nonetheless, that the impression of a successful reconciliation given by the causal theory is illusory.

There is a crucial distinction between giving a *causal explanation* for a certain thing, and giving a *criterially based justification for a candidate description of a certain thing*, or *criterial justification* for short. To respond to "What is that pain in my thigh?" by saying "Remember that hard tackle late in the first half?" is to give a causal explanation, in this case, of the pain in the thigh. To respond to "What is that animal?" by saying "It has whiskers, stripes, and stalks by night; so it is a tiger" is to give a criterial justification — to justify the description "tiger" by deploying the criteria for what it is to be a tiger. I assume the distinction between causal explanation and criterial justification to be a primitive logical distinction. That is, I do not defend it beyond putting it to work in this chapter.

The second species of common sense aesthetics implies that judgments of taste invite (in my terms) criterial justification, not causal explanation. I hope to show, nonnaively, that common sense aesthetics (at least this version of it) is correct on this point. When a critic supports a claim of cardboard characters, dynamic allegro movement, or excessively foreshortened perspective by pointing to features of an artwork, common sense aesthetics says she is engaged in criterial justification, but not in causal explanation. For this reason, the second species of common sense aesthetics is appropriately called the Criterial Theory, and I hope to show that, on this point at least, it is the preferable theory.

The conflict between the causal theory and the criterial theory lies precisely in that the causal theory represents judgments of taste as to be vindicated by accounts of causal relations and processes, not as to be vindicated by reference to features of the artwork after the manner of criterial justification. The causal theory is committed to art criticism being like causal explanation. Sentiments arise in the judge as a result of the experience of the apparent targets of judgments of taste. The task of a theory of taste is to develop a sophisticated account of what properties in the targets of judgment of taste cause what responses in the judger. The causal theory cannot, and does not, represent aright the feature of the logic of judgments of taste to which the criterial theory draws attention. The causal theory of taste cannot therefore be correct as a theory of taste.

Hume and the Causal Theory

By the (admittedly generous) standards stated above, Hume's account of taste in his essay qualifies it as a causal theory. His aim here, as elsewhere in his writings, is to expose the "general and established principles" for the "motion" of the "internal springs" (ST 212) of the mind as regards the acquisition and expression of taste. It might seem perverse to attribute a causal theory of anything to one well known for his skepticism about causality. But the soundness of Hume's account of causality is a quite separate issue. The fact remains that in his resolution of the conflict between the two species of common sense, and in his defense of a standard of taste, Hume gives a definitive role to what are in common sense terms causal processes and relations – never mind the associational terminology which he chooses in his study to deploy.

These are but considerations of a very general kind for attributing a causal theory of taste to Hume. A more textual and tailored argument is needed, and I will now give one. I have suggested already that the causal theory of taste represents itself as a reconciliation of the two intuitively conflicting species of common sense, and that the reconciliation fails. I shall now show through a reading of the language of Hume's essay both how Hume's substantive theory of taste fails to reconcile the conflict, and how the failure is related to the theory being a causal theory. The fact that the passages discussed are all from Hume's essay supports the interpretive aim of this chapter. The commentary on the passages supports the philosophical aim.

The passage where Hume gives his account of the standard of taste is well known:

> [S]trong sense, united to delicate sentiment, improved by practice, perfected by comparison, and cleared of prejudice, can alone entitle critics to this valuable character: and the joint verdict of such, wherever they are to be found, is the true standard of taste (ST 229).[4]

Implicit in the above five-fold criteria indeed being our criteria for the person of good aesthetic taste are certain assumptions about the epistemology and logic of judgments of aesthetic taste, namely, those assumptions found in Hume's second version of common sense aesthetics, the criterial theory. We will go on to

---

4 The words are Hume's summary at the end of the business part of his discussion.

consider a more detailed account which might be given of these five different criteria. Such an account appeals to causal theorists because they think it represents all that the criterial theory can legitimately claim. I will show that, in order to interpret the five criteria for the possession of taste in a way which makes them consistent with its own picture, the causal theory has to transmogrify the criteria, from what I believe are their real selves in their role in the project of criterial justification, into spurious analogues in the project of causal explanation. The causal theory's view makes art criticism far more like the diagnosis and cure of pain, for example, than in fact it is. Such a transmogrification thus deeply misrepresents the activity of art criticism and the making of judgments of aesthetic taste.

I shall proceed by discussing in turn each of the above five criteria[5] for being the person of good taste.

Delicacy of Taste in Judgments of Taste

Hume begins his actual discussion of the standard of taste with what will turn out to be a deeply misleading analogy – that between aesthetic taste and gustatory taste. In regarding delicacy of taste as essential to the person of good taste, Hume has common sense on his side. Part of what we mean by aesthetic taste is exactly the ability to make finer, subtler, more delicate discriminations in the aesthetic qualities of artworks, just as by gustatory taste we mean that same ability with regard to flavors, textures, aromas, and so forth. The following language puts this point very well:

> [W]hen the organs are so fine as to allow nothing to escape them, and at the same time so exact as to perceive every ingredient in the composition, this we call delicacy of taste, whether we employ these terms in the literal or metaphorical [namely gustatory or aesthetic] sense (ST 217).

Nonetheless, as in the previous case of good sense with regard to matters of taste, the propriety of a certain general formula to cover both the causal account and the criterial account disguises very substantial differences between the two accounts. One gets a very good sense of what the model of gustatory taste is supposed to show about aesthetic taste from considering a story from Don Quixote.[6]

---

[5] I follow the order in which Hume actually treats the criteria, rather than in the order in which they appear in his summary.
[6] Cf. Hume, ST pp. 216–217.

The story is well known. Sancho pretends to delicacy of taste as regards wine, and claims it is hereditary. Two of his kinsmen, he relates, each pronounced a certain hogshead excellent. One, though, qualified the claim of excellence by noting a slight taste of leather, while the other qualified it by noting a slight taste of iron. When the hogshead was emptied there was found at its bottom an old iron key with a leathern thong attached. That story, for the purposes of the causal theory, purports to illustrate how it is that a person gets established as a possessor of delicacy of taste, so that his pronouncements become a standard of taste, using an example of gustatory taste as a model. The story indeed does illustrate precisely that point. But how the story illustrates it must be set out carefully. Hume in fact misrepresents the case as originally told by Cervantes.[7] The two kinsmen do not "pronounce the wine to be good." One simply says it has a flavor of iron; the other, merely smelling it, says it has the flavor of leather. No evaluation is made. The misrepresentation is instructive. To see this, let us begin with a simpler case yet. Suppose a number of people are asked to discriminate between two very similar wines. No matter how we mix up the samples, Gabriel gets them right every time, and the others are less successful. Even if we cannot distinguish the wines ourselves, we now do know enough to conclude that Gabriel has a more delicate palate than any of us. He is able to make discriminations we cannot make. So, in the future we take Gabriel's word on the differences between wines. This case, though, is not a matter of applying a taste-predicate to the wines, but just of saying they are different. With actual taste-predicates, the business is trickier. We will be reluctant to take Gabriel's word that the wine is flinty, or impertinent, or has a slight taste of leather or iron, if no one else ever pronounces it to be flinty or ferric, although we would be perfectly within our logical rights to do so.[8] But if several people also so pronounce, then, even if we cannot taste those qualities ourselves, we might well believe Gabriel. If key and thong are produced, of course, or if oenologists correlate tasted flintiness with a certain chemical structure and the wine is shown to have that structure, then Gabriel's reputation as a person of delicacy of taste is made, and is rightly so made.

Why, however, is it necessary to go through all of these complicated routines in order to establish Gabriel's credentials as a possessor of delicacy of taste? Here is another case. Suppose Uri claims to have X-ray eyes. He tells us what is inside all kinds of closed boxes and what is behind brick walls. We do all

---

7 I am grateful to Dabney Townsend for pointing this out to me.
8 Hume himself remarks on the difficulty of proving delicacy of taste under such circumstances, though he insists the delicacy would still have been there. Cf. ST pp. 218–219.

we can to rule out fraud, and Uri still keeps on telling us what is in those boxes and behind those walls. Here, the crucial step in the business is our own ability to see independently what is in the boxes – because a claim about what is in the boxes is a claim about what is in the boxes, not about what is in Uri's head or in ours. This crucial feature is absent in the wine case. There is no way of independently checking on someone else's claims about the wine's flintiness except by exercising that ability which *ex hypothesi* in the Gabriel cases we do not have – the ability to taste the flintiness of wines. This absence of an independent check is part of what inclines philosophers to say that the flintiness of the wine, unlike the toy-containingness of the box, is a matter of what is inside our heads, not what is inside the bottles – that it is, in other words, a secondary quality.[9] We find out that the wine tastes flinty as we find out that the box contains toys – by the testimony of our senses. But for a wine to yield a certain testimony to our senses seems plausibly just what it is for that wine to taste flinty. For a certain box to yield on its being opened a certain testimony to our senses is not at all what it is for that box to contain toys – what it is for the box to satisfy the criteria for toy-containingness – even though it is by the testimony of our senses that we see the box to satisfy the criterion of what it is for a box to contain toys. Now, the crucial issue for understanding judgments of aesthetic taste, and so for philosophical aesthetics, is this: is the possession of an aesthetic quality by an artwork in this respect like the possession of sweetness or flintiness by a wine, or like the possession of toy-containingness by a box? Is the vindication of a judgment of aesthetic taste like the vindication of a judgment of flintiness or like the vindication of a judgment of toy-containingness? The causal theory in fact opts unambiguously for its own version of the wine model: "though it be certain that beauty and deformity, more than sweet or bitter, are not qualities in the object, but belong entirely to the sentiment ..."; "to produce these general rules [namely, general rules of beauty] or avowed patterns of composition, is like finding the key with the leathern thong, which justified the verdict of Sancho's kinsmen, and confounded those pretended judges who had condemned them" (218). But to opt for the wine model in this way is a mistake. Suppose there is a general rule that dynamic tautness as a quality of pieces of music is a function of a range of structural properties of pieces of music. Suppose too one critic who claims to have the complex response of sensing dynamic tautness after hearing Beethoven's *Late Quartets* but not after hearing a set of Sousa marches. Suppose an-

---

9 I do not mean to imply by this that tastes are what philosophers have been calling "secondary qualities" – qualities existing only in the mind. I mean to imply only that the feature of their logic which I refer to is genuinely a feature of their logic. For a fuller statement of my view, see Shiner, "Sense-Experience, Colours, and Tastes."

other critic who claims to have exactly the same non-complex sentiments after hearing the *Late Quartets* as after hearing a set of Sousa marches, and to sense no dynamic tautness in the *Late Quartets*. Then, the discovery of the relevant structural properties in the *Late Quartets* vindicates the judgment of the first critic over the judgment of the second critic, and does something to forward the claims of the first critic to possess delicacy of taste. The process of vindication Hume himself characterizes with perfect accuracy:

> But when we show [the bad critic] an avowed principle of art; when we illustrate this principle by examples, whose operation, from his own particular taste, he acknowledges to be conformable to the principle; when we prove, that the same principle may be applied to the present case, where he did not perceive or feel its influence: He must conclude ... that he wants the delicacy, which is requisite to make him sensible of every beauty and every blemish, in any composition or discourse (ST 219).

There are two stages in bringing out how the procedure of vindicating aesthetic taste is misrepresented by the likening of it to the vindication of Sancho's kinsmen's judgments in the wine case. First, note that the judgment about the *Late Quartets* is vindicated by pointing to properties of the *Late Quartets*, not by pointing to properties of the critic's sentiment. As the above quotation indicates, it is the artwork and not the sentiment which conforms to the principle. In that way, the aesthetic case is like the case where one points out the stuffed bear, nerf ball, and jumping jack to vindicate the claim about the toy-containingness of the box. There is, by contrast, no property of the taste other than its flintiness to which one can point in order to vindicate a claim about its flintiness. One can only again present that property the existence of which is in dispute – its flintiness.[10] It will be said, however, second, that I have failed to grasp the point of the story about Sancho's kinsmen. The point of that story is to bring out how indeed we are no more helpless when faced with the task of vindicating a judgment of gustatory taste than we are when faced with the task of vindicating a judgment of aesthetic taste. In either case there are general rules and principles. The general rule that an old key with a leathern thong tied to it produces a ferric and leathern taste in wine is a pretty unsophisticated general rule. Modern oenology with its understanding of the chemical structure of wine has a repertoire of suitably more sophisticated general rules of the same kind. Likewise, there are general rules connecting certain harmonic structures, meters, and rhythms with dynamic tautness in pieces of music. The vindication of delicacy of taste in either context proceeds by the application to particular cases of general rules. All this

---

10 This too is part of what inclines philosophers to call flintiness a secondary quality.

is true, of course. But it is quite beside the point. The fact that we may at a high level of abstractness describe two processes of vindication as each proceeding by the application to particular cases of general rules is quite compatible with significant differences in underlying logic between the two processes. We may vindicate the claim that two particular triangles are congruent by applying general rules for the congruency of triangles. We may vindicate the claim that a substance will relieve pain by applying general rules for the reduction of pain. It does not follow from that similarity that geometry as a discipline has the same logical form as microbiology. In the geometry case, one is applying general rules of criterial justification, and in the microbiology case one is applying general rules of causal explanation. So also, gustatory taste and aesthetic taste differ in that the general rules appealed to in the search for vindication are in the former case general rules of causal explanation and in the latter case general rules of criterial justification.

The causal theory obscures this fact. It does so in part because in the things it says about delicacy of taste it conflates different senses of the key term "composition." In the passage quoted above (ST 218), we find reference to beauty and blemishes in compositions, and talk of qualities "in a continued composition," and "avowed patterns of composition."[11] There are four different candidates in these different remarks for being a "composition" – the taste-sentiment, the wine, the aesthetic sentiment, and the artwork. The causal theory regards these as logically interchangeable; but that is a mistake. The wine is a "composition" of molecules of this, that, and the other; science, rather than delicacy of taste, will fill out the story. The taste-sentiment may be a "composition" of flinty, ferric, and leathern elements, and delicacy of gustatory taste indeed is what it takes to differentiate the elements in this "composition."[12] Moreover, the two "compositions" are quite different entities, and one may perfectly well be able to perceive every ingredient in the "composition" that is the taste without having the first idea about, or even the first idea about how to acquire the first idea about, the "ingredients" in the "composition" that is the wine. In the aesthetic case, however, it only makes sense to speak of the possessor of aesthetic taste as perceiving every "ingredient" in the "composition" that is *the artwork*. Dynamic tautness or feeble sentimentality are properties of *artworks*, not of sentiments arising in the critic. The critic is claiming to find dynamic tautness in the *Late Quartets,* and not in a sentiment in her head. There are no aesthetic taste-senti-

---

[11] Cf. also the comment about "perceiv[ing] every ingredient in the composition" in the passage on ST pp. 219–220, "a mixture of small ingredients, where we still are sensible of each part."
[12] Wine buffs do after all talk about the "complexity" of wines as tasted; different elements of the taste are correlated with different parts of the palate.

ments which are in the same way as gustatory taste-sentiments "compositions" in their own right, independently of (or, rather, having only causal dependence on) that of which they are sentiments. It is not that there are no aesthetic taste-sentiments. There are: by having them we find out that artworks have aesthetic properties. But in developing and exhibiting delicacy of aesthetic taste, we are discriminating "compositions" that are artworks, not sentiments. The causal theory of judgments of aesthetic taste gets a foothold only because of an illicit parallelism with judgments of gustatory taste.

Practice of Judgment of Taste

Hume believes, as indicated, that practice in the making of judgments of taste is relevant to whether a person can be said to be a possessor of good taste and an exemplifier of the standard of taste. The view is intuitively plausible, and unquestionably a part of common sense about judgments of aesthetic taste. It is well worth inquiring into how such a view might arise. There is of course an important distinction between an obscure and confused sentiment and a clear and distinct sentiment. The more one is presented with a certain artwork or kind of artwork, the more one's sentiments will in all likelihood cease to be obscure and confused, and change to being clear and distinct. True aesthetic appreciation requires clear and distinct sentiments, and not obscure and confused ones. To none of these observations can one really, from either a commonsensical or a philosophical point of view, take exception.

But the same problem arises here as has arisen in other cases of the supposed distinguishing criteria of the person of taste – at first sight all that epistemic terminology (and note that it is epistemic terminology) belongs to the criterial theory. To put forward its own view, the causal theory has to take the terminology over and reconstruct it in its own terms. To see the difficulties that are thereby produced for the causal theory, look again at the terminological shifts. "Practice" may be glossed as the "frequent survey or contemplation of a particular species of beauty," and the inexperienced mind thought of as "obscure and confused," and incapable of pronouncing concerning merits and defects (ST 221). These thoughts are innocent enough, but they must be properly understood. The causal theory does not properly understand them.

The following are plain facts. One will not learn to discriminate between clarets unless one tastes a lot of different clarets. Moreover, one will not learn to discriminate modern Eastern European string quartets unless one listens to a lot of modern Eastern European string quartets. There are, however, different possible philosophical interpretations of these plain facts. On the causal theory's view, in the first case one is learning to discriminate sentiments that arise in one as a result of tasting different wines. The model here is the way that a cook might learn to discriminate the taste caused by the inclusion of nutmeg or cumin in sauces. So also, then, in the second case, surveying a species of beauty is on this same view a matter of examining sentiments that arise in one as a result of listening to modern Eastern European string quartets. However, as part of a line of thought which pretends to respect the intuitions behind the criterial theory, the causal theory claims that practice so understood enables one to "perceive the several excellences *of the performance*," and the merits or defects of the objects. This way lies a fundamental inconsistency. The first type of language deployed by the causal theory can only say that these merits and excellences are other sentiments. But if they are other sentiments, then they are not properties of the object or of the performance. The causal theory borrows from the criterial theory claims that we intuitively want to make, forgetting that its deference to the internalist view makes these claims unintelligible.

We may also talk about the feeling becoming "more exact and nice" (ST 221). This too is equivocal. The feeling itself might become more exact and nice, in the sense that one is able to sense and characterize the feeling itself more nicely and exactly – the pleasure one is now experiencing, one learns to realize, is exquisite in not quite just the same way as the pleasure one experienced five minutes ago. Think how the art of making love is learnt. But the causal theory does not mean only and precisely that. It also wants the feeling to be "more exact and nice" in this further sense, that it is a more exactly and nicely faithful representation of the qualities of that which caused the feeling. As a result of this "more exact and nice" feeling, the theory believes, one will now be able to perceive "the beauties and defects of each part," not just diffusedly perceive the whole object, and to perceive also "the distinguishing species of each quality" (ST 221). But nothing entitles the causal theory to imply in this way that beauty is something that belongs to an object.

We may also speak in terms of "the very degree and kind of approbation or displeasure which each part is naturally fitted to produce" (ST 221). This thought is on one reading perfectly consistent with the causal theory. "Naturally fitted" does not have to be taken as denoting a criterial relation between the properties of an object and the judgment of its artistic merit. The phrase may be taken as referring to an instantiation of laws in what was once called "moral science"; but then such laws must concern what sentiments are caused by what kind of object. The causal theory now however makes the same kind of illegitimate move as it has made before. It follows up such talk with talk about the mist hanging over the object dissipating, and the organ being able to "pronounce, without danger of mistake, concerning the merits of every performance" (ST 222). On the causal theory's view, however, performances, as objects, do not have properties or merits to be accurately discerned.

Prejudice in Judgments of Taste

Another claim that Hume makes is that prejudice can disqualify a person from being a possessor of taste. Again, the criterial theory will not disagree. The intuitively correct core of the way that the thought may be spelled out is two-fold:

> (a) "[A]llow nothing to enter into [one's] consideration, but the very object which is submitted to [one's] examination." (224) That is, do not allow the fact that one was thrown from a horse at the age of six to blind one to the merits of a Stubbs painting; do not allow the fact that a poem seems to describe exactly how one felt when one's cat died to blind one to the feeble sentimentality of the lines.
> (b) Do not use the standards of the twentieth-century post-war New York art world to judge the merits of Attic vase painting, fourteenth-century altar pieces, or Cape Dorset prints: do not rashly condemn what seemed admirable in the eyes of those for whom alone the discourse was calculated.

The causal theory, however, is defending not merely the truth of these truisms. It is defending a particular theoretical account of aesthetic taste. Bearing that in mind, let us ask why, intuitively, one should not do the things the previous paragraph picks out? Why are these pieces of advice to the critic indeed examples of good advice from the point of view of normative aesthetics? The causal theory unsurprisingly gives the answer that its deference to the internalist view requires: "every work of art, in order to produce its due effect on the mind, must be surveyed in a certain point of view" (ST 224). But note the kind of case outside aesthetics to which such words most properly apply. Hume himself mentions such cases. A man in a fever, he tells us, would not insist on his palate as able to decide concerning flavours; nor would one, affected with the jaundice, pretend to give a verdict with regard to colours. In each creature, there is a sound and a defective state ... (215). The cases work like this. Every drug, in order to produce its due effect on the body, must be ingested in a certain condition of the body – my mother, for example, was not allowed to eat cheese because it interfered with the effective operation of certain antidepressant drugs she was taking. Some forms of words make a commitment to the mechanical model clear: "the least exterior hindrance to such small springs, or the least internal disorder, disturbs their motion, and confounds the operation of the whole machine" (213). In this vein, one may also say: "nor have the same beauties and blemishes the same influence upon [a person inflamed by prejudice] as if he had imposed a proper violence on his imagination, and had forgotten himself for a moment" (226). This terminology is unabashedly causal. There is also available terminology which is theory-neutral: the language of a situation for surveying "not conformable to that which is required by the performance," "the point of view which the performance supposes," and the idea that "by this means [namely, not being in the correct position] [one's] sentiments are perverted" (225). These expressions could be interpreted either in terms of the causal theory or the criterial theory opposed to it.

Yet other expressions, which seem to emerge naturally from the foregoing, make sense as proper characterizations of aesthetic appreciation only on the criterial theory, a view which is not compatible with the internalist theory or the causal theory. Such would be talk about "either throwing a false light on objects or hindering the true from conveying to the imagination the proper sentiment and perception" (ST 216). Or the comment that the critic of an orator's performance "must place himself in the same situation as the audience, in order to form a true judgment of the oration." Without doing this, the critic's taste "evidently departs from the true standard, and of consequence loses all credit and authority" (226). The orator needs to attune the speech to the context of the particular audience in order to be a successful orator. The critic of the speech needs to know the same facts about the audience and about how to cause different kinds of effects in different kinds of audiences in order to be a successful critic – that is, one who can judge correctly the quality of a speech.

All these latter remarks show very well what is wrong with a prejudiced judgment: it is not objective; it is not a response to things as they are. The prejudiced judgments turn out to be not true; they do not conform to the true standard, the standard set by those whose judgments are true. These commonplaces, however, have epistemological presuppositions. The presuppositions are that for a set of judgments to be capable of being prejudiced, they must be judgments about the nature of some object: they may be prejudiced or not, just in case they are judgments answerable to and corrigible by facts about features of the object. If a judgment to the effect that a vase is beautiful, for example, satisfies these epistemological presuppositions, then such a judgment cannot be simply an expression of the fact that there is caused to arise in the speaker a certain sentiment. If a judgment about beauty can really be prejudiced, then beauty cannot be simply an internal sentiment merely causally connected to a certain object. In short, certain perfectly correct intuitions about how prejudice is a fault in art criticism cannot be reconciled with the causal theory. When judgments of beauty are reconstructed to make them fit this view, "prejudice" turns out to be analogous to not following proper medical advice. But that is not an available conceptual model for prejudice in judgments of aesthetic taste, nor does that model explain why prejudice is normatively undesirable in art criticism.

Acknowledgments

A complete version of this text, including more additional comparative references to Hume's essay, may be found in *The Journal of Aesthetics and Art Criticism*, Vol. 54, No. 3 (Summer, 1996): 237–249.

Bibliography

Evans, Gareth (1973) "The Causal Theory of Names." *Proceedings of the Aristotelian Society.* Supplementary Volume 47: 187–208.
Hume, David (1967) "On the Standard of Taste." In: Hume, *Essays Moral, Political and Literary*, Eugene F. Miller (Ed.), Indianapolis: Liberty Classics.
Kripke, Saul. (1972) "Naming and Necessity." In: Donald Davidson and Graham Harman (Eds.), *Semantics of Natural Language.* Boston: D. Reidel. 253–355.
Shiner, Roger (1979) "Sense-Experience, Colours, and Tastes." *Mind.* 88: 161–178.
Stoutland, Frederick (1976) "The Causal Theory of Action." In: Juha Manninen and Raimo Tuomela (Eds.) *Essays on Explanation and Understanding: Studies in the Foundations of Humanities and Social Sciences.* Boston: D. Reidel. 272f.

Dabney Townsend
The Problem of a Standard of Taste

"Of the Standard of Taste" has been extensively discussed as if it were the central and virtually the only applicable work by Hume on aesthetics. This is a very misleading way to approach "Of the Standard of Taste" and the other essays that deal with aesthetic issues, especially "On Tragedy" and "On the Delicacy of the Passions." The essays are the consequences of more basic positions worked out in the *Treatise* and the *Enquiries*. Hume's aesthetic epistemology poses problems that were central to the critical discussion of the arts, and he uses the essay form to address those problems in a context that the public was prepared to understand. In particular, "On Tragedy" addresses the problem raised by sentimental enjoyment of piteous and fearful events, and "Of the Standard of Taste" addresses the problem of subjectivity that arises from reliance on sentiment. Neither can be understood fully apart from Hume's more basic account of sentiment and taste. "Of the Standard of Taste" is not about taste, *per se*. The essay is specifically about the problem of a standard – why one must have some standard to settle disputes and how such a standard can be made consistent with the empirical sentimentalism at the heart of Hume's epistemology. I will approach these specialist essays in that light, therefore.

Hume's Defense of Taste

Hume's discussion of taste follows along lines already laid down by Shaftesbury. He is a defender of taste and sentiment. The lines are clearly drawn, therefore. As a critical term, 'taste' is well established. It makes sense and pleasure primary evidence for moral virtue and for beauty. It has a judgmental function, and it is productive in the sense that it is linked to wit and genius. At the same time, it is suspect because it promotes sense and pleasure over any form of rule or reason. Reliance on good taste can be socially conservative, but it is more likely to be associated with free thinking and the rejection of ancient wisdom. If Hume is to vindicate sentiment as evidence, he must account for taste.

In particular, Hume needs a concept of taste as a way to connect his systematic epistemology of impressions and ideas to the normative discrimination of some sentiments from others. Rules cannot make that kind of discrimination. They are limited to empirical indications of order. They can be used to produce sentiment in an orderly fashion and to extend experience both backward for the understanding and forward by expectation. But they cannot distinguish what sentiment itself can alone judge – how the complex of emotions, passions and primary impressions are felt. Taste mediates between felt sentiment and normative discrimination. On the one hand, taste just is a sense at work. It is rooted in its dual sensory meanings of primary sensation and a stimulation of a particular organ. On the other hand, it has acquired an analogical meaning associating it with character and pleasure. That analogy is central to Hume's aesthetic position.

Taste follows imagination.[1] While the primary sensations of taste belong to pure sense, the analogical and normative senses of taste depend on ideas and associations that are controlled by the faculty of the imagination. The simplest distinction is in strength. Sentiments may be stronger or weaker. Taste is not only reflective, therefore; it is subordinate to the passions that control action. "Sentiments must touch the heart, to make them controul our passions: But they need not extend beyond the imagination, to make them influence our taste."[2] Taste in this context is more limited than the direct passions and impressions that would arise if one were immediately involved with action. Because taste is limited in this way, it is subject to fluctuations and variations that can be tolerated whereas strong passions such as anger and love would have to be controlled.

When he wants to refer to purely physical sensation, Hume has available 'relish' as a synonym rather than 'taste' – for example, "A Laplander or Negro has no notion of the relish of wine."[3] 'Relish' retains the purely subjective sense of physical stimulation without bringing into play the analogical and normative meanings of taste. It is worth noting, however, that Hume's examples in this context are not limited to physical impressions. A similar reduction applies to other sentiments or passions of the mind – e.g., anger, cruelty, selfishness. If all that is involved is how one comes to feel an idea, then all that is required is an appropriate stimulation. Absent that stimulation, the passion will not occur:

> A man of mild manners can form no idea of inveterate revenge or cruelty; nor can a selfish heart easily conceive the heights of friendship and generosity. It is readily allowed, that

---

[1] Robert Fogelin points out that the same is true of causal inference. "What we now call Hume's skepticism concerning induction, for all its independent importance, occurs as a step leading to the conclusion that causal inferences (so called) are the product of the imagination and not of any kind of reasoning." See his *Hume's Scepticism in the Treatise of Human Nature*, p. 56. Imagination plays two roles for Hume. It is a way of combining ideas. In that sense, it is a synonym for 'fancy.' But it is also a productive faculty that provides the mind with new ideas. As such, it is essential to understanding basic mental phenomena such as cause and effect.

[2] David Hume, *A Treatise of Human Nature*, 3.3.1, p. 586.

[3] Hume, *Enquiries Concerning Human Understanding* 2, 15/20.

other beings may possess many senses of which we can have no conception; because the ideas of them have never been introduced to us in the only manner by which an idea can have access to the mind, to wit, by the actual feeling and sensation.[4]

Taste in its analogical sense is much more than just sensation, therefore.

Sentiment is basic, but all sentiment is not equal. Since he cannot appeal to a normative reason by itself, Hume is forced to consider the reasoner as well as the reasoning. Differences in sentiment must themselves be translated into sentiment. Hume recognizes the problem. For example,

> In every judgment, which we can form concerning probability, as well as concerning knowledge, we ought always to correct the first judgment, deriv'd from the nature of the object, by another judgment, deriv'd from the nature of the understanding. 'Tis certain a man of solid sense and long experience ought to have, and usually has, a greater assurance in his opinions, than one that is foolish and ignorant, and that our sentiments have different degrees of authority *even with ourselves*, in proportion to the degrees of our reason and experience[5] [my italics].

It is not just that Hume here acknowledges that sentiments have different degrees of authority. It is how he does it. Basically, we have a sentiment in favor of certain kinds of sentiment.[6] We, ourselves, are dependent on our ability to feel the difference in confidence that we have in some sentiments because of our experience. Even though sentiment is itself distinguished, Hume consistently maintains *"that belief is more properly an act of the sensitive, than of the cogitative part of our natures"*.[7] Belief, in turn, endorses certain objects and sentiments and rejects others. Taste is not merely subjective preference. It is founded on a distinction between what the imagination produces that can be believed and what cannot be believed. A person of taste is also a person of good sense.

The problem is that everything is not reducible to judgments that can be traced back to belief. This is particularly the case with beauty and pleasure. In spite of describing beauty as a construction or form that gives pleasure, Hume goes on to say "that beauty like wit, cannot be defin'd, but is discern'd only by a taste or sensation."[8] What beauty lacks is the kind of definition that would allow it to be identified independently of the pleasure it produces. What is missing from a definition of beauty is a specific difference that is an ob-

---

4 Hume, *Enquiries Concerning Human Understanding* 2, 15/20.
5 Hume, *A Treatise of Human Nature*, 1.4.1, pp. 181–182, my italics.
6 Shaftesbury has a similar position.
7 Hume, *A Treatise of Human Nature*, 1.4.1, p. 183.
8 Hume, *A Treatise of Human Nature*, 2.1.8, p. 299.

ject of belief. Hume has no illusion that a sensuous line or uniformity amidst variety could form the kind of specific difference that sensations of color or shape provide for spatial objects. They may be part of a causal expectation, and thus form a rule, but they are not independent of the pleasure they produce. On the other hand, no subjective distinction is available either. Other things cause pleasure without being beautiful. If the pleasure of beauty were qualitatively different, then it would have a defining pleasure that would be at least phenomenologically available. But Hume does not hold that there is a distinctive aesthetic pleasure, so beauty lacks a subjective distinction. Taste fills the gap. It is a *je ne sais quoi*, but one that has roots in sensation.

Hume has recourse to a class of agreeable sentiments that cannot be accounted for except by taste. One can no more account for these effects than one can explain a preference for chocolate over vanilla.

But besides all the *agreeable* qualities, the origin of whose beauty we can, in some degree, explain and account for, there still remains something mysterious and inexplicable which conveys an immediate satisfaction to the spectator, but how, or why, or for what reason he cannot pretend to determine. There is a manner, a grace, an ease, a genteelness, an I-know-not-what, which some men possess above others, which is very different from external beauty and comeliness, and which, however, catches our affection almost as suddenly and powerfully.[9]

This appeal to *je-ne-sais-quoi* is, of course, straight out of the French neoclassical tradition. It finds its place in Hume's theory because sentiment is the final evidence. But that does not make it any more satisfactory as a piece of aesthetic theory. Taste and sentiment are admittedly "blind" at this point. An account of taste that will recognize its judgmental and productive aspect is needed. Pleasure provides that link.

Pleasure and pain are immediate sensations alongside qualities that may be the causes of other impressions. In other words, pleasure is not the same as beauty, nor is it antecedent to beauty. One has a sensation of pleasure, which is a primary sensation and for Hume need not be traced back to anything else. One just feels pleasure. Beauty is an emotion, but it can be treated as a quality because it refers to something that one denominates as beautiful. Now if pain and pleasure are original sensations, and qualities produce calm passions of reflection or secondary impressions that are pleasurable or painful, then qualities alone cannot produce the passions. Otherwise, one would identify certain qualities or objects as pleasurable as well as beautiful. But when we make that kind of reference (as we do), we do not mean that the object or quality is

---

9 Hume, "Enquiry Concerning the Principles of Morals," 8, 216/267.

itself pleasurable but that it regularly produces pleasure in the normal course of producing sentiments. The difficulty this will cause if one takes it seriously is that a quality such as that implied by beauty must have separate identity criteria to distinguish it from other pleasures, and of course Hume does not attempt to supply them, nor on his system could he. Beauty is no more a primary impression than causality or necessity. Hence, taste becomes even more important.

Taste operates in advance of any explanations and principles, either directly in terms of qualities or by extension through rules. Whether principles can be found or not does not affect the evidence of taste. Wit, for example, "is a quality immediately agreeable to others, and communicating, on its first appearance, a lively joy and satisfaction to every one who has any comprehension of it".[10] Wit, in turn, is a mark of good company. Hume's defense of manners and good company could have been given on utilitarian grounds, but it is not. It rests directly on taste.

The role of taste throughout Hume's work remains essentially what it was in the *Treatise*. For example, Hume offers a description of taste in the context of a discussion of wit as a source of pride. Wit presents a problem because it is inexplicable in terms of causes. "No one has ever been able to tell what *wit* is, and to shew why such a system of thought must be receiv'd under that denomination, and such another rejected." In such cases, one has recourse to taste. Taste, then, has two criteria: i) it is distinguished by a sensation of pleasure or uneasiness, and ii) one cannot further justify that pleasure or uneasiness. So taste covers all cases where pleasure is inexplicably present. Taste here is not particularly a form of sensation. Nor is it clear whether our inability to trace the causal sources of taste is an accidental or essential part of taste. It might be the case that if one had better reasons – a causal account, for example – one would not depend on taste. So if one really understood the chemical properties of good wine, wine-tastings would not be required to denominate good and bad wine.[11] But it is more likely that taste should be understood as an association of impressions – there is presumably some corpuscular or micro-explanation for how the mind associates impressions, but one does not need to know it in order to have a full knowledge of the associations. Hume seems to place taste outside rule-governed investigation, but it is not at all certain that he is proposing some proto-Sibleyan position in which taste is a separate area of judgment.

---

10 Hume, "Enquiry Concerning the Principles of Morals," 8, 212/262.
11 Kevin Sweeney has provided a helpful analysis of this example in a paper presented to the American Society for Aesthetics meeting, Santa Barbara, 1993. Unpublished.

The recourse to taste seems to be a matter of empirical necessity, not theoretical isolation for Hume.

Taste enters when one cannot separate multiple causes of the same phenomenon into an ordered set. "There seldom is any very precise argument to fix our choice, and men must be contented to be guided by a kind of taste or fancy, arising from analogy, and comparison of similar instances."[12] Rather than utility, Hume proposes affinity within the mind as the principle that justifies present possession. The mind likes order, and where it finds resemblance or contiguity, it keeps those objects together. So,

> As property forms a relation betwixt a person and an object, 'tis natural to found it on some preceding relation; and as property is nothing but a constant possession, secur'd by the laws of society, 'tis natural to add it to the present possession, which is a relation that resembles it.

Beauty is also a response to this order and natural affinity between objects. Hume promises a more detailed treatment of beauty than he ever supplied, but he hints that it would be based on the impulse to order and resemblance. Deformity would be parts that do not fit; beauty, a product of resemblance and contiguity either in the object or imposed by fancy and imagination. Taste is the guide to the difference.

Taste is also a productive faculty, however. In contrast to reason, which is eternal, taste varies with the constitution of the species, but taste is what gives sentiments. Reason, writes Hume,

> conveys the knowledge of truth and falsehood: [taste] gives the sentiment of beauty and deformity, vice and virtue. The one discovers objects as they really stand in nature, without addition or diminution: the other has a productive faculty, and gilding or staining all natural objects with the colours, borrowed from internal sentiment, raises in a manner a new creation.[13]

How far taste should be treated as some new faculty is questionable, however. The description here fits the imagination and fancy equally well. Given the context, it is probably best to take this description of taste as an unsystematic condensation of the otherwise inexplicable causal role that taste already played.

The productive role of taste is limited to imaginative associations. Hume has a nice tongue-in-cheek reference to a poem on "Cyder"': "Beer wou'd not have been so proper, as being neither so agreeable to the taste nor eye. But he

---

12 Hume, *A Treatise of Human Nature*, 3.2.3, p. 504, n1.
13 Hume, "Enquiry Concerning the Principles of Morals," app I, 246/294.

[the poet] wou'd certainly have preferr'd wine to either of them, cou'd his native country have afforded him so agreeable a liquor." It does seem that 'taste' here has a double meaning – literally the taste of beer; figuratively, a lower class and English preference for beer. Hume, the Francophile, could not resist setting the priorities of taste. More seriously, however, what is agreeable to the senses also appeals to the fancy, according to Hume, and "conveys to the thought an image of that satisfaction, which it gives by its real application to the bodily organs."[14] The workings of taste depicted here proceed from bodily pleasure to an image to the thought of an image, which is the metaphorical taste. The utility of the analogy to physical sensations of taste in this context is not its subjectivity but its ability to supply immediate pleasure. Taste, more than any of the other senses, depends directly on sensual pleasure or uneasiness. The eye and the ear provide images that may be neutral. But taste carries with it its affective quality directly.

Taste also operates through desire, and there, too, the analogy with physical experience is helpful. Hume argues that the effect of beauty is to make one approach or desire something. Hence, he gives as one example that beauty makes us approach food, and thus gives us a keener appetite.[15] In this context, Hume does not suggest that this has anything to do with taste, but it does suggest that the taste metaphor may have some foundation in a desire for pleasure. The path by which the metaphor is developed also supports this association. Alimentary metaphors were common as ways of linking the physical with the spiritual world.[16] The centrality of taste makes it natural to include under taste the desire that essentially pleasurable emotions invoke.

In general, Hume describes movements from one idea to another. If one begins with pleasant ideas, they suggest the person who possesses them. In the case of esteem for riches, for example, one moves from the pleasure associated with riches to esteem for the rich person. (Hume is under no illusion that poverty is blessed.) Beauty or agreeableness are not themselves the most important source of esteem for riches. Beauty is an impression that may produce more violent passions, but it should not be equated with them: "riches and power alone, even tho' unemploy'd, naturally cause esteem and respect: And consequently these passions arise not from the idea of any beautiful or agreeable objects."[17] In this respect, sympathy takes precedence over imagination and fancy in transferring the sentiments from one source to another. One should not expect taste to replace this process. Instead, the analogy of taste expands to include the person.

---

14 Hume, "Enquiry Concerning the Principles of Morals."
15 Hume, "Enquiry Concerning the Principles of Morals," 2.2.11, 395.
16 See Ernst Robert Curtius, *European Literature and the Latin Middle Ages*, pp. 134–136.
17 Hume, *A Treatise of Human Nature*, 2.2.5, p. 359.

In that way, one gets a person of taste, and taste becomes a character trait. In both the moral and aesthetic cases, the production of sentiment is a matter of taste. Taste is the alternative to reason, the internal feeling for good and evil, beauty and deformity. Taste is internal, a motive to action, a source of pleasure and pain. The standard of taste is peculiar to the "nature" of the being that experiences it. Conversely, the character of someone is judged by their taste. In this respect, Hume draws no distinction between moral and aesthetic taste, though there is clearly one to be drawn. Both forms of taste are independent of the understanding. Both are dependent on the way that the individual is constructed and have their source in the complex interaction of imagination and pleasurable sensation. The latter is rooted in the physical sensation exemplified by the senses of 'taste' as a sensual impression, touch, and a testing experience. The former arises from the pleasures that accompany beauty and virtue with an immediacy that makes them otherwise inexplicable.

The Nature of a Standard

The analogy of taste and the role that it plays in supplementing rules to explain moral and aesthetic judgments inevitably leads to a problem of standards. Rules are empirical products of time and habit. They counteract the naive sentimentalism of the moment that is antithetical to Hume's form of empiricism. But they do not supplant sentiment. Taste is not formed by rule, so rules themselves do not provide a standard, and taste is a productive faculty that is itself in need of sorting if one is to avoid a chaos of judgments. Taste produces judgments, but even together with rules it remains idiosyncratic. A standard, on the other hand, must be communal at least. The problem of a standard of taste essentially consists in extending the evidentiary value of sentiment to a community. Du Bos never makes the move from individual sense to communal taste; Hume does. What is at issue is not taste itself, which needs no defense, nor the sentiments produced by taste, which have their own legitimacy and motive force for action, but a way to choose between different tastes – something that is a matter of character and communal value.

Hume's idea of how a standard works is essentially pragmatic. For example, he grants mathematicians a defense of equality of surfaces based on indivisible points. But he calls such a procedure "useless" because it cannot be put into practice by the mind. The mathematical issue is archaic. Hume's failure to distinguish formal from psychological properties of logical systems limits his forays into these issues to an historical interest. But what he says of a standard is important. The purpose of a standard is for the mind to be able to judge. What the mind cannot distinguish and determine conceptually, it cannot use as a standard. His phrase concerning mathematical properties is echoed exactly in the language of "Of the Standard of Taste": "such a composition will never afford us a standard, by which we may judge of proportions."[18] In the case of taste, one requires something that will afford a standard by which one may judge of differing tastes. The operation of a standard in both cases is the same. It must be something that the mind can assemble that will do an essentially pragmatic job – the comparison of two surfaces or the comparison of two tastes. Appeals to *je ne sais quoi* or uniformity amidst variety will help no more than mathematical points.

Hume simply denies that there are really major differences in the sentiments themselves, either in morals or beauty: "None of these revolutions has ever produced any considerable innovation in the primary sentiments of morals, more than in those of external beauty."[19] There are variations, but they amount to no more than what can be accounted for by cultural differences and the influence of circumstances. The basic sentimental reactions are relatively uniform. But agreement in the nature of sentiments does not solve the problem of a standard of taste. In morals and in art alike, the problem is for the mind to be able to compare two sentiments and choose between them. For example, in dealing with property, the need for a standard is to decide disputes. No certain standard exists. One cannot distinguish impossibility from improbability from probability in cases of disputed possession, so the probable knowledge supplied by rules is of no assistance. But a standard is needed to: "Mark the precise limits of the one and the other, and shew the standard, by which we may decide all disputes that may arise, and, as we find by experience, frequently do arise upon this subject."[20] Again, the language is echoed in "Of the Standard of Taste," and the requirement is essentially pragmatic.

Hume extends what he has said about time and fictions to the musician's idea of "a compleat *tierce* or *octave*."[21] The appearance of a perfect standard is a natural but illusory extension of the kind of distinction that the mind can make. "This standard is plainly imaginary ... The notion of any correction beyond what we have instruments and art to make, is a mere fiction of the mind, and useless as well as incomprehensible."[22] This example links together three points.

---

18 Hume, *A Treatise of Human Nature*, 1.2.3, p. 45.
19 Hume, *Enquiries Concerning Human Understanding and Concerning the Principles of Morals*, p. 336.
20 Hume, *A Treatise of Human Nature*, 3.2.3, p. 506.
21 Hume, *A Treatise of Human Nature*, 1.2.4, p. 49.
22 Hume, *A Treatise of Human Nature*, 1.2.4, p. 48.

The musician depends on increasing delicacy. This implies that delicacy is something that can be improved and acquired, and it arises from reflection. With increased delicacy, musicians make comparisons and project a unity that is not actually present apart from the individual impressions. Thus they project a fictional entity, the octave. Thus far, one has a movement of ideas and impressions that produces a new idea – the octave – which is strong enough to be heard as a complex impression even though its reference is essentially fictional. The last move is different. The projection becomes a standard. It is taken as perfect octave, and in spite of the fact that such a thing does not exist and can therefore have no actual use as a standard, it is set up as the ideal. If the question arises which piece of music is the more perfect, it is the delicacy of the musician that issues in a fictional projection that provides a standard. Since what is projected is a fiction, it cannot itself be directly examined. The ability to establish the precise octave as a standard of musical excellence actually depends both on delicacy and on a form of projection that provides a pragmatic standard.[23] The same analogy works for the painter with respect to color and with the mechanic with respect to motion. There is no difference in principle between the artist and the mechanic in this respect. Each is engaged in turning an impression that is essentially non-referential into a representational standard that can be applied to secure a judgment.

Everything turns on the delicacy of the senses of the one who judges. In "Of the Delicacy of Taste and Passion," Hume distinguishes the undesirable effects of a delicacy of passion, which is to be corrected and avoided, from the positive effects of a delicacy of taste. Delicacy of passion is likely to produce a surplus of pains over pleasures. "I believe, however, every one will agree with me, that, notwithstanding their resemblance, delicacy of taste is as much to be desired and cultivated as delicacy of passion is to be lamented, and to be remedied, if possible."[24] Taste is the cure for delicacy of passion because delicacy of taste strengthens our judgment. However, delicacy alone cannot be a standard since it leads only to a fiction. Delicacy of imagination is a product of the influence of sensations of beauty or agreeableness on fancy. The more common ideas of pleasure (which approach impressions in strength) are those that gain strength from resemblance, particularly the common resemblance of human creatures. So one is led from delicacy of imagination to the related objects and thence to the person with whom the objects are associated.[25] This is true of riches, and by ex-

---

[23] Hume is not in a position to consider the musical octave as a relation of frequencies of pitch.
[24] Hume, "Of the Delicacy of Taste and Passion," p. 5.
[25] Hume, *A Treatise of Human Nature*, 2.2.5, p. 358.

tension of critical behavior. In attempting to establish a standard, one is led from the ideal to the one whose taste is able to project it.

When it comes to what can be compared, the parallel between Hume's position in the *Treatise* and in "Of the Standard of Taste" is exact. In the *Treatise*, Hume discusses lines and curves and how they are distinguished. On his psychological principles, no exact comparison is possible because there is no specific idea to compare. But compare we do. What we do, therefore, is produce a rule. This rule is the product of experience in the sense of repeated trials. A rule then has the function of filling the gap between observation and comparison – a rule is essentially the generation of ideal cases from actual experience: "And 'tis from these corrections, and by carrying on the same action of the mind, even when its reason fails us, that we form the loose idea of a perfect standard to these figures, without being able to explain or comprehend it."[26] The same thing happens with respect to taste. The rule is comparable to the musician's perfect octave or the painter's exact color; it is a taste that judges exactly. The evidence that taste issues in a rule is the ability to go on from known cases to unknown cases according to the "same actions of the mind." So what confirms the rule is that new actions of the mind continue to extend the rule. Milton is better than Ogilby. To extend that rule to Bunyan and Addison, one continues to find the same aesthetic objects – elegance, style, precision, etc. By that extension, taste confirms that Addison is better than Bunyan. The failure of the comparison in this case comes only when literature has broadened its scope so that the mind can go on to Bunyan rather than Addison without violating a more comprehensive rule. Hume never says, nor does anything in his procedure imply, that the production of rules is not subject to correction and even change as one changes the scope of experience. Within the scope of the neo-classical rules, Addison *is* better than Bunyan. To change that judgment, one has to change the scope. To change the scope, one must change the observer. Du Bos thought that that required an organic change. Hume needs only a cultural change and a change in taste.

A standard takes precedence over an ideal case. As Hume writes,

> In vain shou'd we have recourse to the common topic, and employ the supposition of a deity, whose omnipotence may enable him to form a perfect geometrical figure, and describe a right line without any curve or inflexion. As the ultimate standard of these figures is deriv'd from nothing but the senses and imagination, 'tis absurd to talk of any perfection

---

26 Hume, *A Treatise of Human Nature*, 1.2.4, p. 49.

beyond what these faculties can judge of; since the true perfection of any thing consists in its conformity to its standard.[27]

This appeal to a standard seems simple until one recalls that the standard itself is only the product of a fictional unity produced by a rule. Thus 'true perfection' works back through sense and imagination to the mind's own operations on its own impressions. Post-modernists might think that they are going to love this, but they won't. Instead of deriving a subjective priority for the observer, Hume derives a standard that will elevate certain observers according to their ability to produce rules.[28]

A standard in Hume's system is absolutely essential. It is not just a social or political necessity, though it is that. It is an epistemological necessity. Without a standard, a whole class of cases would not be explainable. It is not just that one would be unable to settle disputes on the order of Sancho's kinsmen's wine-palates. One would not be able to project a "taste" of the wine at all. One would have only its actual sweetness, acidity, etc., not its goodness or badness. The analogy that extends taste from physical impression to normative judgment would break down. The difference between a wine-tasting machine and a human palate is just taste, just as the difference between a musical spectrum analyzer and a listener is the taste of the listener. The former can say only that such notes are present. The latter can say that they are harmonious or discordant, beautiful or painful to the ear. That is not because the human is a subjective listener but because only with the human projection from experience do such qualities as harmony and beauty come to apply at all. If the machines work, it is because they conform to the rule of human taste. The standard produces the ideal case that has no existence for the machine.

In discussing taste and wit, Hume links taste and a standard in a way that suggests that taste itself is the standard: "Tis only by taste we can decide concerning it [wit], nor are we possest of any other standard, upon which we can

---

27 Hume, *A Treatise of Human Nature*, 1.2.4, p. 51.
28 The usual way of explaining this is to attribute to Hume an ideal observer theory. Thus Annette Baier writes in *A Progress of Sentiments*, "Biases due to our particular historical and social position, and to where our own advantage or affections lie, all must be corrected in our moral discourse and moral evaluations. But it is not a 'view from nowhere'; it is a view from a common human viewpoint, expressing the sentiments of 'the party of humankind against vice or disorder (E. 275),'" p. 182. I suggest that what Hume requires is not an ideal observer, however, but an acute rule-perceiver, which is not quite the same thing. For one thing, it avoids the fact that no observer is ideal and that the conditions for an ideal observer cannot be specified.

form a judgment of this kind."²⁹ Hume seems to be saying that taste is itself the only standard for judgments of what is or is not wit. It is sufficient in the case of wit that if the sally produces pleasure and is not attributable to other causes (for example, flattery), it is true wit; if it produces uneasiness, it is not. Aside from the fact that this is arguably not true because true wit may well produce uneasiness as its legitimate goal (satire, political wit – e. g., Lenny Bruce, George Carlin), one must ask whether in the case of wit there is any other standard than pleasure. If there is not, of course, then not only is there no disputing about wit, but "true wit" is not a real judgment. It is only a subjective preference. If there is a standard, then, it must be more than just a taste. It is someone's taste. No standard gets behind taste to some universal, rational basis for comparison, but that does not reduce the question of a standard to the question of taste. The problem, of course, is that in this context, Hume is not pursuing these questions. They arise only in the context of an example designed to show that wit is a source of pride when one feels pleasure in it.

Elsewhere, Hume takes it for granted that there is a difference between taste and a standard of taste. For example, he acknowledges that moral reasoning takes place. "Truth is disputable; not taste: what exists in the nature of things is the standard of our judgement; what each man feels within himself is the standard of sentiment."³⁰ So a standard is a fact of sentiment and taste. A sentiment is felt immediately. It forms a standard when it is given an authority that extends one person's taste to others. The question is how that extension is possible if taste itself is not disputable. One feels both the beauty of an action and the rightness of that beauty. One might continue to feel the beauty without feeling its rightness, however.

There are two sources of moral judgments: sentiments that arise from the species or sentiments that arise from particular persons. "My opinion is, that both these causes are intermix'd in our judgments of morals; after the same manner as they are in our decisions concerning most kinds of external beauty."³¹ Reflections on tendencies are the stronger, but particular tastes may dominate in specific instances —"in cases of less moment, wherein this immediate taste or sentiment produces our approbation."³² Since all tastes and all impressions are ultimately particular, this can only mean that moral systems extend beyond

---

29 Hume, *A Treatise of Human Nature*, 2.1.7, p. 297.
30 Hume, "Enquiry Concerning the Principles of Morals," 1, 135/171.
31 Hume, *A Treatise of Human Nature*, 3.3.1, pp. 589–590.
32 Hume, *A Treatise of Human Nature*, 3.3.1, p. 590.

what any individual can know. If the system is to be accepted, it must lead to new sentiments in its favor.

Hume clearly believes that such distinctions are not only possible but that they are natural. "But there is this material difference between superstition and justice, that the former is frivolous, useless, and burdensome; the latter is absolutely requisite to the well-being of mankind and existence of society."[33] What is interesting about this passage is not that it has any direct reference to taste or aesthetics but that the problem arises in the same way that the problem of taste arises, and Hume is quite clear that justice is required. He has just acknowledged that differences in justice may be arbitrary from one jurisdiction to another and that they cannot be founded on qualities or objects. Yet some system of justice is necessary. If it can be shown that a similar need arises in the case of taste, and that the erection of a standard is useful, then Hume's argument about justice will go through to taste as well. One might then say that the extreme sentimentalism of a Lawrence Sterne or a Rousseau was like superstition. It fails because it is frivolous, useless, and burdensome. The sentiment that issues in taste and a standard is artificial in the way that justice is artificial, but it is also productive of a standard.

The analogy is not very precise. Taste does not involve property or the regulation of desire. It is more like a state that offers sufficient goods for all indiscriminately. Everyone can enjoy art and nature at will, and my enjoyment does not deprive anyone else of anything. So taste in art is an instance where one is dealing with cases of less moment. In that condition, no justice arises because there is nothing to contend for. So a question continues to arise – why does one need a standard of taste? Certain judgments may seem absurd, but so what? Why not just tolerate absurdity? If art were merely private eccentricity, that might indeed be the appropriate conclusion. But only the most slight forms of art and beauty are isolated. Even landscape gardening is a public art. A partial *ad hominem* argument is appropriate. Hume's own sense of himself as a man of letters implies both reputation and its rewards. It is not the same if Robertson's inferior *History of Scotland* is lauded as highly as Hume's *History of England*. Ideas of intellectual property are just emerging in the eighteenth century.[34] Hume has some concerns along those lines, but even more concerns for the importance of character and reputation. (Shaftesbury shared exactly those concerns.)

---

33 Hume, "Enquiry Concerning the Principles of Morals," 3.2, 159/199.
34 See Martha Woodmansee, *The Author, Art and the Market*, pp. 35 ff.

Two distinctions are drawn in dealing with jurisprudence that have a bearing on this issue. First, jurisprudence turns on close points. Thus the way is opened for taste and imagination to play a role: "The preference given by the judge is often founded more on taste and imagination than on any solid argument."[35] What public utility requires is stability. It is less important how the particulars are settled. Second, one must distinguish the general rule, which must be upheld, and the particular applications of it. From the standpoint of society and justice, property is important, but it is only important who gets the property to the extent that it not seem arbitrary or undermine the general rule. There may be a great many systems of distribution, and they too may depend on imagination. Thus there are two roles for taste and imagination. The first allows variations in specific close cases. The second allows variations in the systems of distribution themselves. Some of the same considerations apply to a standard of taste. In close cases, taste alone will settle the decision between say John Home's *Gordon* and Samuel Johnson's *Irene*. And the preferences assigned to genre – history over landscape, or the preference for comedy in youth – are at best the product of "imagination." But to the extent that a decision is needed in matters of taste, it must come from upholding general rules based on more specific systems.

At the same time, sympathy and sentiment alike dictate that the individual cannot be imposed upon by the standards. The link between taste and the qualities that make up a standard of taste suggests that those qualities ultimately are themselves approved of by taste. No application of a standard can escape the ultimate verdict of sentiment. There is a danger in this. Virtue rests on a feeling of approbation. Hume's analysis of virtues becomes more and more conventional. For example, "indecorum" takes its place alongside wit and beauty. Things are ugly if they are "unsuitable."[36] In Hume's defense, one might say that he is merely cataloguing the agreeable and disagreeable sentiments as he finds them. But there is an unfortunate tendency at this point to take the sentiments at a very superficial level. Hume's more careful analysis gives credit to experience and transfers that to sentiment as well. Hume never thinks that the reliance on sentiment is a reliance on mere sentiment – momentary impulse. Some sentiments are better than others. Hume's reasons why one man reasons better than another have a number of parallels to the criteria for a good critic. They include delicacy (greater powers of observation), the forming of general maxims, freedom from

---

35 Hume, "Enquiry Concerning the Principles of Morals," app. 3, 259/308–309.
36 Hume, "Enquiry Concerning the Principles of Morals," 8, 215/266.

prejudice, and greater experience.³⁷ What is added to this list for moral judgments are abilities to form and sustain arguments. The critic's abilities depend on taste alone. Moral reasoning depends on sentiment, but allows scope for reasoning since it must assess consequences and utility. A standard of taste is a standard for critics.

A Standard of Taste

Hume's attempt to establish a standard of taste is one place where we have an explicit piece of aesthetic theory. It must be approached with care, however. It is an essay rather than a piece of systematic philosophy, and Hume was well aware of the difference in audience that that presupposed. Other essays of the same type, both French and British, also influence it. Instead of belonging explicitly to Hume's own system, the essay is part of a tradition that was already quite extensive. The essay on taste can be regarded as a kind of set piece for *belles lettres*.³⁸ Hume himself encouraged Alexander Gerard's *Essay on Taste*. So one must read "Of the Standard of Taste" as only obliquely related to the *Treatise* and the *Enquiries*. Nevertheless, it is consistent with them, and it offers a clear argument for one aspect of applied aesthetics as Hume advanced it.

Hume's essay has produced a substantial secondary literature.³⁹ Two points lead me to conclude that there is still much work to be done. First, the tendency,

---

37 Hume, "Enquiry Concerning Human Understanding, 9, 84/107n1.
38 See Thomas B. Gilmore, Jr. (Ed), *Early 18th-Century Essays on Taste*, for a collection of essays from the 1730's.
39 It is unnecesary to trace all of this literature here. That in no way diminishes its interest. The most common issues are whether Hume holds a causal theory of taste or not; whether Hume continues to hold to his skeptical conclusions about a standard of taste or compromises them for neo-classical standards; if he does, whether there is an inconsistency between that position and his even seeking a standard; and whether the criteria for true judges are circular, initiate an infinite regress, or impose impossible criteria? Other interesting issues in reading difficult passages bear more or less directly on these questions, and there are also interesting meta-aesthetical questions about the nature of criteria, etc. The causal theory holds that some qualities in the object are suitable to produce a sentiment in an appropriately normal human being and usually retains Hume's location of beauty in the beholder but understands secondary or tertiary qualities as causal in a dispositional analysis. The position is supported in one form or another by Carolyn Korsmeyer "Hume and the Foundations of Taste"; Patricia de Martaelere "A Taste for Hume"; Peter Jones "Another Look at Hume's Views of Aesthetic and Moral Judgments";Theodore Gracyk, and others. Mary Mothersill, "In Defense of Hume and the Causal Theory of Taste," has recently given a brief and straightforward defense of it in reply to Roger Shiner. It is opposed by those who either reject Hume's subjectivism and believe they can find some cri-

even by the most careful readers (and there are some excellent essays in the literature) tend to approach Hume's essay as an essay on taste. In contrast, I want to maintain that it is very important to read the essay as an essay on a *standard* of taste and to keep clearly in view the difference between establishing a standard and taste itself. Hume's theory of taste must be extracted from his whole philosophical corpus. Second, ambiguities in Hume's formulations, equivocation on the nature of rules, and the discursive style of the essay make it seem analytically suspect to the majority of commentators. Yet I believe that Hume is much more consistent and careful than he is given credit for being. There is still much to be said in defense of his approach to the problem of a standard of taste, at least within the larger context of the positions he has staked out in the *Treatise* and the *Enquiries*. It is worthwhile, therefore, to see what kind of contextual case can be made for the essay in the light of the accumulated criticism of twentieth century scholarship.

The reading of Hume's essay that I am offering preserves a consistency with Hume's larger project. If I am right, the essay is a limited portion of an aesthetic and not an aesthetic whole. It presumes a view of beauty and taste that is implicit elsewhere. The price for the consistency I argue for is to make Hume rather more limited in two respects. First, his argument for a standard of taste does not mitigate the potential relativism implicit in his psychology of taste and sentiment. Many of the criticisms directed at Shaftesbury will apply to Hume as well. In particular, Berkeley's fear that while this sentimentalism may be tolerable from extremely able and sophisticated upper and upper middle class philosophers such as Shaftesbury and Hume, it will mislead a less able public is not without foundation. I believe that there is a great difference between Hume's sentimentalism and the more extreme forms represented by Berkeley's Lysicles, but the differences are subtle and easily overlooked. Second, in order to attain a

---

terial grounds in the essay or simply find Hume's position inconsistent with a standard of taste at all. Noel Carroll, "Hume's Standard of Taste," and Roger Shiner (see here, in the current volume), among others, have rejected the causal theory. Circularity is a fairly common complaint. Peter Kivy (see likewise in the current volume), denies the circularity but finds an infinite regress. Carroll and James Shelley accuse Hume instead of redundancy. See Carroll, "Hume's Standard of Taste," p. 191; and Shelley, "Hume's Double Standard of Taste," p. 441. Shelley in "Hume's Double Standard of Taste," and Jeffrey Wieand in,"Hume's Two Standards of Taste," find Hume ambiguous between two standards, but Shelley concludes that "Hume comes no closer to giving us an actual standard of taste in specifying the identifying properties of a true judge than he does in giving us vague instructions on how to formulate the rules of art" (Shelley, "Hume's Double Standard of Taste," p. 444). I am influenced by all of these issues, but I am trying to place Hume's essay in the context of his system and of eighteenth-century thought, so I will not engage them except where they bear directly on what I am arguing.

standard in the face of that relativism, Hume is unable to get beyond a culturally founded hierarchy that is elitist and potentially coercive with regard to standards. A standard does not arise directly from human nature, though it is the uniformity of human nature that makes a standard possible. The standard of taste has to be discovered in the practice of criticism. In order to be able to make choices, one must be willing to establish standards that, however justified they are by history and our culture, could be different. Those standards are natural only in so far as they are the product of our need to judge and avoid the chaos of taste. As with other forms of social contract, we surrender part of our aesthetic independence in order to attain a standard of taste. The only mitigation here is that in aesthetic matters one risks less than in other normative realms.[40] The risks are much higher in moral judgments, and only Hume's optimism about the uniformity of human nature gives morals a more universal, and thus a more uniform, foundation. If I have to concede that even though my taste runs to Stephen King, William Golding gets the critical decision,[41] I still don't have to read Golding unless I am worried about the approval of a very small group of intellectuals. In morals, if my taste runs to acts depicted by Stephen King, I am likely to have to deal with a much more extensive, and coercive, group. My way of reading Hume is thus likely to provide little solace to those seeking aesthetic universals. I doubt that Hume would have found that very disturbing, however.

The whole problem for the essay arises from the location of beauty with "sentiments." "Of the Standard of Taste" retains the basic epistemological structure established in the *Treatise*. Imaginative impressions are sentiments that, while they are part of experience, are not themselves psychological atoms. The pleasure they produce is the qualitative accompaniment of the impressions. Beauty is an emotion, and the word 'beauty' is a class term for calm passions that are sentiments. Thus it is important to note that "sentiments . . . differ with regard to beauty and deformity of all kinds" (ST 204). Beauty is of plural kinds.

When Hume observes that "those who found morality on sentiment, more than on reason, are inclined to comprehend ethics under the former observation" (ST 204), he clearly is among them. The specific sentiments mentioned are justice, humanity, magnanimity, prudence, and veracity. 'Sentiment,' here, is referential to specific situations. If a situation is felt to be just, it is also ap-

---

[40] For example, "No gratification, however sensual, can of itself be esteemed vicious. A gratification is only vicious, when it engrosses all a man's expense, and leaves no ability for such acts of duty and generosity as are required by his situation and fortune." "Of Refinement in the Arts," in *Essays*, p. 279.

[41] Carroll, "Hume's Standard of Taste," p. 187.

plauded, so 'justice' is connotatively positive; but the specific situation that is just varies, and situations that are felt as just or unjust are a matter of taste. The basis for the sentiment is both specific and variable from individual to individual.

The examination of the position that "all sentiment is right" (ST 208) is placed in a hypothetical context. "There is a species of philosophy, which cuts off all hopes of success in such an attempt, and represents the impossibility of ever attaining any standard of taste." (ST 208) But the object of the qualification is to determine whether this position makes a standard impossible, not to suggest that this position is not correct in what it says about taste. This is one of the places where one must keep clear the difference between an examination of taste and an examination of a standard of taste. The position described by Hume as holding that all sentiment is right contrasts with reference to matters of fact. It is exactly what both Hutcheson and Hume have argued for elsewhere. It is still easy in this summary to lose sight of how taste works, however. Hume was writing in a much more popular style than that he employed in the *Treatise*, and there is a consequent looseness in his language that one must be careful to understand. When he writes, "Beauty is no quality in things themselves: It exists merely in the mind which contemplates them; and each mind perceives a different beauty" (ST 230), this does not imply that beauty is the sentiment of taste. What is contemplated is the things themselves or, more accurately, the impressions and ideas that present the things themselves in the mind. Beauty is the emotion or calm passion produced by these impressions. To say that beauty is not a quality in things themselves, then, is also to say that it is a secondary impression as the *Treatise* explained. So when one views Hutcheson's equilateral triangle, what one contemplates is a triangle (given ideationally). Where Hutcheson would find a further idea, uniformity amidst variety, Hume merely finds a taste for triangles. Each mind perceives a different beauty – in this case triangularity as perceived by this observer. Nothing in this implies a separate cause from the impression of the triangle – the beauty of the triangle – but Hume's position is made more difficult, though more consistent and defensible than Hutcheson's, because Hutcheson does have some quality to point to while Hume does not. Hutcheson would, presumably, be able to say that while beauty is indeed not a quality in things, a quality in ideas of beauty (at least for humans) corresponds to qualities in things. Uniformity amidst variety is at once an idea in the mind and a complex quality belonging to the object (though still 'in the mind' in the sense that it is available as a complex idea of sides in relations of triangularity.) Hume's position is similar in its mechanics, but different in that he assigns no specific idea to the sentimental contemplation of the triangle. It only marks a "certain conformity or relation." The emotion it produces is reflective. Hutcheson, one might say, provides a secondary reference for moral and aesthetic sentiments. The sentiments do not refer to anything beyond themselves, but that self-reference takes one back to a primary reference so it is possible to compare beauties on the basis of the primary properties as long as one is dealing with a normal observer. Hume provides a relational theory; beauty extends only to a relation of the secondary impression to an original impression, together with the impression of pleasure, and the reference is solely in terms of the original impression. So nothing in Hume's theory of taste provides a standard, which is the problem that he is considering at this point. Everyone *ought* to acquiesce in his own sentiment. Perceptions of beauty and deformity are not contradictories when they involve more than one observer. It is important to keep this straight, however. If one perceives beauty and another perceives deformity, there are not two different ideas upon which the sentiment rests. If there were, then the disagreement would merely be verbal. The problem would merely be that I do not see what you see. But the problem is deeper. I do see what you see, but my sentiment experiences it as deformity; yours, as beauty. It is very easy, given Hume's language, to slide over into separate ideas of beauty and deformity, but the argument makes a lot less sense that way (though I think Isenbergian types of criticism and many commentators influenced by Wittgenstein take it that way.)

The counter-position from the side of common sense is just that – one would be "thought to defend ... an extravagance" (ST 210) if one denied that some things are more beautiful than others. The basis for this common-sense position is how one would be viewed by one's cultural peers. It is not an absurdity to assert an equality of elegance between Ogilby and Milton if Milton is not established culturally as the superior. For Hume's Muslim, for example, there would be nothing out of the ordinary. Note too that genius and elegance are compared, not beauty as such. Whenever it comes to a specific comparison, there will be specific aesthetic predicates, not just a generalized emotion of beauty. The verdict of absurdity is directed toward the eccentricity of this taste and rests on the widespread agreement of the judges (compare the universal agreement of the faithful). In close cases, the absurdity evaporates. On neither side of the issue, then, is Hume concerned directly with a taste whose evidential power extends beyond itself. On the skeptical side, the difficulty arises because Hume rejects Hutcheson's theory of secondary reference. On the positive side, the only recourse is to that position at which critics have already arrived.

That Hume continues to believe in rules has been widely noted. When he says that they cannot be fixed *a priori*, therefore, he is also acknowledging that there are rules of art discoverable by observation or genius. We have seen above how rules extend experience. What Hume's examples clearly indicate in

"Of the Standard of Taste" are specific aesthetic responses. Once again, as soon as one begins to look closely and compare examples, Hume gives us specific predicates: on the negative side, monstrous and improbable fictions, mixture of styles, want of coherence; on the positive side force and clearness of expression, readiness and variety of inventions, natural pictures (ST 211). These predicates replace uniformity amidst variety, but Hume limits them to empirical rules. So, I read Ariosto. I have an idea of a passage. It is an improbable fiction. My taste, if it conforms to the rules of art, finds this improbable fiction deformed, unpleasant, and an aesthetic fault. I have no taste for improbable fictions, and a wise artist will take note of that. The function of a rule here is to replace the perceptual and qualitative appeal that is at work in Hutcheson. Thus Hume's appeal to rules is not a way of making taste rule-governed but a way of acknowledging that it is not. If taste could be made to conform to rules, one would not need the kind of observation and/or genius that criticism requires. Hume's appeal to rules is a part of the problem of establishing a standard of taste, not a part of the solution, given where he locates rules.

This is made clear when Hume ventures into his quasi-Newtonian explanation of how "the least exterior hindrance to such small springs, or the least internal disorder, disturbs their motion, and confounds the operation of the whole machine" (ST 213). The problem is not that this makes taste variable (though it does) but that it makes us "unable to judge" (ST 213). Trying to establish rules is the aesthetic equivalent of a Newtonian problem of mechanics with three or more bodies. Newton does not pretend to be able to give the internal workings of force and gravity. (He has some marked tendencies toward a physical/theological occasionalism on the matter.) But for a simple two-body problem he can give the empirical laws. There is no aesthetic equivalent of the two-body simplification that makes Newtonian mechanics possible. The only recourse is to what has happened already. "We shall be able to ascertain its influence not so much from the operation of each particular beauty, as from the durable admiration, which attends those works, that have survived all the caprices of mode and fashion, all the mistakes of ignorance and envy" (ST 213). Note again that it is "each particular beauty," not a single idea of beauty that is the object of investigation. The particularity of the ideas is the source of the problem, but it is also the empirical basis for rejecting neo-Platonic causality. Neo-Platonism postulates a single unified idea of beauty with formal and final causes. That is Hume's ultimate opponent in "Of the Standard of Taste."

What one gets from all of this is a shift to consideration of the empirical conditions that may impede agreement. Hume's discussion of internal organs and causal relations does not try to say what or how those organs work to form relations. But "proper sentiment" (ST 216) in this context can only mean common or widely shared sentiment or perception. What is proper is what conforms to normalized, empirical expectations – as in proper manners, or a proper procedure in science.

The role of critical language is to exhibit praise or blame, so aesthetic predicates have an emotive aspect; the application of the terms to which everyone agrees is their emotive connotation. Nothing in these predicates implies reference beyond the secondary impressions that they represent except for their reference, as ideas, to some original impression of sense. The meaning of the specific predicates varies, however. Hume's point is about the greater variance in particulars than in emotive applications, which is the opposite of the situation in "matters of opinion and science" (ST 204) where one can establish agreement about "the facts" but locate those facts differently in complex theoretical ideas. Hume shares with later writers, most notably Kant, the perception that aesthetics is radically particular and not conceptual or theoretical. But in order to make that point, he distinguishes the meaning and application of aesthetic predicates. The meaning is located in the particulars to which "elegance," for example, is applied. The application is the emotively positive connotation shared by "elegance" in all usages.

One source of agreement is human nature, which exceeds the unanimity available to abstract sciences that depend on more difficult observations and reasoning. Hume makes the same argument elsewhere. Human nature is enough alike so that one can count on similar sentiments in moral areas. Abstract reasoning lacks a common human base and is more variable even though it can make use of reason. But a common positive language also can obscure disagreement about "particular pictures of manners" (ST 206). For example, the lying of Odysseus does not produce the sentiment in us that it did in the Achaians. Hume is making a simple distinction: if Odysseus is virtuous, that is good. But I may not concur in the judgment that Odysseus is virtuous if I look directly at Odysseus's behavior. So far, so good. The important thing is to keep distinct the basis for Hume's argument. I do not reason that lying is bad, then fit Odysseus's behavior to that moral rule. I observe, by ordinary means (i.e., external sense or the ideas that the imagination draws from external sense through reference in Homer's text), that Odysseus lies. So I have a complex idea of a lying Odysseus. I form a further idea from that complex idea of a lack of veracity. In my perception, lack of veracity is a matter of taste and moral sentiment. It is linguistically a negative form, and that negative rests upon the feeling that forms the moral sentiment. But Homer has a different moral sentiment and operating by different linguistic rules, locates Odysseus's form of lack of veracity with cunning, and cunning with virtue rather than vice. He would agree with me that if cunning were a vice, it would be a bad thing, but he does not experience the same sentiment with regard to Odysseus's behavior, so he locates cunning differently linguistically as well. Hume presupposes that the complex idea available to external sense and imagination is essentially the same. The evidence, though Hume does not investigate that here, would be that Homer and I would give a common description of the situation. Our causal, habitual, and perceptual patterns as they are evidenced in our language correspond, and reason can confirm that they do so (to the extent that reason gives probable knowledge of matters of fact) by comparing the ideas. But the evidence also indicates that as soon as we begin to form ideas of Odysseus's behavior in the moral sphere, we diverge. Here taste is supreme.

What Hume argues here, however, is not completely consistent with what he says elsewhere. Specifically, he is clearly aware that everyone does not take pride in the same positive way that he takes it.[42] For Hume, pride is the positive. For Hume's Puritan opponents, humility is positive and pride is a sin. One might suspect that the same would be the case with "meekness" (ST 206) in Hume's example from the Koran. So it would appear that even basic emotive responses can vary; we do not all agree as to which are positive and which are negative. That does not change the basic point. A "just sentiment of morals" (ST 207) is one that I perceive as just. "Just sentiment" here can only mean one that I experience when I have that complex idea. It will be the task of the essay to reconcile my "just sentiment" with the variety of other sentiments experienced. Hume complicates the matter by referring to a "steady rule of right," but that must be a rhetorical appeal at this point. Such a rule can only be a consequence of just sentiments, and establishing them is the point at issue. Rather than accuse Hume of begging the question, one must allow him the confidence he shares with his readers that the Koran is selfish, anti-utilitarian, and thus empirically falsified. In the long run, superstition will prove foolish and useless. I take it that this is an instance of a projective application of what the essay will attempt to justify.

We turn now to Hume's strategy to deal with the need for a standard when his consistent theory of sentiments seems to make one impossible. Jeffrey Wieand notes the ambiguity of the phrase "a rule, by which the various sentiments of men may be reconciled; at least, a decision, afforded, confirming one sentiment, and condemning another" (ST 208). Does the second clause refer to a rule by which a decision is afforded, or does it refer all the way back to the standard, in which case the alternatives are a rule, or a standard that will do the job of a rule, at least to provide a decision, but will not be a

---

42 Hume, *A Treatise of Human Nature*, 2.1.5.

rule itself?[43] This may seem crucial, but I take it that both the position of the sentence and its rhetoric dictate that Hume is discussing the possibility of a standard and the question is whether the standard will reconcile the opinions or perform the more limited task of affording a decision between them. A standard could be a rule, but Hume does not expect to be able to give such a rule, nor should we expect it from him if we have followed the rejection of reason's ability to directly affect action in the *Treatise* and the explanation of the variability of taste. Nor is Hume's kind of general rule suitable as a standard because it can only produce expectations and extend ideas and impressions to new contexts. But we can hope for a standard in the sense of a decision confirming one sentiment and condemning another. The key is that confirming is parallel to condemning. Those are the roles assigned to a standard. So the role of a standard of taste is satisfied by a decision between confirming and condemning sentiments. Nothing here implies that sentiments will be corrected or changed. Presumably they will remain just what they were.

The most direct challenge to the way that I am suggesting that "Of the Standard of Taste" be read comes from Anthony Savile. Savile makes an important point by noting that the standard proposed by the *Essay* is evidential for sound criticism, not constitutive of it. Savile writes: "The standard is now, and, I surmise, for Hume always was, conceived of as evidential for sound criticism, not constitutive of it. If you like, "Of the Standard of Taste" is a contribution to the theory of aesthetic evidence, not the theory of aesthetic nature."[44] This is certainly correct. Savile goes on to suggest one way of reading this in which a dispute between Peter and Paul is settled by a decision of good judges in Paul's favor, even though Peter judges it differently.[45] But Savile rejects this alternative as incoherent on the grounds that transmittal of knowledge requires as a necessary condition that the sentiment be shared:

> Hume's standard reconciles varying *sentiments* rather than just *judgments*, and this could only come about by people sharing their experiential responses to something rather than somehow sincerely agreeing in their judgments while differing sentimentally *in petto*.

---

43 Jeffrey Wieand, "Hume's Two Standards of Taste," pp. 129–142. James Shelley returns to this topic, but he takes the passage to be offering Hume's definition of a standard as a rule. He concludes that Hume succeeds in giving us an actual standard neither in terms of true judges or rules of art. James Shelley, "Hume's Double Standard of Taste," pp. 437–445. Hume's rhetoric does not imply that a standard is being defined as a rule when he constructs such parallels, however. 'Rule' is a way of explicating 'standard,' but so is 'decision.' All Hume is asserting is that it is natural for us to seek a standard or a rule, or perhaps only a decision.
44 Anthony Savile, *Kantian Ethics Pursued*, p. 80.
45 Savile, *Kantian Ethics Pursued*, p. 81.

Nor will it do to suppose that Hume thinks that such agreement of sentiment comes about as a result of some prior agreement in judgment secured by consulting good critics first. What he makes plain is that the good judge tries to show the disputing parties what to see.[46]

Savile thinks, therefore, that Hume's appeals to rules and principles are ways that the good critic gets others to see what she sees: "He operates not by enouncing what Peter is to believe, but by getting him to respond to the poem with which he is having difficulty in the light of suggestions about what to look for."[47] Savile quotes Hume's description of what we show the bad critic in support of this view. But I do not think that passage supports Savile's reading at all. First of all, it is addressed not to a reader but to a critic, and for Hume that means not an ordinary reader but one who offers his judgments as in line with the rules of the art. What that critic is shown is that his judgments are not in line with the rules and principles as they have emerged over time. Second, Savile's reading is based on the claim that the transmittal of knowledge requires the replication of sentiment. But on Hume's view of both demonstrative and probable reasoning, all that is required is the replication of ideas. One does not have to feel what Homer felt about Helen in order to understand the *Iliad*. There is a transmittal of knowledge, but it is a knowledge that there is a standard of taste and how that standard can be appealed to. Hume states that explicitly when he says that it is enough to have established that all tastes are not equal. So I conclude that indeed Peter may be left with the judgment against him without sharing the sentiment of Paul, though a good critic will have offered additional ways to experience the work in dispute. If that is incoherent from Kant's point of view, that is part of what is wrong with Kantian aesthetics. It demands that aesthetic intuition, or sentiment in Hume's terms, meet an impossibly high standard. As a result, one is led to look for some special state, contemplative or attitudinal, that ends by separating aesthetics from the real world of art and criticism. Hume is more pragmatic and more useful to real criticism. The Muslim will not be converted to our sentiments by a standard of taste. But our claim to have attained a just sentiment will be affirmed (we hope) by such a procedure. The argument here is about who gets to use the universal terms of approbation – just, virtuous, beautiful. That argument cannot be settled by appeal to the sentiments because the sentiments are just what is experienced. Fenelon is pleased by the honesty of Telemachus in his telling of the tale; Homer is pleased by the lying of Odysseus in his telling. I decide in favor of Fenelon (if

---

46 Savile, *Kantian Ethics Pursued*, p. 82.
47 Savile, *Kantian Ethics Pursued*, p. 82.

I do), not because I share his taste (if I do), but because his taste is confirmed by the standard that at least affords a decision. It is logically possible that I share the taste of Homer (as I do) but conclude that the decision goes to Fenelon.

This is the first crucial divergence from the standard interpretation in my reading of the essay. Hume, I think, is consistent in holding both to his basic ideational principles that make sentiments of taste a privileged, evidential form and to his recognition that a standard is still needed. That separates the question of a standard of taste from taste. Perhaps because Hume's position on aesthetic taste is so scattered outside of this essay, the tendency in the literature has been to try to extract Hume's position on taste from this essay and to take the essay to be about taste itself. But it is not. It presupposes a view of taste. The essay is about standards. There is a primary sense in which taste does not have any standards. One's taste just is what it is. It is an original existence (but not an original impression). Hume holds three compatible positions on this subject. First, taste is not subject to reason or rules. It is formed directly as an immediate response to impressions of pleasure, original impressions of sense, and other secondary impressions and ideas. Second, because human nature is very much the same for everyone, one can look for and expect to find regularities in taste. Finally, within limits, one's taste, as one's character, temper, and physical attributes, can be formed. But that process of formation is extrinsic to particular tastes. I cannot decide what my taste will be, but I can reshape the habits and associations that contribute to my taste in ways that are themselves predictable. Hume is, in this respect, a believer in behavior modification. But given the existence of diverse tastes and the basis for that diversity that Hume has demonstrated in the opening paragraphs of the essay, Hume recognizes both the need for and the possibility of sorting different tastes according to a standard. That standard must be external to particular tastes, and the question of what the standard of taste is cannot itself be a matter of one's taste for a particular work. Nor should one expect a standard of taste to do more than provide a choice. It will not guide the formation of taste itself, though some of the same considerations that establish a standard also may contribute to the behavioral modification program.

This is a point at which Peter Kivy is most helpful when he notes the tendency to a regress.[48] Hume always hovers on the edge of such a regress. If a standard

---

[48] See Peter Kivy, "Hume's Standard of Taste: Breaking the Circle." Kivy's solution for Hume is different from mine, however. He argues that some of the criteria for a good critic apply more widely than to questions of taste and so can be established independently of judgments of taste. I will argue below that the question of a standard raises different questions altogether.

of taste is operative, it will confirm a particular sentiment and condemn another. For example, that the Prophet had not attained a just sentiment will be decided according to what Hume (who shares the prejudice of his age) takes to be the emergent beliefs of human nature. But that in itself also uses moral language, i.e., "just sentiment," and so should be a report of a moral sentiment experienced by Hume, as it clearly is. How then can it be anything but in need of a further standard?[49] We are familiar with this kind argument today when we are told that certain forms of logical reasoning are themselves "Eurocentric" and perhaps "masculine," thus initiating a regress that is supposed to invalidate their status as standards. What makes logical reasoning the standard, we are asked? Hume has available, I think, the same line of reply one sometimes hears to these claims. On the one hand, the substance of his claim is only to provide a standard. It is not to place that standard beyond all dispute. On the other hand, some degree of cultural and biological bias seems inescapable. Hume specifically brings this up at the end of the essay, though it is nation, age, and temperament rather than race and sex of which he seems to be aware. It does not follow from that that one cannot apply a standard, however. In other words, a degree of regress is acceptable, just as a degree of circularity need not be vicious. If it is universalized, a standard of taste may well stand in need of a justification that it cannot attain, but our experience and vision is not universal, and we can push the standard far enough back so that it will work for virtually all of our experience. One cannot escape language into a language-free realm if Wittgenstein is correct; it does not follow from that that language is not referential within very broad language-games. One cannot attain a standard of taste for all cultures and possible beings for all times. But one can make choices in a very large cultural context. Hume believed that context could be extended to be virtually coextensive with human nature. But if it were somewhat narrower, it would still be a standard.

Two problems are evident at this point. First, the only standard that Hume has made possible so far is retrospective. Looking backward, one can fit the

---

That does not mean that Kivy is not correct about the wider application of some of the criteria for good critics.

[49] Noel Carroll rejects this as either a disagreement over a critic (this won't result in an infinite regress because there aren't enough critics) or over the definition of the criteria. (The "conjectured refusal to buy Hume's concept of sense as a mark of a good critic does not show that there is an infinite regress internal to Hume's theory." In Carroll, "Hume's Standard of Taste," p. 190.) I think the real threat of a regress lies in the need for a further standard, this time for good sense, however, and that is different from buying Hume's definition. Whatever definition one has, it will seem to need a standard if it is to serve its function.

data to a pattern that identifies Homer as great. But Hume has provided no grounds at this point for the projection of that standard. His rules are not laws in the Newtonian sense that provides the model here. Second, in the absence of either organs or reference to a standard set of qualities, it is not clear where one should look for clarification. This is where the problem of circularity really enters, not later. Since there are only beauties, not a single, qualitatively defined beauty, the claim that "some objects, by the structure of the mind, [are] naturally calculated to give pleasure (ST 215) does not tell us which objects to examine. Should I consider the pleasures of my mistress, of my dinner, of my horses and dogs? Such suggestions are absurd if one is dealing with criticism and taste, but they certainly predominate empirically. Since Hume identifies neither the structure of the mind, nor a kind of pleasure (except *ex post facto*), nor a single qualitative object, his ideational structure has an empirical problem when he tries to formulate rules that summarize the decisions of taste. The rules are about people's tastes, but those people are just the ones to which one applies the rules in order to choose between competing tastes. The circularity that has been widely noted and debated in the discussion of specific capacities actually should be located earlier. When Hume turns to delicacy, etc., he is really looking for a way out of this empirical problem. Otherwise, he would be able to generate some general rules of art from the past and project them causally (by means of habit, custom, and fixed nature) into a version of neo-classical canons as many of his contemporaries did. What is most remarkable about Hume's procedure at this point is that he comes up with nothing of the sort. At a time when numerous critics in literature and the arts (from Pope to Reynolds, for example) were formulating rules along neo-classical lines, Hume gives us an entirely different approach. I think that this is an attempt to solve the circularity problem, not a fall into it.

Hume's problem is to find a way to extend and generalize the experience of taste. It is clear enough what the standard is once it emerges. Milton is preferred to Ogilby, and any taste that concurs in that decision is confirmed. But a standard must be projective in some way. Even if one cannot predict prior to experience, one must be able to formulate the standard in such a way that it will account for future regularities. Hume's strategy is to examine the characteristics that will convince someone to accept the verdict of a critic, even if that verdict contradicts one's own immediate taste. Thus Hume is not simply trying to describe a good critic. He is trying to describe those characteristics of a critic that have emerged widely as belonging to a good critic because they are consistent with the most stable retrospective judgments. The characteristics that he ends up citing are already widely accepted and are just those that one must appeal to in order to convince both parties to a dispute.

The Problem of a Standard of Taste — 161

Hume begins with delicacy. First, note that it is delicacy of imagination. Imagination can produce a secondary form of impressions. So delicacy of imagination should be an imagination that produces impressions from slighter originals. Since the reflective impressions which are of concern are usually among the calm kind,[50] delicacy is central. However, Hume is interested in delicacy because everyone "would reduce every kind of taste or sentiment to its standard" (ST 216). Thus delicacy can serve as a standard for a critic because "everyone" will acknowledge its relevance. The intention of the essay is "to mingle some light of the understanding with the feelings of sentiment" (ibid.). Presumably this means finding some way for the understanding to operate on sentiments that do not refer beyond themselves. Delicacy thus becomes the central capacity that will link taste and a standard of taste if delicacy can be given "a more accurate definition" (ibid.). I think delicacy is supposed to perform the function for impressions of the imagination that examination of the organs has in primary impressions. One defers to another's visual perception, for example, if it can be shown that the other person's eyes are more acute. Similarly, Hume claims, one defers (naturally) to another's taste if it can be shown to be more delicate. Yet delicacy is not an organ. Delicacy itself is a function of reflection, but its "organ" is the production of sentiments that establish rules – at least rules allow one to examine delicacy. Hume needs a way to make delicacy evident if it is to serve as a standard. How this can be done is the crucial question.

Hume tries to unravel this question with the anecdote of Sancho's kinsmen.[51] Hume presents it as a way of giving a more accurate definition of delicacy. The task is complicated by the fact that delicacy is not directly examinable since we seem to have only introspective access to its operation. The initial conditions of the story are important. Sancho's claim is that his judgment is a hereditary quality. It is acquired only "internally", so it cannot be verified by examining the circumstances under which Sancho acquired it. The wine to be examined is already supposed to be excellent on the grounds of its age and vintage, so the judgment is not directly about the quality of the wine. And the teller of the story is Sancho – whose reputation is that of a buffoon. The gist of the story is that Sancho's kinsmen are ridiculed for their judgment, but they have the last laugh when

---

50 Hume, *A Treatise of Human Nature*, 2.1.1, p. 276.
51 This anecdote has been very widely discussed. Most commentators seem to think that its object is to vindicate a type of critic or a type of judgment. But that cannot be the case because the vindication provided merely confirms the claims of these judges to greater acuteness of taste than others were willing to allow them. I take Hume's object to be to explain what delicacy means. The vindication of Sancho's kinsmen is only a means to that end.

the key with the leathern thong is found and this in turn vindicates Sancho's claim to have inherited his taste from good judges.

Hume's application of the story emphasizes both the similarity and difference between mental and bodily taste. Something is tasted: leather and iron; mental taste would produce correspondingly specific aesthetic qualities – e. g., force and elegance. The discovery of the key only confirms the presence of leather and iron in the wine. It does not confirm the taste of Sancho's kinsmen directly. That is, one still does not have access to the taste itself; one only has access to the cause of the taste. Those who laughed are refuted not by coming to taste the leather and iron but by the discovery of the key. Their taste, not that of Sancho's kinsmen, is the duller. They are wrong to laugh not because their taste is wrong but because it is deficient. This gives Hume his definition: "Where the organs are so fine, as to allow nothing to escape them; and at the same time so exact as to perceive every ingredient in the composition: This we call delicacy of taste" (ST 218). Two things are of note. First, this not a definition in the traditional sense. It remains analogical. There is no organ identified for aesthetic taste, and the ingredients of taste are not specified. Literally, Sancho's kinsmen taste leather and iron; the metaphorical taste is presumably for things like elegance and force. But elegance and force do not have a chemical composition or a natural source. They are predicates assigned to sentiments, and unlike Hutcheson, Hume denies that sentiments can be linked, even experimentally, to some external cause such as uniformity amidst variety. So the appeal to delicacy remains somewhat mysterious. Second, they are Sancho's kinsmen. One presumes that Hume intends that part of the laughter at them arises not just from the pretensions of their taste but from its source. These are not connoisseurs. Literal delicacy is established by what is at the bottom of the barrel. How is metaphorical delicacy to be established?

Hume immediately answers this question, and in answering it confirms what I said above about the role of delicacy in linking general rules to taste:

> Here then the general rules of beauty are of use; being drawn from established models, and from the observation of what pleases or displeases, when presented singly and in a high degree: and if the same qualities, in a continued composition and in a smaller degree, affect not the organs with a sensible delight or uneasiness, we exclude the person from all pretensions to this delicacy (ST 218).

The rules, formed retrospectively, identify the qualities in question. If I want to know what elegance is, I do not ask for its composition or source but for its models. They exhibit it in a high degree. Then delicacy is judged by the ability to find slighter examples that conform to the models. The rules also play the role of the key: "To produce these general rules or avowed patterns of composition is like finding the key with the leathern thong" (ST 218). "Produce" in this context does not mean formulating the rules in the first place. The rules are not themselves a standard. That would make delicacy circular. It means something like being able to cite or demonstrate the application. If I claim that a particular poem is elegant, I confirm my claim by producing – pointing out – the rule that identifies the particular elegance. Hume escapes circularity because the rules themselves are determined independently of the judges by the taste over time of many perceivers.

There is still a problem in Hume's analogy, however. The laughter was not about whether iron had a taste, but whether it could be detected in this wine by these buffoons. Hume forms the analogy by appealing to rules as a "key" to silence the bad critic. Taste is and remains the same regardless of whether it is confirmed or not – whether by rules or discovery of the causal source. Sancho's kinsmen would still taste iron and leather even if no key were found, and their critics do not taste either even after it is found. But Hume is forcing the analogy by asking the rules to do double duty both as exhibition of models and as confirmation of those models (the key). The bridge that makes this plausible is that rules can be used in the same way that discovering the key was used – it convinces the bad critics that the fault lies in themselves rather than in the other.

So we can see what will eventuate in a standard of taste. For a standard to operate in the absence of direct confirmation that is unavailable, a way must be found to convince someone that the fault lies on one side rather than the other. Delicacy can play that role, even if it is not precisely defined. But it can do so only if independent ways of establishing who has delicate taste are found. The circularity often charged to delicacy is not really present because delicacy is never appealed to directly. Sancho's kinsmen do have delicate taste, and their capability allows them to triumph. But the confirmation does not exhibit their delicacy but the key itself. In mental taste, delicacy allows one to triumph as well. But rules and the ability to exhibit precise applications of them serve as the confirmation, the "key." Escaping a circle that would arise if delicacy were both the standard and the means of verification has been the issue all along.

Thus far, Hume has been concerned to show us that delicacy can play the required role as standard. Now he must go on to try to give us a way to tell who has delicate taste. The question now is how the ability to produce rules can play the role of the key and who we can turn to to learn the rules? The answer comes with a twist: "The perfection of the man, and the perfection of the sense or feeling, are found to be united" (ST 220). We are led back to the position explained in the *Treatise* and *Enquiries* where character and temper are the objects of both moral and aesthetic sentiment. If this can be established, not only will it break any circle, since the perfection of the man does not depend on having a *standard* of taste already; it will also relate rules to qualities other than those of the source. The test that determines the qualities of the person is the degree of enjoyment as universally acknowledged. "A delicate taste of wit or beauty ... is the source of all the finest and most innocent enjoyments, of which human nature is susceptible. In this decision the sentiments of all mankind are agreed" (ST 220). Delicacy of taste produces a high quality of enjoyment. Those who do not experience that quality of enjoyment acknowledge that those who exhibit it are in an enviable position. They have the "temper" of the aesthetically perceptive person. So one can tell who has delicate taste by their ability to enjoy things that others do not (but wish they could) enjoy. What they enjoy is established by appeal "to those models and principles, which have been established by the uniform consent and experience of nations and ages" (ST 220).

So now we have completed the connections. Rules do not establish directly that A is better than B. But in so far as rules exhibit models and principles, those who have the ability to produce models and principles with respect to A establish that they are able to enjoy A in a way that someone who does not "see" the models will not. And that enjoyment, resting on one's greater delicacy, is acknowledged as superior, and thus as a standard of taste. There is still a circle evident: delicate taste is an enjoyment of what the rules identify (e. g., Milton) and the rules are rules because they identify what people of delicate taste enjoy (e. g., elegance). But two different senses of "rule" help break the circle. The rules that identify Milton presumably operate because of Milton's elegance, but it is Milton who is the object of the rules. On the other hand, delicacy, while it depends on the rules for its verification, is a response to elegance. It is a delicacy of taste. The rule in the former sense is the cause of Milton's status as "key"; in the latter sense, the rule is the effect of the elegance. "Rule" is able to do both jobs by equivocating on 'rule,' but as long as the rules are pragmatically the same, the technique should work. Hume shifts at this point to the pragmatic side, therefore.

This is the way this is all supposed to work. Consider a country squire who likes horses. He has a taste for horses, gets pleasure from seeing them, riding them, owning them. They are a source of status and enjoyment to him. Confronted with a Stubbs painting of his horse and a Raphael Madonna, we will presume that his taste will prefer Stubbs. He lacks the delicacy to appreciate the more vibrant colors and more refined forms of Raphael, and the mythological and religious symbolism leave him cold. One is not likely to change his taste, and while one can point to features of the Raphael that correspond to its coloration and symbolism, and the squire may even "see" what one is pointing to, there is no reason to think he will feel them. The impressions of sense are simply not accompanied by the level of pleasure required for beauty to be felt. Moreover, the squire can point to features of his Stubbs. What establishes that the ability to respond to Raphael requires greater delicacy of taste and that the taste for Raphael is a desirable quality? Hume's answer is that one must convince the squire that he is missing something and that he is being left out. This is done not by an appeal to an experience that, *ex hypthosesi*, he does not have, but by first pointing out that "everyone" agrees that delicacy is enjoyable, and second, that all the best models – i.e. those established through the ages – fit Raphael better than Stubbs. In other words, the rules are on the side of Raphael and everyone agrees that whatever the rules select also produces the highest kind of enjoyment. So the poor squire is left wishing that he had a more delicate taste, and acknowledging that he is not the best judge of painting. He still prefers Stubbs and presumably will still buy Stubbs, however. There is little point in his buying that for which he has no taste. If he remains unconvinced, no matter. His taste has been condemned all the same. That is why one needs a standard of taste, but unlike moral taste, nothing in particular is harmed by his failure to follow the higher taste. (If, on the other hand, he is cruel to his horses, then his deformed moral taste does matter.)

This can't be the whole answer for a couple of reasons. First, Hume links beauty and utility widely and generally. So in some sense, beauty does matter because utility implies consequences. Second, it still doesn't allow one to project a standard of taste to new instances. Delicacy so far is limited to what the rules can identify, and the rules are essentially conservative. They can only identify that for which there are already models. But Hume is not a neo-classicist. Unlike Johnson, he is not philosophically opposed to new forms like Fielding's novels. By themselves, rules are not sufficient to establish the kind of delicacy Hume needs to provide a standard of taste. Practice provides a kind of projective assurance. Just as one will trust the judgment of a practiced scientist, but question and re-test the experiments of a novice, so practice provides some assurance of the taste of one who goes beyond established models.

Practice remains secondary to delicacy; its function is to improve delicacy of taste. This assumes that delicacy can be improved, so it is not simply an inherited response, though it may be an inherited capacity. "Practice" here means experience of objects. With experience comes a greater ability to distinguish parts from wholes and to assign qualities to species. One's experience becomes more fine-grained, so to speak, and is better able to perceive differences. The mechanics of practice as Hume envisages them do not involve reason. Rather a sentiment "attends" the impressions of the eye or imagination, and that sentiment progresses from confusion to specificity with experience. The sentiment comes to be identified with more discrete and detailed parts of the original impressions. One is led back to the rules that serve as models by practice only because the distinctions that practice allows make possible assigning qualities to species. The rules and models do not dictate to experience. The qualities are those of the object (strictly, those impressions for which the object is a causal source), but beauty is the generic term for those sentiments that "attend" the now much more specific ideas.

With practice comes judgment, the fixing of "the epithets of praise and blame." Hume has shifted gears at this point without quite noticing the shift. The kind of judgment he describes is based on sentiment, but since it is comparative, it really involves reason as well. The picture he gives is one of acquiring more ideas with their attendant sentiments and then arranging them in a hierarchy of greater or lesser beauties. Presumably, this is where imagination comes in. The comparison even extends to making coarse beauties deformities: "a great inferiority of beauty gives pain to a person conversant in the highest excellence of the kind, and is for that reason pronounced a deformity" (ST 224). What results is a pronouncement, and it is for a reason. The evidence is slight, but comparison, while it naturally follows from the earlier discussion, is really somewhat out of place. What Hume is trying to account for at this point is the ability to discriminate tastes within a single observer. But the standard of taste is not about such discrimination. Delicacy is to be the primary criterion for accepting the superiority of someone's taste, even over one's own. But while comparisons follow from delicacy, they do not contribute to it, because delicacy involves response to slighter impressions, not comparative choice. Nor can comparisons be convincing evidence of superiority independently of delicacy. Unless delicacy is established first, one does not have the same objects for comparison. At most, comparison provides a kind of negative evidence: one who does not make comparisons is, *prima facie*, lacking in the experience that leads to comparisons. Peasants or Indians who are pleased with everything (ST 223) are disqualified not because of their sentiment but because of their failure to be judgmental. The accuracy of judgments is not at issue; what one requires in a critic is "one accustomed to see, and examine, and weigh the several performances" (ST 223). People who do not do that can be presumed to lack the requisite delicacy because, if they did have it, they would naturally make such comparisons and exhibit the judgments that follow from them.

Freedom from prejudice is a matter of the situation of the observer. "A critic of a different age or nation ... must place himself in the same situation as the audience, in order to form a true judgment of the oration" (ST 225). What is peculiar here is the goal – a true judgment. On its face, this is puzzling since judgments based on sentiments are not true or false. True judgment, therefore, can only relate to comparison. If one does not take account of the situation of the intended audience, one will form comparisons that lead to judgments based only on one's own situation. In itself, there would seem to be nothing wrong with this on Hume's principles. But Hume finds something wrong, which leads back to the foundation in sentiment.

> By this means, his sentiments are perverted; nor have the same beauties and blemishes the same influence upon him as if he had imposed a proper violence on his imagination and had forgotten himself for a moment. So far, his taste evidently departs from the true standard, and of consequence loses all credit and authority. (ST 239–240)

A perverted sentiment here can only mean one that departs from the models produced by a delicacy of taste. By operating from a self-centered position, an observer is unable to perceive the beauties that produce the models and rules over time. Hume does not really need a disinterested observer; he requires only an acute one. Placing one's self in the position of the audience and being self-aware go together. One does not give up one's own position in the process. Those who read Hume as requiring disinterestedness ask for something that, in Hume's system, cannot be achieved. The true standard is not the rules but the critics who give rise to the rules. The taste of critics who are prejudiced will contribute to no rules, no regularities. Their judgments are not "true" in the sense that a ruler is "true" if it is straight and gives accurate measurements. Such a critic will produce only eccentricities, which, however interesting and self-satisfying they may be, provide no standard. His/her taste loses all credit and authority.

At this point it is interesting to bring Hume into the contemporary debate over critical authority and judgment. There is a school of critical theory that, though it is easily parodied, nevertheless makes a sound point based on audience response. One can never get outside of one's own position as the primary audience, and thus, the argument goes, every "text" is re-made by every audience and every age. There can be no "right" reading of a text because every reading occupies the privileged position of successor to all previous readings. Hume's requirement that one assume the position of the original audience seems on its face a requirement that one occupy a kind of Newtonian absolute space outside of the historical frame of reference, and in contemporary physics and criticism alike, such an absolute frame is deemed impossible. But it is possible to read Hume as actually requiring a different kind of position. The sentiments of critics are not themselves in question. Whether one observes from the standpoint of the original audience or from the standpoint of an idiosyncratic present, the sentiments and beauties observed are still one's own. What is at issue in Hume's treatment is what conditions will allow those sentiments to produce a standard of taste. If they remain idiosyncratic, they cannot produce such a standard. They would be just as idiosyncratic, perhaps more so if, *per impossible*, I tried to become an ancient Greek. Hume holds that appeal to a standard is as natural and necessary as other forms of causal judgment. So his investigation is aimed at disclosing how such a standard is possible even given the radical subjectivity of sentiments (in his terms) or readings and texts (in contemporary terms). The standard itself is not absolute; it is part of what defines the reader-response. Hume incorporates a standard of taste into his radical ideational epistemology, and he argues convincingly that such an incorporation is not only consistent but a natural outcome of taste itself. Therefore, it is wrong to reject Hume as a kind of Newtonian modernist who holds an absolutist view of critical judgment that post-modernism has revealed to be wrong. Many of Hume's contemporary neo-classical opponents were guilty of such absolutism. But Hume's position is much more interesting, and much more radical – which is undoubtedly one reason that it infuriated such writers as Thomas Reid and James Beattie.

The way I am reading Hume's essay is borne out by his reference to good sense. At this point, Hume explicitly acknowledges the reintroduction of reason, which I have noted. Reason is not, Hume grants, an essential part of taste, but it is "at least requisite to the operations of this latter faculty" (ST 226). The question now becomes how reason can be requisite to the operation of good sense on Hume's view without abandoning the priority of the passions over reason in aesthetic and moral experience. The function assigned to reason here is not a direct operation on the ideas of taste or their sentiments. Hume does not argue – and elsewhere specifically rejects – that one can reason oneself into a particular sentiment or even into a pleasurable accompaniment to a sentiment. If I do not like the taste of carrots, no reasoning will make them taste better, and if I do not get pleasure from the taste of elegance, reason will not aid me there either. Nor will reason help me to experience some complex impression of the imagination as elegant if my own taste does not respond to it in that way. Instead, reason operates on prejudice that blocks the way to taste. In effect, I can apply my reason to my prejudices, and reason myself out of them. Then, freed from prejudice, taste *may* operate differently – and correspond more closely to the way it operates in other humans. Thus taste approaches the norm established by human nature as a result of reason. That is what good sense amounts to. "It belongs to *good sense* to check its [prejudice's] influence" (ST 226).

Good sense works in another way as well. Works of art are extensive; "there is a mutual relation and correspondence of parts" (ST 226). Reason cannot produce the sentiment, but there is a possible prior function for reason in putting the parts together and thus making possible the complex ideas of the imagination to which taste responds. If all taste were for simple qualities and from simple ideas from impressions of sense, there would be no need for good sense. But in fact, the imagination is "capacious," and it requires good sense to extend to the kinds of objects that provide taste with its material. The opposite of good sense is simple-mindedness, which is the inability to entertain anything more than simple ideas. Good sense also allows Hume to tie together his two different theories of what beauty is. On the one hand, beauty is simply the species of ideas that taste produces from its imagined impressions together with the pleasure that accompanies them. But on the other hand, Hume holds to a form of utilitarian theory where beauty is fitness for an end. The pattern that the complex ideas have and that reason discovers turns out to be this utilitarian pattern. Reason finds the pattern by matching means and end. The end of poetry, for example, is "to please by means of the passions and the imagination" (ST 227). The function of reason is to recognize the internal relation between means and end. Once the means-end relation is recognized, taste can take over.

All of this is premised on a degree of uniformity in human nature. Given that uniformity, one can see why "it seldom, or never happens, that a man of sense, who has experience in any art, cannot judge of its beauty; and it is no less rare to meet with a man who has a just taste without a sound understanding" (ST 227). It is important to keep the complex line of reasoning straight. Good sense does not judge of the beauty of art. Good sense provides the impressions of sense and the ideas from the "nobler productions of genius" (ST 226); taste experiences them. Judgments of beauty are the result. (Hume does not seem to consider that one might not know that a particular taste was beautiful. At least as a linguistic matter, however, this is beside the point. Some cultures may lack the vocabulary and even the distinctions marked by the generic term 'beauty.' Nevertheless, beauty as the generic reference of taste is as incorrigible as pleasure itself with which it is analytically linked.) Good sense uses one's rational faculties to provide the widest possible impressions based on practice, comparison and freedom from prejudice. Human nature is very nearly the same in all men. So the response of taste to these impressions makes possible rules and models. The rules and models, in turn, establish whose taste is normative and provide a way to convince others that their taste is duller than someone else's.

Again and again, Hume's language is quite precise. Only a few persons have an undistorted delicacy so that their sentiment becomes a standard of beauty. Others "labour under some defect, or are vitiated by some disorder; and by that means, excite a sentiment, which may be pronounced erroneous" (ST 228). Hume does not say simply that the sentiment is erroneous. That would make no sense in his epistemological scheme. A sentiment just is; it cannot be erroneous or true. But given a sentiment, it can be pronounced erroneous. The distinction is subtle but important. If I pronounce a sentiment erroneous,

I disqualify it as a standard – or more precisely, I disqualify the person whose sentiment it is from serving as part of the model that produces the standard. That person's sentiment is condemned and falls outside the rule. But I do not do away with the sentiment as such, and if human nature were different, different sentiments would be pronounced erroneous. The majority does not rule necessarily because mass prejudice and ignorance can intervene to distort the result. Even if everyone were a Nazi and found lamp-shades made of human skin beautiful, they would not be so because it is not human nature but a distorted cultural filter that promotes their taste to the majority position and seems to give it the rule. But such an eccentric taste for what otherwise would be horrible is not impossible, and only time and good sense can correct it.

Thus Hume arrives at the famous five-fold characterization of the true judge and concludes that "the joint verdict of such, wherever they are to be found, is the true standard of taste and beauty" (ST 229). Even though this is as frequently quoted a passage as there is in the literature of aesthetics, it is still important to observe that the joint verdict of the true judges is the standard. The taste of the judges, *per se*, no matter how delicate, cannot provide a standard because their tastes are still only their tastes. A joint verdict can arise from their taste, but there is no guarantee that such verdicts are available. A standard exists only where a joint verdict is to be found.[52] I take this to mean that new forms, such as the novel in the eighteenth century, lack standards at first. They must await the formation of a joint verdict. That is the way that rules re-enter.

Hume has established thus far what the standard of taste is and how it is possible. The five characteristics are not equal. Delicacy at one extreme is the basis since it alone leads directly to sentiments of taste. At the other extreme, good sense operates rationally and cannot affect taste directly. Practice, comparison, and freedom from prejudice help identify delicacy. A true judge is thus one who has delicacy of taste. One who has delicacy of taste will be practiced, unprejudiced, and able to make many comparisons. And in order to qualify for these abilities to have the widest field of operation, a true judge must also have good sense. From true judges arises a joint verdict in the form of rules and models. So we know what the standard of taste is – it is the joint verdict of true judges; and we know how it is possible even though taste remains com-

---

52 James Shelley raises the question whether Hume has not placed himself in an impossible position by appealing to a joint verdict that seems to imply that the good critics can never be wrong (Shelley, "Hume's Double Standard of Taste," p. 443). I think that this is another point where an unacceptable precision is being imposed on Hume's rhetorical tradition. The "joint verdict" means only that there is an emergent consensus. It does not mean that any particular judgment cannot be wrong.

pletely subjective – delicacy, combined with the uniformity of human nature, makes the rules that issue from the sentiment of some observers into a potential standard. But by itself, what we know does not identify the true judges or the rules. In barbarous ages, for example, there may be no true judges and no rules or standards would be evident. In any specific age, the prejudices and cultural perversions of human nature may produce distorted models and standards. How can we defend our right to be considered among the elite and who among us has the right to a place in the pantheon of judges?

Hume's answer gives little comfort to authority. It consists in two parts: one must acknowledge that a standard exists, and then one must present the best factual arguments available for the judgment of the understanding. Beyond that, the result is clearly a matter of who can muster the most support. The existence of a standard of taste does not mean the end of critical disagreement, nor does it guarantee that the best taste will be evident in every case. At this point, Hume is an unabashed optimist about the possibilities of sentiment. Not only is an appeal to sentiment direct and so not subject to the same distortions that one finds in metaphysics and science, but also the "force of nature" is on the side of sentiment. So Hume expects that what ultimately is approved of by a "civilized nation" will be indeed the choice of nature itself. And beyond that appeal, there is no standard.

However, anyone who thinks that Hume has promoted western European civilization to the place of true judge and established a standard for all times and all places ignores the last sections of the essay. Age and national culture place limits on any generalization. Age limits the uniformity of nature, and without that uniformity, there is no standard. National culture limits delicacy, shaping its objects. Nothing could make it clearer that the essay is about discovering a standard and not about taste itself. When the conditions of uniformity that make it possible to arrive at a standard do not exist, "a certain degree of diversity in judgment is unavoidable, and we seek in vain for a standard, by which we can reconcile the contrary sentiments" (ST 233). Outside the limits set out above, "such preferences are innocent and unavoidable, and can never reasonably be the object of dispute, because here is no standard, by which they can be decided" (ST 233). A standard can decide between Milton and Ogilby, each of whom produced epics. If one were to try to extend Hume's argument to Aeschylus and Aristophanes, however, one would have difficulty deciding between them because one produces tragedy and the other comedy. This is in direct contrast to the standard eighteenth-century doctrine that held that there was a hierarchy within the arts, some of which were nobler than others, so that tragedy would be, by rule, always superior to comedy.

Hume's final examples confirm the radical nature of the essay. The only limit on cultural relativity is moral. One cannot respond to and approve what one finds morally offensive, even if it is Homer. Because the standard of taste works as it does, Hume turns at last to a moral standard to correct and limit an aesthetic standard of taste. "Where a man is confident of the rectitude of that moral standard, by which he judges, he is justly jealous of it, and will not pervert the sentiments of his heart for a moment, in complaisance to any writer whatsoever" (ST 237). In other words, if I am morally offended, I will not feel the beauty of a piece, and I will not find the judgments of those who do persuasive, any more than I would find Soviet or Nazi critics persuasive, no matter how uniform their judgments. Their moral disability will disqualify their aesthetic taste. One must not allow Hume's obvious satisfaction in being a civilized European to obscure the limits he places on a standard of taste nor to mislead us about the appeal to moral sentiment. Speculative systems, which for Hume include all theology and positive religion, are perversions. The lack of uniformity in such systems must lead to the strictures on prejudice. But the moral sentiment must take precedence over aesthetic sentiment because moral sentiment issues in action and aesthetic sentiment does not, at least not directly. Hume does not make aesthetic sentiment disinterested. In Hume's thought, aesthetic sentiments are "innocent" rather than disinterested. Within their own sphere, they are a form of private interest; in the public sphere, they are subject to moral disinterestedness. It is wrong to read a Kantian aesthetic disinterestedness back onto Hume. But Hume moves in the direction of disinterestedness by subordinating the aesthetic to the moral sentiment. The taste for beauty has a utilitarian side, and it has consequences – it is productive of the very civilization that judges it, and it is beneficial to the human organism by providing innocent pleasure. But it cannot be detached from moral judgment, and it must be subordinate to that sentiment.

Critics who support moral censure will find no comfort from Hume, however. His moral judgment, like the judgment of beauty, is traceable to a taste and sentiment. Moral law will have to be freed of the same hindrances that interfere with the taste for beauty. A delicacy of taste for beauty will be paralleled by a strong moral sense, and both are subject to the dictates of good sense for a clarification of the impressions that provoke them. Bigotry, superstition, and enthusiasm are Hume's moral enemies.[53]

---

[53] Cf. "Of Superstition and Enthusiasm," for example where Hume writes "In such a state of mind enthusiasm, the imagination swells with great, but confused conceptions, to which no sublunary beauties or enjoyments can correspond." *Essays*, p. 74.

"Of the Standard of Taste" never deviates from its adherence to sentiment as the sole origin of taste. It never pretends that that sentiment can be other than subjective and self-justifying. To look for objective qualities or rules of taste in Hume's essay is to misread him badly in one direction. But the essay attempts to show that nevertheless a standard is possible. A standard of taste is not itself a judgment of taste, nor is it a corrective or guide to good taste. This is Hume's major advance beyond Shaftesbury who is his model in aesthetics even more than Hutcheson.[54] Shaftesbury held to sentiment, but he sought to correct taste by selecting those models that would have a positive moral and aesthetic influence and testing them by raillery. Hume has no such illusions about the force of rules and reason, and his style is neither as convoluted nor as classically satirical as Shaftesbury's. Hume tends more toward irony, though he shares with Shaftesbury a form of soliloquy. So Hume's standard is external to taste itself. It rests on delicacy and the acknowledgment that if taste is a good thing, delicacy must be a good thing as well. But delicacy can be improved and influenced first by practice, comparison, and freedom from prejudice, which shape it, and then by good sense, which regulates it and provides it with an improved set of impressions upon which to work. So rules, models, and the true judges who provide them function as a standard of taste within the limits of age and culture, but their only function is to condemn and confirm. They are never constitutive or productive, as Shaftesbury hoped that they would be. Taste, and not the standard of taste, is the productive sentiment. Hume shares with Shaftesbury and Hutcheson a moral limit, however. Of the two classes of sentiment, moral sentiments must take precedence. Aesthetic sentiments, by themselves, are innocent; moral sentiments define a good nature and character. Innocent enjoyment must give way to moral duty, and if aesthetic enjoyment loses its innocence (as it does, Hume believed, when it indulges in religious superstition), it must be condemned.

It is easy to criticize Hume's aesthetic position in "Of the Standard of Taste" for its obvious prejudices and false judgments. But that is a mistake. I hope I have shown that Hume is consistent here with his epistemology and that he can be defended against most of the charges that arise from a failure to observe how careful he is to stay within the limits set up by his epistemology.

---

54 I don't mean this literally since my evidence as to what Hume thought of Shaftesbury is limited and his dependence on Hutcheson in the literal sense is well documented. I am speaking of affinities of text and approach, not historical influence.

Acknowledgements

This chapter was first published as the conclusion to Dabney Townsend, Hume's Aesthetic Theory: Taste and Sentiment (London: Routledge, 2001)., pp. 180–216. The editor is grateful to the author and to Taylor and Frances for permitting its inclusion here.

Bibliography

Baier, Annette C. (1991) *A Progress of Sentiments*. Cambridge, MA: Harvard University Press.
Carroll, Noel (1984) "Hume's Standard of Taste." *Journal of Aesthetics and Art Criticism*. 43 (2): 181–194.
Curtius, Ernst Robert (1963) *European Literature and the Latin Middle Ages*. Willard R. Trask, trans. New York: Harper Torchbooks.
De Martaelere, Patricia (1989) "A Taste for Hume." *Ratio*. 2 (2): 122–137.
Fogelin, Robert (1985) *Hume's Scepticism in the Treatise of Human Nature*. London: Routledge & Kegan Paul.
Gilmore, Thomas B. Jr. (Ed.) (1972) *Early 18th-Century Essays on Taste*. Delmar, New York: Scholars' Facsimiles and Reprints.
Hume, David (1988) *Enquiries Concerning Human Understanding and Concerning the Principles of Morals*. L. A. Selby-Bigge (Ed.) Revised by P. H. Nidditch. Third edition. Oxford: Clarendon Press.
David Hume (1988) "Enquiry Concerning the Principles of Morals." In: Hume, *Enquiries Concerning Human Understanding and Concerning the Principles of Morals*. L. A. Selby-Bigge (Ed.) Revised P. H. Nidditch. Third Edition. Oxford: Clarendon Press.
Hume, David (1987) "Of the Delicacy of Taste and Passion." In: Hume, *Essays Moral, Political, and Literary*, Eugene F. Miller (Ed.) Indianapolis: Liberty Classics.
Hume, David (1987) "Of Refinement in the Arts." In: Hume, *Essays Moral, Political, and Literary*, Eugene F. Miller (Ed.) Indianapolis: Liberty Classics.
Hume, David (1987) "On the Delicacy of the Passions." In: Hume, *Essays Moral, Political, and Literary*, Eugene F. Miller (Ed.) Indianapolis: Liberty Classics.
Hume, David (1987) "Of Tragedy." In: Hume, *Essays Moral, Political, and Literary*, Eugene F. Miller (Ed.) Indianapolis: Liberty Classics.
Hume, David (1987) "Of Superstition and Enthusiasm." In: Hume, *Essays Moral, Political, and Literary*, Eugene F. Miller (Ed.) Indianapolis: Liberty Classics.
Hume, David (1987) *A Treatise of Human Nature*. L. A. Selby-Bigge (Ed.); revised P. H. Nidditch. Oxford: Clarendon Press.
Jones, Peter (1970) "Another Look at Hume's Views of Aesthetic and Moral Judgments." *Philosophical Quarterly*. 20: 53–59.
Kivy, Peter (1967) "Hume's Standard of Taste: Breaking the Circle." *British Journal of Aesthetics*. 7:1 (Jan.): 57–66.
Korsmeyer, Carolyn (1976) "Hume and the Foundations of Taste." *Journal of Aesthetics and Art Criticism*. 35 (2): 201–215.

Mothersill, Mary (1997) "In Defense of Hume and the Causal Theory of Taste." *Journal of Aesthetics and Art Criticism*. 55 (3): 312–317.
Savile, Anthony (1993) *Kantian Ethics Pursued*. Edinburgh: Edinburgh University Press.
Shelley, James (1994) "Hume's Double Standard of Taste." *Journal of Aesthetics and Art Criticism*. 52 (4): 441.
Wieand, Jeffrey (1984) "Hume's Two Standards of Taste." *The Philosophical Quarterly*. 34, 135, 129–142.
Woodmansee, Martha (1993) *The Author, Art and the Market*. New York: Columbia University Press, 1993.

Howard Caygill
Taste and Civil Society

Taste and the *je ne sais quoi*

> Taste is the capacity for judging the conformity of the power
> of imagination in its freedom with the legitimacy of the understanding.
> Kant, *Reflection* 510

Taste conceived as a 'faculty of judgement' is the precipitate of taste conceived as an activity. This emerges in the *OED's* etymology of the word taste from the Old French *tast* "touching, touch" and the Italian *tasto* "a feeling, a touch, a trial, a taste."[1] Two points of particular interest follow from this derivation. The first is the original active and investigative connotation of taste; it was the activity of feeling or testing and not a passive faculty that tested or felt. The second is the difference between the meanings of taste and aesthetic: both terms denote activities of feeling, touching, and seeing, but while taste produces its own content and gives itself law, aesthetic receives content and law from without.

The transformation of taste into a faculty which mediates between subject and object gives rise to some specific difficulties. The formative aspect of taste as an activity producing its own content and giving itself laws – taste as autopoetic and autonomous – is repressed when it is transformed into a faculty. Yet traces of this repressed activity persist in the exercise of the faculty, and emerge as the difficulties involved in thinking the acquisition of the faculty, its application by the subject, and the peculiar conformity it has with its objects.

However, the most important trace of the reduction of taste to a faculty is the persistent and ineluctable relation of the judgement of taste and pleasure. The influential writings of the Spanish Jesuit, Baltasar Gracian (1601–1658) exemplify the difficulties accompanying the reformulation of the activity of taste into a faculty. Like Hobbes, who saw productive judgement as the creation of illusion, Gracian resolved the formative moment of taste into the production of appearance. In the *Oraculo Manual Y Arte De Prudencia* (1647) taste finds itself between reticence and dissemblance, applying judgment to the shaping of appearances. It is an unknowable faculty, present in the subject in an inexplicable way, and exercised intuitively. The object of its formative activity is the subject as appear-

---
[1] The OED and ODE differ on the Latin root of taste. The OED suggests *taxitare*, to touch, while the ODE suggests a corruption of *tangere*, to touch, and *gustare*, to savour.

ance, the prudent one "who realises that he is being observed, or will be observed" (1647; §297). Much of the pathos of Gracian's writing arises from the necessity of the prudent to dissemble, to represent themselves as appearance, to "Cultivate a happy spontaneity." But what if the object of taste is not the subject itself, but a different object? A similar conclusion follows: the object exists only as appearance, only in so far as it has been produced by taste. And yet this formative activity of taste cannot know itself; it is *only* discernible through the pleasures of producing and manipulating appearances. Gracian's courtly scepticism persists in the French theory of taste which emerged in the second third of the seventeenth century. The French theorists narrowed his view of taste as an art of judgment into a concern with the judgment of art.[2] The adaptation of taste to art was a gesture of aristocratic dissent against the Royal Academy. In place of the conformity of judgment to publicly licensed rules, critics appealed to the *je ne sais quoi* in which the judgment of the work of art was largely a 'matter of taste.' The French critics embraced the difficulties surrounding the possession, application, and object of the faculty of taste as sceptical aporias. We have a faculty of taste, but how we come by it is unclear; we apply it, but how we do so is unclear; it is congruent with objects, but why it is so remains unclear. The *je ne sais quoi* is an admission of the inexplicability of the workings of taste following its restriction to a faculty. The history of taste in the eighteenth century may be seen as the gradual recovery of its formative aspect through the exploration of the difficulties posed in accounting for pleasure. The British development of the theory of taste was from the beginning characterized by an idiosyncratic appropriation of the French model. It is distinguished by its revaluation of the *je ne sais quoi* into the necessary ignorance of the workings of providence. This position is inseparable from the tendency of late seventeenth-century British scepticism to draw activist political conclusions from theoretical scepticism. The *je ne sais quoi* did not justify the apathy and political indifference of a defeated *fronde*, but assumed positive content as a spur to activity. This is apparent in Locke's *An Essay Concerning Human Understanding* (1690), where the premiss that our finite understandings can never hope to gain insight into God's providence does not lead to passivity or renunciation of the world. The very limitation of our understanding is part of His providence, for we have been given the ability to make certain discriminations without knowing their grounds:

---

[2] Remy G. Saisselin, *The Rule of Reason and the Ruses of the Heart: Philosophical Dictionary of Classical French Criticism, Critics, and Aesthetic Issues.*

> For our faculties being suited not to the full extent of being, nor to a perfect, clear, comprehensive knowledge of things free from all doubt and scruple, but to the preservation of us in whom they are, and accommodated to the use of Life: they serve to our purpose well enough if they will but give us certain notice of those things which are convenient or inconvenient to us.[3]

Scepticism does not paralyse the judgement, since it is possible to discriminate with certainty between the convenience or inconvenience of a particular course of action.

This discrimination is an intuition or a sense whose validity is secured by providence. The notion of a providential congruence between our imperfect judgment and self-preservation underlies Locke's account of political judgment in the *Essay*. The emphasis on discrimination leads to the extremely violent view of judgment as the choice between two alternatives:

> We are forced to determine ourselves on the one side or other. The conduct of our lives and the management of our great concerns will not bear delay: for those depend, for the most part, on the determination of our judgement in points wherein we are not capable of certain and demonstrative knowledge, and wherein it is necessary for us to embrace the one side or the other.[4]

The distinction between convenience and inconvenience becomes the necessity to embrace one 'side' or the other in 'great concerns' which brook no 'delay.' The sentiments of this passage are much closer to those of the oligarchy who risked the 1688 Revolution than to the natural rights justification of revolt developed by Locke in the *Two Treatises of Government* The confused debate surrounding the nature of the "Revolution Principles" after 1688 showed that no positive programme united the forces of the Revolution, least of all one of natural rights. The decision to act was not rationally grounded but, as in Locke's case, was legitimated by a providentially guided judgement. Kant shrewdly recognized this emphasis on discrimination without a concept as a "sensualization" of the differential "concepts of reflection,"[5] and saw it as a one-sided restriction of a proper art of judgment. The violence which necessarily accompanied this restriction became apparent in Locke's successors.

The British theory of taste which emerged from the matrix of scepticism, providential argument and "Revolution Principles" was shaped by very specific political and intellectual circumstances. These emerge when the accounts of the

---

[3] John Locke, *An Essay Concerning Human Understanding*, p. 343.
[4] Locke, *An Essay Concerning Human Understanding*, p. 359.
[5] Kant, *Kritik der reinen Vernunft*, A271/B372.

pleasures of art characteristic of the early legitimation crisis of the regime are compared with those following its stabilization through the fiscal and political "Financial Revolution." The difference emerged in the role theorists gave to art in the promotion of the virtues appropriate to civil society. The change in the conception of civil society at the beginning of the eighteenth century was accompanied by a change in the understanding of the pleasures of art. It was never the intention of William's regime to create the conditions for a 'civil society' apart from the state. The emergence of civil society was largely the accident of an oligarchy anxious to limit executive power combined with the successful mobilization of public credit for the finance of foreign military and commercial adventures.[6] Indeed, an important aspect of William's early domestic policy was the disciplining of civil society through a "'Reformation of Manners'" or "'Moral Revolution.'". This policy, initiated after 1688, was a diluted version of continental 'police-state' measures, and although unsuccessful, this was not due to any lack of legislative commitment: "'If Acts of Parliament and orders of justices of the peace could create a moral paradise, England would have been one by 1700.'"[7] Unlike the continental monarchs, William had neither the bureaucratic apparatus nor the standing army required to apply his police measures; the enforcement of the "'Reformation of Manners'" was left to private individuals banding together into "'Societies for the Reformation of Manners'" or to the inconsistent enthusiasm of individual JPs. But this was not the main reason for the failure of the policy; by the beginning of the new century, such direct measures of social control were unnecessary.[8] The burden of legitimation shifted toward the establishment of an autonomous civil society in which the moral policing

---

[6] The standard history of the Financial Revolution is Peter George Muir Dickson, *The Financial Revolution in England: A Study in the Development of Public Credit 1688–1756*. The social and theological implications of the Revolution have been explored within the Arendtian paradigm by J. G. A. Pocock; see his characterization of the revolution in *The Machiavellian Moment*, p. 425, and its ideological confrontation of "the ideology of real property with the threat from the operations not of a trading market, but by a system of public credit," Pocock, *Virtue, Commerce, and History*, p. 68. The subversion of real by mobile property meant the replacement of the 'political' by the 'social' and an emphasis on fantasy over virtue.

[7] Dudley W.R. Bahlman, *The Moral Revolution of 1688*, p. 22.

[8] J. A. W. Gunn however, sees the Moral Revolution more positively as unleashing 'a torrent of social and political criticism that had in some measure been suppressed by the previous regime," Gunn, *Beyond Liberty and Property: The Process of Self-Recognition in Eighteenth Century Political Thought*, p. 10.

of society by the state was considered unnecessary for the establishment of 'throne, religion, happiness and peace'.⁹

The transition from moral revolution to civil society is reflected in the fortunes of the most important theorist of art of the late seventeenth century – John Dennis (1657–1729), *the* Critick. His reputation was a notable casualty of the change in the structure of legitimacy. His writings span from 1692 to 1729, but by the beginning of the new century he had become a distinctly unfashionable, rather comic figure. And although his arguments resembled those of the new theories of taste and civil society, there are important differences of emphasis. Like the theorists of taste, Dennis identified natural law with providential design, but unlike them he saw the design as mediated either through the rules of art or through the legislation of the state. He had no conception of an immediate 'taste' or 'moral sense' valid apart from the rules of art or the direct agency of the state.

Dennis consciously aligned the "Reformation of Modern Poetry," with the "Reformation of Manners": the pleasures evoked by properly regulated arts would contribute to soothing the "jarring passions, of the 'rebellious English." For him as for Pufendorf, natural law is mediated through the institutions of art, religion and the state; it is not disclosed immediately to the individual. This view of the relationship of natural law to civil society was appropriate for the time of "Moral Revolution" which sought to discipline society by institutional means, but became irrelevant after the consolidation of the state through the development of the mechanisms of public credit. The internal mediation of natural law prefigured in Cumberland's text – where providence spoke directly to the conscience of each citizen – was more appropriate to an increasingly autonomous public sphere. The burden of legitimation shifted from the inculcation of piety and virtue from without, to the moral justification of civil society from within, a shift which was registered in the equation of commerce and virtue.¹⁰

---

9 It is important not to overemphasize the autonomy of civil society in Augustan Britain. Leonard Krieger wrote in 1970 that "What distinguished Great Britain from its continental competitors was not so much the obvious difference between limited and absolute sovereignty – since this difference was quite deceptive in terms of effective political power – but rather the difference between a state run by an alliance of social groups and states run by officials who mediated between social groups." Krieger, *Kings and Philosophers 1689–1789*, p. 105. Jonathan Clark more provocatively describes early Hannoverian England as "among the most effectively totalitarian of European states of that time." Clark, *English Society 1688–1832: Ideology, Social Structure and Political Practice during the Ancien Regime*, p. 150.
10 H.T. Dickinson, *Liberty and Property – Political Philosophy in Eighteenth Century Britain*, p. 125; Alfred Hirschmann, *The Passions and the Interests: Political Arguments for Capitalism Before its Triumph*, passim.

Dennis's Horatian view that art contributes to social control by instructing through delight was superseded by the theory of taste. Instead of regarding art as a means for moralizing civil society, the theory of taste saw it as representing the same natural law which directed individual moral judgement. Individual judgement was not ordered by the institutional representation of natural law, but by an intuition or inner sense of it. The axioms of Cumberland's critique of Hobbes reappear in the philosophy of Shaftesbury and his successors. Beauty and order were expressions of a providential natural law mediated through the senses of beauty and obligation. The mediating term, the *sense* of beauty and virtue, was the pleasure of 'taste.'

The British writers saw taste as a faculty, and so fell prey to many of the difficulties surrounding the faculty of taste. These difficulties were complicated by the providential foundation of the British theory of taste, which made the question of how the faculty of taste is given to a subject critical. The chronic equivocation over whether taste was sensible or ideal issues from this complication. As with Locke, providence does not direct individual judgement through reason, but nevertheless determines it according to rational ends. The individual judgement is a sentiment or an inclination to which providence accords the properties of an idea. Shaftesbury, Hutcheson, Kames, and Burke all maintained that the prompting of providence is experienced with the immediacy of a sense; in their writings the 'rational sense' of taste is distributed among a number of discrete senses, including a 'sense of beauty,' a 'sense of virtue,' a 'sense of contract,' and even a 'sense of property.' Individuals behave affectively, according to sentinent, but providence ensures that the sum of their actions realizes the common good. In this way, the freedom and autonomy of the individual at the level of sense is reconciled with the lawlike characteristics of universality and necessity at the level of idea. The price of this solution was the disembodiment of taste; it became an intangible medium of exchange between the rational will of providence and the irrational individual sentiment. The disembodiment of taste affected its relationship to its objects.

Instead of seeing in it a formative activity involving legislation and production, the British theorists interpret the activity of taste as the work of providence. They devolve the responsibility for self-legislation – the ordering of civil society – upon providence, and violently exclude its productive moment. Shaftesbury renders production immaterial by regarding it as the issue of the *je ne sais quoi;* his notion of a providential ordering of civil society and his dematerialization of production were attacked by Mandeville in the *Fable of the Bees*. In defending Shaftesbury, Hutcheson excludes production altogether, placing it outside the operations of taste and subjecting it to entirely different laws. The "benevolent philosopher" considered the moral sense insufficient to ensure labor discipline, and went so far as to advocate slavery for the "slothful." In both cases the giving of the law and the production of its objects are relegated to the *je ne sais quoi;* the formative activity of taste is rendered unthinkable.

Hume and Smith's writings represent attempts to rethink the *je ne sais quoi.* Hume sought to specify the relation between individual and universal without resort to providence. His argument in the *Treatise* that individual moral responses and responses to the beautiful are related through "reflected sympathy" points to a rediscovery of the formative aspect of taste. He later abandoned this project in favor of a sceptical admission that the relation of individual response and universal standard is "obscure." However, on the basis of the *Treatise,* Adam Smith rediscovered the formative aspect of taste, and initiated the transition from the theory of taste and civil society to political economy. He absorbed Mandeville's critique of taste which emphasized need, desire and production, and attempted to unify not only virtue and commerce, but virtue, commerce, and production. His political economy restored the formative aspect of taste by setting out the relation of production and legislation. Production was the suppressed premiss in the theories of taste and civil society, the *je ne sais quoi* which repeatedly undermined their attempts to unify virtue and commerce. And while it is the case that Smith acknowledges the *je ne sais quoi* as both a process of exchange and a labor process, his attempt to know it did not escape providential notions such as the invisible hand and metaphysical proportionalities between production and circulation.

Smith's invisible hand is an apt image for the task of unifying virtue and commerce mounted by the theory of taste. The hand holding the scales, the traditional emblem of justice, is in the act both of weighing the two sides of the case and of giving the law by which it is to be judged. With the disembodiment of taste in the eighteenth century the activity of the investigative and adjudicative hand is dematerialized into the invisible hand of providence. The moments of invention and judgment underlying taste are separated. The surrender of Hobbes's citizens to the judgment of their own creation becomes the surrender to the judgment of providence and the *je ne sais quoi:* the sovereignty of the mask is exchanged for that of the invisible hand.

Whig Hellenism

> When the second system derived from inner subjective grounds, is the system of the moral sense, which has nothing philosophical about it at all. In recent times it is particularly notable in the English Shaftesbury and Hutcheson. It won't catch on so much in Germany, and for this one has Wolff to thank.
> Kant, *Lectures on Moral Philosophy*

The parameters of the British theory of taste and civil society were defined by the writings of Anthony Ashley Cooper, Lord Shaftesbury (1671–1713). The rhapsodic and dialogical form of his texts liberated philosophy from the learned tome, and anticipated the textual practices employed by enlightenment writers to take philosophy out of the schools and into civil society.[11] They also set the agenda for the synthesis of commerce and virtue which occupied British social philosophers during the eighteenth century. In the collection of essays *Characteristics of Men, Manners, Opinions, Times* (1711), Shaftesbury justified the "Revolution Principles" with a philosophy of taste. He followed his tutor Locke in regarding judgment as discrimination, but stated its providential validation in terms of the teleological Platonism of the Cambridge Platonists. More than Locke's, his writings exemplify what Kant later identified as an "amphiboly," identifying not only sense and idea, but extending this equation to individual interest and universal end. The repression concealed in this identification was exposed by Bernard Mandeville (1670–1733) in his *Fable of the Bees*. Mandeville claimed that Shaftesbury's equations of sense and idea, interest and end, and commerce and virtue could only be maintained through violence and deception. His claim was amply borne out by the subsequent defences of Shaftesbury's position, and was eventually conceded by Smith in the *Wealth of Nations*. Shaftesbury's correspondence collected in the *Philosophical Regimen*[12] frames his moral and meta-

---

11 Shaftesbury's influence on the European Enlightenment was both direct and indirect. His *Characteristics* of 1711 went through several English editions and was translated into German in 1768 and French in 1769. As early as 1712 Leibniz had written a critical appreciation of the work, and by 1745 Diderot had translated the "Inquiry Concerning Virtue or Merit" (1699, revised 1711). Shaftesbury's indirect influence was even greater. His work was the main inspiration of the "moral sense" school which dominated English moral philosophy and was exported to Europe, where we shall see it played a major role in the formation of Kant's moral philosophy.
12 The *Philosophical Regimen* is a notebook containing entries from Holland 1698 to Naples 1712. It is described by its editor as "one of the most remarkable unpublished contributions of

physical theories within a definite political setting. While continuing the family's Whig politics of limited monarchy, protestant succession, and the liberty of subjects under law, he was not of the generation of 1688 who considered commerce necessarily injurious to virtue. Shaftesbury's commitment to the "Revolution Principles," his "zeal for the Revolution, and for that principle which effected it"[13] is distinguishable from the vulgar 'enthusiasm' of the moral reformers; he preferred the equation of virtue and beauty over that of virtue and piety. Both virtue and beauty rested on a providential *telos* which ensured the realization of a "beautiful order."

Shaftesbury defends this position in his outline of the three possible approaches to practical philosophy in the essay "The Picture of Cebes," one that

> establishes a providence disposing all things in the most beautiful order, and giving to man a capacity to attend to its laws and to follow them; another that attributes the disposition of things to atoms and chance and that makes the pursuit of pleasure its end, and that which takes neither way, but judges things not to be all comprehensible, and therefore suspends opinion entirely.[14]

Shaftesbury does not reject the Epicurean and Sceptical positions out of hand (positions he later attributed to Hobbes and Locke), but considers their tenets inadequate as foundations for virtue. For him, three elements are necessary for such a foundation: (i) a providence which disposes "all things" into (ii) a beautiful order, and which gives to human beings (iii) a capacity to recognize and to act according to that order. This is close to Cumberland's view of natural law as the providential disposition of the parts of social life into an harmonious whole. But Shaftesbury, unlike Cumberland, sees providence and order as a *telos* in which God is the order of being itself rather than the being who wills that order. For him "All things stand together and exist together by one necessity, one reason, one law; and there is one nature of all things, a common to all."[15] His deistic view of providence naturalized Cumberland's "sentiment of benevolence"

---

modern times in the domain of philosophical thought." Perhaps not, but it is certainly valuable for revealing the social assumptions hidden beneath the stucco of the unctuous rhapsodizing of the *Characteristics*, later criticized by Adam Smith in his lectures on Rhetoric. See Benjamin Rand (Ed.) *The Life, Unpublished Letters, and Philosophical Regimen of Anthony, Earl of Shaftesbury*, p. 311.

13 As written on the back of a letter to Lord Marlborough dated 10 April 1702; Rand (Ed.) *The Life, Unpublished Letters, and Philosophical Regimen of Anthony, Earl of Shaftesbury*, p. 311.
14 Shaftesbury, *Second Characters, or the Language of Forms*, p. 87.
15 Rand (Ed.) *The Life, Unpublished Letters, and Philosophical Regimen of Anthony, Earl of Shaftesbury*.

implanted by the will of the deity into a "sense" of order. Shaftesbury's triple theme of providence, beautiful order, and the sense of order is developed in the writings of Hutcheson, Kames and Burke. He and his successors extend Cumberland's reconciliation of individual interest and the public good through a providential morality. All of them share the ideal of a civil society ordered by a moral sense which providentially ensures the harmonious ordering of individual judgments and the general good apart from the direct intervention of the state. This philosophy provides an account of virtue appropriate to the Whig Hellas, one in which virtue is not the creature of law and the state, but the outcome of the providential orchestration of individual interests through the pleasures of the sense of order.

The relation of teleology and civil society intimated in Cumberland's *De Legibus Naturae* is brought out in Shaftesbury's first work "An Inquiry Concerning Virtue and Merit."[16] This early essay diagnoses the problems of the post-revolutionary social order which the later teleological metaphysics is prescribed to solve. The author of the "Inquiry" elevates the dichotomy of private and public interest into a law of nature: "We know that every creature has a private good and interest of his own, which Nature has compelled him to seek, by all the advantages afforded him within the compass of his make."[17] He argues from this axiom that the "natural" pursuit of self-interest promotes the common good, redefining virtue as the identity of private and public interest: "That to be well effected towards the public interest and one's own is not only consistent but inseparable; and that moral rectitude or virtue must accordingly be the advantage, and vice the injury and disadvantage of every creature."[18] Having established that the private and public interest of a creature "must" coincide, Shaftesbury found the ground of this necessity in the providential *telos*. The *telos* is then interpreted to be a "substantial form" which ensures the harmony of private and public interest.

---

[16] The "Inquiry" was written before 1699 when it was published without Shaftesbury's consent from a manuscript in the possession of John Toland; this forms the basis of Walford's edition. It was revised and appeared among other essays in the *Characteristics*. The accompanying essays are: "A Letter concerning Enthusiasm" (1708), "*Sensus Communis:* An Essay on the Freedom of Wit and Humour" (1709), "Soliloquy, or Advice to an Author" (1710), "The Moralists, A Philosophical Rhapsody" (1709), and finally "Miscellaneous Reflections on the Preceding Treatises" (1711).

[17] Shaftesbury (Anthony Ashley Cooper) 1688, *An Enquiry Concerning Virtue or Merit*, vol. I, p. 243.

[18] Shaftesbury, *An Enquiry Concerning Virtue or Merit*, p. 282.

Shaftesbury argues against Hobbes that the order of providence, with its expressions in virtue and beauty, is prior to any division of individual interests. He is hostile to any suggestion that order may itself be derived or abstracted from individual things:

> Hence Hobbes, Locke, etc., still the same man, same genius at bottom. – "beauty is nothing" – "virtue is nothing" – So "perspective nothing" – "music nothing." – But these are the greatest realities of things, especially the beauty and order of affections.[19]

Instead of beginning with individuals or primary qualities and then deriving general principles of association from their composition, Shaftesbury makes composition prior to individuals. He posits the ultimate reality of beauty and virtue, and claims that individuals embody them. However, this embodiment is equivocal since individuals are not strictly determined to act according to beauty and virtue, but only tend to do so. The difficulties surrounding the determinacy and indeterminacy of individual action collect around the "capacity" to recognize and act according to the beautiful order, in other words, around taste as a faculty of judgment.

Shaftesbury developed his determination of judgment by a substantial form or "beautiful order" against Hobbes's view that order was the consequence of the monopolization of judgment by the sovereign. His essay "*Sensus Communis:* An Essay on the Freedom of Wit and Humour" follows Cumberland in maintaining that a ground of obligation already exists in the state of nature:

> Now the promise itself was made in the state of nature; and that which could make a promise obligatory in the state of nature, must make all other acts of humanity as much our real duty and natural part. Thus faith, justice, honesty, and virtue, must have been as early as the state of nature, or they could never have been at all.[20]

The priority of an objective principle of virtue subordinates the contractual legality of the state to the morality of civil society. But the principle of unity remains inchoate; what is the 'that' which founds obligation? how is it recognized? and how may it be acted upon? The problems of judgment which Hobbes tackled in terms of productive legislation return to trouble Shaftesbury's serene Platonism.

The main problem involves the relation between individual interest and the general good or end. Just as in the case of obligation, Shaftesbury points to a necessity for their congruence without alarming it. This is apparent in the following

---

19 Shaftesbury, *Second Characters, or the Language of Forms,* p. 178.
20 Shaftesbury, *Characteristics of Men, Manners, Opinions, Times,* Vol. I, p. 73.

non sequitur: "There being therefore in every creature a certain interest or good, there must be also a certain end to which everything in his constitution must naturally refer."[21] Neither the *must* nor the unity of *interest and end* have been demonstrated, and it is hard to avoid the suspicion that their natural unity has been discovered after the fact of their difference. This suspicion is reinforced by Shaftesbury's admission that the relation between the interest of the individual and the end to which it tends is unknowable. The individual interest and end *must* be united, but how this may be accomplished is unknowable: it is the work of a *je ne sais quoi* which directs the judgment of taste. Like Hobbes, though with different results, Shaftesbury represents the problem of relating individual and universal in terms of the different positions which artist and audience have to a work of art.

Historians of criticism have taken Shaftesbury's philosophy of art as an important stage in the development away from neo-classical formalism toward a theory of "aesthetic response."[22] However, Shaftesbury does not reject formalism for sensibility, but argues that they are compatible. His argument rests on the distinction between the production and the reception of a work of art. The artist produces the work according to strict rules, remaining in *full* control of the design and ensuring its agreement with nature and propriety:

> Here the unity of design must with more particular exactness be preserved according to the just rules of poetic art that in the representation of any event, or remarkable fact, the probability or seeming truth (which is the real truth of art) may with the highest advantage be supported and advanced[23]

When presented with this highly rational product, the response of the spectator is irrational:

> Though [the artist's] intention be to please the world, he must nevertheless be, in a manner, above it, and fix his eye upon that consummate grace, that beauty of Nature, and that perfection of numbers which the rest of mankind, feeling only by the effect whilst ignorant of the cause, term the *je ne scay quoi*, the unintelligible or the I know not what, and suppose to be a kind of charm or enchantment of which the artist himself can give no account.[24]

The rigorous separation of the production of a work according to strict *rules* from the irrational enjoyment of the same work by the spectator is axiomatic for Shaf-

---

21 Shaftesbury, *Characteristics of Men, Manners, Opinions, Times*, Vol. I, p. 243.
22 Jerome Stolnitz, "On the significance of Lord Shaftesbury in Modern Aesthetic Theory."
23 Shaftesbury, *Second Characters, or the Language of Forms*, p. 33.
24 Shaftesbury, *Characteristics of Men, Manners, Opinions, Times*, vol. I, p. 214.

tesbury's philosophy of art. The same "feeling only by the effect whilst ignorant of the cause" also founds Shaftesbury's social philosophy. The beautiful order is the rational design of providence which ensures balance and harmony but can only be known through its pleasurable effect of unifying private and public interest. For, Shaftesbury maintains,

> Virtue has the same fixed standards [as art]. The same numbers, harmony, and proportion will have place in morals, and are discoverable in the characters and affections of mankind; in which are laid the just foundations of an art and science superior to every other of human practice and comprehension.[25]

Like art, virtue follows a rational design; and like the response to a work of art, the act of virtue is irrationally determined: it is a 'certain just disposition or proportionable affection of a rational creature towards the moral objects of right and wrong'.[26] Ignoring the inconsistency in the most important characteristic of a rational creature being not reason but disposition or affection, the question remains of how a disposition may be just, or an affection proportionable; how, in other words, a rational order can also be a *je ne sais quoi*.

The capacity which mediates between the laws of providence and individual judgment, between individual interest and rational end, is itself irrational. It is a "proportionable" affection, one with the properties of rationality. Shaftesbury develops this notion in terms of the ability of an affection or "sense" of discrimination. The rational "senses" of beauty and virtue, for example, discriminate between beauty and ugliness, or between good and bad actions, without being aware of the grounds for their discrimination. Yet in order to work the discrimination must be both a sense and an idea. Shaftesbury embraces this equivocation in the person of Theocles in the dialogue "The Moralists, A Philosophical Rhapsody":

> Nothing surely is more strongly imprinted on our minds, or more closely interwoven with our souls, than the idea or sense of order and proportion. Hence all the force of numbers, and those powerful arts founded on their management and use. What a difference there is between harmony and discord! cadency and convulsion! What a difference between composed and orderly motion, and that which is ungoverned and accidental! Now as this difference is immediately perceived by a plain internal sensation, so there is withal in reason

---

25 Shaftesbury, *Characteristics of Men, Manners, Opinions, Times*, vol. I, pp. 227–228.
26 Shaftesbury, *Characteristics of Men, Manners, Opinions, Times*, vol. I, p. 258.

this account of it, that whatever things have order, the same have unity of design, and concur in one; all parts are constituent of one whole or are, in themselves, entire systems.[27]

A sense or idea of proportion is brought to each discrimination, but the relation between the perception of sense and the law of the idea is not spelt out. How is the perception of differences by the senses aligned with the unity and design of reason? Shaftesbury consistently describes their relation in terms of a "proportion" between the manifold of sense and interests, and the unity of idea and end. But he nowhere considers the difficulty involved in establishing this proportion. He sees that the activity of establishing a proportion between sense and idea is pleasurable, but does not explore what this activity involves.

By regarding the activity of establishing a proportion as a *je ne sais quoi*, Shaftesbury separates production from enjoyment. Pleasure issues from objects which are mysteriously brought forward for discrimination according to unknowable laws. The feeling of pleasure dictates, through an unknowable law, which actions will most contribute to the public good. With such theses Shaftesbury reaches a definition of virtue as the harmony of private and public interests, one appropriate to the transition from an aristocratic dominion based on agriculture to an oligarchic dominion based on agriculture and commerce. His writings describe a virtuous state in which the pursuit of private interest providentially result in the general good. But the vision of a Whig Hellas, the virtuous commercial state, requires that the difficult and perhaps contradictory relations of sense and idea, interest and end, be obscured beneath a fog of equivocation, *non sequitur, petito principii* and I know not what.

One outcome of the equivocation of sense and idea is a passive or consumptive rather than active or productive view of action. The product of an action, its "end," is separated by a *je ne sais quoi* from immediate activity or "interest." Shaftesbury's individuals are not autonomous artists rationally producing a work, but spectators of the beautiful order in which they are fortunate to find themselves. In pursuing their individual interests, they constitute the beautiful order, but disown the product of their activity by contemplating it as a spectacle; at no point do they consider themselves as producers or legislators. Shaftesbury's individuals inhabit the realm Arendt termed the "social," producing neither material nor political works. Compared with Aristotle, for whom political activity is the prerogative of the free, productive activity, the burden of the slaves, Shaftesbury's individual are neither free nor slaves, but intermediate – mer-

---

[27] Shaftesbury, "The Moralists, A Philosophical Rhapsody" in: *Characteristics of Men, Manners, Opinions, Times*, Vol. II, p. 63.

chants subject to the laws of exchange. Smith's observation that in a commercial society "every man becomes in some measure a merchant" holds for Shaftesbury's synthesis of virtue and commerce.

The discourse of "interest" which underlies Shaftesbury's redefinition of virtue shows the distance between his and classical accounts of virtue, or between the original and the Whig Hellas. In the latter, citizens are merchants exchanging according to individual interest, and finding these interests disposed toward the end of the public interest. The classical distinction between the productive and political classes is dissolved into the unity of civil society. Mandeville's critique of Shaftesbury restates the classical distinction by emphasizing the problem of producing to satisfy desire, and the necessity of politically ordering the collisions in civil society arising from the obstruction of desire. The *Fable of the Bees: or, Private Vices, Publick Benefits* unmasks Shaftesbury's philosophy as aristocratic domination by demonstrating that idea and sense, or "interest" and "end," can only be reconciled through violence and deception.[28]

The moral of Mandeville's fable is well known. The hive thrived when catering for vice and luxury, but when it experienced a "reformation of manners," when the "knaves turned honest" tthe inhabitants were left virtuous but destitute. In an essay added to the fable in 1723, 'A Search into the Nature of Society,' Mandeville turned the moral of the *Fable* against Shaftesbury:[29] "This Noble Writer (for it is the Lord Shaftesbury I mean in his *Characteristicks*) Fancies that a Man is made for Society, so he ought to be born with a kind of Affection to the whole, of which he is a part, and a Propensity to seek the Welfare of it."[30] Mandeville is not persuaded by the equivocal moral sense which harmonizes private and public interest; he suggests instead that "The Sociableness of Man arises from only these two things, *viz.*, the multiplicity of his Desires and the continual Opposition he meets with in his Endeavours to gratify them."[31] Mandeville enlists appetite and desire against the claims of virtue; they are the basis of all human activity – against them not even Shaftesbury's "greatest realities" are safe:

---

28 "At bottom, he was saying that the real world of economy and polity rested on a myriad of fantasy worlds maintained by private egos." J.G.A. Pocock, *The Machiavellian Moment*, p. 465.
29 Mandeville's critique of Shaftesbury was emphasized in the German translation of the *Fable* known to Kant, which was titled: *Anti-Shaftesbury oder die entlarvte Eitelkeit der Selbstliebe und Ruhmsucht in philosophische Gesprachen nach der Englandischen*, published in 176 1.
30 Mandeville, *The Fable of the Bees*, p. 324.
31 Mandeville, *The Fable of the Bees*, p. 344.

> What I have endeavour'd hitherto, has been to prove, the *pulchrum et honestum*, excellency and real worth of things are most commonly precarious and alterable as Modes and Customs vary; that consequently the Inferences drawn from their Certainty are insignificant, and that the generous Notions concerning the Natural Goodness of man are hurtful, or they tend to mislead and are merely Chimerical.[32]

Beauty and virtue are revealed as screens for desire and appetite, masks of domination and not the "greatest realities" eulogized by the philosophical lord.

Mandeville restates the classical division of the political and the productive classes in his distinction between the interests of civil society and the reason of the state. Civil society consists in the pursuit of desire and production for the satisfaction of desire; but since this pursuit leads inevitably to conflict – there being no pre-established harmony between "interest" and "end" – it is necessary for the state to channel and restrain the energies of civil society. Not content with denying Shaftesbury's argument that civil society is intrinsically harmonious, Mandeville insists that such harmony can only be achieved through violence:

> All sound Politicks, and the whole Art of governing, Are entirely built upon the Knowledge of Human Nature. The great Business in general of a Politician is to promote and, if he can, reward all good and useful Actions on the one hand: and on the other, to punish or at least discourage, everything that is destructive or hurtful to Society.[33]

Mandeville replaces the *je ne sais quoi* with a cynical I know only too well; in place of providence he puts the manipulative politician. His exposure of the violence of the *je ne sais quoi* served to put Shaftesbury's successors on the defensive.[34]

Mandeville's critique of the equation of virtue and commerce had a considerable impact on eighteenth-century social and political theory. By pointing to the necessity of satisfying desire through production, and of regulating civil society politically, Mandeville restored the distinction of the productive and political classes to social and political theory. The theorists of civil society sought to incorporate certain elements of his critique into a restatement of Shaftesbury's position. Hutcheson's first work explicitly defends Shaftesbury against Mandeville, but the problem of the productive class's place in civil society manifested

---

[32] Mandeville, *The Fable of the Bees*, p. 343.
[33] Mandeville, *The Fable of the Bees*, p. 321.
[34] "It was because he posed the conflict between virtue and commerce so starkly that he had such a great influence upon the most important moral philosophers of the later part of the century – Hutcheson, Hume, and Smith – all of whom had to rejoin what Mandeville had torn asunder" Thomas A. Horne, *The Social Thought of Bernard Mandeville*, p. 33.

itself in his exclusion of labor discipline from the working of the moral sense. The most sophisticated response to the problem of production and civil society transformed moral philosophy into political economy. Smith took over Mandeville's insights into production and the division of labor and unified them with Shaftesbury's reconciliation of commerce and virtue. Smith distributes the equivocation of the moral sense across the realms of circulation and production: the object of individual "interest" was the work produced in the division of labor, while the "end" of public interest was achieved through the invisible hand of the market. However, the "beautiful order" of the market and the division of labor are still proportioned through a *je ne sais quoi*, since it is not possible for either the entrepreneurial or the productive classes to have a proper understanding of the rationality of their beautiful orders.

The Critic on the Bench

> When the point to be explained is taken for a cause.
> *Vis plastica*. instinct, *horror vacui*, the sense of truth (idiosyncrasy).
> Home's diverse senses: the sense of justice, the sense of honour, participatory.
> Kant, *Reflection* 316

Henry Home, Lord Kames, combined the careers of judge and critic. The "search for principles underlying particular rules as they were to be applied to particular cases in practice" which characterized his early writings on law and equity[35] was extended to the philosophy of art in his influential *Elements of Criticism* of 1762.[36] The *reform* of Scottish law through principles of equity and the establishment of the elements of criticism were closely related. The principles of law and the elements of criticism were derived from providence, and were identified with the rational senses of "beauty," "property," and "contract" discovered by Shaftesbury and Hutcheson. As with these authors, Kames's search for 'principles' of legal and moral judgement appropriate to the new civil society is mirrored by his search for teleologically guaranteed "elements" of criticism which would channel the "luxurious appetites" stimulated by commercial society into a virtuous "ordering of the ranks." Kames crudely fuses natural law, provi-

---

35 William C. Lehmann, *Henry Home, Lord Kames, and the Scottish Enlightenment*, p. 27.
36 One overenthusiastic reviewer in the *Scot's Magazine* wrote: "We entertain no kind of doubt but that the Elements of Criticism may one day supersede the critical labours of the Stagirite" (cited in Lehmann, *Henry Home, Lord Kames, and the Scottish Enlightenment*, p. 228). Adam Smith did entertain all kinds of doubts, and is reputed to have said of Kames's books in general and of the *Elements* in particular "They are all bad, but this is the worst."

dence and the institutions of civil society. The coarseness of his exposition is evident in the *Essays in the Principles of Morality and Natural Religion* published in 1751. The *Essays* are divided into two groups: the first contains essays on "Our Attachment to Objects of Distress," "The Foundations and Principles of the Law of Nature," and "Of Liberty and Necessity" which defend Hutcheson's moral sense theory against Hume's critique; while the second extends the critique into natural religion and other areas. Kames's main line of defence, as Kant observed, consists in multiplying the inner senses and linking them with an extremely crude teleological naturalism:

> A lion is said to purchase the means of life by his claws. Why? because such is his nature and constitution. A Man is made to purchase the means of life by help of others in society. Why? because from the constitution both of his body and mind he cannot live comfortably but in society. It is thus we discover for what end we were designed by nature, or the author of nature.[37]

Adam Smith must have groaned at this indiscretion. That the author of nature designed us for an "end" was a commonplace of eighteenth century moral philosophy; but it was hardly polite of Kames to express it quite so bluntly. For put that way, it exposes more than just the banality of the providential argument.

Kames compounds the indiscretion by deriving the ensemble of 'senses' from the 'ends' which we are providentially determined to follow. These are suddenly identified with the institutions of civil society; just as providence gives the lion his claws, so it bestows on us the "senses" or "feelings" of property and contract:

> We have a feeling of property; we have a feeling of obligation to perform our engagements; and we have a feeling of wrong on encroaching upon property, and in being untrue to our engagements[38]

God commends the institutions of property and contract through the implantation of property and contract feelings. From these feelings Kames develops a robust theory of justice in which "Justice is the moral virtue which guards property, and gives authority to covenant."[39]

The pleasure of beauty is an important cog in the divine clock of Kames's universe. After the performance of the primary virtues of property and contract come the nobler sentiments of beauty. Virtue is beautiful, but the pleasures of

---

[37] Lord Kames (Henry Home), *Essays in the Principles of Morality and Natural Religion*, p. 41.
[38] Lord Kames (Henry Home), *Essays in the Principles of Morality and Natural Religion*, p. 119.
[39] Lord Kames (Henry Home), *Essays in the Principles of Morality and Natural Religion*. p. 103.

beauty are insufficient to ensure virtue. Virtue must be founded in obligation, and obligation in pain.

However, the pleasures of beauty are not irrelevant to virtue and obligation. Beauty rewards the "fine points" of virtue; but, more interestingly – as will be seen in the discussion of the *Elements* – a certain amount of pleasure in the beautiful softens up the moral sense, making it more susceptible to pain. But too much softening can weaken the moral sense itself, which is the threat posed by luxury. As in Hutcheson's thought, pleasure and pain are inseparable for Kames. The sense of beauty, then, aids obligation but threatens to degenerate into luxury, tragically ceasing to be virtue's ornament and becoming its adversary:

> We find him [humanity] sensible of beauty, in different ranks and orders; and eminently sensible of it, in its highest order, that of sentiment, action and character. But the sense of moral beauty is not alone sufficient. The importance of morality requires some stronger principle to guard it; some checks and restraints from vice, more severe than mere disapprobation. These are not wanting. To the sense of beauty is superadded a sense of obligation; a feeling of right and wrong, which constitute a law within us. The law enjoins the primary virtues, those which are essential to society, under the strictest sanctions. Pain, the strongest monitor we have is employed to check transgression: while in the sublimer, more heroic points of virtue, where strict obligation ends, pleasure is employed to reward the performance.[40]

Kames, like Hutcheson, supplements the pleasures of the senses of beauty and morality with the pains of right and obligation. The contemplative pleasures of the imagination cannot secure order – they must be supplemented by the pain of morality. The existence of the sense of beauty shows that humans are not Hobbist beasts, like the aforesaid lion, but must still be tamed by a sense of obligation. This is a discriminative "sense," being at once (in one sentence) a "*sense* of obligation," a "*feeling* of right and wrong" and a "*law* within us."[41] The law is said to be constituted by the feeling of right and wrong, but the relationship between the principle of law and discrimination is left completely unexplored, being the work of a mysterious providence. But just as Hutcheson's moral sense was supplemented by violence, so is Kames's inner law attended by the "strictest sanctions." Only after the stern maxims of justice are fulfilled ("guard property," "observe contracts") may the pleasures of the senses be indulged.

---

40 Lord Kames (Henry Home), *Essays in the Principles of Morality and Natural Religion*, pp. 380 – 381.
41 Kames, *Essays in the Principles of Morality and Natural Religion*, p. 381.

The teleology of property and contract developed in the *Essays* is carried over into the *Elements of Criticism*. The "dedication" of the work to George III offers some Machiavellian advice concerning beauty's contribution to order:

> The Fine Arts have ever been encouraged by wise Princes, not simply for private amusement, but for their beneficial influence in society. By uniting different ranks in the same elegant pleasures, they promote benevolence: by cherishing love of order, they enforce submission to government: and by inspiring a delicacy of feeling, they make regular government a double blessing.[42]

The Fine Arts encourage a unity of sentiment which unites the "different ranks" in a benevolent love of order; but the pain implied by the pleasure is never far away since the Fine Arts "*enforce submission* to government." The unity of ranks in the elegant pleasures soften manners, and makes the ranks more sensitive and easy to order, and more desirous of order. By establishing the "elements" of universal and necessary judgements of taste, and promoting a sensitively mannered unity of sentiment, Lord Kames makes his contribution to the love of order.

Kames is not blind to the dangers of an excessive delicacy of feeling and, using the *topos* of the corruption of virtue by commerce, warns the King that unregulated commerce may lead to overrefinement and luxury. All is not lost though, for the proper development of the sense of beauty offers a new basis for virtue which does not threaten the progress of commerce (property and contract):

> To promote the Fine Arts in Britain, has become of greater importance than is generally imagined. A flourishing commerce begets opulence; and opulence, inflaming our appetite for pleasure, is commonly vented on luxury, and on every sensual gratification: selfishness rears its head; becomes fashionable; and infecting all ranks, extinguishes the *amor patriae*, and every spark of public spirit. To prevent or retard such fatal corruption, the genius of an Alfred cannot devise any means more efficacious, than the venting opulence upon the Fine Arts; riches employ'd, instead of encouraging vice, will excite both public and private virtue. Of this happy effect Ancient Greece furnishes one shining instance; and why should we despair of another in Britain?[43]

This return to the fantasy of the Whig Hellas[44] relieves the agonizing problem Shaftesbury had of how to regulate luxury without law. The excess of wealth threatening virtue may be vented on art. But for this to work, Kames has to

---

[42] Kames, *Elements of Criticism*, Vol. I, v.
[43] Kames, *Elements of Criticism*, Vol. I, p. vii.
[44] Caygill, *The Art of Judgment*, pp. 44–53.

show that beauty has the qualities of an inner law which is universal and necessary. He achieves this through a demonstration of the teleological foundation of taste and criticism.

Kames insists that the sense of beauty is grounded in a rational principle, and describes his *Elements* as "attempts to form a standard, by unfolding those principles that ought to govern the taste of every individual."[45] The standard has a prescriptive force derived from the moral sense, to which it is related in being a discriminative feeling governed by a mysterious principle:

> A taste in the fine arts goes hand in hand with the moral sense, to which indeed it is nearly allied; both of them discover what is right and what is wrong: fashion, temper, and education have an influence to vitiate both, or to preserve them pure and untainted; neither of them are arbitrary nor local; being rooted in human nature, and governed by principles common to all men.[46]

The alliance of taste and the moral sense is based on three common characteristics. The first is their shared origin in a "human nature" characterized by universally shared "principles." They are, additionally, both discriminative faculties prone to corruption and open to improvement. The third is less a common characteristic than a mutual support agreement: the moral sense gives taste its prescriptive power while taste enhances the susceptibility of the moral sense. The first chapter of the *Elements* expands Kames's earlier model of "human nature," locating the various senses and passions within a providential order. What was previously discussed in terms of Lions and clocks is now elaborated into a moralistic theory of art wherein God, human nature, and the elements of criticism are brought face to face. Their meeting is described in chapter 10 on "Congruity and Propriety":

> The God of nature, in all things essential to our happiness, hath observed one uniform method to keep us steady: in our conduct, he hath fortified us with natural laws and principles, preventive of many aberrations, which would daily happen were we totally surrendered to so fallible a guide as is human reason. Propriety cannot rightly be considered in another light, than as the natural law that regulates our conduct with respect to ourselves; as justice is the natural law that regulates our conduct with respect to others.[47]

The *Elements* continue in this way for hundreds of pages, discussing God's providential arrangement of the senses, of society, and of the artistic representation

---

45 Kames, *Elements of Criticism*, Vol. I, p. i.
46 Kames, *Elements of Criticism*, Vol. I, p. 6.
47 Kames, *Elements of Criticism*, Vol. I, p. 348.

of them. Volume I discusses such principles as "Dignity and Grace," "Ridicule," "Custom and Habit" in the light of their relation to providence; volume II relates these principles to a neo-classical rhetorical poetic. It is in the conclusion, "On the Standard of Taste," that Kames returns specifically to the question of the relation of beauty and virtue, moral sense and sense of beauty, introduced in the "Dedication" of the *Elements*.

The excursus on the "Standard of Taste" is undoubtedly the most original and interesting part of the *Elements*. In it Kames reconsiders the three common elements of the moral sense and the sense of beauty: origin in human nature, their discriminative character, and mutual support. Beneath the shared characteristics is the providential teleology, unknowable except through its effects. The "principle" of taste follows from human nature, but can only be known intuitively: "the conviction of a common standard is universal and a branch of our nature, we intuitively conceive a taste to be right or good if conformable to the common standard, and wrong or bad if disconformable."[48] However, we cannot know the common standard except where we "intuitively conceive" a taste to be right or good. The intuitive conception is a discrimination of the conformity or disconformity of a particular taste, and it is only because we make such discriminations that we are convinced that there is a standard underlying them. The nature of the principle which enables the discrimination to take place remains hidden.

The principles of morality and taste must be at once subjective and objective: subjective as a feeling of discrimination but objective as law. This leads to some patent difficulties, as in this passage: "every man, generally speaking, taking it for granted that his opinions agree with the common sense of mankind, is therefore disgusted with those who think differently, not as differing from him, but as differing from the common standard."[49] The common standard begins to wobble, for if one individual can take it for granted that their taste represents common sense, what prevents another individual with a different taste from doing so? The possibility of a discursive search for consensus conducted by individuals lodging different claims to represent the universal is ignored in favour of a providentially established common conviction of human nature. Human nature is not a common ground of consensus from which individuals may judge the merits of different claims to represent the universal, but is the providential law which legislates the universal:

> upon a conviction common to the species, is erected a standard of taste, which without hesitation is applied to the taste of every individual. That standard, ascertaining what actions

---

[48] Kames, *Elements of Criticism*, Vol. II, p. 492.
[49] Kames, *Elements of Criticism*, Vol. II, p. 493.

are right what wrong, what proper what improper, hath enabled moralists to establish rules for our conduct, from which no one person is permitted to swerve. We have the same standard for ascertaining in all the fine arts, what is beautiful or ugly, high or low, proper or improper, proportioned or disproportioned; and here, as in morals, we justly condemn every taste that deviates from what is thus ascertained by the common standard.[50]

The elision of conviction and rule is characteristic; the universal cannot be known, but must be seen to rule. The individual judgement must be subsumed "without hesitation" under a general standard.

This governs the long series of discriminative oppositions (beautiful/ugly, high/low, etc.) which reduce to the opposition of pleasure and displeasure. The conviction behind the discriminations is described as the "standard" of taste or virtue, and no more can be said of it than that it is ordained by the same providence which gave the lion his claws. The standard is not open to negotiation, only application through discrimination. Unfortunately, establishing such discriminations upon a conviction or sentiment gives them an extremely weak basis, making them vulnerable to the corruption of sentiment. The vulnerability of sentiment to corruption requires that it be underwritten by the violence of the firmest sanctions.

Kames's work ventures a settlement between the traditional fear of the luxurious corruption of virtue and the aspiration to justify the virtues of a commercial society through the moral sense. Here beauty and virtue complement one another: virtue provides the prescriptive force for the discriminations of taste, while the pleasures of beauty hone the discriminations of virtue. These complementary activities rest on a providential teleology that raises a standard which is felt but not known in the act of judgment. While beauty vents the tendencies to luxury and sensitizes manners, the order of the commercial society is ensured by the feelings of property, contract, etc., which are unthinkable without the strictest sanctions. The equivocation of "sense" and "reason" identified by Kant as the main philosophical inadequacy in Shaftesbury, Hutcheson, and Kames, dissolves reason into the unknowable yet unnegotiable conviction behind the discriminations of sense, which can only be maintained through force.

---

50 Kames, *Elements of Criticism*, Vol. II, pp. 496–497.

Form and Discrimination

> Whether Hume is right: that great beauties are exceptional because exceptional beauty (or beauty in itself) is alone called great, that is, tautologously. Whether beauty is only called great comparatively, or whether it has its ideal in itself.
> Kant, *Reflection* 986

The difficulty of legitimating a discriminative sentiment with a law or standard is uppermost in the theory of taste. All the theorists point to a "conformity" or "proportion" between sentiment and reason which is a *je ne sais quoi*, or gift of providence. Hume's writings on criticism address this problem, but attempt to solve it without recourse to divinity. In the *Treatise of Human Nature* (1739) he considers the "conformity" between the discrimination of sense and the law of reason to lie in an artificially produced form. He justifies the problem of the relation of form and the production of objects with reference to production in general, but ends by privileging the production of fine art. In his later texts the insight into the source of the conformity between sentiment and reason is abandoned. In *An Inquiry Concerning the Principles of Morals* (1751) Hume figures the distinction of reason and sentiment in terms of God's being and His will, while in "Of the Standard of Taste" (1757) he sees the conformity between them as unknowable, yet leaving a trace or "mark" in history. Hume envisaged the *Treatise of Human Nature* as five books, billed in the "Advertisement" to the *Treatise* as: (i) "Of the Understanding," (ii) "Of the Passions," (iii) "Of Morals," (iv) "Of Politics," and (v) "Of Criticism." The complete performance depended on "the approbation of the public," which was, alas, not forthcoming. Following the lack of acclaim for the first three books, those on politics and criticism remained unpublished, probably unwritten. As a consequence, the existing *Treatise* gives only a partial picture of Hume's projected "science of man." Hume makes the following division of the science in the "Introduction" to the work:

> The sole end of logic is to explain the principles and operations of our reasoning faculty, and the nature of our ideas: morals and criticism regard our tastes and sentiments: and politics consider men as united in society, and dependent on each other. In these four sciences of *Logic, Morals, Criticism, and Politics,* is comprehended almost everything, which it can any way import us to be acquainted with, or which can tend either to the improvement or ornament of the human mind.[51]

---

51 Hume, *Treatise*, pp. xv-xvi.

Although the criticism and politics[52] were not completed, it is possible to conjecture their contents from scattered passages in the *Treatise* and from those essays in *Essays, Literary, Moral, and Political* intended to correct and supplement it. The place of criticism within the science of human nature can be established by plotting its relation to other parts of the science. In the *Treatise* Hume emphasizes the similarities between criticism and morals over the differences between criticism and logic. In the later writings he is concerned more to distinguish logic from taste than to point to similarities between morals and criticism. In the *Treatise*, both criticism and morals are founded upon the discrimination of pleasure and pain. Both sciences have to show that this discrimination is regular and lawlike, but they also have to establish whether pleasure and pain are the origin or the consequence of the ideals of beauty and virtue.

Book II, Part I, section viii of the *Treatise* considers the distinction of beauty and deformity. The difficulties of this chapter are important for drawing out the relation of Hume's theory of taste to morals. It begins by ascribing beauty to whatever "gives us a peculiar delight and satisfaction"[53] and deformity to whatever causes pain. The distinction of beauty and deformity is immediately allied to pleasure and pain, these "are not only necessary attendants of beauty and deformity, but constitute their very essence."[54] Pleasure and pain are not predicated in a judgment of taste but define its terms. They also constitute the distinction of virtue and vice; but what is vital to both discriminations is that they are regular, and indicate the presence of a hidden law.

Hume establishes the regularity of the discriminations of pleasure and pain by aligning them with a "principle." He follows Hutcheson in relating pleasure to the principle of utility, but refrains from deriving utility from providence. He favours a form of teleological argument which maintains the *effect* of providence in utility while overlooking what the tradition saw as the *source* of utility in the providential being (Shaftesbury) or will (Hutcheson) of God. For Hume pleasure is a subjective response to utility; he ignores the theological question of the ultimate source of this utility. This discretion leads to difficulty, since – by separating utility from the being of God – Hume raises the problem of the relative priority of pleasure and utility: it is equally plausible that a thing is useful because it gives pleasure, as that it gives pleasure because it is useful.

---

52 Hume's political philosophy has been reconstructed by David Miller, *Philosophy and Ideology in Hume's Political Thought*.
53 Hume, *Treatise*, p. 298.
54 Hume, *Treatise*, p. 299.

Adam Smith later oscillated between the two positions, eventually opting for the former. Hume, however, embraced both relations of pleasure and utility, and presented them in two distinct accounts of pleasure and its objects.

The problems of the precedence of pleasure or utility and the source of the regularity of the discriminations of pleasure and pain are highlighted in Hume's illegitimate deductions of the rules of art from utility. For example: "the rules of architecture require, that the top of a pillar shou'd be more slender than its base, and that because such a figure conveys to us the idea of security, which is pleasant; whereas the contrary form gives us the apprehension of danger, which is uneasy."[55] Here the rules of architecture are derived from utilitarian considerations of security and danger (a distinction Burke later used to found the distinction of the beautiful and the sublime). Yet earlier on the same page Hume stated that pleasure and pain constitute the essence of beauty and deformity; now they seem to follow from utilitarian considerations of security and apprehension of danger. The subordination of pleasure and beauty to utility is underlined in the comment that although beauty may only be discerned and not defined, it is "nothing but a form, which produces pleasure" just as "deformity is a structure of parts, which conveys pain."[56] Pleasure and pain no longer "constitute" beauty and deformity, but are "produced" and "conveyed" by form and deformity; but then these follow in their turn from the "power of producing pain and pleasure." Hume's description of these intellectual contortions as an "argument I esteem just and decisive"[57] is unconvincing.

The restless movement between pleasure as constitutive and constituted betrays difficulty in conceiving how a discrimination can be regular, and where the source of its regularity lies. The problem of the precedence of pleasure or utility has not been addressed, nor have the theoretical transitions from utility to a form of utility, and from the form of utility to beauty and pleasure. The main difficulty lies in the spurious validity given utility by renaming it the "form" of utility. To speak of a form of utility gives to individual utility an objective universality and necessity. However, the transition from individual to formal utility requires a principle, a theoretical substitute for providence which would articulate each individual utility within an harmonious whole. Once the providential guarantee for the form of utility has been abandoned, beauty is prone to be dispersed among the particularities of the useful. As Burke was to point out, the equation of beau-

---

55 Hume, *Treatise*, p. 299.
56 Hume, *Treatise*, p. 299.
57 Hume, *Treatise*, p. 300.

ty and utility overextends the category of beauty: ploughs and saddles are useful and give pleasure, but this does not make them beautiful.

At some points in the *Treatise* Hume recklessly endorses the wide equation of utility and beauty and, forgetting his earlier definition of beauty as a *form*, identifies it with useful *objects:* "This observation extends to tables, chairs, scritoires, chimneys, coaches, saddles, ploughs, and indeed to every work of art; it being a universal rule, that their beauty is chiefly deriv'd from their utility, and from their fitness for that purpose, to which they arc dcstin'd."[58] This "universal rule" prefers the beauty of useful objects over the form of beauty; all works of art, all produced objects, which are appropriate to the end for which they were produced, are beautiful. This argument falters when it specifies the beauty and utility of those peculiar objects which form the fine arts. Hume's philosophy of fine art is usually read as the crude Horatian argument that works of art are beautiful because they promote morality. He does indeed approach such a position in his essays "Of Refinement in the Arts" and "Of Tragedy" but these by no means exhaust the resources of his theory of taste.

Beyond the "saddle and plough" account of the beauty of all useful objects, it is possible to discern another more interesting argument in the *Treatise*. In this Hume confronts the problem of the origin of *form* in pleasure and utility, and revises his understanding of the utility of fine art. This argument, recognized by Adam Smith as Hume's real achievement in the philosophy of art, derives its formal principle of utility from a theory of society.

Before excavating this argument it is necessary to consider briefly Hume's moral philosophy. The relationship between the critical and the moral departments of Hume's "science of man" is more subtle than is usually acknowledged. Virtue gives a sensation of pleasure and is in accord with utility; the specific utility determining virtue is the good of the whole:

> Now justice is a moral virtue, merely because it has that tendency to the good of mankind; and, indeed, is nothing but an artificial invention to that purpose. The same may be said of allegiance, of the laws of nations, of modesty, and of good manners. All these are mere human contrivances for the interest of society.[59]

Such an account of utility holds only if there be a principle or prior determinant of the public interest – the role played by providence in Shaftesbury, Hutcheson and Kames. In rejecting providentialist argument Hume is left with the problem

---

58 Hume, *Treatise*, p. 364.
59 Hume, *Treatise*, p. 577.

of the form of utility, of how to relate individual with social utility or the "good of mankind."

Hume discovered such a principle in sympathy:

> as the means to an end can only be agreeable, where the end is agreeable; and as the good of society, where our own interest is not concern'd, or that of our friends, pleases *only* by sympathy: It follows that sympathy is the source of the esteem, which we pay to all the artificial virtues.[60]

As the basis for the esteem paid to the artificial virtues which ensure the equivalence of individual and social utility, Hume's theory of sympathy seems an intermediate stage between the unification by providence employed by his predecessors and Smith's "invisible hand." Indeed, the synthesis of universal and individual in sympathy is figured, as is the moral sentiment of Smith's early *The Theory of Moral Sentiments* (1759), in terms of the catoptric trope of mutually reflecting mirrors.

The development of Hume's account of the form of beauty in the *Treatise* is inseparable from his philosophy of sympathy: "Thus it appears, *that* sympathy is a very powerful principle in human nature, *that* it has a great influence on our taste of beauty, and *that* it produces our sentiment of morals in all the artificial virtues"[61]. Sympathy has a "great influence" on the taste of beauty and "produces" our sentiments of morals. Hume uses a metaphor of catoptric illusion to explain how sympathy moves between individual and general utility. The sum of individual reflections on each other's actions produces a reflected utility or "form of utility" which is re-experienced by the individual as sympathy, a feeling for the whole:

> In general we may remark, that the minds of men are mirrors to one another, not only because they reflect each others emotions, but also because those rays of passions, sentiments and opinions may often be reverberated, and may decay away by insensible degrees. Thus the pleasure which a rich man receives from his possessions, being thrown upon the beholder, causes a pleasure and esteem; which sentiments again, being perceiv'd and sympathis'd with, encrease the pleasure of the possessor; and being once more reflected, become a new foundation for pleasure and esteem in the beholder.[62]

In this passage, later criticized by Smith, the infinity of past and present reflections assumes independence from the individual mirrors, becoming a form

---

60 Hume, *Treatise*, p. 577.
61 Hume, *Treatise*, pp. 577–578.
62 Hume, *Treatise*, p. 365.

whose effect is felt through the sentiment of sympathy. The field of mutual reflection is held to be the sublimated utility which forms the ground of pleasure in the fine arts. The utility of works of art differs from that of useful objects in being a highly mediated expression of the form of utility. The utility lying at the source of the pleasure in the fine arts is not immediate and personal, like that of enjoying a saddle, but issues from a form produced by reflection and experienced as sympathy.

This argument is analogous to the providentialist ascription of pleasure to the affective experience of the *telos* or unifying principle of society. One of its consequences is that an individual may, through sympathy, find something beautiful and pleasant which for them has no immediate utility, and carries with it the apprehension of danger: "as when the fortifications of a city belonging to an enemy arc esteem'd beautiful on account of their strength, tho' we could wish that they were entirely destroy'd."[63] On this occasion, immediate and reflected utility may be said to conflict. This position marks another stage in the development of the argument for 'disinterested perception' as a source for beauty: in Shaftesbury such disinterest resulted from a contemplation of the *je ne sais quoi*, while in Hume the "unknowable" has been specified as the artificial, historically produced, formal utility of society.

Hume now bases the rules of art on the refinement of sympathy; we do not use the fine arts as we would a scritoire or a saddle since their utility is formal, end-directed without an immediate end:

> There is no rule in painting more reasonable than that of balancing the figures, and placing them with the greatest exactness on their proper centres of gravity. A figure, which is not justly balanc'd, is disagreeable; and that because it conveys the idea of its falt, of harm, and of pain: Which ideas are painful, when by sympathy they acquire any degree of force and vivacity.[64]

This explains how Hume was able to maintain a theory of beauty resting on saddles and scritoires alongside one demanding the strictest rules of decorum: the former is based on immediate, the latter on reflected utility. Hume's dual theory of art seems to contain both Shaftesbury's enjoyment of the *je ne sais quoi* abstracted from desire and immediate utility, and Mandeville's identification of beauty and desire for objects. But he is careful to keep the two philosophies apart: the enjoyment of a useful object is rigorously distinguished from the formal and contemplative pleasures of "fine art." The "ordering of the ranks" advo-

---

63 Hume, *Treatise*, pp. 586–587.
64 Hume, *Treatise*, pp. 364–365.

cated by Karnes is maintained in Hume's two-tiered philosophy of art. We shall see below how Smith, in his critique of Hume, sought to synthesize the two arts of immediate and reflected utility. The separation of the two arguments is the result of Hume's not fully exploring the source and character of the regularity between sentiment and reason. He attributes such regularity to utility, and relates utility to desire for an end, seeing the origin of pleasure to lie in the realization of ends. But his distinction between material utility – the pleasures of a good saddle – and formal utility – the pleasure of fine art – remains tied to the dichotomy of sentiment and reason. The nature and the source of their conformity remains unexplained. The impasse reached in relating the discriminations of sense and the laws of reason is renegotiated in the first appendix to *An Inquiry Concerning the Principles of Morals,* "Concerning Moral Sentiment." Now, when discussing the relation of logic, morals, and criticism, Hume emphasizes the differences between criticism and logic over the former's similarity with morals.

Hume offers five distinctions between logic (the science of reason) and criticism (the science of taste). These are stated in terms of (i) the knowledge claims of each faculty, (ii) their modes of representation, (iii) the connection of each with moral action, (iv) their procedures and (v) their "standards" or sources of validity. In terms of knowledge claims, reason "conveys the knowledge of truth and falsehood" while taste "gives the sentiment of beauty and deformity, vice and virtue."[65] Although both faculties are discriminative, reason distinguishes between truth and falsehood in terms of knowledge, while taste distinguishes between beauty/deformity and vice/virtue according to sentiment. The distinction is then developed in terms of the modes of representation pertaining to reason and sentiment:

> reason 'discovers objects, as they really stand in nature, without addition or diminution' while taste 'has a productive faculty; and gilding and staining all natural objects with the colours, borrowed from internal sentiment, raises in a manner, a new creation'[66]

The perceptions of reason neither add nor subtract from its objects; it is in some sense objective and mimetic, while those of taste are productive, re-producing its objects by adapting them to its desire. Hume's third distinction contrasts the influence of reason and taste on the passions. Reason can only determine the means for attaining the ends given by the passions, but taste can establish ends, and constitute desire, "as it gives pleasure and pain, and thereby constitutes happiness or misery, becomes a motive to action, and is the first spring or im-

---

[65] Hume, *An Inquiry Concerning the Principles of Morals,* p. 484.
[66] Hume, *An Inquiry Concerning the Principles of Morals,* p. 484.

pulse to desire and volition."⁶⁷ Reason is disinterested, and neither alters its object of perception nor offers any motive for action; taste, on the other hand, changes its object and motivates actions. This leads Hume to his fourth distinction of reason and taste. The disinterestedness of reason allows it to be used as an investigative instrument: "From circumstances and relations, known or supposed ... [reason] leads us to the discovery of the concealed and unknown." Taste however, does not follow the train of demonstrative argument, but judges subjectively, and "makes us feel from the whole a new sentiment of blame or approbation."⁶⁸ Reason is an analytical faculty following objective judgments, while taste is synthetic, adding to the perception a subjective sentiment of praise or blame. Yet the nature of the synthetic judgment of taste is even more complicated than it seems here. The exposition of the differences between taste and reason takes an astonishing turn in the discussion of their sources of validity. Here the sceptical Hume is found distinguishing critical and logical validity in terms of the difference between the ontological and voluntarist views of God. Reason and the validity of logic are founded on the *being* of God while taste and the standard of criticism depend on His *will*. Hume is a Thomist or Spinozist in matters of reason, and a Scotist or Cartesian in matters of taste. The validity of reason is eternal and unchangeable, issuing from the divine being whose laws are independent of even God's will: "The standard [of reason] ... being founded on the nature of things, is eternal and inflexible, even by the will of the Supreme Being." The standard of taste, by contrast, is subjective, not fixed in being but ordained by the divine will: "the standard [of taste] ... is ultimately derived from that Supreme will, which bestowed on each being the peculiar nature, and arranged the several classes and orders of existence."⁶⁹

But not only does the singularity of each being issue from God's will, but also the classification and ordering of beings. These are the province of reason and should be independent of even God's will; but here they are found to share an origin with the pleasures of taste. The validity of reason, it is suggested, is in some way subordinate to that of taste.

There is one God for reason, another for taste. This equivocal divinity has implications for criticism. Taste is subjective and capricious, but evinces a regularity which suggests it possesses a validity similar to logic. The addition of a subjective sentiment to a perception occurs with regularity and possesses the properties of universality and necessity. But then again it seems as if God's

---

67 Hume, *An Inquiry Concerning the Principles of Morals*, p. 484.
68 Hume, *An Inquiry Concerning the Principles of Morals*, p. 484.
69 Hume, *An Inquiry Concerning the Principles of Morals*, p. 484.

will, the source of the regularities of taste, the law of the distinction of pleasure and pain, also founds the classificatory system and validity of reason. The regularities of the discriminations of taste in a sense underlie those of reason. How might this be thought?

In the essay "Of the Standard of Taste" (1757) Hume transforms the two utilities of the *Treatise* and the divided God of *Concerning Moral Sentiment* into a play of sceptical paradoxes. The standard of taste is recognized to be indeterminate: it has neither the understanding's concern with the universal nor sentiment's dispersal in particulars, yet possesses characteristics of both. Hume hopes to "mingle some light of the understanding with the feelings of sentiment" (ST 216) by establishing a rational standard or rule of taste, but says he would be content with a convincing sensible discrimination: "It is natural for us to seek a *Standard of Taste*; a rule, by which the various sentiments of men may be reconciled; at least, a decision afforded, confirming one sentiment, and condemning another" (ST 207–208). The difficult relation of rule and discrimination is separated into a desire for a rule and a voluntaristic decision confirming a particular discrimination. The rule is only perceptible through the conviction of the discrimination.

In his exploration of the relation of rule and discrimination, Hume finds that although the judgments of reason and the responses of sentiment differ, there is nevertheless a "conformity" between objects and sentiment. And this conformity, which regularizes the discriminations of sentiment, is analogous to the rule of reason:

> The difference, it is said, is very wide between judgement and sentiment. All sentiment is right; because sentiment has a reference to nothing beyond itself, and is always real, wherever a man is conscious of it. But all determinations of the understanding are not right; because they have a reference to something beyond themselves, to wit, real matter of fact; and are not always conformable to that standard. Among a thousand different opinions which different men may ascertain of the same subject, there is one, and but one, that is just and true; and the only difficulty is to fix and ascertain it. On the contrary, a thousand different sentiments, excited by the same object, are all right: because no sentiment represents what is really in the object. It only marks a certain conformity or relation between the object and the organs or faculties of the mind; and if that conformity did not really exist, the sentiments could never possibly have being (ST 208).

The judgments of reason must be conformable to "real matter of fact" and this conformity must be "fixed and ascertained." But sentiment is first denied any such conformity with objects, since it does not represent what is really there. Its pleasure is produced in the encounter with an object. But then this encounter, in its myriad forms, nevertheless marks a "certain conformity or relation" without which, indeed, sentiment could not exist. The existence of sentiment depends on a prior regularity between the object and the mind; the discriminations of sentiment are as conformable as those of reason. And while Hume does not identify the source of this regularity as "providence," his argument is formally similar to that of the providentialists who argued that proportion preceded both sentiment and its object. The "certain conformity or relation" registers the return of the *je ne sais quoi*. By letting sentiment "mark" an unknown order or design – a pre-established harmony – Hume allows it to mediate between universal rule and individual discrimination; either universal nor individual but marks a "relation" which includes both.

The sentiment of the beautiful is not self-referential, nor does it bow to an external rule; it marks a "certain conformity" which exceeds both reason and sentiment. The "certain conformity or relation" leaves marks which may be traced over time. The regularity or "form" of discrimination which is felt only as conviction at the moment of decision, becomes manifest in history:

> The relation, which nature has placed between the form and the sentiment, will at least be more obscure; and it will require greater accuracy to trace and discern it. We shall be able to ascertain its influence, not so much from the operation of each particular beauty, as from the durable admiration, which attends those works, that have survived all the caprices of mode and fashion, all the mistakes of ignorance and envy (ST 213).

Hume attributes the obscurity of relation between form and sentiment – the law of discrimination – to prejudice and the capricious distraction of fashion. This attribution enables him to translate the problem of "marking" the relation into that of marking the critic:

> But where are such critics to be found? By what marks are they to be known? How to distinguish them from pretenders? These questions are embarrassing; and seem to throw us back into the same uncertainty, from which during the course of this essay we have endeavoured to extricate ourselves (ST 229).

The question of judging judges cannot be answered if the difficulty of judgment has itself not been tackled. For by what criteria do we distinguish between judges? For both judgment in general and the judging of judges Hume appeals to history; time not only manifests the conformity of sentiment and form, but also vindicates the righteous judge.

The source of the obscurity of the relation of form and sentiment, of rule and discrimination, may lie elsewhere. In the distinction of the validities of reason and taste, Hume sees God as both subject to the laws of the universe and creating them by His will. The conformity of reason to its objects rests on universal law, but then both the objects and the laws of reason are creatures of God's will. A similar structure of argument, without the divinity, underlies the distinctions of form/sentiment and rule/discrimination. The conformity of reason is univocal, but that of taste and the sentiments is plural. Taste produces its objects, and the laws under which they are enjoyed; reason on the other hand is given its objects and its law. It is possible to be more specific and say that reason is given its objects and laws by taste, by the sentiments. Objects are produced according to the pleasure which they will give, but pleasure is determined by the attainment of an end. But the end is also legislated by pleasure, so there is a relation or conformity between legislation of ends and the production of objects. It is this relation which is marked in the regularities between the form of law and the discriminations of sentiment.

For Hume the relation of law and production was unknowable, and the source of the obscurity of the relation between law and discrimination. The obscure relation was not immediately dissolved into the workings of providence, but left open. As with Shaftesbury and Hutcheson, the relation was marked by pleasure, but Hume also intimated that it was formed by pleasure. There was the pleasure of attaining an end, but the ends themselves were constituted by pleasure. Hume divided the pleasures according to those in an object which satisfied an end, and those of contemplating ends apart from any object. The relation between the two was not openly acknowledged, although it was conceded to be "obscure." Hume's scepticism regarding the knowledge of this conformity met with two responses. The first, represented by Burke, was a forceful restatement of the providential character of this relation. The second, worked through by Smith, pointed to a notion of productive legislation underlying the obscure conforming and relating of law and sentiment.

Acknowledgements

A longer version of this chapter appears in Howard Caygill, *Art of Judgment*, (Oxford: Blackwell, 1989).

Bibliography

Bahlman, Dudley W.R. (1957) *The Moral Revolution of 1688*. New Haven: Yale University Press.
Caygill, Howard (1989) *The Art of Judgment*. Oxford: Blackwell.
Clark, Jonathan (1985) *English Society 1688–1832: Ideology, Social Structure and Political Practice during the Ancien Regime*. Cambridge: Cambridge University Press.

Dickinson, H.T. (1977) *Liberty and Property – Political Philosophy in Eighteenth Century Britain*. London: Weidenfeld and Nicolson.

Dickson, Peter George Muir (1967) *The Financial Revolution in England: A Study in the Development of Public Credit 1688–1756*. London: Macmillan.

Gunn, J. A. W. (1983) *Beyond Liberty and Property: The Process of Self-Recognition in Eighteenth Century Political Thought*. Kingston/Montreal: McGill-Queen's University Press.

Hirschmann, Alfred (1977) *The Passions and the Interests: Political Arguments for Capitalism Before its Triumph*. Princeton: Princeton University.

Horne, Thomas A. (1978) *The Social Thought of Bernard Mandeville*. London: MacMillan.

Hume, David (1739) *Treatise*. London: John Noon.

Hume, David (1751) *Enquiry Concerning the Principles of Morals*. London: A. Millar.

Kant, Immanuel (1781) *Kritik der reinen Vernunft*. Riga: Johann Friedrich Hartknoch.

Lord Kames (Henry Home) (1751) *Essays in the Principles of Morality and Natural Religion*. Edinburgh: R. Fleming, for A. Kincaid and A. Donaldson.

Lord Kames (Henry Home) (1762) *Elements of Criticism*. Edinburgh: A. Kincaid and J. Bell.

Krieger, Leonard (1970) *Kings and Philosophers 1689–1789*. Chicago: Chicago University Press.

Lehmann, William C. (1971) *Henry Home, Lord Kames, and the Scottish Enlightenment*. The Hague: Nijhoff.

Locke, John (1977) *An Essay Concerning Human Understanding*. John W. Yolton, (Ed.) London: J.M. Dent & Sons. [1690]

Mandeville, Bernard (176 l) *Anti-Shaftesbury oder die entlarvte Eitelkeit der Selbstliebe und Ruhmsucht in philosophische Gesprachen nach der Englandischen*.

Mandeville, Bernard (1924) *The Fable of the Bees: or, Private Vices, Publick Benefits* (2 vols). F.B. Kaye (Ed.) Oxford: Oxford University Press. [1714]

Miller, David (1981) *Philosophy and Ideology in Hume's Political Thought*. Oxford: Oxford University Press.

Pocock, John G.A. (1985) *Virtue, Commerce, and History*. Cambridge: Cambridge University Press.

Pocock, J.G.A. (1975) *The Machiavellian Moment*. Princeton: Princeton University Press.

Rand, Benjamin (Ed.) (1900) *The Life, Unpublished Letters, and Philosophical Regimen of Anthony, Earl of Shaftesbury*. New York: MacMillan, 1900.

Saisselin, Remy G. (1970) *The Rule of Reason and the Ruses of the Heart: Philosophical Dictionary of Classical French Criticism, Critics, and Aesthetic Issues*. Cleveland: Press of Case Western Reserve University.

Shaftesbury (Anthony Ashley Cooper) (1977) *An Enquiry Concerning Virtue or Merit*, David Walford (Ed.) Manchester: Manchester University Press. [1711] [1688]

Shaftesbury, (1711) *Characteristics*.

Shaftesbury, 'The Moralists, A Philosophical Rhapsody.' In: *Characteristics of Men, Manners, Opinions, Times*, Vol. II, 63.

Shaftesbury (1914) *Second Characters, or the Language of Forms*. Benjamin Rand, (Ed.) Cambridge: Cambridge University Press.

Stolnitz, Jerome (1961) 'On the Significance of Lord Shaftesbury in Modern Aesthetic Theory.' *The Philosophical Quarterly*, Vol. 11: 97–113.

Babette Babich
Nietzsche's Aesthetic Science and Hume's Standard of Taste

> "Aber alles Leben ist Streit um Geschmack und Schmecken!"
> — Nietzsche

Classical Philology as "Aesthetic Science," Styles, and Scholarly Tastes

David Hume foregrounded standardly classical names, like Homer and like Milton in his "Of the Standard of Taste." Where Hume is concerned to raise the question of a standard or measure that would permit one to assess a poet or an author of lasting value, i.e., of the rank of a Homer or Milton, Nietzsche raised the traditional "Homer question" as a question to his own discipline of Classics, in his 1869 inaugural lecture at the University of Basel, "Homer and Classical Philology," asking very literally: what standard does one employ when identfying a poem or a fragment as composed by Homer as author of an ancient text? How do scholars judge or decide such questions of identity, assign textual attributions? Nietzsche adverts to the "taste" of those same classical scholars, arguing that it is by means of subjective taste or judgment that expert authorities determine a text fragment to be Homer's own, relying as they do on a very cultivated if however "subjective taste [Geschmacksrichtung]"[1]. The "science" of aesthetics as Nietzsche speaks of it, qua scholarly subjective affair determines what will and what will not count as Homer.[2] For Nietzsche, to raise the question of the scientific value of such aesthetic science is for this reason a question of taste as it is also an epistemological concern regarding what is subsequently taken to be historical fact or true. We recognize Nietzsche's concern with the status of classical philology *as a science* – the same language that recurs in his "Attempt a Self-Critique" added as a new preface when he republishes his first book on tragedy, underscoring that in that same first book,

---

[1] Friedrich Nietzsche, "Homer und die klassische Philologie," p. 299.
[2] See the section entitled "Nietzsche's Homer Question and Darwin's Origin of Species out of the Spirit of Language" in the author's "Towards a Critical Philosophy of Science: Continental Beginnings and Bugbears, Whigs, and Waterbears," pp. 345–351.

where he also raises the question of Homer's status, that he had been the very first to raise the question of science as a question.

The coincidence of the epistemic with the aesthetic is key for Nietzsche who argues that scholarly discernment is *aesthetic* judgment.³ The connection with Hume⁴ is immediate and just as Hume observes that the passage of time allows us to confirm a successful aesthetic appraisal as successful, Nietzsche similarly invokes the passage of time in the second of his *Untimely Meditations*, "Vom Nutzen und Nachtheil der Historie für das Leben," "On the Uses and Liabilities of History for Life," and in which essay Nietzsche opposes Hegel's understanding of the union of art *and* science as absolute knowledge as Nietzsche explicates Hegel:⁵ "the race is now at its height, for only now does it possess knowledge of itself, only now is it revealed to itself."⁶ For Nietzsche, the achievement defers knowledge and life to an end stage, valuing above all, the view from the end, the perspective of twilight:

> I believe there no dangerous vacillation or transformation of German culture in this century that has not been rendered yet more dangerous by the enormous and to this moment ongoing influence of this philosophy, the Hegelian. Truly, crippling and depressing as the belief is that one is a latecomer of the ages, it must appear however dreadful and devastating

---

3 As Kant observes in a footnote to the *Critique of Pure Reason*, The Germans are the only people who currently make use of the word 'aesthetic' in order to signify what others call the critique of taste. KdrV A21/B36. I will come back to this issue below.

4 In addition to Daniel Breazeale's *Toward a Nihilist Epistemology, Hume and Nietzsche*, see Craig Beam, "Hume and Nietzsche: Naturalists, Ethicists, Anti-Christians." And see Mark T. Conard, "Nietzsche and Hume in the Genealogy and Psychology of Religion." Consider, in addition, Louise Mabille's chapter "Hume on the Use and Abuse of Skepticism for Life," as well as Ivan Broisson, "*Ressentiment* und Wille zur Macht Nietzsche und Hume über Moral- und Religionskritik," and further on to an early essay by Eric Blondel and several general analytic studies as well. See too emphasizing the historical commonalities of Hume's view of morality and Nietzsche's genealogy, David B. Allison, "Nietzsche's Aesthetic Taste for Moral Metacritique." Intriguingly, although Hume is not a reference, Anthony Ludovici, *Nietzsche and Art* follows Humean divisions, attending to the refinements of 'Fine Art' just on the terms of artist, public, and critic.

5 "One has scornfully named history conceived in this Hegelian fashion God's sojourning on the earth, which deity however was himself first created solely by history. This god, however, became transparent and comprehensible interior to the Hegelian crania and is already ascended through all the dialectically possible steps of his evolution up to this very self-revelation: such that for Hegel the highpoint and culmination of the world-process coincided with his own Berlin existence." Nietzsche, *Vom Nutzen und Nachtheil der Historie für das Leben*, § 8, *Kritische Studienausgabe*, [KSA], 1, p. 308.

6 Nietzsche, KSA 1, p. 308. Nietzsche writes here of gnomic significance of Hegelianism for German culture as "einer gewissen sehr berühmten Philosophie." See for a discussion: Babich, "Nietzsche (as) Educator."

when such a belief one day by a bold inversion elevates this latecomer to godhood as the true meaning and aim of all previous events, equating his miserable condition with a consummation of world-history.[7]

There are parallels with Hume's derision of our tendency to ignore the particular phases, powers, constitutions of life for the sake of an ideal springtime, strangely supposed as still to come and in which anything is always 'still possible.'

> And from the dregs of life hope to receive,
> What the first lightly running could not give.[8]

Hume makes a similar observation regarding time and the volatility of enjoyments in his essay, "The Epicurean" – "the roses have lost their hue; the fruit its favour"[9] – as Hume emphasizes nature, the effects of satiation and not less, when it comes to the appetite for love, of the passage of time on the expression of and capacity for the passions. Nietzsche emphasizes the limits of satiety and its coordination with a given physiological constitution in the case of the Italian theorist of sobriety (and long life), Luigi Cornaro.

As with Hume's own writerly style, style is key to Nietzsche's work. Thus David Allison could champion the "New Nietzsche" by foregrounding Jacques Derrida's discussion of Nietzsche's textual or rhetorical "style"[10] and which stylistic emphasis is similarly foregrounded in Alexander Nehamas's more analytically styled and very influential *Life as Literature*.[11]

This reference to style is complicated by Nietzsche's stylistic achievements in language, argued by some such as Gottfried Benn and Hans-Georg Gadamer as

---

7 Nietzsche, KSA 1, p. 308.
8 Cited from Nietzsche, *Vom Nutzen und Nachtheil der Historie für das Leben* ["es sind die, von denen David Hume spöttisch sagt: 'And from the dregs of life hope to receive, / What the first lightly running could not give."], KSA 1, p. 255.
9 Hume places a song in the mouth of Damon, sung to faded roses and wine (among his other examples): "Ye happy youth, he sings, ...deluded mortals, thus to lose your youth, thus to throw away so invaluable a present, to trifle with so perishing a blessing. Contemplate well your recompence. Consider that glory, which so allures your proud hearts, and seduces you with your own praises. It is an echo, a dream, nay the shadow of a dream, dissipated by every wind, and lost by every contrary breath of the ignorant and ill-judging multitude. You fear not that even death itself shall ravish it from you. But behold! while you are yet alive, calumny bereaves you of it; ignorance neglects it; nature enjoys it not; fancy alone, renouncing every pleasure receives this airy recompence, empty and unstable as herself." Hume, "The Epicurean," p. 143.
10 David B. Allison (Ed.), *The New Nietzsche*.
11 Alexander Nehamas, *Life as Literature*. It is relevant perhaps that it is more the question of desire or eros than that of style and taste that bears on Nehamas' later reflection, *Only a Promise of Happiness: The Place of Beauty in a World of Art*.

having "changed" the German language, an achievement not all scholars regard as a "good thing."[12] In addition, and this also matters with respect to Hume's "style," Nietzsche's "stylizing" or "stylization" also signifies exaggeration, misdirection or lying, which also brings in a set of additional issues when comes to political questions regarding Nietzsche and our own standards in reading him.[13] For Nietzsche such questions are epistemological ones as Nietzsche not only encourages us to think about the origins of moral judgments, i.e., to go *beyond* good and evil, but urges us to ask why we seek what we take to be the truth? Why, apart from morality, do we not inquire into the status of the lie, epistemologically, scientifically, speaking?

The Homer Question

What have truth and lie to do with aesthetic questions? Surely the entire point of art is, as Nietzsche also argued, that with art the lie, illusion, deception as such, has a good conscience. Thus, it was as a classical philologist that Nietzsche sought to reflect in the case of Homer on the subjective basis of scholarly attribution as the (individual and authoritative) basis on which classicists distinguish between ancient texts, and in the case of the doing of history, determine dates and (this is the case of Homer) undertake the determinative ascription of a text to a given author, and, beyond the Homer question, to raise the further question as Nietzsche raised it concerning the historical presumptions of doxography, depending as they do on the notion of specific teachings as of suc-

---

12 For an indictment of Nietzsche on these grounds: Heinz Schlaffer, *Das entfesselte Wort: Nietzsches Stil und seiner Folgen*. The point is not without relevance to questions of Hume's own ironic style. And see on Nietzsche's reception the contributions to Ekaterina Polyakova and Yulia Sineokaya (Eds.), *Фридрих Ницше: наследие и проект*. М.: Культурная революция, / *Friedrich Nietzsche: Heritage and Prospects*, including questions of style in Babich, "Nietzsche's Influence and Meaning Today – With Weight on the Sameness of the Eternal Return," pp. 391–406.

13 Tracy B. Strong has made this point in his reflections on rhetoric in Nietzsche, citing Brian Leiter's dismissal of Nietzsche's style owing to what Leiter calls Nietzsche's "penchant for hyperbolic rhetoric and polemics" and hence Nietzsche's tendency to "overstate" his case, as Leiter puts it in his own contribution to Stanford's Internet Encyclopedia of Philosophy. See Strong, "In Defense of Rhetoric; or, How Hard it is to Take a Writer Seriously: The Case of Nietzsche." For a contrasting point of view, see Berel Lang's "Misinterpretation as the Author's Responsibility (Nietzsche's Fascism, For Instance)." Indeed, political scholarly battles some assume to be long finished are by no means concluded – think in the case of the theme of the present volume of the disputes between Hume and Rousseau but also as yet more salient in the case of Hume's essay "Of the Standard of Taste," of Warburton and Hume.

cession or schools, the *diadochai* in philosophy (the assessment that permits the scholar to determine who may be called the student of whom) relevant as this is for ascription of historical precedence and influence.[14]

In his inaugural lecture, Nietzsche's theoretical emphasis on the "so-called Homer question," involves stylistic matters articulated in terms of "personality," arguing that given the limitations of or absence of texts or material foundations, solely discussion of the person (including ancient reports of the same in Diogenes Laërtius and his sources as Nietzsche had investigated the same) survives the refutation of this or that philosophical system or doctrine.[15]

But what do we mean by *personality* in this sense? Does this not seem the quintessential question of taste, a matter that may not be disputed – we can go back to Descartes for this – that is to say: the question of the self, the sovereign constatation of our modern subjectivity?

To avoid such quandaries, today's classical philologists favor those they read authoritatively: this generates today's canon and this canon is even more focused than it was in Nietzsche's day and thus, as received, we read certain ancient Greek philosophers, Plato, Aristotle, and today and increasingly, the Stoics. In addition, there is the turn to the study of ancient cosmology and science, including engineering and architecture (among the more exciting manifestations of this trend). Beyond this, must be considered the increasingly monotone character of philosophy, today almost exclusively analytic as this reflects a dominant or mainstream taste determining what counts (or ought to be counted) as "philosophy" in the academy.[16] To this extent, we read our ancients the way we read our Hume and our Nietzsche – in terms of what we suppose as their "arguments" and it is on these terms, again: as we suppose them to be articulated, that we evaluate what we then suppose them to be saying.

Perhaps in consequence, some have found it difficult to read Nietzsche's texts. In particular, some find it hard to follow his discussion of Homer's "*personality.*" By contrast, there has been considerable discussion of Homer's *agon* (especially with respect to Hesiod, where the contest seems closer to one David Hume would appreciate) by contrast with the traditional *Homer question*

---

14 Nietzsche has notes on this theme in each of his lectures but especially in his lecture on Anaxagoras in the courses he gave on early Greek philosophy at the University of Basel over a period of seven years, *Die vorplatonische Philosophen*, KGW, II/4, pp. 207–362. Cf., too, Nietzsche's lecture notes for his course on the succession or διαδοχαί of Preplatonic philosophers, Winter Semester 1873–1874, KGW, II/4, pp. 615–632.
15 Nietzsche, *Philosophy in the Tragic Age of the Greeks* in KSA, 1, p. 801; cf. p. 803.
16 See for a broader discussion Babich, "Are They Good? Are They Bad? Double Hermeneutics and Citation in Philosophy, Asphodel and Alan Rickman, Bruno Latour and the 'Science Wars.'"

in Nietzsche's inaugural lecture in Basel articulated with respect to the existence/nonexistence of the historical poet himself (the personality) by contrast with the creative spirit of a people (the folk origination of poetry).[17]

A similar distraction is at work when one approaches "the subject" of the poet (especially the lyric poet), in the context of the larger overall stylistic contrast or contest between epic and lyric poetry and thus the relation between Homer and Archilochus as Nietzsche associates these two names in his first book on tragedy.[18] On the face of it, this seems not unlike Hume's original comparison in his "Of the Standard of Taste" between Homer and Fenélon (ST 205) but, Nietzsche argues, and this is the ultimate point to be sure of Hume's own project, that it is *scientific*, that is to say, *philological* attribution that is at stake in such standard disputation concerning scholarly esteem: which texts are to be attributed to Homer, which not? Given Nietzsche's search for an 'aesthetic science' that may be counted as a science, as Nietzsche refers to this in just such Kantian terms at the start of his *Die Geburt der Tragödie aus dem Geist der Musik* [*The Birth of Tragedy out of the Spirit of Music*], it may be argued that a similarly 'scientific' sensibility likewise animates Hume's search for a standard. For Nietzsche's part, speaking of the conflict between the sexes – the allusion is to Hölderlin – Nietzsche will also foreground, and this adds complexity, the pleonastic nature of aesthetics in the realm of "aesthetische Wissenschaft [aesthetic science]."[19]

Hume argues in "Of a Standard of Taste" that we generally require such a standard and not merely for the practical or economic purposes of estimating a likely future literary success in the realm of theater or poetry (or, indeed wine futures). Although Hume's examples are largely literary ones, they may be extended to art as such, painting and sculpture and architecture and Hume himself highlights more subjective public signifiers of taste, with his parable

---

17 See Friedrich Nietzsche, "Homer und die klassische Philologie," p. 290. For discussions of the notion of the contest (less then, a matter of Homer himself), see Christa Davis Acampora, *Contesting Nietzsche* and compare Yunus Tuncel, *Agon in Nietzsche* and Larry Hatab, "Prospects for a Democratic Agon," and highlighting the militaristic force of such disputes, the contributions to Herman Siemens and James Pearson (Eds.) *Conflict and Contest in Nietzsche's Philosophy*.
18 See further on Archilochus (including further literature), Babich, "Nietzsches Lyrik. Archilochos, Musik, Metrik" and, in English, "Nietzsche's Archilochus."
19 This is characterized in Nietzsche's inaugural lecture by invoking classical philology's "centauric" nature. See Nietzsche, "Homer und die klassische Philologie," p. 289.

of wine, including one's gustatory powers of discrimination (judgment) or "delicacy" in resolution and appreciation of fine distinctions.[20]

Nietzsche had argued that the expert "distinguishes" works of art or literary texts by identifying *stylistic differences*, in order, morphologically, to locate poetic or plastic works historically: thus classified, the historian can date coins, temple offerings, cylindrical seals, and so on. Stylistic differences similarly permit characterizations in kind: poetic or religious or philosophical and historical, etc., and yet monumental discoveries like the Derveni Krater (along with the much more discussed Derveni papyrus) blurs past identifications leading to conflicts that can upset scholarship for decades.[21]

Stylistic questions of taste may thus be read as a *critique* of scholarly judgment and to this extent Nietzsche's Homer question goes back to Friedrich August Wolf and, before Wolf, to the philological tradition of the Hellenistic Greeks in their Alexandrian "grammarian" twilight.[22] Nietzsche frames the question thus: Was Homer a product (or construct) of scholarly taste, a figure created

---

[20] See Steven Shapin, "The Sciences of Subjectivity" and see too Deborah Gigante's broader, *Taste: A Literary History*.

[21] If traditional distinctions are thus questioned such "monumental" witness changes the discipline. "Text philology," à la Ritschl is problematic enough but physical discoveries compound those difficulties. I refer here to the gold funerary leaves found in Thurii, Hipponium, Thessaly, and Crete (and even Geoffrey S. Kirk, John E. Raven and Martin Schofield, in their very traditionally classical account in *The Presocratic Philosophers*, discuss the Hipponium text in their first chapter on orphic tradition [p. 29 ff.]). For a discussion of context regarding the difficulty of specifying the "fragment," not unrelated to some of Nietzsche's own concerns in his own reflections on Preplatonic philosophy, see Charles Kahn's *Anaximander and the Origins of Greek Cosmology* as well as Catharine Rowan Osborne's important *Rethinking Early Greek Philosophy*. But note Richard Janko's assessment of the recalcitrance of scholarly habits when he notes the silencing of alternate readings in the production of the definitive transcription of the Derveni papyrus: "By using a simple but bizarre expedient, P. and T. have contrived not to acknowledge that scholars other than themselves have toiled to reconstruct this text. They include no apparatus criticus!" Janko concludes that the authors "have chosen to benefit neither from the scholarship of the past decade nor from recent advances in reconstructing and reading carbonized papyri." Janko, "Review of *The Derveni Papyrus*." In his own philological reflections Nietzsche argues against drawing conclusions of a positive kind on the basis of no evidence.

[22] As Nietzsche explains: "The zenith of the historical-literary studies of the Greeks, and hence also of their point of greatest importance – i.e., the 'Homer question'—was reached in the age of the Alexandrian grammarians." Nietzsche, "Homer und die klassische Philologie," p. 291. This regime began with a return to the ancient institution of a contest between Homer and Hesiod and thence and also a return to the origination of the texts themselves, instituting philology as such, which may, as Nietzsche reminds us, be dated to the reign of Pisistratus, as it was then that the oral compositions associated with Homer were first "gathered together" in "bookish form."

by selecting fragments, thus attributing them to his "authorship" under his name, or was he an individual whose originating achievements compelled the attention to his name that would endure over millennia, such that, quite as Hume, writes the "same *Homer* who pleased at *Athens* and *Rome* two thousand years ago, is still admired at *Paris* and at *London* (ST 213)?

Hume's question concerns this very standard durability, such that (and this very historical aesthetic invariance under temporal and cultural transformations is the confirmation of taste) "All the changes of climate, government, religion, and language, have not been able to obscure his glory" (ST 213). The Homer question for Nietzsche is not unrelated to the way he distinguishes the "pure or unmix't" thinkers among the Preplatonic philosophers (as opposed to the more complex amalgam of influences as these are represented or declared by Plato, according to Nietzsche).[23] By contrast, note the negative value of Hume's esteem for Shakespeare contra Warburton's valorization, as Hume criticizes the achievements to be ascribed to Shakespeare's invention:

> If Shakespeare be considered as a MAN born in a rude age and educated in the lowest manner, without any instruction either from the world or from books, he may be regarded as a prodigy; if represented as a POET capable of furnishing a proper entertainment to a refined or intelligent audience, we must abate much of this eulogy.[24]

Framing what still plays a role in the ongoing and provocative Shakespeare authorship question, where Hume appeals to taste, Nietzsche answers by attributing authorship (in a letter he writes to Cosima Wagner), not to Shakespeare but to Lord Bacon. The parallel is relevant as Nietzsche, speaking of Homer, invokes a similarly Humean convention of genial individuality to argue on these terms that Homer, the individual, the genial poet, the personality, the man, "could in no wise be the first of his kind."[25]

The question for Nietzsche is less the historiological contest between *folk poetry* or *individual poets* than Hume's question of aesthetic esteem, as Shakespeare may be accounted a "prodigy" given his achievements just if his origins are "rude," that is, if, as Hume reflects he was indeed (*qua* Shakespeare Shakespeare) "educated in the lowest manner," Nietzsche observes with respect to

---

23 "Plato ist der erste großartige Mischcharacter sowohl in seiner Philosophie als als philos. Typus." Nietzsche, KGW II/4, p. 214.
24 Hume, *The History of England, from the Invasion of Julius Caesar to the Revolution in 1688*, Vol II, p. 249.
25 Nietzsche, "Homer und die klassische Philologie," p. 281.

Homer that "poetic genius may not create folk poetry" to the extent that the sheer notion of 'folk poetry' is itself already a traditional aesthetic judgment.[26]

The critical is the heart of Nietzsche's epistemological rigor, arguing that scholarship turns out to be dedicated less to discovery than to *reducing* the *unknown* to the *known*. The result, as Nietzsche writes in *Twilight of the Idols*, is a sclerotic science: "First basic principle: any explanation is better than none."[27] The reading Nietzsche offers, after his own teacher, Friedrich Ritschl, is a hermeneutic one, where critique, Ritschl emphasizes, follows hermeneutics. Thus the connection to Hermes, to whom, as Nietzsche notes, classical philology as a science must be dedicated: not the 'muses' and still less the Erinyes (the 'furies' or 'kindly ones'). As noted in the introduction above, Hermes is the "messenger of the gods."[28] If Hermes matters to Hume, it is not only in terms of his deathbed reading of Lucian, as the one to whom one gives what excuses one has to give (in addition to Clotho, and, ultimately, to Rhadamanthus), but stylistically, if we may recall the Celtic Heracles/Ogmios in Lucian, rhetorically relevant when it comes to a universal grammar, a "standard."

Hume and Nietzsche – and Kant

"Naturwissenschaft als eine
Symptomatologie —"
— Nietzsche, KGW VIII/1, 2 [69], S. 90.

Beyond Hume's references to Homer in "Of the Standard of Taste," Hume's original critique of causality[29] inspires Nietzsche's own account of causality.[30] Thus

---

26 Nietzsche, "Homer und die klassische Philologie," p. 276. Nietzsche marvels here that with this question one discovers "for the first time the wondrous capacity of the people's soul" ("Homer und die klassische Philologie," p. 291; cf. pp. 294–95 and pp. 298 ff), later asking what led the people to abandon this genial capacity.
27 Nietzsche, *Götzen-Dämmerung*, "Die vier grossen Irrthümer," § 5 [1888], KSA 6, p. 93
28 Nietzsche, "Homer und die klassische Philologie," p. 305. Nietzsche thus resuscitates the Homer question by directing it contra the philologists. And this is the primary reason that the classicist William Arrowsmith was so concerned to have his discipline engage Nietzsche. See Arrowsmith's "Nietzsche on Classics and Classicists." With few exceptions, classicists have not responded to this "challenge" in either Nietzsche's original or, more latterly, Arrowsmith's spirit.
29 "I have found that such an object has always been attended with such an effect, and I foresee, that other objects, which are, in appearance, similar, will be attended with similar effects. I shall allow, if you please, that the one proposition may justly be inferred from the other; I know, in fact, that it always is inferred. But if you insist that the inference is made by a

Nietzsche contends with explicit reference to Hume, almost as if the divisions of today's analytic-continental distinction in professional, university philosophy were at stake, that "Kant made the epistemological skepticism of the English *possible* for the Germans," suggesting that "Locke and Hume were in themselves [*an sich*] too luminous, too clear, that means, as judged according to German instinctive values: 'too superficial'."[31]

---

chain of reasoning, I desire you to produce that reasoning." David Hume, *An Enquiry Concerning Human Understanding* (1772).

30 While Raoul Richter, Fritz Mauthner and Hans Vaihinger already made this observation which is patent enough in Nietzsche more than a hundred years ago, in English Arthur Danto points out that Nietzsche's notion of the concept of causality is "very much like Hume's." Danto, *Nietzsche as Philosopher*, p. 75. Yet no sooner do scholars begin to talk about Hume and Nietzsche than Hume's discussion of causation tends to be excluded or minimized, perhaps to avoid the caricature, as one scholar described it, of "Hume as hard-nosed protological positivist and hero of 'analytic' philosophy." Peter Kail, "Nietzsche and Hume: Naturalism and Explanation," here p. 5. The reference "hard-nosed" echoes David Miller's characterization of Hume in his "Being an Absolute Skeptic." Kail is largely concerned, as his title indicates, with the thorny – to analytic Nietzscheans – question of whether Nietzsche is a naturalist and does not make much of Hume on causation, thus he presents, as caricature, a description of Nietzsche (heavens to Betsy) as "antiscience, a "postmodernist" and doyen of "Continental' philosophy." Kail usefully mentions some of the literature on Nietzsche and Hume, leaving out the one monograph on Nietzsche and Hume by Daniel Breazeale, cited above, *Toward a Nihilist Epistemology: Hume and Nietzsche*. Peter Bornedal offers another useful reading of Nietzsche and Hume in his "A Silent World: Nietzsche's Radical Realism: World Sensation Language." For a specific discussion of causation from an analytic perspective (which means that much of this very useful article is dedicated to explaining Nietzsche's failure to develop a "revised account of causality along the lines of ... regularity theory," see Peter Poellner, "Causation and Force in Nietzsche," here p. 291. Here Poellner is more concerned with Boscovich than Hume. On force Reinhard Löw remains useful along with Reinhold Grimm. I cite both scholars in my study of *Nietzsche's Philosophy of Science*.

31 Nietzsche, KGW VIII/2, 9 [3], p. 4. The question concerning Nietzsche's acquaintance with Hume is not unlike the industry that asserts that Nietzsche never read Kant while arguing that Nietzsche read shelves and shelves of secondary literature (including literature on Kant) in order to sidestep the impression that he might have read Kant. I maintain that Nietzsche read pretty much the Kant most scholars in Nietzsche's day had read or (this at very least) the Kant my students and colleagues have read. Scholars like to claim that Nietzsche did not read Kant and they do this, because, shades of the influence Kant tells us that Hume had on his critical philosophy, Nietzsche does not take the conclusions from Kant one prefers to take today. Nietzsche reads Kant as dangerously skeptical and precipitously nihilistic, rather in the spirit of most of the scholarship of the early 19th century. In this spirit, so Nietzsche contends, speaking of the categories of "Zweck," Einheit," Sein" (KGW VIII/2, 11 [91], 1, p. 290), that "the belief in the categories of reason [*Glaube an die Vernunft-Kategorien*] is the cause of nihilism," to the extent that "we have measured the valued of the world un categories which refer to a purely invented [*eine rein fingirte*] world." (KGW VIII/2, 11 [91], 2, p. 291) Nietzsche's "Critique of

In the *Prolegemena*, Kant tells us that, via David Hume, what "woke" him from his "dogmatic slumber" was the question of causality as such:

> Hume proceeded primarily from a single but important concept of metaphysics, namely, that of *the connection of cause and effect* ..., and he challenged reason, which here pretends to have generated this concept in her womb, to give him an account of by what right she thinks that something could be so constituted that, if it is posited, something else must necessarily also be posited thereby; for this is what the concept of cause says.[32]

As Nietzsche puts it "Hume doubted the legitimacy of causality altogether,"[33] whereby Kant's contribution, as Nietzsche argued, would be to rescue the functionality of causation, which was the very service of his critical philosophy, but which nevertheless entailed that Kant placed "a monstrous question mark after the concept of 'causality'."[34]

As Nietzsche argues here, seeming to anticipate P.F. Strawson, Kant delimited the sensible realm within which the concept of causality "can" make sense, adding that "even now we are not done with the fixing of such limits."[35] However, as Nietzsche also reminds us in his notes, Hume explained causality by means of habit or "custom [*Gewohnheit*]," whereby, as Nietzsche parallels the point, "Kant with great calm said 'it is a capacity [*es ist ein Vermögen*]."[36] At issue is hardly that Kant disproves (or disagrees) with Hume: instead, and much rather: he undertakes to rescue the concept of causation and yet, as Nietzsche argues, "Causality escapes us: to assume a direct connection between two ideas, as logic does – that is the consequence of the grossest and coarsest observation."[37]

Nihilism," as he puts it betrays the era in which Nietzsche happened to have lived. What is also almost certainly the case, and we do well to reflect on this as our appetite for reading decreases with our passion for networked or digital 'scholarship,' there was by any standard more reading done in Nietzsche's day than scholars seem able to imagine doing today. And as one's temper or appetite for reading varies from person to person, this was especially the case for Nietzsche who reminds of the need for slow reading, a *lento* which presupposes, both leisure and depth, or what he called philology, but such liberality, such freedom is the ancient meaning of scholarship. See further Babich, "Nietzsche's Critique: Reading Kant's Critical Philosophy."

32 Kant, *Prolegomena to Any Future Metaphysics*, 4, 257; 7.
33 Nietzsche, *Die fröhliche Wissenschaft*, §357, KSA 3, p. 598.
34 Nietzsche, *Die fröhliche Wissenschaft*, §357, KSA 3, p. 598.
35 Nietzsche, *Die fröhliche Wissenschaft*, §357, KSA 3, p. 598.
36 Nietzsche, KSA 11, 34 [82], p. 445.
37 Nietzsche, KGW VIII/2, 11 [113], p. 295.

Hume distinguishes between "relations of ideas, and matters of fact."[38] And relations of ideas include "the sciences of geometry, algebra, and arithmetic," including in sum "every affirmation which is either intuitively or demonstratively certain."[39] Hume bluntly explains what counts as a matter of fact, which he specifies as "the second objects of human reason," adding that, by contrast with relations of ideas, matters of fact "are not ascertained in the same manner; nor is our evidence of their truth, however great, of a like nature."[40] On Nietzsche's reading, Kant does not resolve the problem Hume raises here and the trouble we have with contradiction as such, that is to say: "to affirm and to deny one and the same thing" is only a matter, as Nietzsche puts it, of "'subjective experience'." Thereby, as Nietzsche emphasizes, "no sort of necessity is articulated, *but only an incapacity* [*ein Nicht-Vermögen*]."[41] The principle of contradiction in this sense, which Nietzsche interprets as a sentence that either assumes its content in advance, taking it for granted ("just as if he *already* knew the same from another source") or else as one might read it, partly as one is inclined to read Parmenides, father of logic, who tells us what can and what cannot be said (and here Nietzsche plays with moral modalities): "that is to say: a contradictory predicate *ought* not be attributed," from which it follows that the principle of contradiction cannot be a "*criterium of truth* but rather an *imperative* concerning that which *should be counted as true.*"[42]

In a parallel to Mach, Nietzsche observes that "our belief in things is the presupposition for our belief in logic. The A of logic is like the atom, a subsequent construct of the 'thing.'"[43] Hume's point as we recall, and this argument we recognize as recurring in Kant and his demand, by contrast, for apodeictic certainty – that is: Hume's necessity – and matters of fact are sheerly contingent, what is more, as Hume argues, the "contrary of every matter of fact is still possible, because it can never imply a contradiction, and is conceived by the mind with the same facility and distinctness, as if ever so conformable to reality."[44] Nietzsche takes the same kind of reasoning "There is no contradiction: we only have the concept of contradiction derived from that of logic – from which we've falsely

---

[38] Hume, *Enquiry Concerning Human Understanding*, pp. 25–26.
[39] Hume, *Enquiry Concerning Human Understanding*, pp. 25–26.
[40] Hume, *Enquiry Concerning Human Understanding*, pp. 25–26.
[41] Nietzsche, KSA 11:9 [97], p. 389.
[42] Nietzsche, KSA 11:9 [97], p. 389.
[43] Nietzsche, KSA 11:9 [97], p. 389.
[44] Hume, *Enquiry Concerning Human Understanding*. Sec. IV, Part 1.

translated it into 'things.'"⁴⁵ In this sense, for Nietzsche: "necessity is in no wise a matter of fact, but [only] an interpretation."⁴⁶

Where I like to broach this point modestly, with reference to the ineluctable contingency of the breakfast cereal, say, as I might suppose this to be on hand among the other contents of the cupboard (which cereal I might be counting on eating tomorrow, with or without spouses, room-mates, and mice to interfere), Hume's example is of apocalyptic, cosmic proportions:

> That the sun will not rise tomorrow is no less intelligible a proposition, and implies no more contradiction, than the affirmation, that it will rise. We should in vain, therefore, attempt to demonstrate its falsehood. Were it demonstratively false, it would imply a contradiction, and could never be distinctly conceived by the mind.⁴⁷

This is great stuff – and there is here no space, alas, to talk about the most fascinating search in cosmological physics to date, the hunt for neutrinos, including the theoretical multiplication of neutrinos, levelling up with different sorts (thereby increasing rates of detection using the same data and, much more significantly, as this is a non-spurious issue, building an array of neutrino detectors of various kinds across the globe, such that this constitutes a physics growth industry in Japan, China, Germany, and of course CERN etc.), and just such puzzles are, at least in part, why we love philosophy. We are also in a bit of hot water at the same time as Hume ties this to causality, very problematic when it comes to modern science and the ideal of explicating, predicting, and controlling what we can of the world (or, maybe, just the weather).

Matters of fact are contingent matters of experience and not necessity. Hence Hume argues that the knowledge of the causal relation is never "in any instance, attained by reasonings *a priori*, but arises entirely from experience."⁴⁸ Ad hoc. And ad hoc, empirical as it is, is pretty weak ale if what we want is certain knowledge.

> Were any object presented to us, and were we required to pronounce concerning the effect, which will result from it, without consulting past observation, after what manner, I beseech you, must the mind proceed in this operation? It must invent or imagine some event, which it ascribes to the object as its effect, and it is plain that this invention must be entirely arbitrary. The mind can never possibly find the effect in the supposed cause, by the most accurate scrutiny and examination. For the effect is totally different from the cause, and con-

---

45 Nietzsche, KSA 11:9 [91], p. 384.
46 Nietzsche, KSA 11:9 [91], p. 383.
47 Hume, *Enquiry Concerning Human Understanding*. Sec. IV, Part 1.
48 Hume, *Enquiry Concerning Human Understanding*. Sec. IV, Part 1.

sequently can never be discovered in it. Motion in the second billiard ball is a quite distinct event from the motion in the first, nor is there anything in the one to suggest the smallest hint of the other.⁴⁹

Not content with this, Hume takes on gravity:

> A stone or piece of metal raised into the air, and left without any support, immediately falls: but to consider the matter a priori. Is there anything we discover in this situation which can beget the idea of a downward, rather than an upward, or any other motion, in the stone or metal?⁵⁰

We assume that the future will resemble the past but, as Hume argues and it is this connection that will take us back to taste, it is no more than custom that leads us to assume that similar events will have similar consequences and for our empirical predictions we count on habit not reason. As Hume reminds us, *looks like, sounds like* is not the best bet in every case, as he puts it "Resemblance is the most fertile source of error; and indeed there are few mistakes in reasoning which do not borrow largely from that origin."⁵¹

Bread and Nourishment: On Nietzsche's Cornaro and the Physiology of Taste

Physiology was Hume's reference when he invoked the nourishing properties of bread in a person's life experience in the past and as bread in the future might or might not have the same properties for the same person. Bread and its nutritional properties seem proportionate or at least innocuous references considered from Hume's day to Nietzsche's day to our own. If such "properties" are also variously interpreted by the fashions of nutrition science, what is certain is that that science of nutrition seems to have made little progress since the days of either Nietzsche or Hume. Thus current nutritional theory would seem to corroborate the claim argued by the French "physiologist of taste," Anthelme Brillat-Savarin as he argues that no matter whether solid or liquid, consuming bread (starch) leads to weight gain: "All animals that are fed on food become fat whether

---

49 Hume, *Enquiry Concerning Human Understanding*. Sec. IV, Part 1.
50 Hume, *Enquiry Concerning Human Understanding*. Sec. IV, Part 1.
51 Hume, *A Treatise of Human Nature*, p. 61.

they will or not. Man is subject to the same law."[52] Brillat-Savarin quickly adds what we may call the cake corollary, as Atkins or paleo diet fans will also note: "Farinaceous food has a much quicker effect when mixed with sugar," observing further that "Farinaceous matter (grain) is not the less fattening when absorbed in liquids, as in beer. Beer drinking nations may boast the biggest stomachs" and adding that "Another cause of corpulency is too much sleep and a want of sufficient exercise."[53]

The skeptical Hume, is not writing his own physiology of taste and he has other concerns than the weight gain we can see in the difference between the portraits of Hume (young) and Hume (portly):[54]

> The bread, which I formerly ate, nourished me: that is, a body of such sensible qualities was, at that time, endued with such secret powers; but does it follow, that other bread must also nourish me at another time, and that like sensible qualities must always be attended with like secret powers? The consequence seems nowise necessary.[55]

Hume foregrounds the betrayal built into food and its seemingly occult properties: food that serves one well at one point in time, can prove less nourishing and, given the risks of diabetes and other glutinous afflictions, even fatal at another. Bread is thus a classically duplicitous food, good for you *and* bad for you, like the sweet/bitter that Hume despairs of resolving into "the real sweet or the real bitter" (ST 209): the staff of life and yet the same thing that can induce pancreatic and other troubles especially if one adds one's preferred accoutrements, in whatever combination of fats and sugars.

In *The Philosopher's Diet*, Richard Watson draws on important points in order to manage to side with then-current nutrition science (not likely utterly ac-

---

52 Jean Anthelme Brillat Savarin, *The Handbook of Dining; or Corpulency and Leanness Scientifically Considered*. [Brillat-Savarin's "Physiologie Du Gout" is cited on the title page of the translation], p. 105, and indeed this translation is taken from the *Physiology of Taste*. Brillat-Savarin notes this as the second and principle cause of corpulency the first being a matter of natural physiological tendencies in particular individuals, of which a pug or upturned nose seems to be a sign.
53 Jean Anthelme Brillat Savarin, *The Handbook of Dining; or Corpulency and Leanness Scientifically Considered*, p. 106. The effects as Brillat-Savarin points out are by no means immediate, a delayed efficacy compounded by a 'natural' (today we prefer to say genetic but by substituting genetic for natural we have added nothing to the explanation) 'tendency' to gain weight. Brillat-Savarin's example is the (sexist) observation that the rounded cheeks and charming dimples in the young lady one is courting may have a very different aspect sooner rather than later in life.
54 This has been cited in the introduction above, but see, again, for illustration, David Fordham, "Allan Ramsay's Enlightenment: Or, Hume and the Patronizing Portrait."
55 Hume, *An Enquiry Concerning Human Understanding*, II.

curately) in a more than incidentally off-the-cuff sentence to explain of Hume that: "In his twenties he had a skeptical crisis, wrote one of the classics of Western philosophy (*A Treatise of Human Nature*), gained 60 pounds in six weeks to becomes a fat jolly fellow for the rest of his life." As Watson goes on to insist, "Hume would surely maintain that the likeliest cause for weight gain is not a sluggish metabolism but the total intake of food."[56] Watson is wrong, despite the bald plausibility of the notion (the calories-in/calories out theory of weight gain), bread is not quite in the same calorie categoric as one of Hume's other favorite foods, the oyster which he famously consumed in great numbers with Adam Smith, in the eponymously named Edinburgh club. Thus to cite nutrition researchers, "although in theoretical terms a calorie is a calorie, in practice this is not the case."[57]

Hume is by no means as absolute as Watson, observing in "Of Suicide" (one of the texts cut and replaced with "Of the Standard of Taste"), but a bit more sensitive, adverting to a modest *vanitas* that points to more complexity than simple causality: "the lives of men are shortened or extended by the smallest accident of air or diet, sunshine or tempest."[58] Thus "A hair, a fly, an insect is able to destroy this mighty being whose life is of such importance."[59] Thus Hume argues that in great scheme of things, suicide makes no difference from one perspective (that of the universe), while making all the difference from the smaller perspective (that is the point of view of the individual).[60]

At issue is not that these differences make no difference whatsoever in terms of causation but rather with respect to the ultimate terms of blame or dietary prohibition. And the focus here being nutrition, it may be useful to note that what I have elsewhere characterized as Nietzsche's "eco-physiology"[61] includes en-

---

56 Richard A. Watson, *The Philosopher's Diet: How to Lose Weight & Change the World*, p. 67.
57 John Hollis and Rick Mattes, "Are All Calories Created Equal? Emerging Issues in Weight Management."
58 Hume, *Essays On Suicide, And The Immortality Of The Soul, Ascribed To The Late David Hume, Esq., Never before published. With Remarks, intended as an Antidote to the Poison contained in these Performances, By The Editor. To Which Is Added, Two Letters On Suicide, From Rosseau's* Eloisa, p. 8.
59 Hume, *Essays On Suicide, And The Immortality Of The Soul*, p. 11.
60 "When I shall be dead, the principles of which I am composed will still perform their part in the universe, and will be equally useful in the grand fabrick, as when they composed this individual creature. The difference to the whole will be no greater than betwixt my being in a chamber and in the open air. The one change is of more importance to me than the other; but not more so to the universe." Hume, *Essays On Suicide, And The Immortality Of The Soul*, pp. 16–17.
61 Babich, *Nietzsche's Philosophy of Science*, and, for a later, revised edition, *Nietzsche's Wissenschaftsphilosophie*, see especially Chapter Three.

gagement with the lived world, bodily as Hume speaks of it in fine detail (the "hair" that can have lethal effect) but also as Nietzsche interpreted his own 19th-century scientific physiology of nutrition, the basis of which remains scientifically influential, as we read in Watson's account of *The Philosopher's Diet*, to this very day.

What makes Nietzsche more interesting than the conventional Watson, and this despite the century of difference between them, is that Nietzsche would seem to have anticipated the development of physiology less as a given or already determined science than as a 'future' science to be differentiated in accord with further research and with respect to each physiological type or individual and dependent in addition on a range of environmental factors.[62] As Hume points to the nefarious complex of dependent questions in his reflections on vulnerability as in his reflections on both the conditions for taste (delicacy, critical reception), what Watson left out in his quick account of the circumstances in which Hume made his spectacular weight gain was both his transition from youth to maturity (one's twenties can be a time for this, for others this takes place in one's thirties and so on) which changes one's metabolism, the three years in France (age 23 to 27), a part of which was spent in considerable abstemiousness, as prefatory to the sedentary occupation that is writing, producing a prodigious weight gain in a relatively short time: six weeks. It is painful and sobering to note, on the other hand, that Hume would lose even more weight in approximately the same length of time at the end of his life.

As Hume writes in "On the Immortality of the Soul":

> The weakness of the body and that of the mind in infancy are exactly proportioned, their vigour in manhood, their sympathetic disorder in sickness; their common gradual decay in old age. The step further seems unavoidable; their common dissolution in death. The last symptoms which the mind discovers are disorder, weakness, insensibility, and stupidity, the fore-runners of its annihilation. The farther progress of the same causes encreasing, the same effects totally extinguish it.[63]

To develop a science of this all-too-human, bodily condition, Nietzsche sought a specialized science of-and-for the specific individual, a science which, to be

---

[62] For Nietzsche, who wrote about the relation between metabolism and perception drawing on then current physiology and psychology to do so, biologists and medical scientists were charged to consider the individual in all its ineffable manifestation as such, in terms of a multifarious variety of types (and I note that such an emphasis was characteristic of 19th century science) rather than as contemporary sciences focus on genetic specification, numerical assays, statistically calculated in terms of general typology.

[63] Hume, *Essays On Suicide, And The Immortality Of The Soul*, p. 34.

a science, would have to be adjusted from moment to moment, or at least day to day, in terms of a particular regime regarding activity and dietetics. Nietzsche's attention to the condition of decadence is very much a part of this, as is his reading of Socrates and not less of Epicurus and indeed as we shall see of Cornaro's theory of diet and life-extension. Today, when it comes to such dietetic science, it is not as if we lack such all together, given applied or sports physiology, a science limited because the concern is less the health or flourishing of the individual than a very specific and often very short-term matter of performance.[64]

But apart from sports (and to a certain extent, experimental animal physiology and research undertaken for the food industry), the specificity of Nietzsche's demands do not correspond to current nutritional science as this follows *more* rather than less *generalization*, expressed, so common is this, by the catch phrase favored by medical advice: *individual results may vary*, often applied in place of reviewing the specific effects of medication, or nutrition or even nutrition *and* exercise for any given individual. Nietzsche, who arguably thought more of science's promise than might have been justified, anticipated a well-articulated *science* dedicated to studying the interaction between nutrition and one's environment over time along with one's specific constitution. In its place, we have a generalized nutrition science, which to be sure varies from country to country, albeit usually deferring to the US or the UK,[65] standardized such that a medical practitioner merely need allow only for body weight, in order to argue that the same food value (or drug) might be imagined to suit all physiological or metabolic types.

Just this conventional habit is of course increasingly recognized (this is in theory, if not in practice) as scientifically, methodologically problematic. On the basis of such generalizations, extant scientific studies almost universally equated not only different male types but men and women. Thus critics challenge that women (and children and the elderly) are in effect treated in the medical realm (for want of anything like the comprehensive range of differential

---

64 I should add that Nietzsche wanted this science to cover the course of a lifetime, youth, maturity, age and death and to include particular geographic loci in terms of health for each individual, considered across the seasons as well. And this too is a very 19th century idea of the charge or responsibility of physiological science as a science.

65 A number of authors have written on related topics. See for a range of references Babich, *Nietzsche's Philosophy of Science*, pp. 77–134 as well as the reflections of Graham Parkes and Gary Shapiro in addition to Peter Sloterdijk, Jacques Derrida, Friedrich Kittler, Greg Moore, Heinrich Schiperges, Ric Brown, Alphonso Lingis, etc., etc.

studies Nietzsche had imagined would be needed) as so many cases of the standardized adult male.⁶⁶

Nietzsche, pointing to typological metabolic differences, argued contra the general rule of simple caloric restriction, countering the wisdom of Cornaro's *Sobriety*, that some, like the "birdlike Cornaro," might thrive, others not.

For Nietzsche, this constitutional difference raised the question of causality because as, he argues, Cornaro's theory inverts the direction of causality:

> Everybody knows Cornaro's famous book in which he recommends a meager diet for a long and happy life – a virtuous life, too. Few books have been read so widely; even now thousands of copies are sold in England every year. I do not doubt that scarcely any book (except the Bible) has done as much harm, has shortened as many lives, as this well intentioned oddity. Why? Because Cornaro mistakes the effect for the cause. The worthy Italian thought his diet was the cause of his long life, whereas the precondition for a long life, the extraordinary slowness of his metabolism, was the cause of his slender diet. He was not free to eat little or much; his frugality was not a matter of "free will" – he made himself sick when he ate more. But whoever has a rapid metabolism not only does well to eat properly, but needs to. A scholar in our time, with his rapid consumption of nervous energy, would simply destroy himself on Cornaro's diet. *Crede experto.*⁶⁷

In this passage, Nietzsche argues that even the usual Humean *post hoc, ergo propter hoc* is itself complicated in human perception through the complications of memory and desire and not less through prejudice and projection, to conscious intentionality and will. Thus by concluding as Luigi Cornaro did that his spare diet was *the* cause of his long life, Nietzsche argues that "Cornaro mistakes the effect for the cause."

As Cornaro goes, so do we all, and Watson similarly argues in this fashion in his diagnosis of Hume's corpulence. Thus, and no matter whether we do or not diet, we are inclined to mistake the effect for the cause. Thus it is common to find individuals supposing themselves in need of some kind or other physical transformation to imagine that by force of will they can resolve to "get back" into shape (by eating/drinking/smoking less, etc.). But such individuals are like Cornaro, oblivious, Nietzsche would argue, to the wide range of other factors involved in addition to 'force of will.' These other factors are (often) ill-understood

---

[66] See F. A. Arain et al., "Sex/gender medicine. The biological basis for personalized care in cardiovascular medicine," E. Ortona, et al., "Redox State, Cell Death and Autoimmune Diseases: A Gender Perspective," as well as the contributions to Flavia Franconi (Ed.), *La salute della donna. Un approccio di genere*, etc.

[67] Nietzsche, *Götzendämmerung*, KSA 6 pp. 88–89.. Cited in what follows as TI, *The Four Great Errors*, §1. Nietzsche is referring to Luigi Cornaro's *Trattato de la Vita Sobria* [Discourses on the Life of Sobriety] (1558), see Louis Cornaro, *The Art of Living Long*.

physiological differences between individuals (nationality, body type, gender), emotions, disposition, the quality of food consumed (a calorie is not a calorie, some are fats, some are proteins, some carbs are better than other carbs), the role of hormones at different ages of life, insulin levels, etc., and as Hume himself reliably observed, the overall difference age makes, a difference itself only adding to the range of differences. Thus, what makes the most difference when it comes to health is not body weight per se but youth as such. Here we recall that the twenty-three year old Hume had an advantage over the twenty-seven year old, to which may be added his earlier lifetime of Scots foodstuffs as opposed to the more refined French fare he enjoyed abroad.[68]

The problem with causal thinking for Nietzsche is that we begin by thinking that we already know what counts as a cause. But, Nietzsche asks here, "from whence did we derive our knowledge," or, and here he speaks very like Hume, "more precisely our belief that we possessed this knowledge?"[69] For Nietzsche this is the basis of the same problem of the will qua immediately given that still exercises so much effort in philosophy: "We believed ourselves to be causal agents in the act of willing; we at least thought we were there *catching causality in the act*."[70]

Of course, the scientific darling of analytic philosophy, cognitive neuroscience has done nothing to secure this last conviction in the interim, quite the contrary. And this was so even for the physio-psychological empirical research of Nietzsche's own 19th century: "The 'inner world' is full of phantoms and false lights: the will being one of them."[71] Thus Nietzsche concludes on the basis of the same then-contemporary scientific debunking of the convictions of philosophy, "There are no spiritual causes at all! The whole of the alleged empiricism which affirmed them has gone to the devil." [72]

The problem for philosophy was the metaphysics it had invented on the basis of this empirical error of judgment: "we had made a nice misuse of that 'empiricism,' we had created the world on the basis of it as a world of causes, as a world of will, as a world of spirit."[73] We catch the concision of the trend

---

68 See, for an argument as to the difference this locational transformation might have made, although the contrast is between the French and the Swiss, the chapter on "Bread" in Siegfried Giedion's *Mechanization Takes Command*.
69 Nietzsche, TI, *The Four Great Errors*, §3.
70 Nietzsche, TI, *The Four Great Errors*, §3.
71 Nietzsche, TI, *The Four Great Errors*, §3.
72 Nietzsche, TI, *The Four Great Errors*, §3.
73 Nietzsche, TI, *The Four Great Errors*, §3.

Nietzsche traces: Hume and Kant, thence to Schopenhauer, thence to Hegel. But Nietzsche writes,

> the human being derived the concept 'being' only from the concept 'ego,' posited 'things' as possessing being according to his own image, according to his concept of the ego as cause. No wonder he later always discovered in things only that which he had put into them.[74]

And just when the enlightened, up-to-date, scientific philosopher is nodding in agreement contra the sensibilities driving such 18th and early 19th century "nonsense," Nietzsche interrupts to conclude with an ellipsis in a move that would have pleased Ernst Mach, "...And even your atom, messieurs mechanists and physicists, how much error, how much rudimentary psychology, still remains in your atom!"[75]

In the case of the most common of philosophy's great errors, i.e., the error of mistaking the cause for the effect, personal resolve is foremost in dieting and physical fitness.

Like the ancient philosopher of diet and abstemiousness for the sake of happiness, Epicurus, Nietzsche argues that the Italian Cornaro got sick when he attempted to eat more than a limited amount, thus in both advocates for abstemiousness, their physiology produced a built-in equivalent of lap-band surgery. Neither Cornaro nor Epicurus were particularly robust men and yet, and perhaps dictated by their physiological sensitivity to diet, both of them managed to live, in the case of Epicurus a *relatively* long life (sickly from youth, Epicurus lived to be 71) and even, in Cornaro's case, an *extremely* long life. Nietzsche argued that Cornaro's long life had more to do with his specific constitution than his diet. This should be expanded as Nietzschean also argues that someone who exercises does so, in a certain sense, because he or she cannot help but do so, as an expression of energy or vitality or youth. The point is not to deny the value of exercise. Rather the metabolic system of an athlete is such that more calories are burned at rest, meaning that a more muscular person has both more capacity *and* more inclination to burn energy. The fitter you are, the easier it is and the more appealing it is for you to exercise. Thus, like Cornaro, we invert cause and effect.

Fitness clubs use this error in reasoning to their advantage, employing youthful physical fitness trainers (and I am far from meaning to discredit physical fitness). So too, cosmetic counters feature youthful and attractive salespersons to market their cosmetics.

---

74 Nietzsche, TI, *The Four Great Errors*, §3.
75 Nietzsche, TI, *The Four Great Errors*, §3.

Nietzsche's own reflections on diet (and climate!) invokes differences between specific physiological constitutions, including nationalities and body types, varying cultural appropriations or formations of the body. Hume, as we have seen, lists the general propensity to decay, showing an allegiance to Heraclitus matching Nietzsche's and which also alludes to Lucian, "every thing however seemingly firm is in continual flux and change, the world itself gives symptoms of frailty and dissolution."[76] Here it may be instructive, especially given Hume's 18th century misogyny, to note Simone de Beauvoir's *The Second Sex* where she writes, echoing not only Tertullian who is himself following Pindar: "On ne *naît* pas *femme*, on le deviant [One is not *born* a *woman*, one becomes one]."[77] Feuerbach too drew upon classical influences in the physiological cliché usually associated with him and coined in reaction to the philological play on the relation between being and eating as well as early 19th century physiology: "Du bist, was Du isst,"[78] reducing Brillat-Savarin's already pithy aphorism, "Tell me what you eat, and I will tell you what you are" [*Dis moi ce que tu manges, je te dirai qui tu es*].[79]

Taste, Light Pleasures, and Wine

From causality and the occult properties of bread, I turn to a reflection on wine. Hume is almost universally cited with reference to estimations or speculations supposed or attested (this is also related to the question of delicacy) in wine and other speculated-upon works of art. And Nietzsche is also worth reflection just to the extent that he too draws on the commonplace that is the estimation of wine and the conventional standardization that is involved with being a wine

---

76 Hume, *Essays On Suicide, And The Immortality Of The Soul*, p. 34.
77 Simone de Beauvoir, *Le deuxième sexe*. De Beauvoir's phrase echoes Tertullian's *Apologeticus* – "one is not born, but becomes a Christian," which echoes for its own part Seneca *De ira*, "… no one is born wise but becomes so." It was, earlier still Pindar's 2nd *Pythian Ode*, "Now that you have learned, become who you are," which inspired Nietzsche's *Werde, der bu bist*.
78 Feuerbach used the phrase in his review of Jakob Moleshott's *Lehre der Nahrungsmittel:* "Der Mensch ist, was er ißt." On Nietzsche and Feuerbach, see Richard Brown, "Nietzsche 'that profound physiologist,'" in addition to Wolfgang Wahl, *Feuerbach und Nietzsche: Die Rehabilitierung der Sinnlichkeit und des Leibes in des 19. Jahrhunderts*. Thomas Brobjer includes an account of Nietzsche's reading of Feuerbach in his "Nietzsche as German Philosopher."
79 Already mentioned above, Anthelme Brillat-Savarin's *Physiologie du goût ou Méditations du gastronomie transcendante. Ouvrage théorique, historique, et à l'ordre du jour*" was first published anonymously in 1825 and then after Brillat-Savarin's death in 1826 under his name. This is the fourth of twenty aphorisms affixed to the beginning of the text.

drinker. As Nietzsche writes early in the section of the first volume of *Human, All too Human* entitled "Tokens of Higher and Lower Culture" – and wine drinking is nothing if it is not perhaps the quintessential such token – reflecting on nothing less Humean, if one will, than the "fetters" of "habit," Nietzsche reflects in an aphorism entitled *Origin of Faith:*

> [A man] is a Christian, for example, not because he has knowledge of the various religions and has chosen between them; he is an Englishman not because he has decided in favor of England: he encountered Christianity and Englishness and adopted them without reasons, as a man born in wine-producing country becomes a wine-drinker.[80]

It is helpful to recall that the Naumburg-raised Nietzsche grew up in German wine country.[81]

Here, I turn to a cognate distinction Hume makes to underline that Hume not only awakens Kant from his "dogmatic slumber" (as everyone observes) but that Hume is the reason Kant adverts to the distinction between German *aesthetics* and what the French and English call *taste*.[82] In his own account, Nietzsche connects the language of taste with morality – speaking of aesthetic judgments in terms of taste [*Geschmack*] and not less its negative dimensionality, likewise as Hume emphasizes related to "delicacy," to disgust [*Mißhagen*]. Hume, who focuses his argument on standards for, objectively speaking, what may be assessed or valued as 'good' or 'bad,' by framing his question ironically, highlighting Cervantes' twofold allusion to the judgment power involved in the claim to discriminating taste, including the issue of causation – the leather thong and metal key a discerning palate, two of them no less – as Nietzsche says, truth begins with two – distinctively, identifying the objective components at work in the mélange of flavors in "good wine" in his *Don Quixote*.

In a related reflection alluding to Winckelmann, Wilhelm Amann speaks of the "quiet work" [*stille Arbeit*] of taste, invoking the Abbé Du Bos's "ragout" comparison (241ff.) which last determinative identification is the clear reference for Hume's "delicacy" in taste.[83] For Du Bos, one does not invoke theoretical rules to judge a stew but arrives in an unmediated judgment at an exact ver-

---

80 Nietzsche, *Human, All too Human*, §226, p. 109.
81 Although Nietzsche famously mocks the beer-drinking habits of the Germans, he was himself, so we have it on eyewitness report, fond of Kulmbacher.
82 "The Germans are the only people who currently make use of the word 'Aesthetic' in order to signify what others call the critique of taste." Kant, *Critique of Pure Reason*, A21/B36$_a$.
83 Wilhelm Amann, in *"Die stille Arbeit des Geschmacks": Die Kategorie des Geschmacks in der Aesthetik Schillers und in der Debatte der Aufklärung*, pp. 241ff.

dict.⁸⁴ In the same way, one can taste the ingredients in a sauce directly, even where they are mixed, providing one has a sufficiently discerning or "delicate" palate. For Hume as we shall see, only objective precision will matter.

Given the focus on Lucian noted in the introduction, we may note a 'science fiction style' stylization apparently indebted to Lucian's "Ἀληθῶν διηγημάτων" ["A True Story"], both where Nietzsche cites Hume in German, and where, likewise himself referring to Lucian, Hume suggests that a traveller landing on our planet would find it hard to distinguish between our species' capacity for suffering – given our hospitals, our battlefields and prisons, and the ordinary corruptions and messes of life – and the particular virtues of our institutions for cultural enjoyment. How, Hume asks, would one show "the cheerful side of life" to such an alien, how "give him a notion of its pleasures"?⁸⁵ Where would one take an alien to show him a good time, as it were (and remember this is an alien visiting Hume's 18th- century Scotland, so perhaps to a performance of *Douglas* or Shakespeare), "to a ball, to an opera, to court?"⁸⁶ This alien "might reasonably think," so Hume argues, he was only being shown "other kinds of distress and sorrow."⁸⁷

Here, I am referring, as almost every one who writes on Hume and taste also refers, to Cervantes, *Don Quixote*. Thus Nietzsche reflects more generally on Cervantes as a poet, contrasting this characterization with the pretensions of the poseur,⁸⁸ and criticizing him, not unlike Hume's reference to Shakespeare, in terms of quality or artistic genius. For Nietzsche, Cervantes instantiates the artist's capacity for "taking play seriously,"⁸⁹ and is accordingly a conventional figure for the Enlightenment and its "battle" less with "stupidity than imagination: vanquishing the phantoms of the mind."⁹⁰ For Nietzsche, the novel's picaresque lampooning of the dispossessed in the wake of the inquisition – the same "in-

---

84 Du Bos, *Réflexions critiques sur le poésie et sur le peinture*. In the broader context of philosophical reflection on taste, Amman also cites Alfred Baeumler, *Das Irrationalitätsproblem* and Ernst Cassirer, *Die Philosophie der Aufklärung*. For a comprehensive contextualization of this question, with only a passing reference to Bauemler and without reference to Du Bos, see Jean-Marie Schaeffer, *Art of the Modern Age: Philosophy of Art from Kant to Heidegger*.
85 Hume, *Dialogues Concerning Natural Religion*, pt. 10, quoted in Nietzsche's posthumous notes, KSA 7:29[86], p. 667. For a discussion with a glance at Hume, see Babich, "Le Zarathoustra de Nietzsche et le style parodique: A propos de l'hyperanthropos de Lucien et du surhomme de Nietzsche."
86 Nietzsche, KSA 7:29[86], p. 667.
87 Nietzsche, KSA 7:29[86], p. 667.
88 In Nietzsche, *Untimely Meditations*, II: 5.
89 Nietzsche, KSA 8:4[4], p. 40.
90 Nietzsche, KSA 9:5[16], p. 184.

quisition Cervantes might well have fought against"[91] – reflects not the historical era but the artist's invention as such set off contra an entire genre (in Cervantes' case these are *Ritterromane* – knightly tales or chivalric romances) and, thus as Nietzsche implies, to Cervantes' credit, "contra the whole of Spain."[92] From such a perspective, Nietzsche describes Cervantes as a "national disaster."[93]

Nietzsche's reading does not valorize Cervantes' *Don Quixote* and the "knight's" relationship with his ideals – nor his Dulcinea nor his loyal squire, Sancho Panza, or any of the other people he meets to the extent that Nietzsche follows his own vision of the knightly qua 'noble' poetic aphorism as distinguished in "What is Romanticism?" The artist's achievement may not be assessed in terms of his depiction of the nature of the "things themselves," as they are or were (or as they are or were not), but only in the light of art – and life itself.

In just such a fashion, Hume does not cite Cervantes to illustrate artistic writerly prowess (i.e., as exemplar on the level of Homer or Milton). What adumbrates the standard qua standard for Hume, as exemplifying the referentiality demonstrated over time (in the case of literature) and thus as itself a standard for the rightness of evaluative judgment between authors such as (to use Hume's own examples) Homer (contra Fenélon), John Ogilby (contra Milton), or John Bunyan (contra Addison) and certainly we may add: John Home (contra Shakespeare) or indeed, adding the critic's standard to the list, Warburton (contra Hume). For Hume, the question of an author's relative "quality" and the desired *objective* standard for determining the same qualities turns on the capacity to distinguish a writer of outstanding and not less durable – that is, "classic" – importance from a candidate doomed to have no more than a temporary or passing influence, and it is the "objective" or universal rather than the subjective or individual judgment or capacity for discernment that preoccupies Hume in "Of the Standard of Taste."

The text from Cervantes as Hume cites it on the matter of rightly opining or judging is as follows:

> It is with good reason, says *Sancho* to the squire with the great nose, that I pretend to have a judgment in wine: This is a quality hereditary in our family. Two of my kinsmen were once called to give their opinion of a hogshead, which was supposed to be excellent, being old and of a good vintage. One of them tastes it; considers it; and after mature reflection pronounces [217] the wine to be good, were it not for a small taste of leather, which he perceived in it. The other, after using the same precautions gives also his verdict in favor of

---

91 Nietzsche, KSA 8:23[140], p. 454.
92 Nietzsche, KSA 8:23[140], p. 454. For Nietzsche, such devastation is always the risk, intended or not, of *successful* satire.
93 Nietzsche, KSA 8:23[140], p. 454.

the wine; but with the reserve of a taste of iron, which he could easily distinguish. You cannot imagine how much they were both ridiculed for their judgment. But who laughed in the end? On emptying the hogshead, there was found at the bottom, an old key with a leathern thong tied to it (ST 216–217).

Everyone knows the drill on this one. Hence the relatives called to discriminate (for what else are they asked to do) are in the right, demonstrating – this is more than assessing – the pedigreed judges' assessment to have been wrong.

In a related reflection comparing Homer's verse and Archilochus's verse, the classicist Martin Steinrück illuminates another kind of assessment or judgment as that between Odysseus and the suitors in Homer's *Odyssey* by highlighting the structural relevance of mockery, obviously in the Iambic (Archilochus). Thus pride/mocking – in this classical context – goeth before the mocker's classical comeuppance: all the suitors are slain (death), the girl who refuses an offer of marriage is herself exposed to ridicule.[94] Stylistically, the best vantage point is classical mockery (and this is also useful when it comes to a reading of Lucian whereby everyone, seemingly, is fair game, Jews and Christians, Greeks and Romans): mocking Sancho Panza's relatives (they are rude judges), in turn mocking the more estimable scoffers when the iron key/leathern thong finally is brought to light.

In Hume's case, the standard judgment survives objective test as the test of time. Because the "standard" is standardized across variations, invariant over time, as in the fictitious but obviously versimilar example of the key with its leather thong found only at the end, i.e., when it is too late for those others of indelicate taste who have not only failed to detect the foreign body in the wine but who have drunk, whilst singing its praises, physically, in what Hume calls "real matter of fact," what turns out, quite objectively, to have been *contaminated* wine.

Cervantes' Sancho Panza claims a genealogy of judgment: this talent is in his "blood." In the process, Cervantes lampoons *both* blood-based *and* arriviste pretensions. But the only basis or standard of proof, were it to be had when it comes to subjective claims (qua claims of taste) is neither a matter of hereditary constitution nor the imperative qualification of wealth (polite as it may be), but empirical corroboration.[95] The wine has a leathern or iron taste *if and only if*, at the end of the day – at the bottom of the cask – there is found "an old key with a

---

[94] Martin Steinrück, *The Suitors in the Odyssey: The Clash Between Homer and Archilochus*, pp. 7 ff.
[95] In the broader spirit of Scruton's chapter above and further in his, *Beauty: A Very Short Introduction*, is the need to distinguish, in beauty's case, between the true and the fake.

leathern thong tied to it." (ST 216–217) The "discovery" is icing on the cake, as Hume does not hesitate to underline and we can imagine that a key or other object may have fallen in only to be swiftly fished out, so that its contaminating presence might never come to light. Still: for Hume there is only one cause (and hence only one true assessment) of the objective presence of leather and iron in the wine.

> A thousand men may have a thousand different opinions about some one thing; but just exactly one of the opinions is true, and the only difficulty is to find out which one that is (ST 208).

Questions of objectivity in judgments of taste when it comes to wine are so conventionally patent as to be numerical (Parker points or monetary value) as Steven Shapin has analysed this for his own part.[96] The judgment of wine, good or bad, also serves as a social indicator of class or wealth – the aristocratic subtext of Cervantes' text.

I mentioned Nietzsche's upbringing in Naumburg as relevant to assessing his own reflections on wine drinkers (and of use in reading what he writes about Germans and beer), recall Hume's own formation in wine in the region of the Loire, where he spent the years 1734–1737 writing what would be his doomed *Treatise on Human Nature*. The ability to judge or discern good wine or indeed, and by analogy, and this would have been the point here, *good* essays by *good* authors, is both essential and dangerous: Hume who writes about this observes that delicacy in passion is perhaps a less-than-ideal trait for the bearer. Still what stands to this day is the presumption of discernment in the wine-pouring ritual at table (even given California-style wine production protocols, i.e., industrial standardization, duly signified in its ubiquity by twist-off caps).

The objective illustration of Sancho Panza's kinsmen's *good* taste highlights Hume's exposition of a needed "standard" of taste for the sake of distinguishing between judgments in Hume's objective search for "a rule by which the various sentiments of man may be reconciled; at least a decision afforded, confirming one sentiment and condemning another." (ST 232)[97]

I began by recalling Nietzsche's inaugural Homer lecture and his observation that a specifically subjective presumption influences the scholarly assumption "that the problem of the contemporary circumstances of [Homer's] same epic is to be solved using the standpoint of an aesthetic judgment."[98] As a result,

---

96 Steven Shapin, "The Sciences of Subjectivity."
97 Cited after Hume, "Of the Standard of Taste," p. 282.
98 Nietzsche, "Homer und die klassische Philologie," p. 296.

we may recall Nietzsche's conclusion once again: every historical foray into the question of Homer comes to the same end, leaving today's scholar with nothing more than "a series of especially beautiful and prominent loci, chosen according to subjective taste [*subjektive Geschmacksrichtung*]."[99]

Like the wine connoisseurs who "know" the cask to be excellent, the classical scholar who makes a judgment regarding the author he takes to be the author of the Derveni Papyrus or a popular reviewer evaluating a new translation of Homer's *Odyssey* or else, to less fanfare, of Diogenes Laërtius,[100] or regarding how one might resolve the status of a translated word or phrase, the judgment in each case is made on the basis of, it is an expression of, the scholar's (or the reviewer's) subjective taste. This subjective judgment becomes the standardizing foundation of scholarship:

> The epitome of aesthetic singularity which each scholar was capable of discerning with his own artistic gifts, he now named Homer.[101]

Such judgments are the fruit of scholarly expertise not only in classics but in archaeology, anthropology, especially physical or biological anthropology, comparative anatomy, palaeontology and evolution, and art history and so on.

For this reason, Nietzsche thinks it essential to focus on the role of style in matters of scholarly taste or judgment, just as Hume articulated the question of taste as a matter not solely of subjective estimation but precisely *objective* confirmation.[102] Where wine flavors and olfactory notes are commonly described referring to hints and tastes of elements – tobacco, vanilla, oak, flint – distant from wine, an objectively specific tension is foregrounded in the assessment of Sancho's kinsmen, whose "reserve of a taste of iron" turned out at the moment of what modern media culture likes to call "the reveal" – "upon emptying the hogshead" – to have had an objectively descriptive *literality*. At the same time, there is the stylistic place of irony and Hume and Nietzsche both invoke Cervantes as they invoke Lucian, *ironically*.

Hume's original *Five Essays* was reduced by two essays, forcing him to compose a purpose-writ essay fit to the length needed just in order to be able to pub-

---

99 Nietzsche, "Homer und die klassische Philologie," p. 299.
100 See, for example, Emily Wilson's new translation of Homer's *Odyssey* or the oversize format and extensively illustrated translation of Diogenes Laërtius, *Lives of the Eminent Philosophers* by Pamela Mensch and edited by James Miller.
101 Nietzsche, "Homer und die klassische Philologie," p. 299.
102 For Nietzsche, the error, indeed the "*Mittelpunkt*" of the errors in this context, is the precipitation of objective rather than subjective judgment on this same basis.

lish the remaining essays as a book: *Four Essays.* The essay he wrote was directed to the kinds of assessments that could force such cuts. For his part, Nietzsche maintained his own stylistic insight into the *aesthetic* basis of science [*die aesthetische Wissenschaft*] and in his *Thus Spoke Zarathustra* he recalls both his inaugural lecture and the beginning of his first book, cautioning his readers (thereby echoing Kant's critical philosophy of the power of judgment, the epigraph to this chapter: "Yet all of life is a struggle of taste and tasting."[103]

It is a struggle of taste and tasting because claims of taste are contested. As a result of this contestation of claim and counterclaim – countered in Nietzsche's case by Ulrich von Wilamowitz-Möllendorff, in Hume's case by William Warburton – we need a standard of taste.

Robert Browning echoes the quandary of distinction in his 1864 poem, *Rabbi ben Ezra,*

> Now who shall arbitrate?
> Ten men love what I hate;
> Shun what I follow, slight what I receive:
> Ten, who in ears and eyes
>   Match me we all surmise, —
> They, this thing, and I that ; whom shall my soul believe?

If David Hume called his first book "dead-born," the judgment of tradition, that is the standard of time as this was his own standard for such, has vindicated him. I would hold that the same holds for Nietzsche's philosophy and perhaps the same may prove to hold for his philological reflections as well.

Acknowledgments

Sections of this chapter grow out of reflections that appear in of "On Nietzsche's Judgment of Style and Hume's Quixotic Taste: On the Science of Aesthetics and 'Playing' the Satyr," *Journal of Nietzsche Studies*, 43:2 (2012): 240–259 and "Towards a Critical Philosophy of Science: Continental Beginnings and Bugbears, Whigs, and Waterbears," *International Studies in the Philosophy of Science*, 24:4 (2010): 343–391.

---

103 [*Aber alles Leben ist Streit um Geschmack und Schmecken*] Nietzsche, *Thus Spoke Zarathustra:* II, "On Those Who Are Sublime."

Bibliography

Acampora, Christa Davis (2013) *Contesting Nietzsche*. Chicago: University of Chicago Press.
Allison, David Blair (2005) "Nietzsche's Aesthetic Taste for Moral Metacritique." *Symposium*. 9(2): 153–167.
Allison, David Blair (Ed.) (1985), *The New Nietzsche*. Cambridge: MIT Press. [1977]
Amann, Wilhelm (1999) *"Die stille Arbeit des Geschmacks": Die Kategorie des Geschmacks in der Aesthetik Schillers und in der Debatte der Aufklärung*. Würzburg: Königshausen und Neumann.
Arain, F. A. et al. (2009) "Sex/gender medicine. The biological basis for personalized care in cardiovascular medicine," *Circ J*. 73(10): 1774–82. Sep 4.
Arrowsmith, William. "Nietzsche on Classics and Classicists," *New Nietzsche Studies*, 10:3 and 4 (2017): 127–137.
Babich, Babette (2016) "Nietzsche's Archilochus," *New Nietzsche Studies*, 10(1 and 2): 133–170.
Babich, Babette (2017) "Nietzsche's Critique: Reading Kant's Critical Philosophy." In: Mark Conard (Ed.) *Nietzsche and the Philosophers*. Lanham: Rowman & Littlefield. 171–192.
Babich, Babette (2017) "Are They Good? Are They Bad? Double Hermeneutics and Citation in Philosophy, Asphodel and Alan Rickman, Bruno Latour and the 'Science Wars'." In: Paula Angelova, Andreev Jaassen, Emil Lessky (Eds.), *Das Interpretative Universum*. Würzburg: Königshausen & Neumann. 259–290.
Babich, Babette (2017) "Nietzsche's Influence and Meaning Today – With Weight on the Sameness of the Eternal Return." In: Polyakova, Ekaterina and Yulia Sineokaya (Eds.) *Фридрих Ницше: наследие и проект*. М.: Культурная революция, / *Friedrich Nietzsche: Heritage and Prospects*. Moscow, LRC Publishing House. 391–406.
Babich, Babette (2017) "Nietzsches Lyrik. Archilochos, Musik, Metrik." In: Christian Benne and Claus Zittel (Eds.), *Nietzsche und die Lyrik. Ein Kompendium*. Frankfurt am Main: Springer/Metzler. 405–429.
Babich, Babette (2011)"Le Zarathoustra de Nietzsche et le style parodique: A propos de l'hyperanthropos de Lucien et du surhomme de Nietzsche." *Diogène: Revue internationale des sciences humaines*. 232 (October): 70–93.
Babich, Babette (2010) *Nietzsche's Wissenschaftsphilosophie. "Die Wissenschaft unter der Optik des Künstlers zu sehn, die Kunst aber unter der des Lebens"*. Oxford/Bern: Peter Lang.
Babich, Babette (2010) "Towards a Critical Philosophy of Science. Continental Beginnings and Bugbears, Whigs, and Waterbears." *International Studies in the Philosophy of Science*. 24(4): 343–391.
Babich, Babette (1994) *Nietzsche's Philosophy of Science: Reflecting Science on the Ground of Art and Life*. Albany: State University of New York Press.
Beam, Craig (1996) "Hume and Nietzsche: Naturalists, Ethicists, Anti-Christians." *Hume Studies*. 22(2): 299–324.
Baeumler, Alfred (1923) *Das Irrationalitätsproblem*. Tübingen: Max Niemeyer.
Beauvoir, Simone de (1949) *Le deuxième sexe*. Paris: Gallimard.
Bornedal, Peter (2005) "A Silent World: Nietzsche's Radical Realism: World Sensation Language." *Nietzsche-Studien*. 34: 1–47.

Breazeale, Daniel (1975) *Toward a Nihilist Epistemology: Hume and Nietzsche*. New Haven: Yale University Press. [1971]
Brillat-Savarin, Jean Anthelme (1865) *The Handbook of Dining; or Corpulency and Leanness Scientifically Considered*, L. F. Simpson trans. New York: D. Appleton and Company.
Brillat-Savarin, Jean Anthelme (1848) *Physiologie du Goût*. Paris: Gabriel de Gonet.
Brobjer, Thomas (2003) "Nietzsche as German Philosopher." In: Nicholas Martin, (Ed.), *Nietzsche and the German Tradition*. Oxford/Bern: Peter Lang. 39–82.
Broisson, Ivan (2006) "*Ressentiment* und Wille zur Macht. Nietzsche und Hume über Moral- und Religionskritik." In: Volker Gerhardt and Renate Reschke, (Eds.), *Friedrich Nietzsche – Zwischen Musik, Philosophie und Ressentiment*. Berlin: Akademie. 117–128.
Brown, Richard S. G. (2004) "Nietzsche 'that profound physiologist.'" In: Thomas Brobjer and Gregory M. Moore, (Eds.) *Nietzsche and Science*. Aldershot: Ashgate. 51–70.
Cassirer, Ernst (1932) *Die Philosophie der Aufklärung*. Tübingen: Mohr.
Conard, Mark T. (2017) "Nietzsche and Hume in the Genealogy and Psychology of Religion." In: Conard (Ed.), *Nietzsche and the Philosophers*. London: Routledge. 146–168.
Cornaro, Louis [Luigi] (2005) *The Art of Living Long*. Frankfurt: Springer, 2005. [1558]
Danto, Arthur (1965) *Nietzsche as Philosopher*. New York: Columbia University Press,
Diogenes Laërtius (2018) *Lives of the Eminent Philosophers*. Pamela Mensch trans. Oxford: Oxford University Press.
Du Bos, Abbé (1967) *Réflexions critiques sur le poésie et sur le peinture*. Geneva: Slatkine [1719].
Fordham, David (2006) "Allan Ramsay's Enlightenment: Or, Hume and the Patronizing Portrait." *Art Bulletin*. 88(3): 508–524.
Franconi, Flavia (Ed.) (2010) *La salute della donna. Un approccio di genere*. Milan/Rome: Franco Angelli.
Giedion, Siegfried (1948) *Mechanization Takes Command: A Contribution to Anonymous History*. Oxford: Oxford University Press.
Hatab, Lawrence (2002) "Prospects for a Democratic Agon: Why We Can Still Be Nietzscheans." *Journal of Nietzsche Studies*. 24 (Fall): 132–147
Hollis, John and Rick Mattes (2005) "Are All Calories Created Equal? Emerging Issues in Weight Management." *Current Diabetes Reports*. 5,5 (Oct.): 374–378.
Homer (2017) *The Odyssey*. Emily Wilson trans. New York: W. W. Norton & Company.
Hume, David (1985) "The Epicurean." In: Hume, *Essays Moral Political and Literary*, Eugene F. Millar (Ed.) Indianapolis: The Literary Fund. 138–145.
Hume, David (1941) *A Treatise of Human Nature*. L. A. Selby-Bigge, (Ed.) Oxford: Clarendon Press [1888].
Hume, David (1824) *The History of England, from the Invasion of Julius Caesar to the Revolution in 1688*, Vol. II. London: Thomas Kelly.
Hume, David (1783) *Essays On Suicide, And The Immortality Of The Soul, Ascribed To The Late David Hume, Esq., Never before published. With Remarks, intended as an Antidote to the Poison contained in these Performances, By The Editor. To Which Is Added, Two Letters On Suicide, From Rosseau's* Eloisa. London: Printed for M. Smith; and sold by the Booksellers in Piccadilly, Fleet-street, and Paternoster-row.
Hume, David (1772) *An Enquiry Concerning Human Understanding*.

Janko, Richard (2006) "Review of *The Derveni Papyrus*, edited by Theokritos Kouremenos, George M. Parássoglou, and Kyriakos Tsantsanoglou." *Bryn Mawr Classical Review*, October 29.
Kahn, Charles (1960) *Anaximander and the Origins of Greek Cosmology*. New York: Columbia University Press.
Kail, Peter (2009) "Nietzsche and Hume: Naturalism and Explanation." *Journal of Nietzsche Studies*. 37: 5–22.
Kant, Immanuel (2004) *Prolegomena to Any Future Metaphysics*. Gary Hatfield, trans. Cambridge: Cambridge University Press.
– (1929) *Critique of Pure Reason*. Norman Kemp-Smith, trans. London: Macmillan.
Kirk, Geoffrey S. John E. Raven and Martin Schofield (1984) *The Presocratic Philosophers*. Cambridge; Cambridge University Press, 1984.
Lang, Berel (2002) "Misinterpretation as the Author's Responsibility (Nietzsche's Fascism, For Instance)." In: Jacob Golomb and Robert S. Wistrich (Eds.) *Nietzsche, Godfather of Fascism? On the Uses and Abuses of a Philosophy*. Princeton, NJ: Princeton University Press. 47–65.
Ludovici, Anthony (1911) *Nietzsche and Art*. London: Constable.
Mabille, Louise (2011) "Hume on the Use and Abuse of Skepticism for Life." In: Mabille, *Nietzsche and the Anglo-Saxon Tradition*. London: Continuum.
MacIntyre, Alasdair (Ed.), (1965) *Hume's Ethical Writings*. New York: Collier.
Miller, David (1999) "Being an Absolute Skeptic." *Science* 284:5420 (4 June): 1625–1626.
Nehamas, Alexander (2007) *Only a Promise of Happiness: The Place of Beauty in a World of Art*. Princeton: Princeton University Press.
Nehamas, Alexander (1985) *Life as Literature*. Cambridge: Harvard University Press.
Nietzsche, Friedrich (1970) KGW VIII/2. Berlin: de Gruyter.
Nietzsche Friedrich (1995) KGW II/4. Berlin: de Gruyter.
Nietzsche, Friedrich (1994) "Homer und die klassische Philologie." In: *Frühe Schriften*, Carl Koch and Carl Schlechta (Eds.) Munich: Beck, Vol. 5, 290.
Nietzsche, Friedrich (1986) Nietzsche, *Human, All too Human*, Reg Hollingdale, trans. Cambridge: Cambridge University Press.
Nietzsche, Friedrich (1983) "On the Uses and Disadvantages of History for Life," *Untimely Meditations*, R. J. Hollingdale, trans. Cambridge: Cambridge University Press.
Nietzsche, Friedrich (1980) *Kritische Studienausgabe*. Giorgio Colli & Mazzino Montinari (Eds.) Berlin: de Gruyter.
Nietzsche Friedrich. *Die fröhliche Wissenschaft*. KSA 3.
Nietzsche, Friedrich *Götzen-Dämmerung*. KSA 6.
Ortona, Elena et al. (2008) "Redox State, Cell Death and Autoimmune Diseases: A Gender Perspective." *Autoimmun Rev.* 7: 579–584.
Osborne, Catharine Rowan (1987) *Rethinking Early Greek Philosophy*. London: Duckworth.
Poellner, Peter (1999) "Causation and Force in Nietzsche." In: Babette Babich, (Ed.) *Nietzsche, Epistemology, and Philosophy of Science: Nietzsche and Science II*. Dordrecht: Kluwer. 287–297.
Polyakova, Ekaterina and Yulia Sineokaya (Eds.) (2017) Фридрих Ницше: наследие и проект. М.: Культурная революция, / *Friedrich Nietzsche: Heritage and Prospects*. Moscow, LRC Publishing House.

Schaeffer, Jean-Marie (2000) *Art of the Modern Age: Philosophy of Art from Kant to Heidegger*, trans. Steven Bendall. Princeton, NJ: Princeton University Press.

Schlaffer, Heinz (2007) *Das entfesselte Wort: Nietzsches Stil und seiner Folgen*. Munich: Hanser.

Scruton, Roger (2011) *Beauty: A Very Short Introduction*. Oxford: Oxford University Press. [2009]

Shapin, Steven (2016) "The Sciences of Subjectivity." In: Babich (Ed.), *Hermeneutic Philosophies of Social Science*. Berlin: de Gruyter. 123–142.

Siemens, Herman and James Pearson (Eds.) (2018) *Conflict and Contest in Nietzsche's Philosophy*. London: Bloomsbury.

Steinrück, Martin (2008) *The Suitors in the Odyssey: The Clash Between Homer and Archilochus*. Oxford: Peter Lang.

Strong, Tracy B. (2013) "In Defense of Rhetoric; or, How Hard it is to Take a Writer Seriously: The Case of Nietzsche." *Political Theory*. 41(4): 507–532.

Tuncel, Yunus (2013) *Agon in Nietzsche*. Milwaukee: Marquette University Press.

Wahl, Wolfgang (1998) *Feuerbach und Nietzsche: Die Rehabilitierung der Sinnlichkeit und des Leibes in des 19. Jahrhunderts*. Würzburg: Ergon Verlag.

Watson, Richard A. (1998) *The Philosopher's Diet: How to Lose Weight & Change the World*. Boston: David R. Godine Publisher [1985].

V Comparisons, Art, Anatomies

Andrej Démuth and Slávka Démuthová
The Comparison as the Standardization of Aesthetic Norms

Beauty and options for its research represent an ancient philosophical issue, combining not only questions of methodology, but also a significant number of metaphysical questions and obstacles. One of those essential questions is definitely: what is beauty and is it possible to objectively examine beauty? If yes, then how?

Recently, it has been possible to observe an increase in interest in the interdisciplinary and multidisciplinary scientific research of the aesthetic experience – its content, creation, origin and process, as well as the possibilities to assess it mathematically and objectively approach beauty or an aesthetic experience. We can also witness the use of statistics and mathematics in aesthetics and art, or mathematical research on the proportions of an attractive face,[1] body, or any other subject of cultural anthropology, evolutionary psychology, and aesthetics. The core issue of the stated research is whether beauty (or its characteristics) is something objective and measurable,[2] or purely subjective, a thing of feelings and individual emotions. Is it possible to mathematize the experience of beauty and aesthetics? Are they mathematical? Does an aesthetic experience hold any cognitive-mathematical content? Is it possible to deal with it cognitively?

As we believe, the key contribution to such "mathematical" and statistical approaches can be found in Hume's essay "Of the Standard of Taste" and in the reactions it has caused. This study tries to describe two historical approaches to continuity and the mathematization of beauty, which can be identified in the analyses of beauty in the period when aesthetics was formed as an independent philosophical field, and which can be observed in approaches to the mathematics of aesthetic experience research even today. Despite the fact that they all came about in the same period [David Hume: "Of the Standard of Taste" (1757) and Immanuel Kant: *Die Kritik der Urteilskraft* (1790)] the same enlightened, intellectual climate, represents different epistemological and ontological concepts of beauty and its potential research. But what they are associated by (apart from their ideological and historical influence) is the discovery of tools of relatively trivial mathematics, especially mathematical statistics, to clarify beauty and the emergence of aesthetic norms.

---

1 Andy Calder, et al. (Eds.), *The Oxford Handbook of Face Perception*.
2 Archie J. Bahm, "Is a Universal Science of Aesthetics Possible?"

The very first and essential approach to this field is Hume's "mathematization" of taste and his search for objective aesthetic standards.

Hume and Standardization of Taste

If we are to understand Hume's work "Of the Standard of Taste,"[3] we have to take into account the historical context of the writer's views. It is especially important when we are setting out Hume's ideas on what we today call Aesthetics.

Aesthetics in the broad sense goes back at least as far as Pythagoras and Plato's contemplations on different types of beauty and ratio between their parts. However, the history of modern Aesthetics starts in the eighteenth century, when aesthetics was established as an individual philosophical discipline,[4] the subject of which was beauty, taste and aesthetic emotion. Beauty has once again become a philosophical issue par excellence[5], and thinkers have not only primarily directed their attention to the extent of its rationality, or its irrationality and relationship to emotions, but also to whether it is an objective quality of an object or the subjective aspect of thinking, evaluation, and feeling, and whether

---

[3] Humes's essay "Of the Standard of Taste" is an elaboration of his ideas from *An Enquiry Concerning the Principles of Morals* and was issued as a part of *Four Dissertations* (together with the essay "Of Tragedy" in 1757). It is also a reaction to the decision of the Edinburgh Society for Encouraging Arts, Sciences, Manufacturers and Agriculture in Scotland, which awarded the essay of Alexander Gerard *"Dialogue on Taste"* with the title of "best essay on taste" in 1755 (Hume was a member along with Adam Smith, Lord Kames, William Robertson, Alan Ramsay and Adam Ferguson) which was issued together with three similar dissertations by Voltaire, d'Alembert and Montesquieu in the seventh volume of *Encyclopédie* in 1759 after Hume's prompting. Cf. Peter Jones, "Hume on the Arts and 'The Standard of Taste': Texts and Contexts," in: David Fate Norton & Jacqueline Taylor (Eds.), *The Cambridge Companion to Hume*. 2nd edition, here 431–432.

[4] What remains unclear for the historians is whether the establishment of aesthetics dates back to the 18th century (Leibniz-Wolf tradition together with Gottsched's essays on the truth and imagination after Baumgarten's *Aesthetica* (1750), or the Addison-Schaftesbury-Hutcheson-Burke tradition) and whether it was established as a discipline on the British Isles (as Criticism) or in the continental Prussia (see Paul Guyer, *A History of Modern Aesthetics*, Vol. 1), or whether it is necessary to go further back, e.g., to the renaissance or 17th century France [see Rudolf A. Makkreel "Aesthetics" in: K. Haakonssen (Ed.), *The Cambridge History of Eighteenth-Century Philosophy*, Vol. 1].

[5] According to a Czech mathematician Peter Vopěnka, beauty was the reason why Greek mathematicians (arithmeticians and acousmaticians) began examining the relationships between the objects and their proportions (Petr Vopěnka, *Úhelný kámen evropské vzdělanosti a moci*, p. 54). Similarly, later in the Renaissance, research focused on partial findings (science) rather than 'the' original beauty.

(and under which conditions) an aesthetic judgement may be considered universally applicable and binding.

As we know, for British schools in Hume's time, taste was one of the key human intellectual skills.[6] Taste was a question of the reason, sentiment, and judgment. Aesthetics labeled *Criticism* in Hume's nomenclature, therefore could have become a Newton-type science if the subject of its research had been the analysis of mind patterns, the ways in which we think or the ways in which we perceive beautiful things and how our mind processes information in this regard. Aesthetics could have become a logic of feeling and appreciations. However, some philosophers (in the Cartesian tradition, for instance) associated taste with rational skills and a certain natural skill of judgment. As an empiricist, Hume believed that the only way to examine this skill – undoubtedly interesting and important in everyday life – is through experience and observation. It could be either introspection, analyzing one's own experience of beauty, or it could be an objectification of the aesthetic experience of other individuals.[7]

Like many other philosophers of the Scottish Enlightenment, Hume was aware of the fact that there are a wide variety and diversity of opinions that consider the issue of perceived beauty and the aesthetic judgments we make. That was true for both the members of the same community, whose opinions were formed by identical or very similar personal and cultural experiences, as well as for the cultural and social environments where these individuals grew up or actively participated in. This variety and diversity is revealed to be the point of departure for reflections, and not as itself a problem into which Hume has been led by his own assumptions.[8] According to Hume, the reasons that cause this diversity belong mainly to the domain of emotional affection and the unconscious replacement of subjects of aesthetic judgments with the emotions they cause. The situation is similar to when, in considering causality, we exchange *post hoc* with *propter hoc*. In taste judgments, we identify the subject of perception along with the emotion generated and we demand that we make judgments about the subject, not the emotions.

---

[6] In the introduction to his *Treatise*, Hume states four basic disciplines – philosophical fields (logic, morals, criticism and politics), describing the mind and its abilities or researching the phenomena that are connected to these skills.
[7] Like the other representatives of Scottish Enlightenment, Hume avoids the term "aesthetic experience", but he speaks of beauty and taste in connection with it. From the historical point of view, the term "aesthetic" is related to Baumgarten's book "*Aesthetica*" and it was established in the English language thanks to the translation of Kant's works, mostly *Kritik der Urteilskraft* and *Kritik der reinen Vernunft*.
[8] See: O. Dadějík, "David Hume a logika soudů vkusu."

Hume was aware that the perception of beauty was connected to sensibility under the influence of Lockean epistemology and Hutchinson's aesthetics. His sensualism results in the fact that the subject of an aesthetic judgment is not something external but, on the contrary, the impression we perceive as subjects.[9] Therefore, the quality of our perception is not the quality of the object. That leads to polemics regarding the nature of secondary qualities.

Similar to Berkeley, Hume believed that taste judgment, the attribution of qualities to objects, is a result of rational generalization and abstraction. However, it can often be incorrect. That which is infallible and true is our perception. Therefore, if I claim that some object is beautiful, I cross the boundary of sensual experience and emotion in my judgment and I attribute qualities to something that I might perceive incorrectly. Emotion (opinion, *impression*) is the only real and epistemically infallible thing and thus taste judgments should apply only to perception:

> Among a thousand different opinions which different men may entertain of the same subject, there is one, and but one, that is just and true; and the only difficulty is to fix and ascertain it. On the contrary, a thousand different sentiments, excited by the same object, are all right: Because no sentiment represents what is really in the object. It only marks a certain conformity or relation between the object and the organs or faculties of the mind; and if that conformity did not really exist, the sentiment could never possibly have being (ST 208).[10]

The subject of our thoughts should be thus perception and a certain taste psychology. According to Hume, the ontology of beauty is (referring to Shakespeare's *"Beauty is in the eye of the beholder"*) a matter of impression, it "is no quality in things themselves: It exists merely in the mind which contemplates them [...]" (ST 209).

It thus seems that aesthetics is based on perceptions and therefore there is a risk that it must be fundamentally subjective and relative. The reason why it is so lies in the fact that we do not have receptors that are developed at the same level of sensitivity, or they might be contaminated and thus the resulting perceptions can be (and often are) very different. In addition, we are also very different in the question of preference, and thus,

> each mind perceives a different beauty. One person may even perceive deformity, where another is sensible of beauty; and every individual ought to acquiesce in his own sentiment, without pretending to regulate those of others (ST 209).

---

[9] A. Démuth, "David Hume a asociačné 'škandály' jeho myslenia."
[10] Hume, *Selected Essays*, p. 136.

Can a science about beauty and the "pleasant" even exist? Or can we only provide descriptions of our own subjective emotions?

As Peter Jones shows,

> In "Of Standard of Taste" Hume, in effect, extends his reflections from An Enquiry concerning the Principle of Morals on the respective roles of reasons and sentiment in the realm of values. Some so-called judgements of taste are, he believes, palpably foolish and indefensible: "the taste of all individuals is not upon an equal footing," and we should not give unrestricted license to the claims that it is "fruitless to dispute concerning tastes." He recognizes that those who introduce the sentiment into the analysis must nevertheless avoid claiming that everyone is equally right in matters of sentiment. Indeed, if rational discourse is even to be possible, there must be some "standard," rule," or criterion by which disputes can be resolved. Consequently, Hume hopes to show that criticism is a factually based, rational, social activity, capable of being integrated into the rest of intelligible human discourse, and he attempts to establish that sentiment can be a criterion. Of course, if there are "rules," whether of composition or criticism, they must not be thought of as "fixed by reasoning a priori, or ... be esteemed abstract conclusion of the understanding.[11]

If Hume wanted to give succor to aesthetics as a science, the judgments of which could claim objective validity, he could opt for at least two solutions. He partially opted for both. The first solution was the analysis of "beautiful," that is, the thing which beautiful emotions and the objects that cause them have in common.

Hume realized that despite the indisputable diversity of our tastes (ST 208–209), it is possible to find objects and crafts that appeal to almost everybody in various observation contexts within history and across cultures. These classics are beautiful because our subjective tastes probably have something in common. The "statistical intersection" of individual tastes could be a solution to the search for a potential general taste, if it exists, or at least general attributes of what we like. It is obvious from the nature of his epistemology that what we like are not the objects themselves,[12] but the structure or form of our emotions. And thus we have to rivet our attention to them. However, Hume does not analyze "beautiful" objects by means of a specific phenomenology of the perception of appealing objects, that is, what we experience when we like something, or through the intersection of attributes of objects we perceive as "beautiful", and not even through our desires or for what purpose we have for liking something when we like something. He pays attention to another aspect of the sub-

---

[11] Jones, "Hume on the Arts and 'The Standard of Taste.'"
[12] "Though some objects, by the structure of the mind, be naturally calculated to give pleasure, it is not to be expected, that in every individual the pleasure will be equally felt." Hume, *Selected Essays*, p. 140.

jective perception of beauty – its atypicality and *excellence*[13] in comparison to other, up until that point, aesthetically neutral objects.

The term excellence is, to philosophy, special. On the one hand, excellence is everything which is not common, that is rare. Thus our preferences in perceiving various aesthetic objects can be rare. Hume is aware that there are individuals who might like things which others do not like or even that disgust them. He assumes that this anomaly in taste could be caused by sickness or an individual oddity. Individual anomalies in taste are more likely to be an error than the standard. Hume expects that the majority would reject such an unusual taste judgment because it is in contrast to a certain generally accepted standard of perception. And here is the core of the issue. We consider everything which is excellent to be beautiful, however, this excellence is considered (or might be considered) beautiful by the majority of those who perceive it. It seems that our nature forces us to search for generally accepted standards of perception in our judgments (ST 209). The question is: does such a standard even exist and how are these aesthetic standards established?

We believe that Hume's fundamentals of aesthetic judgment are more or less mathematical. Its core is the comparison.[14] Just by comparing one's own experience, the standard of taste is created. Hume assumes that perceptual standards as well as standards of taste really do exist. He documents it by the statement that

> If, in the sound state of the organ, there be an entire or a considerable uniformity of sentiment among men, we may thence derive an idea of the perfect beauty; [...] (ST 215).

The idea of beauty could therefore be derived statistically from the unity of feeling of pleasure in the perception of the same object by different individuals

> in like manner as the appearance of objects in day-light, to the eye of a man in health, is denominated their true and real colour, even while colour is allowed to be merely a phantasm of the senses (ST 215).

But in what manner are the aesthetic standards established?

Regarding the famous example of Sancho Panza tasting wine, it is obvious that our taste is standardized by practice and the quantity of observations. Even

---

[13] Hume uses the term *excellence* in two meanings. Firstly, it conveys rareness – uncommonness as an opposite to usualness (standard). Secondly, it conveys rareness in the sense of perfection.

[14] "We judge more of objects by comparison, than by their intrinsic worth and value." Hume, *A Treatise of Human Nature*, p. 238.

individual taste is, in fact, a result of the standardization of judgments. If the inexperienced individual is to deal with some notion, he compares it with the notions he has already experienced and therefore his individual taste might differ from that of others:

> A man, who has had no opportunity to compare different kinds of beauty, is indeed totally unqualified to pronounce an opinion with regard to any object presented to him. By comparison alone we fix the epithets of praise or blame, and learn how to assign the due degree of each (ST 223).

Therefore, our perception is a standardization of our experiences. Our scale for beautiful and ugly develops with a quantity of material "already perceived." We consider beautiful those things which are not average, and in this manner they meet or even exceed the established standards. This is just the first part of Hume's solution – the less visible one. The second one is the standardization of tastes between individuals.

If our experience is limited to only some types of objects, it is obvious that our taste will be determined and limited by this particularly narrow experience. This is valid for each individual and therefore by sharing aesthetic experiences and taste judgments (and comparing them!) it is possible to rectify the individual taste and thus it is possible to establish generic taste and aesthetic feelings for a community or nation on the same principles of comparison and standardization. The standardization of standards of taste is therefore done on an individual as well as an inter-individual level by the same means.

Hume believes that any assessment is always a social activity. Not only because the evaluation awaits agreement from others but mainly because we learn to appreciate what we appreciate from others by using language. Supporting this idea is an ancient insight, much trumpeted in the eighteenth century, that we all begin by learning what to say from others, and no one can begin by being a pretender: pretence is a parasitic knowledge, and knowledge in principle is public. Hume has already emphasized that it is by comparison that we learn how to assign "the epithets of praise or blame" (ST 223) In brief, no human being can proclaim special authority for a self-absorbed report of her or her thoughts about the world, without first having learned from others how to formulate and express thoughts of such a kind; in this respect, judgment about art differs not at all from anything else.[15]

It could seem that the result of such standardization would, in the end, be an average of the aesthetic judgments. However, we would only face this situation if

---

15 Cf. Jones, "Hume on the Arts and 'The Standard of Taste,'" p. 439.

each person had completely different individual aesthetic judgments. The truth is that we like the same things, thanks to various – for instance, historical or social – influences. Thus, Hume believes that beauty is everything that exceeds the standard and it is therefore (like the Gaussian distribution of intelligence and genius) everything which is (positively) perceived as rare, not only by a single individual but also by a group of observers. The inter-subjective taste is formed by a process of standardization and synchronization of individual tastes. Practice, education and expert opinions play a vital role in this process.

Hume's philosophy is often criticized because his definition of taste, as stated by experts – critics – is circular.[16] However, considering previous thoughts, it is obvious that the relevance of any taste judgment is dependent on the level of experience of the person who perceives it. According to Hume, the opinions of critics are more authoritative than the opinions of inexperienced or partially experienced individuals. Although it would be sufficient, this is not caused only by the expertise of the critic in his field, nor by his having incomparably more experience in it and therefore a better overview of the matter. The greater and more diverse set of aesthetic experiences the critic has, the more reliable his judgment is.

The second important factor of Hume's preferences in experts' opinions lies in the subtlety and education they use in their judgments. Hume presents the example of the perception and judgment of flavors (ST 217–218). It is clear that almost everybody is able to identify the significant and common flavors. However, the critic is able to identify not only the rare and uncommon ingredients, but he can also sense them with greater (or greatest) subtlety. It is the subtlety and the ability to distinguish that is necessary for taste relevancy and expertise. The subtle senses and imagination are given by physiology as well as by education and practice. The task of the experts, for authoritative opinions, is not only to classify and organize our experiences, but for their experiences and subtlety to also compensate for our missing individual experiences which we are unable to perceive due to our absence of subtle receptors or imagination. Thanks to the value of their experience, our individual standard of experience becomes closer to the expert's standard. I believe that somewhere here (in these mathematical evaluations of individual experience with the experience of experts) lies the source of Kant's ability to distinguish between high and low art and the experts' task for the development of taste.

---

[16] Guyer, *A History of Modern Aesthetics*, p. 129; Alexander Broadie, "Art and Aesthetic Theory" in: Broadie, (Ed.), *The Cambridge Companion to The Scottish Enlightenment*, p. 289.

Mathematical Composition

Kant himself, who, as he stated, was awoken by Hume from his dogmatic sleep, directly reacted to Hume's philosophy in the aesthetic sphere. Kant undoubtedly conceived the first part of his Kritik der Urteilskraft [*Critique of Judgement*] as a response to Hume, whose essay on taste Sulzer translated for him.[17] Kant is considered to be a philosopher who rejects any rational interventions in taste judgments[18]. Pure aesthetic judgment is a matter of reflective evaluation (in contrast to a defining one) which is deprived of terms or intellectual purposes.

If we look into Kant's thesis about beauty and ideal, we will come to the conclusion that the idea of beauty is a cognitive concept and the ideal is a vision identical with this. But how do we come to the ideal of beauty—*a priori* or empirically; cognitively or by means of imagination?

In his *Critique of Judgment*, Kant suggests a notable (as he calls it) psychological explanation:

> Notice how in a manner wholly beyond our grasp our imagination is able on occasion not only to recall, even from the distant past, the signs that stand for concepts, but also to reproduce [an] object's image and shape from a vast number of objects of different kinds or even of one and the same kind. Moreover, all indications suggest that this power, when the mind wants to make comparisons, can actually proceed as follows, though this process does not reach consciousness: the imagination projects, as it were, one image onto another, and from the congruence of most images of the same kind it arrives at an average that serves as the common standard for all of them.[19]

What is more, from the image of the standard origin of a handsome man's stature, Kant specifies in his analysis of the origin of the standard idea:

> Someone has seen a thousand adult men. If now he wishes to make a judgment about their standard size, to be estimated by way of a comparison, then (in my opinion) the imagination projects a large number of the images (perhaps the entire thousand) onto one another. If I may be permitted to illustrate this by an analogy from optics: in the space where most of the images are united and within the outline where the area is illuminated by the colour applied most heavily, there the average size emerges, equally distant in both height and

---

17 See Jones, "Hume on the Arts and 'The Standard of Taste'," p. 445.
18 On the other hand, he preferred the thesis of beauty's role in mathematics until 1790, however, he later rejected it (compare Christian Helmut Wenzel, "Beauty, Genius, and Mathematics: Why Did Kant Change His Mind?")
19 Kant, *Kritik der Urteilskraft*, p. 75.

breadth from the outermost bounds of the tallest and shortest in stature; and that is the stature for a beautiful man[20]

Therefore, the standard idea originates from an unconscious mathematical calculation.[21] The unconsciousness is documented not only by the mentioned conviction about *the real comparison* (though *insufficient for the consciousness*), but also by Kant's note that

> The same result could be obtained mechanically, by measuring the entire thousand, adding up separately all their heights and their breadths (and thicknesses) by themselves and then dividing each sum by a thousand. And yet the imagination does just that by means of a dynamic effect arising from its multiple perception of such shapes on the organ of the inner sense.[22]

It could be said that this act is carried out intuitively with an unspoken algorithm for the solution.[23] However, Kant clearly unfolds this mathematical algorithm. Our creation of aesthetic standards is tied to mathematical operations of which we are unaware because they are performed by the imagination.

Nevertheless, the significant issue is whether it is done on the basis of previous experiences (as suggested by Hume) or *a priori*. Although Kant states that the creation of the ideal is determined by previous experience (according to Kant, the Chinese ideal is different to the European one) based on the perceptions that one might encounter in his or her environment. This fact is valid not only for the standards of human physique, but for all aesthetic standards and patterns (for instance the standards of horses, dogs, etc.). On the other hand, at the same time he says that

> this standard ideal is not derived from proportions that are taken from experience as determinate rules. Rather, it is in accordance with this ideal that rules for judgment become possible in the first place.[24]

The creation of an algorithm of aesthetic standards probably takes place *a priori*,[25] but its material is obtained by experience.

---

20 Kant, *Kritik der Urteilskraft*, p. 75.
21 Cf. Démuth, "Poznanie, vedenie alebo interpretácia?"
22 Kant, *Kritik der Urteilskraft*. p. 75.
23 Démuth, "Intuícia ako výpočet so zastretým algoritmom riešenia? "
24 Kant, *Kritik der Urteilskraft*, p.75.
25 Similar to "A judgment of taste rests on a priori bases" Kant, *Kritik der Urteilskraft*, pp. 64–65.

Nevertheless, there is Kant's other remarkable note that

> the standard idea is by no means the entire archetype of beauty within this kind but is only the form... Nor is it because of its beauty that we like its exhibition, but merely because it does not contradict any of the conditions under which a thing of this kind can be beautiful.[26]

What is more, he suggests an example in a footnote:

> It will be found that a perfectly regular face, such as a painter would like to have as a model, usually conveys nothing. This is because it contains nothing characteristic and hence expresses more the idea of [human] kind than what is specific in one person.[27]

However, as the numerous observations of psychologists and cognitive scientists show, people perceive faces that are the closest to Kant's described average as a standard of beauty as beautiful. This knowledge has been well-known since the times of Galton and his almost Kantian experiment with the composite images of criminals who were more attractive than the faces of individuals, but it was proved by repeated observations carried out by Langlois and Roggman,[28] and by many others.[29] The explanation of why we like faces which are close to or identical to faces created according to the Kantian standard is not only mathematical, but also evolutionary. However, the fact remains that throughout the history of art (for instance in the Baroque period) opinions can be found that for "perfection," the perfectly average and symmetrical face very often requires the violation of symmetry and the average by means of a certain beauty spot which would make the object distinctive and unforgettable.

Conclusion

We have tried to present two historical models of aesthetic (taste) judgment, the ideal of beauty, and their relationship with mathematization in this study. As we have shown, the crucial idea of the mathematization of beauty and aesthetic

---

26 Kant, *Kritik der Urteilskraft*, p. 75.
27 Kant, *Kritik der Urteilskraft*, p. 75.
28 Judith H. Langlois and Lori Roggman "Attractive faces are only average."
29 G. Rhodes, et al., "Facial Symmetry and Perception of Beauty" and Rhodes et al., "Are Average Facial Configurations Attractive Only Because of Their Symmetry?" and Devendra Singh "Body Shape and Women's Attractiveness. The Critical Role of Waist-to-Hip Ratio."

norms lies in Hume's idea of standardization of taste via comparison and standardization of norms.

Hume's idea of statistical standardization provides the context for many contemporary psychological and cultural-anthropological studies aimed at the understanding of taste creation, its influences and the significance of rareness and excellence, as a desire for specific positive deviation. At the same time, it highlights the potential for aesthetic studies concentrated on the analysis of cognitive structures of the subject, its perceptions, and the subjective as well as inter-subjective nature of aesthetic experience. He believes that expert opinion might help widen our limited experiences and guide us through our own, insufficiently organized aesthetic experiences. The judgment of taste is based on experiences, rational[30] social participation[31] and social interaction.

Acknowledgments

This work was supported by the Slovak Research and Development Agency under the contract No. APVV-15-0294.

Bibliography

Bahm, Archie J. (1972) "Is a Universal Science of Aesthetics Possible?" *Journal of Aesthetics and Art Criticism*. 31 (1): 3–7.

Broadie, Alexander (2010) "Art and aesthetic theory." In: Broadie (Ed.) *The Cambridge Companion to The Scottish Enlightenment*. Cambridge: Cambridge University Press, 280–297.

Calder, Andy J. et al. (2011) *The Oxford Handbook of Face Perception*. Oxford: Oxford University Press.

Dadějík, Ondřej (2017) "David Hume a logika soudů vkusu." *Filosofický časopis*. 2: 275–296.

Démuth, Andrej (2009a) "Intuícia ako výpočet so zastretým algoritmom riešenia?" In: David Krámsky (Ed.) *Kognitivní věda dnes a zítra*. Liberec: Nakladatelství Bor. 81–86.

Démuth, Andrej (2009b) *Poznanie, vedenie alebo interpretácia?* Pusté Úľany: Schola Philosophica.

Démuth, Andrej (2013) "David Hume a asociačné "škandály" jeho myslenia. In: Démuth, et al. (Eds.) *Rozpravy o Humovej filozofii*. Pusté Úľany: Schola Philosophica, 9–23.

Graham, Gordon (2014) "Aesthetics as a Normative Science." *Royal Institute of Philosophy. Supplement*, 75: 249–264.

---

30 Meaning to be able to explain.
31 Jones, "Hume on the Arts and 'The Standard of Taste'," 433.

Guyer, Paul (2014) *A History of Modern Aesthetics*. Vol. 1. Cambridge: Cambridge University Press.
Hume, David (2012) *A Treatise of Human Nature*. Create Space Independent Publishing Platform.
Hume, David. (1757) *Four Dissertations*. London: Millar, in the Strand.
Hume, David (2008) *Selected Essays*. Oxford World's Classics, Oxford: Oxford University Press.
Jaffro, Laurent (2008) "Some Difficulties with the Reidian Argument for Aesthetic Realism." *14th Conference of Japan-Korea Aesthetic Studies Society*, Japan. 129–142.
Jones, Peter (2011) "Hume on the Arts and 'The Standard of Taste': Texts and Contexts. In: David Fate Norton & Jacqueline Taylor (Eds.) *The Cambridge Companion to Hume*. Second edition. Cambridge: Cambridge University Press, 414–446.
Kant, Immanuel (1922) *Kritik der Urteilskraft*. Fünfte Auflage. Leipzig: Verlag von Felix Meiner.
Kivy, Peter (2004) Reid's Philosophy of Art. In: Cuneo & Woudenberg (Eds.) *The Cambridge Companion to Thomas Reid*. Cambridge: Cambridge University Press. 267–288.
Langlois, Judith H. and Lori Roggman (1990) "Attractive Faces are Only Average." *Psychological Science*. 1: 115–121.
Makkreel, Rudolf A (2011) "Aesthetics." In: Knud Haakonssen, (Ed.) *The Cambridge History of Eighteenth-Century Philosophy*. Vol. 1., Cambridge: Cambridge University Press. 516–556.
Norton, David Fate and Jacqueline Taylor (Eds) (2011)., *The Cambridge Companion to Hume*. 2nd edition (Cambridge: Cambridge University Press)
Rhodes, Gillian, Fiona Proffitt, Jonathan M. Grady, & Alex Sumich, (1998) "Facial symmetry and perception of beauty." *Psychonomic Bulletin & Review* 5: 659–669.
Rhodes, Gillian, et al (1999) "Are Average Facial Configurations Attractive Only Because of Their Symmetry?" *Psychological Science*. 10: 52–58.
Singh, Devendra (1993) "Body Shape and Women's Attractiveness. The Critical Role of Waist-to-Hip Ratio." *Human Nature*. 4(3): 297–321.
Vopěnka, Petr (2000) *Úhelný kámen evropské vzdělanosti a moci*. Praha: Práh.
Wenzel, Christian Helmut (2001) "Beauty, Genius, and Mathematics: Why Did Kant Change His Mind?" *History of Philosophy Quarterly*. 18(4): 415–432.

Bernard Freydberg
Plato and Hume's Philosophy of Art

In the Platonic dialogues, poetry is discussed almost exclusively in terms of whether it helps or harms the souls of the people who hear it (reading was not, of course, widespread among the ancients). For David Hume, poetry is discussed in terms of how its more or less ingenious presentation of the human sentiments engages those same sentiments in its readers and/or spectators, and the best match of poem to listener is characterized by the innocence of the pleasure it brings. İn addition, reason plays a larger *positive* role in Hume's aesthetics than in either the theoretical or moral philosophy. In the former, the arguments of reason result one and all in the ongoing discovery of our ignorance. In the latter, which is guided by the right/wrong imagery of the human heart, reason has little to do other than to concur in the discovery of most of the moral qualities. Only justice and political society tax it, and do so not very heavily. While aesthetic judgment is primarily a matter of sentiment, reason must be actively present. As will be shown, the necessary "sound state" requires it, the art object includes it, and the overall view of the subject entails it.

A difficulty in approaching this work that is common to all philosophies of art from the modern period concerns its suitability for our much more recent age. Hume addresses one such matter when he asserts that philosophers give way to other, better ones in future ages, but poets retain their lustre. Here, I disagree with Hume's suggestion that "ARISTOTLE, and PLATO, and EPICURUS, and DESCARTES, may successively yield to each other..." (ST 231) There are many resources in Hume's aesthetics for any philosophy – and in the other thinkers mentioned.

Another difficulty arises with respect to what at least seems to be a radically altered artistic landscape beginning in the late nineteenth and early twentieth centuries. Artists themselves have challenged the central tenets of their predecessors in their work. Questions of continuity, of the nature of the work of art (if indeed it has a nature), of art's relation to politics, of the relation of the artist to the work of art she or he creates – these questions, among others, lead me to ask how is Hume's philosophy of art relevant to a century that has seen the so-called Aristotelian unities and their offspring in the visual and aural arts disappear? How, for example, can the Humean view of art deal with Kafka, Virginia Woolf, Duchamp, Schoenberg, Merce Cunningham, Ornette Coleman, not to mention their even more unorthodox heiresses and heirs and *their* postmodernist descendants – if indeed it can?

A different matter that requires attention, perhaps not unrelated to the latter one, is also raised by Hume's text. I would like to agree with the second part of the sentence cited above, "...But TERENCE and VIRGIL maintain an universal, undisputed empire over the minds of men." (ST 231) Earlier, he makes the same claim for Homer. Unless the first two names happen to coincide with that of a current celebrity just as the third coincides with an obtuse cartoon character, there is a strong likelihood that fewer than 1% of Americans would recognize these names and a larger but dwindling minority would recognize them in Europe and in the rest of the world. As to their "maintaining an empire over the minds of men," only a miniscule percentage of that very small group has sufficient command of Greek and Latin to respond to Hume's encomium.

Are there more recent modern works to which we can turn that fulfill Hume's lofty criterion? Perhaps most of Shakespeare; perhaps most of Mozart and Beethoven as well; perhaps also works of Da Vinci and Michelangelo. Whether or not the work of such relatively recent but widely celebrated modern painters might qualify, or that of early 20th century choreographers, seems undecidable. In our era, the visual arts tend to be more accessible. Of Homer, Terence, and Virgil, perhaps we can conditionally admit Hume's praise, i.e., *if* classical knowledge were as common among educated people as it *should* be. In any case, Hume is correct that there are clear cases of superiority. These are especially plain when the difference in quality is obvious, e.g., when comparing the compositions of Beethoven with those of his contemporary, the violin virtuoso Paganini. Less plain but no less decisive is the superiority of Mozart to the good Salieri, a comparison popularized by the imaginative dramatization in the play and film *Amadeus*.

Hume begins by employing the above as an *elenchus* to the accustomed view that taste is no more than a matter of opinion. Taste among human beings differs widely even within homogeneous groups, and terms of praise for works of art are alike (i.e., elegance, spirit, etc.). "But when critics come to particulars, this seeming unanimity vanishes; and it is found, that they had affixed a very different meaning to their expressions." (ST 204) However, the existence of clear cases, together with the agreement that such cases exist, results in the impossibility of maintaining the accustomed view.[1] Thus, in a one-sentence paragraph

---

[1] The main issue of the essay, according to Dabney Townsend, "is not about taste per se. The essay is specifically about the problem of a standard – why one must have some standard to settle disputes and how such a standard can be made consistent with the empirical sentimentalism at the heart of Hume's epistemology." Dabney Townsend, *Hume's Aesthetic Theory*, p. 180. To solve the problem, Townsend distinguishes what might be called three tiers of aesthetic response: first pleasure, an immediate impression for which no account is required; then beauty, which has no definition and which follows upon pleasure but only in response to certain ob-

Hume writes: "It is natural for us to seek a *Standard of Taste*; a rule by which the various sentiments of men may be reconciled; at least a decision afforded confirming one sentiment, and condemning another" (ST 208).

To those who would defend the accustomed view by asserting that beauty does not exist in things themselves but only in the eye of the beholder, just as preferences for certain taste sensations in food issue only from the predilections of the diner, Hume presents these clear cases as a refutation that convinces:

> Whoever would assert an equality of genius and elegance between OGILBY and MILTON, or BUNYAN and ADDISON, would be thought to defend no less an extravagance, than if he had maintained a mole-hill to be as high as TENERIFFE, or a pond as extensive as the ocean. Though there may be found persons, who give the preference to the former authors; no one pays attention to such a taste... (ST 210).

These two English writers, whose work appeared within one hundred years of Hume's life, had not passed the test of time; yet they presented clear cases. Can we replace those British names today with the poetry of rock-singer JEWEL and that of ELIZABETH BISHOP, or with JAMES PATTERSON and SAUL BELLOW? I certainly hope so ... but I am just as certainly mistaken, so distant from us has the standard of taste withdrawn.

At the very least, however, Hume's essay recollects and affirms this standard for us today, and serves as a valuable resource even apart from its other noteworthy features. Perhaps its most striking such feature is the claim that aesthetic standards are firmer and more lasting than either philosophical, moral, or scientific ones. Philosophical standards have always been open to dispute. While moral language seems well-fixed, i.e., virtue is always praised and vice is always blamed, this fixity is primarily attributable to the nature of language. The particular qualities and actions that constitute virtue are variable across cultures and history. Natural science features discoveries that improve upon and often supplant their predecessors. But the decidedly pre-classical Homer still holds all of its centuries-long recognition for artistic excellence, and new discoveries are always shedding more light on the remarkable epics.

The same source that determines Hume's theoretical and moral philosophies also determines his aesthetic philosophy, in a word, "experience; nor are [the rules of composition] any thing but general observations, concerning what has

---

jects; then finally taste, "which operates in advance of any explanations and principles, either directly in terms of qualities or by extension through rules" (183). One problem with Townsend's interpretation may be merely verbal: Hume calls the Standard of Taste "a rule." If I were to attempt to reconcile Townsend's view with my own, I would say that the standard cannot be stated propositionally but experienced as a ruling image arising from the requirements of delicacy, etc.

been universally found to please in all countries and in all ages" (ST 210). However, "experience" extends differently in each of the three realms. In the first *Enquiry*, experience extends only to impressions and ideas. When subjected to enquiry, we find that our "knowledge" is restricted to constant conjunction and the belief that such conjunction will continue. In other words, our enquiry into experience ulimately yields only a non-rational psychological connection; in a way, experience as connected perception disappears on the foundation of "experience." In the second *Enquiry*, moral philosophy springs from experience as the common recognition of right/wrong moral imagery in the human heart. Experience is always subject in some way to the sentiment of humanity, in Hume's words. This image-based experience is sustained throughout, and leads to a catalogue of desireable qualities. In neither case does Hume's "experience" require an abundance of sophistication to grasp, although the first *Enquiry* displays unmatched subtlety of argument while the latter offers the most rigorous image-play in modern philosophy.

What is required for genuine aesthetic experience in accord with the standard toward which Hume has so strongly gestured? The most general answer is: a very great deal. On the part of the spectator, every one of these conditions must be met concurrently: (1) it must occur at a proper time and place; (2) the imagination must be suitably disposed; (3) the mind must be perfectly serene; (4) thought must duly recollect what is germane; and (5) proper attention to the object must be paid. "…[I]f any of these circumstances be wanting, our experiment will be fallacious, and we shall be unable to judge of the catholic and universal beauty." (ST 213) I am sure that this holds true for me, and I venture to say that it also holds for the vast majority of even those who love art the most, not only that these five conditions have not ever been met concurrently but that it is a rare and happy occasion indeed when more than two are operative at any one time.

Hume does not himself claim to have achieved this state. It is an experience that requires a mix of exacting discipline and exceptional good fortune to have enjoyed this particular "experience." In this light, it does not surprise when Hume turns immediately to Homer as a model in order to illustrate it:

(1) we are at sufficient distance from it in virtually every way to make "now" a proper time and place
(2) when we pick up either epic, it is assumed that our imagination is disposed toward it
(3) this can never be established certainly, but the transport to the ancient Greek language facilitates equanimity of mind
(4) thought recollects the mythical material
(5) the epic fully engages our attention with respect to its prosodic and rhythmic qualities.

That Hume uses an example from a "dead" language is no accident. Anything English, European, Asian, or African is either too close or altogether too distant. As we "all" have access to a langauage and two poems that are complete in themselves, the Homeric epics are almost uniquely able to provide an occasion for a display of the aforementioned concurretly required qualities. Through them, one can enjoy genuine aesthetic experience.

What happens in cases when the aesthetic experience does not occur, which – one must say – is in almost every case? A sound state in each person consists of the aforementioned collection of qualities. A defective state consists of...well... everything else! Hume declares "want of delicacy" to be one obvious cause. Once again, he gives a convincing example, a vicarious image – this one from a comic scene in *Don Quixote* – instead of a definition. Sancho Panza relates his hereditary excellence in the discernment of wine quality to a squire with a large nose: one of his ancestors correctly identified a leathern taste and the other a metallic one in a quantity of wine. Though ridiculed by the others present, a key tied to a strip of leather was later found. Therefore, though beauty and deformity belong to sentiment rather than to objects, "it must be allowed, that there are certain qualities in objects which are fitted by nature to produce those particular feelings." (ST 217) Delicacy requires the sensitive apprehension of those quailties that produce those particular feelings:

> Where the organs are so fine as to allow nothing to escape them, and at the same time so exact as to perceive every ingredient in this composition, this we call delicacy of taste, whether we employ these terms in the literal or metaphorical sense (ST 217–218).

This quality serves also, as was shown in the second *Enquiry*, as a particularly useful quality that might even exceed philosophy in the happiness it brings at least as a result of the pure pleasure it affords. Once again, however, Hume speaks of exceptionally attuned organs, compared to which mine, at least, are painfully discordant though my experiences of art are among my most treasured. When I attend the Pittsburgh Symphony Orchestra, I can never say that my sensibility has missed nothing and has perceived every ingredient. In a live jazz concert, which involves spontaneous improvisation, such delicacy may be impossible in principle. Even when I read and reread a short poem of, e.g., Louise Glück or Gwendolyn Brooks, I never feel that all the pieces have somehow come together. While these experiences have brought me the widest and deepest pleasure, I cannot claim delicacy in Hume's sense.

Further tests make the attainment of the already virtually impossible standard of taste still "more virtually impossible." One requires the widest possible experience within a particular species of beauty. Another requires frequent re-experiences of an object of that species in many different lights so as not to be overly influenced by a first or second impression before making one's judgment. Still another requires "comparisons between the several species" for "by comparison alone we fix the epithets of praise or blame, and learn how to assign the due degree of each." (ST 223) Finally, delicacy necessitates freedom from prejudice, the ability to regard oneself apart from all affiliations and enmities as "a man in general," Where this does not occur, the judgment is perverted.

Thus, if one were to meet Hume's requirements set by the standard of taste, one must spend one's entire leisure several times over perfecting one's organs, studying and comparing numberless works of art in every species, and all the while – or first of all? – purifying one's outlook of every taint of prejudice. There is no time to work, certainly no time to write philosophical texts, no time to read them one after one has read this text and signed on to the achievement of meeting Hume's standard of taste. All this for a quality that is useful to oneself but one without which a person can live a good moral life? What on earth is going on here? Is Hume serious?

I confess that I am not certain. I will venture to say, however, that the virtual impossibility of achieving the standard is – intentionally or not (and I would wager *something* on the former) – another instance of Hume's playfulness within which the deepest seriousness is concealed, akin to the playfulness of the Platonic dialogues. I say "akin," because the similarity here crosses from Hume's judgment in philosophy of art to Socrates' judgment in his pursuit of wisdom generally. If we stipulate that wisdom in the realm of artistic apprehension consists of meeting the standard of taste, then *no one is wise*.[2] To provide an oversimplified but useful example, suppose a reasonable but monolingual English speaker holds the opinion that, e.g., Homer's *Iliad* lacks poetic merit because its lines don't seem to sing. Tell that person that in order to render a proper judgment, one must be quite conversant in Greek. The person "must conclude, upon the whole, that the fault lies in himself..." (ST 219) Extend this example as far as you like, and the most one can say is that there are greater and lesser degrees of delicacy, and that ultimately even the most specialized judge must concede the fallibility of her or his judgment or risk a legacy of folly, e.g., by deriding French Impressionism as madness, if indeed there is such a legacy.

---

[2] Timothy M. Costelloe writes: "The standard...is an abstraction from the activity itself and presents in propositional form what good taste would consist in were individuals free of the imperfections of their nature." Costelloe, *Aesthetics and Morals in the Philosophy of David Hume*, pp. 16–17.

Recall Plato's *Apology:* "It is likely that the god is really wise and by his oracle means this: 'human wisdom is of little or no worth.'"[3] Where is the kinship with Hume? It is here: the achievement of the standard of taste, just as the achievement of real wisdom, is closed off to human beings. Yet another playful, perhaps even comic element is this: even supposing one could do the impossible and fulfill every listed critierion, works of art continue to be made, requiring ongoing comparisons which, we may assume, would require ongoing alterations in the tasks required to achieve the standard. What, then, is the outcome? Negatively, we must always be prepared to draw the inference against ourselves when presented with a work that we are for some reason unprepared to judge. At the least, we must say "I don't know."

In this regard, Hume's thought offers a rebirth of Socratic ignorance in aesthetic matters. Is there a person anywhere who can claim Humean "delicacy" with respect to the burgeoning of unprecedented forms of artmaking? One might object that delicacy is no longer a relevant quality. In response and opposition, this is a mere quarrel about a word, in light of the clear matter of fact that curators make decisions concerning what works deserve to be shown, conductors and chamber groups make decisions on what music deserves to be played and heard, respected literary and poetry organizations award prizes to works that they believe merit them.

I have little doubt, for example, that the much-celebrated Elliott Carter is a superb composer, and have no regret about my compact-disc purchases of performances of his music. Nor am I sorry about the hours I spent listening – trying to listen – to his music. Why can't I hear it, enjoy it? Why is it honored and enjoyed by critics and aficionados of avant-garde "classical" music? (1) I lack the required...something, and (2) the critics and aficionados do not. This is the best answer I can give. However, I have long loved the music of Ornette Coleman, who only recently has achieved official recognition from the established judges,[4] though this music presents formidable barriers to access for many people. However, in this case I have been a steady "comparer" of jazz performances, and so find myself concurring confidently with this recognition of his genius. Again, this confirmation represents only the best I, and the critics, can do at this time. There can be no doubt that the decision to award the prize was based upon the cultivated sensibility of the judges, call it "delicacy" or call it something along similar

---

3 Plato, *Apology*, 23a.
4 His musical effort *Sound Grammar* (2006) recorded live in Germany in 2005, is the first jazz album to receive a Pulitzer Prize. Like many artists with distinctive styles, Coleman endured much ridicule for his composing, his horn and violin playing, and his general approach to music. Obviously, he had his champions as well.

lines. Without providing much in the way of transition (and so strengthening my hunch), Hume goes on to observe that "few are qualified to give judgment on *any* work of art." (ST 228 – emphasis mine) He implicitily admits that the actual existence of a single qualified critic of any work of art is not necesary to his argument:

> It is sufficient for our present purpose, if we have proved, that the taste of all individuals is not upon an equal footing, and that some men in general, however difficult to be particularly pitched upon, will be acknowledged by universal sentiment to have a preference above others (ST 230).

Here are two other crossings back to Platonic philosophy, though along somewhat different lines. The issues do not directly concern images and image-play, but rather trace the general limits of human judgment.

The first concerns the rare or non-existent judge who has its counterpart in *Republic* V, in the course of Socrates' distinguishing the lovers of sights from the philosophers:

> The lovers of hearing and the lovers of sights, on the one hand, I said surely delight in beautiful (*kalas*) sounds and colors and shapes and all that craft makes from such things, but their thought (*dianoia*) is unable to see and delight in the nature of the beautiful itself. That, he said, is certainly so.
> Wouldn't, on the other hand, those who approach the beautiful itself and see it by itself be rare (*spanioi*)?
> Very much so (*kai mala*)[5]

The lovers of hearing and of sights are said to be asleep though they think they are awake; the only ones who are called "awake" are those who can both distinguish the beautiful itself and beautiful things, and can see how beautiful things participate in beauty itself. The latter are the analogues of Hume's superior judges. Regarding the "very rare" one who can see beauty itself by itself, one finds telling silence. Such a one may not be a human being at all. One who fully measures up to Hume's standard of taste – may we not suspect the same?

The second crossing occurs from Hume's discussion of the task of the true critic, whose superior judgment is always open to challenge:

> Whether any particular person be endowed with good sense and a delicate imagination, free from prejudice, may often be the subject of dispute, ...but that such a character is valuable and estimable, will be agreed in by all mankind. Where these doubts occur, ...men

---

5 Plato, *Republic*, 476b–c.

must produce the best arguments that their invention suggests to them; they must acknowledge a true and decisive standard to exist somewhere, to whit, real existence and matter of fact; and they must have indulgence to such as differ from them in their appeals to this standard (ST 230).

This passage echoes Plato in the *Phaedo* where Socrates "assumes" or "lays down" (*hupothemenos*) what he judged to be the strongest (*errōmenestaton*) *logos*.[6] That the beautiful itself by itself exists, this he affirms as the strongest *logos*.[7] Whatever harmonizes (*sumphōnein*) with this "assumption" he will call true, and what does not he will regard as untrue.

For Hume, the matter of fact and real existence of a standard of taste conforms to the Socratic presupposition of "beauty itself in itself, goodness itself in itself," and the like. The repeated and very frequent Socratic recourse to the first person in these lines strongly suggests that Socrates is not claiming anything resembling objective truth; indeed, truth could only be said to occur given the assumption. What makes Socrates' "assumption" strongest, then, is not its truth, but rather its ability to fend off all challengers in the contest of *logoi*, or in most current translations, of "arguments." Hume's "best arguments" occur under the power of the matter of fact/real existence of the standard of taste. This matter of fact/real existence cannot be beheld directly any more than Platonic beauty can. Rather, its acceptance must be granted once the phenomenon of clear cases is granted.

With this measuring of Hume's claim, disputes of taste – at least those of a certain kind – do not admit of a decisive answer. A helpful example may be the mid-nineteenth century vitriolic dispute between music critic Eduard Hanslick, champion of Brahms and Mendelssohn and despiser of Wagner and Liszt, and Richard Pohl, enthusiastic partisan of Wagner and Liszt and antagonist of Brahms and Mendelssohn.[8] Though Hanslick is read more frequently today as

---

6 Plato, *Phaedo*, 1a—e.
7 There are others along this line, the *eidē*.
8 The overall view of critic Eduard Hanslick that there is no such thing as an extra-musical emotion, and who championed Brahms and denounced Wagner, is captured in the following citations from *On the Beautiful in Music*, "[Music's] nature is specifically musical. By this we mean that the beautiful is not contingent upon nor in need of any subject introduced from without, but that consists wholly of sounds artistically combined" (p. 47). "For the object of these pages, it is enough to denounce emphatically as false Wagner's principle theorem as stated in the first volume of *Oper und Drama*," in which Wagner argued that drama was the end and music the mere means. Hanslick continues: "An opera...in which the music is really and truly employed as a medium for dramatic expression is a musical monstrosity" (p. 44). By contrast, Richard Pohl, champion of Wagner and "the music of the future," was "swept off his feet

a result of his provocative formalism that admits the aesthetic validity only of purely musical emotions and that rules out what he calls "program music" as well as all music designed to elicit "human" emotions, it can be said that in the actual world of music programming Pohl draws even with his antagonist. Though these two critics certainly showed no "indulgence to such as differ from them in appeals to this standard," less partisan and passionate music directors and conductors have implicity indulged each of them.

What are we to make of this comment, offered almost as self evident, in considering Hume as a Platonic philosopher (and 'Continental' ancestor):

> Every work of art has [like all noble works of genius] also a certain end or purpose for which it is calculated; and is to be deemed more or less perfect, as it is more or less fitted to attain this end. The object of eloquence is to persuade, of history to instruct, of poetry to please, by means of the passions and the imagination (ST 226–227).

This view resists reinterpretation along either path. Hume never gives a description of what he calls "genius." One cannot be certain whether it points to a creative ability that differs in kind from a high degree of technical facility, or only in degree. The Platonic dialogues, while not having such a word at their disposal, nevertheless clearly point to divine inspiration as its source – or what we would call a qualitative distinction. One of its key features is a kind of madness, as we have seen, and not calculation toward a pre-determined end. Similarly, Continental philosophy of art, although discourses on genius are not an important part, clearly acknowledges a gift that is special and peculiar to certain arists such as Cezanne, Van Gogh, Klee, and Kandinsky as visual artists, and Hölderlin, Celan, and Keats as poets.

A far more noteworthy difference emerges in Hume's comment on the object or purpose of poetry. Neither in the Platonic dialogues nor for recent Continental philosophy does poetry have as its goal merely "to please by means of the passions and the imagination," (ST 227) though it *may* have this quality as a second-order effect. In both, the close relation between poetry and *truth* constitutes the crux of the issue, which (accordingly) plays a much larger role. In either the traditional interpretation of Plato that regards poetry as dangerous to the soul, or the newer one that regards poetry in a friendly and complementary way, the detrmination concerning the connection of poetry to truth is a central concern.

And in one of the most influential strains of Continental philosophy, poetry – great poetry – is one of the preeminent sites at which truth happens. In this

---

by the passionate ideals of the musical romanticists..." Edwin N. Waters, "Franz Liszt to Richard Pohl," p. 193.

strain, established earlier by Martin Heidegger, truth is interpreted as the Greek *alētheia* – *a-lētheia* – un-forgottenness or un-hiddenness. This is the most originary sense of truth; truth as correspondence or coherence are mere second-order offshoots in which *their* origin conceals itself. Untruth, darkness and ignorance, belong essentially to truth's disclosure. Hölderlin ("*Was bleibet aber, stiften die Dichter*")[9] and Stefan George among the Germans, and especially Sophocles among the Greeks receive sustained interpretive elucidation.

Hume does not have the slightest scruple concerning the celebration of *beauty* in its wondrous capacity to shine upon the souls of those who behold it, and at one point links it in a way to reason, from which it is otherwise distinct:

> Not to mention, that the same excellence of faculties which contributes to the improvement of reason, the same clearness of conception, the same exactness of distinction, the same vivacity of apprehension, are essential to the operations of true taste, and are its infallible concomitants. It seldom or never happens, that a man of sense, who has experience in any art, cannot judge of its beauty; and it is no less rare to meet with a man who has a just taste without a sound understanding (ST 227).

As the large majority of Hume's examples are literary, it scarcely surprises that he notes the requirement of being able to follow a series of propositions in a work of imagination just as is required in following a chain of inferences in the sciences. Add to that the above citation that claims their close affinity in the mind of the person of sound sense and one might ask: "What, then, is the difference after all?"

Here, we find another instance of Hume's text working against itself with an unexpected and significant result. It appears that sound understanding and true taste, while aligned in the person of acumen, are nonetheless distinct. Sound understanding refers to the operations of reason, true taste refers to the fineness of sentiment. However, what Hume in the first *Enquiry* calls "sound understanding" has a very limited sense. Strictly speaking, its only positive meaning can be found in relations of ideas. With respect to matters of fact, the person whose understanding is actually sound has full awareness of its profound limits.

Our best insights amount to no more than customs, which are reducible to fictions that repeat themselves such that we must believe that they will continue to occur. No other distinction can be made regarding those fictions and the ones we cannot (and therefore do not) believe. According to sound understanding, the phenomenon we call "cause" is nothing other than constant conjunction and the "new" impression (read: sentiment) that it generates. The unavoidable conclu-

---

[9] "What remains, the poet establishes." Friedrich Hölderlin, *Werke und Briefe*, Band 1, p. 196.

sion – at least so it seems to me (this is surely not Hume's own view) – is that there is no difference in kind at all between the theoretical and the aesthetic experience. Both are fundamentally aesthetic, though the nature of the first does not become apparent until Hume's *Enquiry* reaches its zenith.

One can even find early traces of finite imagination and finite transcendence in Hume's discussion of what he calls "innocent and unavoidable" performances that "can never reasonably be the object of dispute, because there is no standard by which they can be decided" (ST 234). One's nationality, for example, or the time in which one lives, or—most thought-provoking – one's chronological age, can give rise to preferences among works that are otherwise judged as meeting the standard. Hume writes:

> At twenty, OVID may be the favourite author, HORACE at forty, and perhaps TACITUS at fifty. Vainly would we, in such cases, endeavour to enter into the sentiments of others, and divest ourselves of those propensities which are natural to us. We choose our favourite author as we do our friend, from a conformity of humour and disposition. Mirth or passion, sentiment or reflection; whichever of these most predominates in our temper, it gives us a peculiar sympathy with the writer who resembles us (ST 223).

In other but doubtlessly accurate terms, as one nears death one's preference – one's need, perhaps? – for different kinds of vicarious imaging undergoes change. In still other words, as the body gradually declines from its prime, there is less desire for the erotic vicarious imagery such as offered by Ovid. In middle age, the imagery of the comforts of bourgeois life is more welcome. Finally, as one reaches the threshhold of death – *epi gēraos oudō* as Socrates has it in *Republic* I[10] – one seeks the larger picture, given in history rather than poetry, into which one can meaningfully locate one's life. One can therefore speak of a standard that engages both spectator and artwork, but one cannot specify the preference of either the spectator or the artwork, nor can one ultimately match them. The best one can do in this regard is to invoke the standard as establishing certain works as meeting the test of time. With respect to those works, an *elenchus* awaits: if the spectator does not admire these works, then the defect is in *him*.

Hume further bows to finitude in his discussion of "the celebrated controversy concerning ancient and modern learning" (ST 235) that takes place toward the end of his essay. Earlier, he appeared to assert that the proper appraisal of the great classical poets requires looking away from the "false content" of some of their lines while concentrating entirely on the conveyance of sentiment and

---

[10] Plato, *Republic*, 328e.

the pleasure that ensues. Here, he seems to alter this position as least to a degree, admitting that:

> [t]he want of humanity and decency, so conspicuous in the characters drawn by several of the ancient poets, even sometimes by HOMER and the GREEK tragedians, diminishes considerably the merit of their noble performances, and gives modern authors an advantage over them (ST 236).

I disagree immediately and sharply with Hume's "considerably." Quite apart from any content, the matchless music of Homer alone lifts his epics above all of the modern authors available in Hume's time, with arguments possible (but not likely, in my view) only for Shakespeare and Milton in English, and though I do not know their languages, Dante and Cervantes and a few others. Even regarding content, Hume's aesthetics does not include an analogue to the Platonic *huponoia*, or underlying sense. Rather, one must *allow* for more or less straightforward falsehoods or age-related moral defects, i.e., one must somehow overlook them. When it comes to appraising the matter in terms of ancient and modern *learning*, Hume seems to say, the modern authors clearly prevail. Only a somewhat tortuous distinction between artistic excellence and the incorporation of "learning" into artistic production saves Hume from outright contradiction.

Here, the bouquet goes to the ancients – due to their greater sophistication, no less. The way Homer's "Achilles in Hades" passage yielded two different interpretations – one "negative" and the other "positive" in two different contexts suffices to settle the contest in favor of the ancient, especially in light of the positive interpretation occurring for the human being who has been liberated from the cave. Two more among others: For the training of the guardians as delineated in *Republic* III, Socrates would ban *Odyssey* X, 444–45, since the city does not need guardians who believe that they would become insubstantial nothings should they be slain:

> …[Tiresias] alone has intelligence even after death,
> but the rest of them are flittering shadows.[11]

However, the *Meno* concludes by recommending this identical passage: there are no teachers nor will any be found "unless there is someone among our statesmen who can make another into a statesman. If there were one, he could be said to be among the living what Tiresias was said to be among the dead, namely that 'he alone retained his intelligence while the others are flitting shadows.' In

---

11 Plato, *Republic*, 386d.

the same manner such a man would, as far as virtue is concerned, here also be the only true thing compared with shadows" (100a).

One more: the *Republic* finds Socrates deploring poetic depictions of gods undergoing all kinds of transformations, concerned that the guardians' steadfastness would be compromised by such images. However, he employs the same passage playfully from *Odyssey* XVII, 485 to question the Eleatic Stranger's identity in the *Sophist:*

> For the gods take on all sorts of transformations, appearing as strangers from elsewhere, and thus they range at large through the cities, watching to see which men keep the laws, and which are violent (216a–b).

Elsewhere, I note the distortion – or more neutrally, the alteration – that results from the end of what is outrageously called "paganism" and the onset of Christianity, a change that runs so thoroughly deep that even an atheist as resolute as Hume cannot resist it. The playful relation of the Greeks to their gods, which includes making them subject to interpretations of all kinds – even Hermes, the messenger god, the "god" of interpretation is interpreted in many ways[12] – is a relation that is alien to Hume's age, though Hume himself is always ready to ridicule superstition, a.k.a. religion as customarily practiced. His thought also undermines the entrenched sensible/intelligible distinction and its offshoots in a momentous manner.

Thus, he has also left "Of Tragedy" for us, a work on aesthetics that serves only to cement his bond to the distinctions his thought so successfully confounded. For Hume, the skill of the author and/or playwright goes no further than her or his ability to manipulate the passions of the spectators. Hume praises Shakespeare highly for this skill, and praises the turning point of *Othello* for the intensification the poet achieves by focusing upon the hero's impatience, which only serves to magnify his jealousy.[13] However, Hume also criticizes Shakespeare for "great irregularities, and even absurdities, [that] so frequently disfigure the ani-

---

12 Homeric hymns to Hermes give special emphasis to his status as messenger between human beings and gods, while acknowledging his other service as lord over all animals and as conductor of souls into Hades. His role as messenger features prominently in Socrates' recollection of Diotima's speech in Plato's *Symposium*. In the Orphic hymns to Hermes, there is no mention of his role as intermediary, but he sings of his role as the god of discourse and of sleep. Further, the Homeric hymns claim that Zeus and Maya parented Hermes; the Orphic hymns attribute this parentage to Dionysus and Aphrodite.
13 Hume, "Of Tragedy," 130.

mated and passionate scenes intermixt with them."[14] He refers to Shakespeare's rudeness and lack of theatrical knowledge, and wonders whether he and his contemporaries overrate him by concentrating too much on his most moving moments.

Though echoing the Aristotelian trope "imitation is always of itself agreeable,"[15] Hume's analysis makes no mention of plot, character, or thought – perhaps presupposing them as prerequisites for any worthy such drama. He does, however, place greater emphasis on Aristotle's less highly regarded elements, called diction, song, and spectacle. In his explanation of the paradoxical pleasure that melancholy scenes often produce in the spectator, he writes:

> The genius required to paint objects in a lively manner, the art employed in collecting all the pathetic circumstances, the judgment displayed in disposing them: the exercise, I say, of these noble talents, together with the force of expression, and beauty of oratorical numbers [*rhythms*], diffuse the highest satisfaction on the audience, and excite the most delightful movements.[16]

Another necessary element of this peculiar enjoyment is the constant awareness – dwelling, however, in the background – that one is watching a *play*, i.e., that the events are contrived, that it is false, e.g., that a real man named Othello kills a blameless real woman named Desdemona, his wife. To show how this unstated but operative background awareness works, he contrasts any theatrical production with Cicero's 70 B.C. successful prosecution of Verres on numerous corruption charges with respect to his behavior as a leading official in Sicily. While the audience awareness of the background "unreality" of the play before them makes the spectacle of human misery peculiarly pleasurable, Cicero's "actual" artful and convincing rhetoric in detailing Verres' disgraceful malfeasance[17] before the court did not (and would not) bring pleasure.

When one recasts this example in Hume's own terms from the first *Enquiry*, one finds the perspective altered significantly. The difference between, e.g., a theatrical experience of Shakespeare's *Othello* and Cicero's oration against Verres is one of degree and not one of kind; we have direct experience of neither. Of *Othello* and of theatrical and literary productions generally, we have the con-

---

14 Remarks of David Hume on Shakespeare in Brian Vickers, ed., *The Critical Heritage*, Volume IV: 1753–1765, p. 176.
15 Hume, "Of Tragedy," p. 129.
16 Hume, "Of Tragedy," pp. 128–29.
17 Verres was successfully prosecuted for violations in taxation of wheat farmers, of fostering false allegations against leading landowners during a war by means of taking their slaves—some of which he killed. See Cicero, *The Verrine Orations*, Vol. 1.

stant conjunction of the theatrical framework and of the kinds of works that occur within it that occasions the background sense of unreality. Of actual orations, we have the belief instilled by habit of their reality. And when we consider the Ciceronian oration from this great chronological distance, we may be forgiven if we take the latter to be a theatrical performance.

The irony concealed in Hume's aesthetics concerns its essental conventionality. While giving an acute and thought-provoking account of the standard of taste and saving the idea of beauty in the course of his analyses, he esteems aesthetic experience far less than he does theoretical or moral experience. Delicacy of taste is the most innocent and the purest pleasure, and so gives the most sublime enjoyment to the one who has it. But it ranks below the pursuit of truth, the one passion that does not admit of excess, and below moral rightness, which suffuses human life with light and worth. One would not go too far wrong in saying that the higher two philosophical aspects concern themselves with questions of the nature of reality, while aesthetics concerns itself with the effect of imitations, "mere images," upon their sapient beholders.

But both the theoretical and moral apects of his philosophy, when followed through in the very way that he established them, give way to insights – "principles" – that are fundamentally aesthetic. That is to say, as reason recedes as it must, imagination and images move to center stage and shape everything of real consequence. In other words, Hume's philosophy presents human experience as *art* – except when it comes to art.

However, one phrase offered almost in passing suggests something more and other, though it leaves the general structure intact:

> In like manner, a quick and acute perception of beauty and deformity must be the perfection of our mental taste; nor can a man be satisfied with himself while he suspects that any excellence or blemish in a discourse has passed him unobserved. In this case, *the perfection of the man, and the perfection of the sense of feeling, are found to be united* (ST 220, emphasis mine).

In the perception of beauty, the human being who is divided into reason and sense (passion or sentiment) finds this division overcome, overtaken by what Continental philosophy has called *ecstasy*.

Ecstasy in Hume? Yes – and thus another testament to his Continental philosophy ancestry.

Acknowledgments

This chapter was originally published in a more complete version in Bernard Freydberg, *David Hume Platonic Philosopher, Continental Ancestor* (Albany: SUNY Press, 2012).

Bibliography

Cicero, (1959) *The Verrine Orations*. Vol. 1., L. H. G. Greenwood, trans. Cambridge: Harvard University Press.
Costelloe, Timothy M. (2007) *Aesthetics and Morals in the Philosophy of David Hume*. New York: Routledge.
Hanslick Eduard (1959) *On the Beautiful in Music*, Gustav Cohen, trans. Indianapolis: Bobbs-Merrill.
Hölderlin, Friedrich (1969) *Werke und Briefe*, Band 1. Frankfurt am Main: Insel Verlag.
Hume, David (2008) "Of Tragedy." In: Hume, *Selected Essays*. Stephen Copley and Andrew Edgar (Eds.) New York: Oxford World Classics.
Hume, David (2008) "Of the Standard of Taste." In: Hume, *Selected Essays*. In: Hume, *Selected Essays*. Stephen Copley and Andrew Edgar (Eds.) New York: Oxford World Classics.
Hume, David (1995) "Remarks on Shakespeare." In: Brian Vickers (Ed.) *The Critical Heritage: Shakespeare*. Volume IV: 1753–1765. London: Routledge.
Phaedo (1911) *Phaedo*, John Burnet, trans. Oxford: Clarendon Press.
Plato (1924) *Euthyphro, Apology of Socrates and Crito*, John Burnet, trans. Oxford: Clarendon Press.
Plato (1991) *Republic*, Alan Bloom, trans. New York: Basic Books. [1968]
Townsend, Dabney (2001) *Hume's Aesthetic Theory*. New York: Routledge.
Vickers, Brian (Ed.) (1995) *The Critical Heritage*. Volume IV: 1753–1765 (London and New York),
Waters, Edwin N. (1967) "Franz Liszt to Richard Pohl." *Studies in Romanticism*. Volume VI, (Summer): 193–202.

Emilio Mazza
"Cloathing the Parts again": The Ghost of the Treatise in the Standard of Taste

> "Certes, j'ay non seulement des complexions en grand nombre, mais aussi des opinions assez, desquelles je desgouterois volontiers mon fils, se j'en avois. Quoy, si les plus vrayes ne sont pas tousjours les plus commodes à l'homme, tant il est de sauvage composition!"
> — Montaigne, "Des Boyteux"

> "My enemies, you know, and I own, even sometimes my friends, have reproached me with the love of paradoxes and singular opinions"
> — D. Hume, "Dedication" to "The Natural History of Religion"

Anatomy and Delineation: Different Images of the Same Philosophy

"Self-love is the love of oneself, and of all things for the sake of oneself," François de La Rochefoucauld proclaims: "its transformations surpass those of metamorphoses, its refinements those of Chemistry."[1] La Rochefoucauld is ready to make "the anatomy of all the recesses of the heart."[2] The selfish philosopher, Hume remarks, allows that there is such a thing as friendship, "though he may attempt, by a philosophical chymistry, to resolve the elements of this passion, if I may so speak, into those of another, and explain every affection to

---

1 La Rochefoucauld, *Réflexions, Sentences et Maximes Morales*, p. 64; see *Les Œuvres de M. L'Abbé de Saint Real*, Vol. II, p. 223. Hume remarks that the French express pride, self-love, and vanity by the same terme *amour propre:* "there arises thence a great confusion in Rochefoucault, and many of their moral writers" (Hume, An *Enquiry Concerning the Principles of Morals* in: *Enquiries Concerning Human Understanding and Concerning the Principles of Morals*. App.4.3n; SBN 314n.1).
2 La Rochefoucauld, *Maximes*, p. 579. Fénelon accounts for a preacher that made "an anatomy of the passions which is equal to M. de La Rochefoucauld's Maximes" (Fénelon, "Dialogues sur l'éloquence en général et sur celle de la chaire en particulier" [1718], in *Œuvres*, 2 vols., J. Le Brun (Ed.), Vol. 1, p. 4). Mme de Sévigné maintains that "never was the human heart anatomized better than by these Messieurs [Nicole and Pascal]" (*Recueil des Lettres de Madame La Marquise de Sévigné*, Vol. I, p. 251).

https://doi.org/10.1515/9783110585575-015

be self-love."³ Like chemistry, anatomy can be an image for (moral) philosophy. Montaigne aims "to penetrate into the opaque depths of the inward recesses of the human mind,"⁴ and Madame de Gournay promptly praises "his perfect anatomy of the passions and inward movements of men."⁵ The "famous Gracian," as Addison calls him,⁶ entitles a chapter of his *Critick*, "The Moral Anatomy of Man".⁷ In the *Inquiry Concerning Virtue*, Shaftesbury accounts for an "inward anatomy" ("few of us endeavour to become anatomists of this sort") and an "anatomy of the mind,"⁸ and Mandeville, in the *Fable*, celebrates "the curious, that are skill'd in anatomizing the invisible Part of Man."⁹ According to Voltaire's *Lettres philosophiques*, Locke "has developed human reason to man, as an excellent Anatomist explains the springs of human body."¹⁰ Even Swift, in a Swiftian manner, dedicates himself to the "Dissection of Human Nature,"¹¹ and in the "Digression in the Modern Kind" he confesses:

> I have some Time, with a World of Pains and Art, dissected the Carcass of *Humane Nature*, and read many useful Lectures upon the several Parts, both *Containing* and *Contained*; till at last it *smelt* so strong, I could preserve it no longer. Upon which, I have been at a great Expence to fit up all the Bones with exact Contexture, and in due Symmetry; so that I am

---

3 Hume, *An Enquiry Concerning the Principles of Morals*, App.2.4; SBN 296. Adam Smith immediately detects "a little philosophical chemistry" in the *Discourse* of the Mandevillian Rousseau (A. Smith, *Essays on Philosophical Subjects*, p. 251). Some selfish "spiritual chemists", Shaftesbury observes, transform humanity into mutual hatred (*Sensus Communis*, in *Characteristics of Men, Manners, Opinions, Times*, pp. 62–63). On the chemistry image, see R. Descartes, *Meditationes de prima philosophia*, in *Œuvres de Descartes*, Vol. II, p. 277.
4 Michel de Montaigne, "De l'exercitation," *Les Essais*, Vol. II, p. 378.
5 M. le Jars de Gournay, "Preface" to Montaigne, *Les Essais*, p. [7]. She also praises Montaigne's "painting", and underlines his "freedom in anatomizing love," which was blamed as "impudent and dangerous" (p. [5]).
6 *The Spectator*, vol. IV, no. 293, p. 238.
7 Balthasar Gracián, *The Critick*, p. 151; see, p. 168; B. Gracián, *L'Homme Detrompé, ou Le Criticon*, p. 155. "By means of this moral anatomy he is able to judge soundly of things and to measure reputation by the square of truth" (B. Gracián, *L'Homme du Cour*, p. 26; see B. Gracián, *The Art of Prudence: or, A Companion for a Man of Sense*, p. 22bn.1). "It's a Sort of curious Anatomy thus to search and penetrate into Things, and to sound their Insides and Bottoms." (Gracián, *The Compleat Gentleman*, p. 5).
8 Shaftesbury, *An Inquiry Concerning Virtue or Merit* [1711], in *Characteristics*, p. 194; *Miscellaneous Reflections*, p. 419 (see *Soliloquy, or Advice to an Author*, pp. 92–93, p. 115).
9 Bernard Mandeville, *Fable of the Bees*, Vol. I, rem. N [1723], p. 145.
10 Voltaire, *Lettres philosophiques*, p. 125.
11 In the *Tale of a Tub* Swift announces his "Lectures upon a Dissection of Human Nature" among the "Treatises [...] most of them mentioned in the following Discourses; which will be speedily published" (J. Swift, *A Tale of a Tub. Written for the Universal Improvement of Mankind*, p. [3]).

ready to shew a very compleat Anatomy thereof to all curious *Gentlemen and others*. [...] having carefully cut up *Humane Nature*, I have found a very strange, new, and important Discovery; That the Publick Good of Mankind is performed by two Ways, *Instruction*, and *Diversion*.[12]

It is not surprising that every book of Hume's *Treatise* presents itself as an "anatomy of human nature" or "anatomy of the mind."[13] And the *Abstract* follows them: the *Treatise* "proposes to anatomize human nature."[14] The *Philosophical Essays concerning Human Understanding* (in 1758 Hume retitles it *Enquiry*)[15] do not completely abandon the anatomy image[16] and use it in defence of abstruse philosophy; yet they prefer to call themselves a "mental geography, or delineation of the distinct parts and powers of the mind."[17] Following the *Philosophical Essays*, Kant calls Hume a "geographer of human reason."[18]

Hume's "mental geography or delineation" departs from the deep and minute Mandevillian anatomy ("small trifling Films and little Pipes"),[19] which dis-

---

12 Swift, *A Tale of a Tub*, p. 123.
13 Hume, *A Treatise of Human Nature*, 1.4.6.23, 2.1.12.2, 3.3.6.6; SBN 263 ("accurate anatomy of human nature"), 326 ("anatomy of the mind"), 621 ("anatomist [...] [of] human nature"); HL I, 33 ("examining the Mind [...] as an Anatomist"). According to Jennifer Herdt, Hume "drawing on Mandeville, suggested that moral philosophers may be either painters or anatomists; he declared himself, in the *Treatise of Human Nature*, to be an anatomist." (J.A. Herdt, *Putting On Virtue. The Legacy of the Splendid Vices*, p. 221).
14 Hume, *An Abstract of a Book Lately Published An Abstract of a Book lately Published, entituled "A Treatise of Human Nature."* 2; SBN 646.
15 Hume, *Philosophical Essays concerning Human Understanding*. I use the first title to underline that both the *Enquiries* were originally conceived as a series of philosophical essays. Unlike the *Enquiry* on morals, the *Enquiry* on the understanding was also originally published under the title of *Philosophical Essays*; yet, unlike the 1741 *Essays, Moral and Political*, the reader cannot (completely) consider each essay "as a Work apart" and free himself from that "tiresome Stretch of Attention and Application" which is required to grasp the connection among the different essays (David Hume, "Advertisement" to *Essays, Moral and Political*, p. v.; see E. Mazza, "The eloquent *Enquiry*. Merit or virtue in its proper colours.").
16 Like the *Abstract* (A 2; SBN 646), and the *Dialogues* (1.13, 7.8–9; p. 136, p. 177) both the *Enquiries* preserve the expression "to anatomize." See: Hume, *An Enquiry Concerning Human Understanding*, in *Enquires*, 4.4; SBN 27; *An Enquiry Concerning the Principles of Morals*, App.1.5; SBN 287.
17 Hume, *Enquiry Concerning Human Understanding*, 1.13; SBN 13. The expression *géographie mentale* was also used (with a different meaning) by Claude Buffier, *Géographie Universelle*, p. 76.
18 Immanuel Kant, *Critique of Pure Reason*, p. 702.
19 Like those who "study the Anatomy of Dead Carcasses," those who "examine into the Nature of Man, abstract from Art and Education," may observe that "the chief Organs and nicest Springs [...] are not hard Bones, strong Muscles, and Nerves, nor the smooth white Skin that so beauti-

tinguishes itself from Shaftesbury's inward elitist anatomy and is attacked by Hutcheson ("[Mandeville] has 'Anatomised the invisible part'").[20] Hume's mental geography gets closer to Pope's "*Map* of Man" and less minute "Anatomy of the mind" ("the large, open, and perceptible parts").[21] Pope's *Essay on Man* is a "*temperate* [...] short [...] System of *Ethics*", where "much of the *Force*, as well as *Grace* of Arguments or Instructions depends on their *Conciseness*": "What is now publish'd, is only to be considered as a *general Map* of Man, marking out no more than the *Greater Parts*, their *Extents*, their *Limits*, and their *Connection*, but leaving the particular to be more fully delineated in the Charts which are to follow."[22] Poetry and a precise chain of reasoning, ornament and perspicuity: Pope wishes he "can unite all these without diminution of any of them."[23] And Warburton remarks: it is "a true *delineation* of human Nature, or a general, but exact map of Man."[24] Pope, Hume acknowledges in 1742, has found the "just mixture," the "*proper medium*" between simplicity and refinement: he is able to indulge in the greatest refinement and wit "without being guilty of any blameable excess."[25]

According to the *Philosophical Essays*, Hutcheson and Butler are those who successfully "delineate" the parts of the mind, and Hume (*à la* Hobbes) is the one who wishes to "unite the boundaries" of the abstruse and obvious philoso-

---

fully covers them, but small trifling Films and little Pipes that are either over-look'd, or else seem inconsiderable to Vulgar Eyes": the "vilest and most hateful Qualities" of men are the "most necessary Accomplishments" to fit them for the largest, happiest and most flourishing society (Mandeville, "Preface" to *Fable of the Bees*, pp. 3–4).

20 Frances Hutcheson, *Hibernicus's 'Letters'*, 19 February 1724, n. 47 (1725), in *Opera Minora*, p. 396. Hutcheson criticizes Mandeville's "*Anatomizing of Passions*" (p. 402): Mandeville "has seen the 'Chief Organs and nicest Springs of our Machine,' which are yet but 'trifling Films, and little Pipes, not such gross strong things as Nerves, Bone, or Skin'" (p. 395).

21 Alexander Pope, "The Design [1734]," *An Essay on Man [...]. With Notes by William Warburton*, p. 19. "In the Anatomy of the Mind [...] more Good will accrue to mankind by attending to the large, open, and perceptible parts, than by studying too much such finer nerves and vessels as will for ever escape our observation" (p. 19).

22 Pope, "The Design," p. 20.

23 Pope, "The Design," p. 20.

24 William Warburton, in Pope, *An Essay on Man*, p. 2n (my own italics).

25 David Hume, "Of Simplicity and Refinement in Writing." Essays, p. 193. Hume thinks that all the questions concerning the "proper medium" are "difficult to be decided," not only because the extremes often run "so gradually into each other, as even to render our *sentiments* doubtful and uncertain", but also because "it is not easy to find *words* proper to fix this medium" (*Essays*, p. 45).

phy, and to reason in an "easy manner."[26] Like the *Abstract* ("those few simple principles, on which all the rest depend"),[27] the *Philosophical Essays* still look for a careful philosophical search for principles: "may we not hope, that philosophy [...] may carry its researches still farther, and discover, at least in some degree, the secret springs and principles, by which the human mind is actuated in its operations?"[28] Newton, from the "happiest" reasoning, seems to have determined the laws and forces which govern the revolutions of the heavenly bodies:

> there is no reason to despair of equal success in our enquiries concerning the mental powers and œconomy, if prosecuted with equal capacity and caution. It is probable, that one operation and principle of the mind depends on another; which, again, may be resolved into one more general and universal.[29]

The *Philosophical Essays* justify the attempt of the moralists ("to find some general principles into which all the Vices and Virtues were justly to be resolv'd")[30] by appealing to the example of natural philosophers, critics, logicians and politicians. This tension between an impossible illegitimate search and a probable legitimate one was already at work in the "Introduction" to the *Treatise*:

> And tho' we must endeavour to render all our principles as universal as possible, by tracing up our experiments to the utmost, and explaining all effects from the simplest and fewest causes, 'tis still certain we cannot go beyond experience; and any hypothesis, that pretends to discover the ultimate original qualities of human nature, ought at first to be rejected as presumptuous and chimerical.[31]

---

26 Hume, *Enquiry Concerning Human Understanding*, 1.14, 1.17; SBN 14, 16. "I have known— writes Hobbes—clearness of judgement, and largeness of fancy; strength of reason, and graceful elocution" (Thomas Hobbes, *Leviathan*, p. 468).
27 *A* 1; SBN 646. Like the *Treatise* (Intro.8–10, 1.1.7.11, 1.3.5.2; SBN xvii–xviii, 22, 84), the *Abstract* distinguishes between the acknowledged impossibility of knowing the ultimate principles and the desire and satisfaction of going as far as possible: "tho' we can never arrive at the ultimate principles, 'tis a satisfaction to go as far as our faculties will allow us" (*Abstract* 1; SBN 646). Hume's aim is to examine several phænomena and find that they "resolve themselves into one common principle"; to "trace this principle into another" and "at last arrive at those few simple principles, on which all the rest depend" (*A* 1; SBN 646).
28 Hume, *Enquiry Concerning Human Understanding*, 1.15; SBN 14.
29 Hume, *Enquiry Concerning Human Understanding*, 1.15; SBN 14–15. According to the moral *Enquiry* it is "not probable", and scarcely "possible", that the principles of human nature, like humanity, can be "resolved" into principles "more simple and universal" (*Enquiry Concerning the Principles of Morals*, 5.2.17n; SBN 219).
30 Hume, *Enquiry Concerning Human Understanding* 1.15; SBN 15.
31 Hume, *Treatise*, Intro.8; SBN xvii (see *T* 1.4.7.6; SBN 266).

We should acknowledge that we have arrived at "the utmost extent of human reason," Hume admonishes, and we can give "no reason for our most general and most refined principles, beside our experience of their reality."[32] Then, in a Lockean manner, we should "sit down contented."[33] The *Enquiry Concerning the Principes of Morals* seems to get rid of the difficult balance of the *Treatise*: it insists on the experienced reality of moral principles and asserts the peculiarity of morals: "the case is not the same in this species of philosophy."[34] Hume settles down, content with some original general principles, and asks: *why we should ever seek farther?* Even if it were probable (and he suggests it is not) that these principles could be resolved into more simple and universal ones, this is no longer his aim.

The *Enquiry*, with its catalogue of qualities and its four sources of moral sentiment, calls itself a "true Delineation or Description of [...] human Nature," a "compleat Delineation or Description of Merit," a "Delineation or Definition of VIRTUE."[35] In the *Enquiry*, while he rejects the selfish philosophical chemistry, Hume cannot advocate his previous philosophical anatomy. Anatomy and chemistry are too close to each other: the "moral dissecting table" and the "*chemistry* of the moral [...] conceptions" are so close that Nietzsche celebrates their union.[36] The time has come for moral delineation. And while Hume attacks Wollaston's too rational *Religion of Nature Delineated* (the author calls it "only a Delineation"), his *Enquiry* is attacked by Balfour's *Delineation of the Nature and Obligation of Morality*[37] (Hume ironically defines it "full of [...] sublime ideas").[38] Hume answers Balfour that there can be virtue even upon his "more confined system" and that he "always found, that more simple views were sufficient to make [him] act in a reasonable manner."[39]

In a 1739 letter to Hutcheson and in the third book of the *Treatise* Hume asserts that the anatomical "abstract" reasoning can be useful to a pictorial

---

32 Hume, Intro 9; SBN xviii.
33 Hume, Intro 9; SBN xviii; see John Locke, *An Essay Concerning Human Understanding*, p. 45.
34 Hume, *An Enquiry Concerning the Principles of Morals*, App.2.7; SBN 299.
35 Hume, *An Enquiry Concerning the Principles of Morals*, p. 22, p. 172, p. 184 (*EPM* App.2.13, 9.1, 9.12; SBN 302, 268, 277). In 1764 Hume turns "Delineation or Definition of VIRTUE" (Hume, *An Enquiry*, 1751, p. 184) into "Delineation or Definition of PERSONAL MERIT" (David Hume, *Essays and Treatises on Several Subjects*, Vol. II, p. 350).
36 Friedrich Nietzsche, *Human, All Too Human. A Book for Free Spirits*, p. 12, p. 32.
37 William Wollaston, *The Religion of Nature Delineated*, p. 6, p. 211; James Balfour, *A Delineation of the Nature and Obligation of Morality*, p. 28, p. 58, p. 137.
38 J. Y. T. Greig (Ed.), *The Letters of David Hume*, I, p. 173.
39 Greig (Ed.), *The Letters of David Hume*, I, p. 173.

"practical" morality, even though it must remain something different from it.⁴⁰ The *Philosophical Essays* assent to this assertion, and the moral *Enquiry* puts it into practice. *À la* Hobbes, (in moral sciences "reason and eloquence [...] may stand very well together"),⁴¹ Hume seems to take more seriously his previous intention "to make the Moralist & Metaphysician agree a little better": yet, rather than adding the required "warm Sentiment of Morals," he renders his enquiry less "abstract."⁴² He delineates, rather than painting. The benevolent *Monthly Review* detects the change and remarks that the *Enquiry* is "free from that sceptical turn which appears in his other pieces", and the "manner of treating" the subject is "easy and natural."⁴³

In 1751 abstruseness and paradoxicality, systematic attitude and "unity of principle"⁴⁴ have disappeared, together with the "Heat of Youth & Invention"⁴⁵ which attended the *Treatise*. Now, the abstruse manner and the dangerous consequences of an opinion can be a presumption of falsehood (they actually are, even though they ought not to be such).⁴⁶ He who ignores it, has "but a bad grace."⁴⁷ The "Delineation," which gets closer to painting, is still founded on the anatomical *Treatise:* by "cloathing the Parts again," this foundation is set "more at a distance" in appendices and footnotes, where it is "more cover'd up from sight"⁴⁸ – Cicero censures "the people who place their less strong points first."⁴⁹ Like the fables of poetical pagan religion, which "were, of themselves, light, easy, and familiar; without devils, or seas of brimstone,"⁵⁰ Hume's advantageous philosophical truths "represent virtue in all her genuine and most engaging charms, and make us approach her with ease, familiarity, and affec-

---

40 Greig (Ed.), *The Letters of David Hume*, I, p. 33; *T* 3.3.6.6; SBN 263.
41 Hobbes, *Leviathan*, p. 468.
42 Greig (Ed.), *Letters of David Hume* I, 33 (see *T* 3.3.6.3, 3.3.6.6; SBN 619, 620–621; Hume, *Enquiry Concerning Human Understanding* 1.8, 1.17; SBN 10, 16). According to those (Hutchesonians) who "would resolve all moral determinations into *sentiment*", if we "extinguish all the warm feelings and prepossessions in favour of virtue [...] morality is no longer a practical study, nor has any tendency to regulate our lives and actions" (Hume, *An Enquiry concerning the Principles of Morals* 1.8; SBN 172).
43 W. Rose, "Review of *Enquiry Concerning the Principles of Morals*," p. 28. The hendyadis "easy and natural" does not occur in the *Enquiry*.
44 Hume, *An Enquiry concerning the Principles of Morals* 5.2.16–17; SBN 218–219.
45 Greig (Ed.), *The Letters of David Hume* I, p. 151.
46 Hume, *Enquiry Concerning Human Understanding* 11.27; SBN 147.
47 Hume, *An Enquiry concerning the Principles of Morals* 9.14; SBN 279.
48 Hume, Treatise, 3.3.6.6; SBN 621.
49 Cicero, *De Oratore*, Vol. I, pp. 436–437.
50 D. Hume, *The Natural History of Religion*, in *Four Dissertations*, p. 85.

tion."⁵¹ Like Montaigne ("there is nothing gayer, more agile, more cheerful and I might say more frolic some [than philosophy]")⁵² and his "Epicurean" ("the gay, the frolic *Virtue*"),⁵³ Hume concludes: "The dismal dress falls off, with which many divines, and some philosophers had covered [virtue]; and nothing appears but gentleness, humanity, beneficence, affability; nay even, at proper intervals, play, frolic, and gaiety."⁵⁴

No more opinions that may "appear somewhat extraordinary,"⁵⁵ after the *Treatise*. No more "lewd" Humean "liberties" with his neighbour's wife (and the precaution of shutting the windows).⁵⁶ No more promoting himself as a "disturber" of the philosophical public peace, or a "subverter" of established philosophy, like Arcesilaus according to Bayle and Cicero.⁵⁷ No more excessive shocking paradoxes "to raise Attention" or increase the sale of a work, as in Mandeville's *Fable of the Bees, or Private Vices, Publick Benefits*.⁵⁸ No more reason "slave of the passions," which Reid considers as Hume's "favourite paradox":⁵⁹ reason, says the *Enquiry*, "directs only the Impulse, receiv'd from Appetite or Inclination."⁶⁰ No more impressions and ideas (in the moral *Enquiry* the term "impression" is almost gone): like the third book of the *Treatise*, the *Enquiry* "requires not that the reader shou'd enter into all the abstract reasonings" of the

---

51 Hume, *An Enquiry concerning the Principles of Morals* 9.15; SBN 279.
52 Montaigne, "De l'institution des enfans," *Les Essais*, vol. I, XXVI, p. 160.
53 Hume, "The Epicurean," *ES*, p. 142.
54 Hume, *An Enquiry concerning the Principles of Morals* 9.15; SBN 279.
55 Hume, *Treatise* 2.3.3.4; SBN 415.
56 Hume, *Treatise* 3.1.1.15; SBN 461–462 and n.1; see W. Wollaston, *The Religion of Nature Delineated*, pp. 141–2, pp. 171–2.
57 Bayle, "Arcesilas," *Dictionnaire historique et critique*, Vol. I, p. 285; Rem. E, p. 285b; Cicero, *Academica*, in *De Natura Deorum/Academica*, pp. 484–485.
58 "The true Reason why I made use of the Title [...] was to raise Attention: As it is generally counted to be a Paradox, I pitch'd upon it in Hopes that those who might hear or see it, would have the Curiosity to know, what could be said to maintain it; and perhaps sooner buy the Book, than they would have do otherwise" (Bernard Mandeville, *A Letter to Dion*, p. 39; see also, p. 41, p. 49).
59 Hume, *Treatise* 2.3.3.4; SBN 414–415. "It appears – Reid remarks – a shocking paradox, repugnant to good morals and to common sense; but [...] it is nothing but an abuse of words": like Mandeville, Hume "insinuate[s] the most licentious paradoxes with the appearance of plausibility" (Thomas Reid, *Essays on the Active Powers of Man*, p. 184, p. 212, p. 479; see Mandeville, "A Search into the Nature of Society," p. 333; Bernard Mandeville, *An Enquiry into the Origin of Honour, and The Usefulness of Christianity in War*, p. 31, p. 80).
60 Hume, *An Enquiry concerning the Principles of Morals* App.1.21; SBN 294.

first two books; unlike the third book of the *Treatise*, it does not continue "to make use of the terms, *impressions* and *ideas*, in the same sense as formerly."[61]

Yet, as Hume remarks, it is "almost impossible for the mind to change its character in any considerable article,"[62] and some tensions remain. The young abstruse paradoxical Hume seems to revive in his literary and more mature friends: the Epicurean lover of skeptical paradoxes (and his "curious" principles) in the *Philosophical Essays*;[63] the careless skeptic Philo (and his "out-of-the-way difficulties") in the *Dialogues Concerning Natural Religion*;[64] the great skeptical rambler Palamedes (and his "artifice") in the *Dialogue* appended to the moral *Enquiry*;[65] and the voice of doubt (and her "embarassing" questions) in "Of the Standard of Taste." (ST 229) No sooner Hume finds the true standard in the joint verdict of the true critics, the voice comes out:

> But where are such critics to be found? By what marks are they to be known? How distinguish them from pretenders? These questions are embarrassing; and seem to throw us back into the same uncertainty, from which, during the course of this essay, we have endeavoured to extricate ourselves. (ST 229–233)[66]

This is not the only skeptical voice in "Of the Standard of Taste," which can be seen as a skeptical process of limitation of different skeptical views including: the traditional natural equality of tastes and the imperfection of our faculties, and the more Humean embarassing (answerable) questions and two (unavoidable) sources of variation. Even when the embarassing questions seem to be answered, the skeptical voice is not silenced:

> But notwithstanding all our endeavours to fix a standard of taste, and reconcile the discordant apprehensions of men, there still remain two sources of variation [...]. The one is the different humours of particular men; the other, the particular manners and opinions of our age and country [...] where there is such a diversity in the internal frame or external situation as is entirely blameless on both sides, and leaves no room to give one the preference above the other; in that case a certain degree of diversity in judgment is unavoidable, and we seek in vain for a standard, by which we can reconcile the contrary sentiments. (ST 232)

---

61 "Advertisement" to *Of Morals*.
62 Hume, *Treatise* 3.3.4.3; SBN 608.
63 Hume, *EHU* 11.1; SBN 132.
64 Hume, *Dialogues Concerning Natural Religion* P.6, p. 128; 7.17, p. 181.
65 Greig (Ed.), *Letters of David Hume* I, 173; Hume, *A Dialogue* in *Enquiries*, 1, 18; SBN 324, 330.
66 See Mazza, "Fluctuations, Manners, Tastes, and Religion in the Standard of Taste."

The *Standard* is composed nearly twenty years after the first book of the *Treatise* and, strictly speaking, is Hume's last philosophical published work. Hume has learned that a civilized nation "may easily be mistaken in the choice of their admired philosopher" (ST 232) (is he also thinking about himself?) and he is taught not to draw his philosophy from "too profound a source." (ST 216) The happy aim of the *Philosophical Essays* seems to be achieved: "reconciling profound enquiry with clearness" and "reasoning in this easy manner."[67] Hume seems to extend to the province of criticism the advice of the moral *Enquiry*: skepticism, abstruseness, and paradoxicality are unfit for taste; at least on the surface, where the essay flows cool and clear. At the bottom the skeptical process is still at work. Thus, when in 1757 Hume accounts for the *Four Dissertations*, the place of the *Standard* is not immediately identifiable: "some of these Dissertations are Attempts to throw Light upon the most profound Philosophy: Others contain a greater Mixture of polite Literature, & are wrote in a more easy Style & Manner."[68]

Discovery and Paradox: The Unsteady Status of Sensible Qualities

In the Preface to his *Sermons*, Butler allows that some of them are "very abstruse and difficult": abstruseness may be "unavoidable" and therefore "not always [...] inexcusable."[69] On the contrary, in the sermon "Upon Compassion," he points out "the Danger of over-great Refinements; of going besides or beyond the plain, obvious, first Appearance of Things, upon the Subject of Morals and Religion."[70] Morality must be "somewhat plain and easy to be understood": "It must appeal to plain common Sense [...] because it appeals to Mankind."[71] In the Preface to the *Essay on the Nature and Conduct of the Passions*, Hutcheson denies that his inquiry is "too subtile for common Apprehension, and consequently not neces-

---

67 Hume, *Enquiry Concerning Human Understanding* 1.17; SBN 16. "Happy, if we can unite the boundaries of the different species of philosophy, by reconciling profound enquiry with clearness [...] reasoning in this easy manner", the *Philosophical Essays* declare (*EHU* 1.17; SBN 16); "Happy, if we can render all the consequences sufficiently plain and perspicuous!", the *Enquiry* echoes (*EPM* 5.2.17n.19; SBN 219).
68 Hume, *Further Letters of David Hume*, pp. 40–41.
69 Joseph Butler, "Preface" to *Fifteen Sermons Preached at the Rolls Chapel*, pp. iv-v; see, pp. iii–vi, p. xiii.
70 Butler, "Upon Compassion," in *Fifteen Sermons*, p. 98.
71 Butler, "Upon Compassion," *Fifteen Sermons*, p. 99.

sary for the Instruction of Men in *Morals*."[72] All its difficulty chiefly arises from "some *previous Notions*, equally difficult at least, which have been already receiv'd":[73] "ingenious speculative Men, in their straining to support an *Hypothesis*, may contrive a thousand *subtle selfish Motives*, which a kind generous Heart never dreamed of."[74]

According to Hume's *Philosophical Essays*, Butler and Hutcheson are among those who, "with so much Success, delineate and describe the Parts of the Mind."[75] By "ordering and distinguishing" (as Hume defines his own task),[76] and dispelling some previous confusions, they both "show us the Nature and Importance of this Species of Philosophy."[77] Butler and Hutcheson are also that "great Name or Authority" Hume was looking for to recommend his *Treatise*.[78] When Hume asks Hutcheson's opinion, he immediately and cheekily declares that he cannot "entirely promise to conform" himself to it.[79] Hutcheson remarks that the third book of the *Treatise* "wants a certain Warmth in the Cause of Virtue, which [...] all good Men wou'd relish."[80] Hume replies by calling himself an anatomist and a metaphysician rather than a painter and a moralist: he praises a minute anatomy to someone who had already blamed it in Mandeville.[81] What an interesting paradox.

The "fundamental" principle of modern philosophers – says the first book of the *Treatise* – is that colours, sounds, tastes, smells, heat and cold are "nothing

---

72 Francis Hutcheson, "The Preface" to the *An Essay on the Nature and Conduct of the Passions and Affections. With Illustrations on the Moral Sense*, p. 3.
73 Hutcheson, "Preface", p. 3.
74 Hutcheson, [Introduction to] *Illustrations*, p. 135.
75 Hume, *Philosophical Essays*, 1748, p. 14 (*EHU* 1.14; SBN 14).
76 Hume, *Philosophical Essays*, 1748, p. 13.
77 Hume, *Philosophical Essays*, 1748, p. 16n. Hume refers to Butler's *Sermons* and probably to Hutcheson's *Illustrations*; in 1756 he deletes the footnote (D. Hume, *Essays and Treatises on Several Subjects*, Vol. II, p. 14).
78 Greig (Ed.), *Letters of David Hume* I, 27–28; see R. Klibansky and E.C. Mossner, eds., *New Letters of David Hume*, I, p. 25, p. 29, p. 34, pp. 36–37, p. 43.
79 Greig (Ed.), *Letters of David Hume* I, p. 40.
80 Greig (Ed.), *Letters of David Hume*, I, p. 32.
81 Hume's 1739 account of anatomy recalls Mandeville's description of it: "to discover its [i.e. of the mind] most secret Springs & Principles [...] Where you pull off the Skin, & display all the minute Parts, there appears something trivial, even in the noblest Attitudes & most vigorous Actions" (Greig, ed., *Letters of David Hume* I, p. 32). The account of the *Treatise* is similar: "[an] accurate dissections and portraitures of the smaller parts of the human body [...] There is even something hideous, or at least minute in the views of things, which he [the anatomist] presents" (Hume, *Treatise* 3.3.6.6 ; SBN 620–621).

but impressions in the mind."[82] As a modern philosophical performance the *Treatise* asserts that necessity "lies merely in ourselves, and is nothing but that determination of the thought."[83] And this, Hume allows, is the "most violent" paradox he could advance.[84] The second book compares ("reflective") impressions to "sensible qualities."[85] In a 1740 letter to Hutcheson, affecting to follow his example, Hume compares virtue and vice to those sensible qualities, "which, according to modern Philosophy, are not Qualitys in Objects but Perceptions in the Mind."[86] *Of Morals* repeats almost verbatim the letter to Hutcheson.[87] In both texts, *à la* Addison ("that great Modern Discovery [...] indeed one of the finest Speculations in that Science [of natural philosophy]"),[88] Hume calls it a "Discovery in Morals," which, like the preceding discovery in natural philosophy, must be regarded as "a mighty Advancement of the speculative Sciences," though it has "little or no Influence on Practice."[89] Hutcheson had already reassured his readers: "Let none imagine [...] [it] does diminish [the] *Reality*" of the ideas of virtue and vice.[90] In a footnote to *The Sceptic*, after expressing the fear of "appearing too philosophical," Hume recalls "that famous doctrine, supposed to be fully proved in modern times," that sensible qualities "*lie* [...] *merely in the senses.*"[91] Hume compares beauty and deformity, virtue and vice, to these qualities. This "discovery," he argues, "takes off no more from the reality of the latter qualities [virtue and vice], than from that of the former [beauty and deformity]";

---

82 Hume, *Treatise* 1.4.4.3; SBN 226 (see *T* 1.4.2.12–13; SBN 192).
83 Hume, *Treatise* 1.4.7.5; SBN 266. Necessity "is something, that exists in the mind, not in objects" (*T* 1.3.14.22; SBN 165); it it "lies only in the act of the understanding [...] lies in the determination of the mind [...] belongs entirely to the soul" (*T* 1.3.14.22–23; SBN 165–166).
84 Hume, *Treatise* 1.3.14.24; SBN 166.
85 Hume, *Treatise* 2.2.6.1; SBN 366 .
86 Greig (Ed.), *Letters of David Hume* I, p. 39.
87 Hume, *Treatise* 3.1.1.26; SBN 468–469. On the comparison with secondary qualities, see Francis Hutcheson, *An Inquiry into the Original of Our Ideas of Beauty and Virtue in Two Treatises*, p. 27, p. 42, pp. 147–148, pp. 177–178.
88 *The Spectator*, vol. VI, n. 413, p. 97.
89 Greig (Ed.), *Letters of David Hume* I, 39. The letter calls it a "mighty," the *Treatise* a "considerable" advancement (Hume, *Treatise* 3.1.1.26, 469).
90 Hutcheson, *Illustrations*, 4, p. 177.
91 Hume, "The Sceptic," *ES*, 166n; see *ES*, 163, 166. According to Hutcheson sensible ideas of colours, sounds, tastes and smells etc. "denote the Sensations in our Minds", the "Modifications of the perceiving Mind", and beauty "properly denotes the Perception of some mind" and has a relation to a "Mind which perceives it" (*An Inquiry*, p. 27): "All Beauty is relative to the Sense of some Mind perceiving it" (*An Inquiry*, p. 42), and the sensible ideas of colours, sounds, tastes and smells etc. are "only *Perceptions* in our Minds", and the ideas of virtue and vice "Perceptions of a *Sense*" (Hutcheson, *Illustrations*, p. 177).

it makes "no alteration on action and conduct" in moral as well as in natural philosophy.⁹²

According to Addison the discovery is "at present universally acknowledged by all the Enquirers into Natural Philosophy," and "this is a Truth which has been proved incontestably by many Modern Philosophers."⁹³ Similarly in the *Philosophical Essays* Hume declares that "it is universally allowed by modern enquirers, that all the sensible qualities [...] are perceptions in the mind."⁹⁴ Hume advances a "philosophical" skeptical objection to the opinion of external existence, an objection that derives from the "most profound" philosophy and which does not admit of "so easy a solution."⁹⁵ This objection represents the opinion of external existence as contrary to reason, "at least, – Hume adds – if it be a principle of reason, that all sensible qualities are in the mind";⁹⁶ namely, if this principle be the conclusion of a causal consistent reasoning. In the *Treatise* it was a conclusion that we reach "when we reason from cause and effect."⁹⁷

The *Philosophical Essays* ascribes to Hutcheson the discovery in morals:

> [He] has taught us, by the most convincing Arguments, that Morality [...] is entirely relative to the Sentiment or mental Taste of each particular Being; in the same Manner as the Distinctions of sweet and bitter, hot and cold, arise from the particular Feeling of each Sense or Organ.⁹⁸

Since we find this discovery in the first section of the third book of the *Treatise* ("Moral distinctions not deriv'd from reason"), we would expect it in the first Appendix of the moral *Enquiry* ("Concerning moral sentiment"), where Hume re-

---

92 Hume, "The Sceptic," *ES*, 166n.
93 "Light and Colours, as apprehended by the Imagination, are only Ideas in the Mind, and not Qualities that have any Existence in Matter" (*The Spectator*, n. 413, p. 97).
94 "All the sensible qualities of objects, such as hard, soft, hot, cold, white, black, &c. are merely secondary, and exist not in the objects themselves, but are perceptions in the mind" (Hume, *Enquiry Concerning Human Understanding* 12.15; SBN 154; see ibid., 12.16; SBN 155).
95 Hume, *Enquiry Concerning Human Understanding* 12.6, 12.15; SBN 151, 154.
96 Hume, *Enquiry Concerning Human Understanding* 12.16; SBN 155.
97 Hume, *Treatise* 1.4.4.15; SBN 231 (see *T* 1.4.4.4; SBN 227).
98 Hume, *Philosophical Essays*, 1748, p. 15. In March 1740 Hume writes to Hutcheson: "Morality, according to your Opinion as well as mine, is determin'd merely by Sentiment" (Greig, ed., *Letters of David Hume* I, 39). According to Reid the "analogy" between the "external senses" of touch and taste and the "internal sense" of beauty "led Dr. Hutcheson, and other modern Philosophers, to apply to beauty, what Des Cartes and Locke had taught concerning the secondary qualities, perceived by the external senses" (Thomas Reid, *Essays on the Intellectual Powers of Man*, p. 740).

calls the *Treatise* and the Hutchesonian sentimentalist arguments: in the first Appendix Hume discusses "how far either *reason* or *sentiment* enters into all decisions of praise or censure," and accounts for the views of "those who would resolve all moral determinations into *sentiment*."[99] Yet, there there are but remote traces of the Hutchesonian comparison between moral qualities and sensible secondary qualities, which seemed so important in the *Treatise:* for example, the assertion that the matter of fact, which we call "crime," "resides in the mind of the person,"[100] evokes an assertion of the *Treatise*.[101] Again, the assertion that "Beauty is not a quality of the circle. It lies not in any part of the Line"[102] repeats verbatim a passage of *The Sceptic*.[103]

Does Hume deem the discovery of modern philosophy in morals, and the comparison between moral and secondary qualities, a too philosophical principle (it is the fear expressed by *The Sceptic*), with no practical influence and therefore (*à la* Butler) unfit for a moral *Enquiry*? Certainly, Hume is no longer seeking Hutcheson's authority to recommend his work. Unlike the *Treatise*, the *Enquiry* seems to be calculated for Butlerian rather than Hutchesonian readers, and sometimes stands in direct opposition to Hutcheson's moral sense (there is sympathy behind the curtain of utility and humanity).[104] Like Butler in the dissertation *Of the Nature of Virtue* ("such a Moral Faculty [...] whether considered as a Sentiment of the Understanding, or as a Perception of the Heart, or which seems the Truth, as including both"),[105] the moral *Enquiry* declares that "*reason* and *sentiment* concur in almost all moral determinations and conclusions."[106] As Hume puts it in "Of the Standard of Taste," the intention is "to mingle some light

---

99 Hume, *Enquiry Concerning the Principles of Morals* 1.6, App.1.1; SBN 171, 285 (see ibid., App.1.12; SBN 291).
100 Hume, *Enquiry Concerning the Principles of Morals*, App.1.6, 287.
101 Hume, *Treastise* 3.1.1.27; SBN 469.
102 Hume, *EPM* App.1.14; SBN 291.
103 Hume, "The Sceptic," *ES*, 165.
104 See Luigi Turco, "Hutcheson and Hume in a recent polemic"; Luigi Turco, "La virilità perduta del *Trattato* di Hume," p. 252 n. 50.
105 Joseph Butler, *Of the Nature of Virtue*, in *The Analogy of Religion, Natural and Revealed to the Constitution and Course of Nature*, p. 452.
106 Hume, *Enquiry Concerning the Principles of Morals* 1.9; SBN 172. In many species of beauty, especially in the artistic and moral beauty, which partakes of the artistic, "much reasoning" and the "assistance of intellectual faculties" are "requisite" (Hume, *Enquiry Concerning the Principles of Morals* 1.9; SBN 173): in all moral decisions there is a clear "partition between the faculties of understanding and sentiment" and reason must "enter for a considerable share" and is "often requisite" (Hume, *Enquiry Concerning the Principles of Morals*, App.1.2, App.1.4; SBN 285–286).

of the understanding with the feelings of sentiment" (ST 216): reason is "at least requisite to the operation" of taste. (ST 226)

"Of the Standard of Taste" also discusses a species of sentimental unlimited "sceptical" philosophy ("all sentiment is right"), which maintains that "beauty is no quality in things themselves: It exists merely in the mind which contemplates them"; and that "to seek the real beauty, or real deformity, is as fruitless an enquiry, as to pretend to ascertain the real sweet or real bitter." (ST 209) [107] Hume's attitude appears to be different from the *Treatise*. "Though it be certain," he says correcting Hutcheson, that beauty and deformity, "more than" sweet and bitter (originally he writes "no more than" [ST 217]),[108] "belong entirely to the sentiment, internal or external," yet, he immediately adds, "it must be allowed, that there are certain qualities in objects, which are fitted by nature to produce those particular feelings." (ST 217)[109] The appeal to traditional topics (fever and jaundice), like that to the skeptical "trite topics" against the senses in the *Philosophical Essays*, serves only to remind us that the sound state of the organ "alone can be supposed to afford us a true standard of taste": "a man [...] affected with the jaundice, [would not] pretend to give a verdict with regard to colours." (ST 215)[110] To the sentimental unlimited skepticism Hume opposes his own limited reasonable skepticism (there is "a difference in the degrees of our approbation or blame"), which is drawn from "two sources of variation": the different humours of particular men, and the particular manners and opinions of our age and country. (ST 232)

---

107 This argument leads to the unlimited sceptical conclusion of the "natural equality of tastes" (ST 210); in the *Treatise* the argument leads modern philosophy into the most extravagant skepticism with regard to external continued and independent existence (Hume, *Treatise* 1.4.4.6, 1.4.4.15; SBN 227–228, 231).
108 Cf. Hume, "Of the Standard of Taste," in *Essays and Treatises on Several Subjects*, Vol. I, p. 296. Unlike Hume (beauty and deformity are probably more mental than sweet and bitter), Hutcheson maintains that "perhaps there is no resemblance" in the objects to mental sensations like sweet and bitter; while the idea of beauty, as a mental perception, "may indeed have a nearer resemblance" to objects than these sensations (Hutcheson, *An Inquiry*, p. 27). In the 1742 essay "The Sceptic," Hume thinks that, notwithstanding a considerable diversity, there is more "uniformity" in the sentiments of the mind than in most feelings of the body, and that in mental taste there is "something approaching to principles", and critics can reason and dispute "more plausibly" than cooks or perfumers (Hume, "The Sceptic," *ES*, 163).
109 According to Hume, also Locke and Malebranche maintain that in the bodies there are only the "Causes or something capable of producing [the sensible Qualities of Heat, Smell, Sound, & probably Colour] in the Mind" (Paul B. Wood, "David Hume on Thomas Reid's *An Inquiry into the Human Mind, On the Principles of Common Sense:* A New Letter to Hugh Blair from July 1762," p. 416).
110 See Hume, *Enquiry into Human Understanding* 12.6; SBN 151.

In 1762, Hume abandons virtue and beauty and brings the matter back to ist original metaphysical field. After reading some chapters of Reid's *Inquiry*, *à la* Hobbes ("this opinion hath been so long received, that the contrary must needs appear a great paradox"),[111] Hume observes that "Philosophy scarce ever advances a greater Paradox in the Eyes of the People, than when it affirms that Snow is neither cold nor white: Fire hot nor red" – a quite traditional but un-Humean example.[112] Philosophers, especially Malebranche and Locke, Hume observes, did not believe the sensible qualities "to be really in the Bodies, but only their Causes or something capable of producing them in the Mind", and it did cost them some pains to establish this principle; by supposing that the vulgar share this philosophical principle, Hume objects, Reid imagines them "to be Philosophers & Corpuscolarians from their Infancy."[113] Reid had better followed Cicero's recommendation: "in this place we shall speak like the vulgar [...] for, in speaking of the popular opinion, we must use popular and accepted words."[114] In Hume's words: Reid he had better "entirely conform" himself to the vulgar's "manner of thinking and of expressing themselves" and "accommodate" himself to their notions.[115]

That color "is not a quality of bodies, but only an idea in the mind," Reid declares in the *Inquiry*, is "one of the most remarkable paradoxes of modern philosophy, which hath been universally esteemed as a great discovery."[116] Reid also

---

111 Hobbes, *Human Nature*, p. 23.
112 Wood, "David Hume on Thomas Reid's *An Inquiry*", p. 416 (see *T* 1.4.2.13; SBN 192). The *Philosophical Essays* refer to "flame and heat, snow and cold" as objects always "conjoined together" (Hume, *Enquiry concerning Human Understanding* 5.8; SBN 46); yet in his discussions of modern philosophy Hume never uses the snow-and-fire example. According to Reid, philosophers "discarded all secondary qualities of bodies" and "found out by their means, that fire is not hot, nor snow cold"; Berkeley "advanced them a step higher", and "the triumph of ideas was completed" by Hume (Thomas Reid, *An Inquiry into the Human Mind, On the Principles of Common Sense*, see p. 35). Malebranche makes the example of the white snow and hot fire, and thinks it certain that these sensible qualities have not a real existence external to us (Nicolas Malebranche, *Recherche de la vérité*, 3rd ed., 3 vols., G. Rodis-Lewis (Ed.), vol. I, p. 133; vol. III, p. 62). Locke makes the example of the "*Flame* [...] denominated *Hot* and *Light*; *Snow White* and *Cold*", and remarks that "it would by most Men be judged very extravagant' if one should not say that these qualities are "the same in those Bodies, that those *Ideas* are in us" (Locke, *An Essay*, pp. 137–138, 372); and Philonous-Berkeley cannot help thinking that "snow is white, and fire hot" (George Berkeley, *Three Dialogues Between Hylas and Philonous*, p. 108).
113 Wood, "David Hume on Thomas Reid's *An Inquiry*", p. 416.
114 Cicero, *De officiis*, pp. 202–203.
115 Hume, *Treatise* 1.4.2.31; SBN 202 (see ibid., *T* 1.4.2.43; SBN 209).
116 Reid, *An Inquiry*, p. 196.

thinks that this paradox is "nothing else but an abuse of words."[117] Philosophers say that color is in the mind, the vulgar that it is a quality of bodies, but the difference is "only about the meaning of a word":[118] the vulgar, as well as philosophers, think and believe that the qualities which cause the sensations are in the bodies. And Philosophers, recommends Reid, should better speak, as well as think, with the vulgar; they should not "shock them by philosophical paradoxes, which, when put into common language, express only the common sense of mankind."[119] Yet, philosophers are not able to follow Reid's advice, and keep on producing their paradoxes. To plain sensible men the "paradoxes of the ideal philosophy" appear to be "palpable absurdities," to their adepts they are "profound discoveries":[120] among these paradoxes there is also the "important modern discovery,"[121] "one of the noblest discovery of modern philosophy": the shocking "strange paradox [...] universally received" that qualities are not in the bodies, but only in the mind.[122]

The discovery of modern philosophy is first ascribed to causal reasoning by the first book of the *Treatise*, then suspected not to be a principle of reason by the last of the *Philosophical Essays*. It is extended to morals by the third book of the *Treatise*, and excluded from morals by the moral *Enquiry*. Then both Hume and Reid turn it into a paradox; and Reid turns the paradox into an abuse of language. Finally, Reid proclaims, we can successfully reconcile philosophy with common sense; by turning the vulgar into philosophers, Hume ironically replies.[123] Even when he is politely distancing himself from modern philosophy, Hume does not give up attacking those who attack it.

---

117 Reid, *An Inquiry*, p. 196. According to Reid the paradoxes of the modern or ideal philosophy are but an abuse of words and language (Reid, *An Inquiry*, p. 161, pp. 98–201, p. 203, p. 209).
118 Reid, *An Inquiry*, p. 198.
119 Reid, *An Inquiry*, pp. 198–199.
120 Reid, *An Inquiry*, p. 75.
121 Reid, *An Inquiry*, p. 161.
122 Reid, *An Inquiry*, pp. 198–199. "The ingenious Mr Addison, in the Spectator, N° 413, speaks thus of it. 'I have here supposed that my reader is acquainted with that great modern discovery, which is at present universally acknowledged by all the inquirers [....]'" (p. 199).
123 Reid, *An Inquiry*, pp. 196, 198–199. According to Reid the distinction between primary and secondary qualities was made by Democritus, Epicurus, and their followers (Hume corrects him: "there are but obscure Traces of it among the Antients viz in the Epicurean School"); Aristotle and the Peripatetics abolished it (Hume agrees: "The Peripatetics maintained opposite Principles"); Descartes, Malebranche, and Locke, "revived it, and were thought to have put it in a very clear light" (Hume admonishes him: "You know what pains it cost Malebranche & Locke to establish that Principle") (Reid, *An Inquiry*, pp. 131, 160; Wood, "David Hume on Thomas Reid's *An Inquiry*", p. 416).

Acknowledgments

I'm grateful to Babette Babich for her suggestions. A different and longer version of this chapter was published in *David Hume and Contemporary Philosophy*, I. Kasavin (Ed.) (Cambridge: Cambridge Scholars Publishing, 2012), pp. 278–309.

Bibliography

Balfour, James (1753) *A Delineation of the Nature and Obligation of Morality*. Edinburgh: Hamilton, Balfour and Neill.
Bayle, Pierre (1740) "Arcesilas," *Dictionnaire historique et critique*. 5th edition, 4 vols. Amsterdam-Leyde *etc.*: P. Brunel *et alii*. Vol. I.
Berkeley, George (1713) *Three Dialogues Between Hylas and Philonous*. London: G. James for H. Clements.
Buffier, Claude (1732) *Géographie Universelle*. Paris: P.-F. Giffart. [1616]
Butler, Joseph (1729) *Fifteen Sermons Preached at the Rolls Chapel*. 2nd edition, London: W. Botham for J. and J. Knapton.
Butler, Joseph (1736) *The Analogy of Religion, Natural and Revealed to the Constitution and Course of Nature*. London: J. and P. Knapton.
Cicero (1979) *De Natura Deorum/Academica*. London: Harvard University Press.
Cicero (1967) *De Oratore*, 2 vols. London: W. Heinemann.
Cicero (1928) *De officiis*. London: W. Heinemann.
Descartes, René (1996) *Meditationes de prima philosophia*, in *Œuvres de Descartes*, 11 vols., C. Adam and P. Tannery, (Eds.) Paris: Vrin.
Fénelon, François (1983) "Dialogues sur l'éloquence en général et sur celle de la chaire en particulier" [1718], In: *Œuvres*, 2 vols., Jacques Le Brun, (Ed.) Paris: Gallimard (1983–1997).
Gournay, M. le Jars de (1652) "Preface." In: Montaigne, *Les Essais*. Paris: I.B. Loyson.
Gracián y Morales, Baltasar (1953) *The Oracle: A Manual of the Art of Discretion*. L.B. Walton, trans. London: J.M. Dent & Sons [1647].
Gracián y Morales, Baltasar (1730) *The Compleat Gentleman*. London: T. Osborne.
Gracián y Morales, Baltasar (1728) *L'Homme du Cour*. Rotterdam: J. Hofhout.
Gracián y Morales, Baltasar (1714) *The Art of Prudence: or, A Companion for a Man of Sense*. London, D. Browne.
Gracián y Morales, Baltasar (1705) *L'Homme Detrompé, ou Le Criticon*. La Haye: J. van Ellinckhuysen.
Gracián y Morales, Baltasar (1681) *The Critick*. London: T.N. for H. Brome.
Greig, J. Y. T. (Ed.) (1932) *The Letters of David Hume*, 2 vols. Oxford: Clarendon Press.
Herdt, Jennifer A. (2008) *Putting On Virtue. The Legacy of the Splendid Vices*. Chicago: The University of Chicago Press.
Hume, David (1947), Dialogues concerning Natural Religion. Norman Kemp Smith (Ed.). Edinburgh: T. Nelson.

Hume, David (2014) *Further Letters of David Hume*. Felix Waldmann (Ed.) Edinburgh: Edinburgh Bibliographical Society.
Hume, David (1998) *Enquiry Concerning the Principle of Morals*. Edinburgh: A. Millar.
Hume, David (1978) *Treatise of Human Nature*. L.A. Selby-Bigge (Ed.), P.H. Nidditch (Rev.) Oxford: Clarendon Press. [1739]
Hume, David (1975) *Enquiries Concerning Human Understanding and Concerning the Principles of Morals*, L.A. Selby-Bigge (Ed.) P.H. Nidditch (Rev.) Oxford: Clarendon Press.
Hume, David (1770) *Essays and Treatises on Several Subjects*, 4 vols. London: T. Cadell, Edinburgh: A. Kincaid and A. Donaldson.
Hume, David (1764) *Essays and Treatises on several Subjects*. 2 vols. London: A. Millar.
Hume, David (1757) "Of the Standard of Taste" in: *Four Dissertations*. London: A. Millar.
Hume, David (1985), *Essays Moral, Political, and Literary*. E.F. Miller (Ed.). Indianapolis: Liberty Classics.
Hume, David (1748) *Philosophical Essays concerning Human Understanding*. London: A. Millar.
Hobbes, Thomas (1996) *Leviathan*, J. C. A. Gaskin (Ed.) Oxford: Oxford University Press.
Hutcheson, Francis (1990) *Opera Minora*. Hildesheim: G. Olms Verlag (1725).
Hutcheson, Francis (2002) "The Preface" to *An Essay on the Nature and Conduct of the Passions and Affections. With Illustrations on the Moral Sense*. A. Garrett (Ed.) Indianapolis: Liberty Fund.
Hutcheson, Francis (2004) *An Inquiry into the Original of Our Ideas of Beauty and Virtue in Two Treatises*. W. Leidhold (Ed.) Indianapolis: Liberty.
Kant, Immanuel (1996) *Critique of Pure Reason*. Indianapolis: Hackett.
Klibansky, Raymond and Ernest Mossner (Eds.) (1954) *New Letters of David Hume*. Oxford: Clarendon Press.
La Rochefoucauld, François (1743) *Réflexions, Sentences et Maximes Morales*. Paris: Veuve Ganzeau.
La Rochefoucauld, François (1992) *Maximes*. J. Truchet (Ed.) Paris: Garnier.
Locke, John (1985) *An Essay concerning Human Understanding*, P.H. Nidditch (Ed.). Oxford: Clarendon Press.
Malebranche, Nicolas (1991) *Recherche de la vérité*, 3rd ed., 3 vols., G. Rodis-Lewis (Ed.) Paris: Vrin.
Mandeville, Bernard (1732) *A Letter to Dion*. London: J. Roberts.
Mandeville, Bernard (1732) *An Enquiry into the Origin of Honour, and The Usefulness of Christianity in War*. London: J. Brotherton.
Mandeville, Bernard (1924) *Fable of the Bees: or, Private Vices, Publick Benefits*. 2 vols., F.B. Kaye (Ed.) Oxford: Clarendon Press.
Montaigne, Michel de (1992) *Les Essais*. 3 vols., P. Villey (Ed.) Paris: PUF.
Mazza, Emilio (2018) "The Eloquent *Enquiry*. Merit or Virtue in its Proper Colours." In: J. Taylor (Ed.) *Reading Hume on the Principles of Morals: Essays on "An Enquiry concerning the Principles of Morals."* Oxford: Oxford University Press.
Mazza, Emilio (2018) "Fluctuations. Manners, Tastes, and Religion in the Standard of Taste." In: Angela Coventry and Alexander Sager, (Eds.) *The Humean Mind*. London: Routledge.
Nietzsche, Friedrich (1996) *Human, All Too Human. A Book for Free Spirits*. Cambridge: Cambridge University Press.

Pope, Alexander (1745) "The Design [1734]" In: *Of An Essay on Man [...]. With Notes by William Warburton*. London: J. and P. Knapton.
Reid, Thomas (1788) *Essays on the Active Powers of Man*. Edinburgh: J. Bell.
Reid, Thomas (1785) *Essays on the Intellectual Powers of Man*. Edinburgh: J. Bell.
Reid, Thomas (1764) *An Inquiry into the Human Mind, On the Principles of Common Sense*. Edinburgh: A. Millar et alii.
Rose, W. (1752) "Review of *Enquiry Concerning the Principles of Morals*," The Monthly Review, January. 1–19.
Sévigné, Mme de (1736) *Recueil des Lettres de Madame La Marquise de Sévigné*. Leide: Verbeel.
Shaftesbury, Anthony Ashley Cooper (1999) *Characteristics of Men, Manners, Opinions, Times*, L. E. Klein (Ed.) Cambridge: Cambridge University Press. (1964) [1711].
Smith, Adam (1982) *Essays on Philosophical Subjects*. W.P.D. Wightman and J.C. Bryce (Eds.) Indianapolis: Liberty Fund.
Swift, Jonathan (1710) *A Tale of a Tub. Written for the Universal Improvement of Mankind*. London, J. Nutt, [1704]
Turco, Luigi (2007) "Hutcheson and Hume in a Recent Polemic." In: Mazza and E. Ronchetti (Eds.) *New Essays on David Hume*. Milano: Franco Angeli. 171–198.
Turco, Luigi (1997) "La virilità perduta del Trattato di Hume." I *castelli di Yale* 2. 231–252.
[Vichard, César] (1757) *Les Œuvres de M. L'Abbé de Saint Réal*. 8 vols. Paris: Libraires Associés.
Voltaire (1734) *Lettres philosophiques*. Amsterdam: E. Lucas.
Wollaston, William (1724) *The Religion of Nature Delineated*. London: S. Palmer. [1722]
Wood, Paul B. (1986) "David Hume on Thomas Reid's An Inquiry into the Human Mind, On the Principles of Common Sense: A New Letter to Hugh Blair from July 1762." *Mind*. 95, 380. (Oct): 411–416.

Notes on Contributors

Babette Babich teaches at Fordham University in New York City and occasionally at the Humboldt University in Berlin, Germany. She is Visiting Professor of Theology, Religion, and Philosophy at the University of Winchester, England. Her most recent book in English, *The Hallelujah Effect* (2016 [2013]) raises the question of beauty (including male-female desire), theorizes Adorno (on broadcast technologies, including digital media), and Nietzsche (on ancient Greek music and Beethoven) along with the culture of the musical 'cover'.

Howard Caygill teaches at Kingston University in London. He studied at the Universities of Bristol, Sussex and Oxford and has taught at the University of East Anglia and Goldsmiths College, University of London. He has published on Kant, 20th century philosophy, aesthetics, and political philosophy. Select recent titles include *Kafka: In Light of the Accident* (2017), *Walter Benjamin: The Color of Experience* (2016); *On Resistance: A Philosophy of Defiance* [2015 (2013)].

Timothy M. Costelloe is Professor of Philosophy at the College of William & Mary. His primary research and teaching interests are in aesthetics and history of philosophy, with particular emphasis on Hume and the modern period. He is the author of *Aesthetics and Morals in the Philosophy of David Hume* (2007), *The British Aesthetic Tradition: From Shaftesbury to Wittgenstein* (2013), and, most recently, *The Imagination in Hume's Philosophy: The Canvas of the Mind* (2017).

Andrej Démuth studied philosophy and psychology. He is a Professor of Philosophy and Head of Department of Philosophy at the Trnava University (Slovakia). His research is focused on modern philosophy, epistemology, and cognitive studies. He is the author of several books: *Homo – anima cognoscens* (2003); *Perception Theories* (2013); *Introduction to the Study of the History of Epistemology* (2015); *Prolegomena to the Study of Modern Philosophy* (2015) as well as articles on cognition and history of philosophy.

Slávka Démuthová is an Associate Professor of Psychology and the Head of the Department of Psychology at the Faculty of Arts, University of Ss. Cyril and Methodius in Trnava, Slovakia. Her professional orientation focuses on the history of psychology and on Thanatology. She is an author of several monographs, scientific articles and regularly gives invited lectures at universities abroad (University of Edinburgh, Scotland; Masaryk University in Brno and Prague College of Psychosocial Studies, Czech Republic; Cardinal St. Wyszynski University in Warsaw, Poland; University of Ljubljana, Slovenia).

Bernard Freydberg has published nine books, most recently *A Dark History of Modern Philosophy* (2017). Previous books include: *David Hume: Platonic Philosopher, Continental Ancestor* (2008), *The Thought of John Sallis* (2008), *Schelling's Dialogical Freedom Essay* (2005), *Philosophy and Comedy* (2005), *Imagination in Kant's Critique of Practical Reason* (2005) and *The Play of the Platonic Dialogues* (1997). He is currently Visiting Scholar at Duquesne University.

Peter Kivy (1934–2017) was professor emeritus of musicology and philosophy at Rutgers University. Among many other monographs, he was author of *The Seventh Sense: A Study of Francis Hutcheson's Aesthetics, and its Influence in Eighteenth-Century Britain* (1976), *The Corded Shell: Reflections on Musical Expression* (1980), and *Music Alone: Philosophical Reflections on the Purely Musical Experience* (1990). One of his last books was a collection, *Sounding Off: Eleven Essays in the Philosophy of Music* (2012).

Carolyn Korsmeyer is the author or editor of twelve books, including *Making Sense of Taste: Food and Philosophy* (1999), *Gender and Aesthetics* (2004), *Savoring Disgust: The Foul and the Fair in Aesthetics* (2011), and *Things: In Touch with the Past* (forthcoming 2018). She is Research Professor of Philosophy at the University at Buffalo, State University of New York, and a past president of the American Society for Aesthetics.

Christopher MacLachlan was born and educated in Edinburgh, where he attended university; his doctoral thesis was supervised by John Valdimir Price. In 2013 he retired after nearly forty years service in the School of English, University of St Andrews. He has published essays on Ramsay, Hume, Burns, Scott, Hogg, Stevenson, Buchan and Spark. He helped to edit conference papers on Edwin Muir, George MacDonald and eighteenth- and nineteenth-century Scottish and Gaelic literature. He also edited *Before Burns*, an anthology of eighteenth-century Scottish poetry in addition to a selection of Burns's poetry (jointly with Robert Crawford). He has edited Matthew Lewis's Gothic novel *The Monk*, Robert Louis Stevenson's *Travels with a Donkey* and *The Amateur Emigrant*, and is author of a book on Tolkien and Wagner.

Emilo Mazza is Associate Professor at the Libera Università di Lingue e Comunicazione IULM in Milan. He works primarily on Hume and modern philosophy (scepticism, relativism, travel, and national characters). He has published several papers on Hume including contributions in *Impressions of Hume* edited by Frasca-Spada and Kail (2005), *The Continuum Companion to Hume* edited by Bailey and O'Brien (2012), *Reading Hume on the Principles of Morals: Essays on "An Enquiry concerning the Principles of Morals"* edited by Taylor (2018), and *The Humean Mind* edited by Coventry and Sager (forthcoming). He is the co-editor (with Ronchetti) of *New Essays on David Hume* (2007). He has translated into Italian and edited Hume's *Dialogues concerning Natural Religion* (1996) and Descartes' *Discours de la méthode* (2012). His recent works on Hume include: *La peste in fondo al pozzo. L'anatomia astrusa di David Hume* (*The pestilence at the bottom of a well: The abstruse anatomy of David Hume*) (2012), and *Gazze, whist e verità. David Hume e le immagini della filosofia* (*Magpies, whist and truth: David Hume and the images of philosophy*) (2016).

Roger Shiner taught Philosophy at the University of Alberta for 35 years before moving to the Okanagan Valley in 1999. He used to say that he would leave Alberta only for somewhere that had a serious wine industry: he has kept his word. Since then he has been Adjunct Professor of Philosophy at the Okanagan campus of the University of British Columbia as well as teaching part time at that campus and at Okanagan College. He served as a Trustee for the American Society of Aesthetics from 1984–87 and as Secretary-Treasurer from 1988 to 1996. He is the author of "Wittgenstein on the Good, the Beautiful and the Tremendous" (1974), "On Giving Works of Art a Face" (1978) and "The Mental Life of a Work of Art" (1982) as well as other essays in aesthetics. His interest in Wittgenstein was sparked by studying with Renford Bambrough and John Wisdom at Cambridge. He is also the author of *Norm and Nature:*

The Movements of Legal Thought (1992), *Freedom of Commercial Expression* (2003) and *Legal Institutions and the Sources of Law* (2005), as well as numerous other essays in legal theory.

Roger Scruton is a writer and philosopher, who has written widely on aesthetics, including *The Aesthetics of Architecture* (1979), *Sexual Desire* (1986) and *The Aesthetics of Music* (1997). Works of fiction include: *A Dove Descending*, *Xanthippic Dialogues* and *The Disappeared*. Roger Scruton is a Fellow of the Royal Society of Literature, a Fellow of the European Academy of Arts and Sciences, and a Fellow of the British Academy. His collection of stories, *Lost Causes* is forthcoming with Beaufort Books, New York.

Dabney Townsend was educated at Duke, Drew, Emory, and Oxford. He has taught in the University of Texas System and the University of Georgia System and as a visiting lecturer at the University of Auckland in New Zealand. He was Executive Director of the American Society for Aesthetics from 2007 to 2016. His books include *Aesthetic Objects and Works of Art*, *An Introduction to Aesthetics*, *An Historical Dictionary of Aesthetics*, *Aesthetics A to Z*, and *Hume's Aesthetic Theory* as well as numerous papers in aesthetics and eighteenth-century British philosophy.

Research and Citation Bibliography

Acampora, Christa Davis (2013) *Contesting Nietzsche.* Chicago: University of Chicago Press.
Addison, Joseph (1712) "Taste." *The Spectator.* 409. June 19.
Addison, Joseph (1957) In: Robert J. Allen (Ed.) *Addison and Steele: Selections from The Tatler and The Spectator,* New York: Holt, Reinhart, and Winston.
Agamben, Giorgio (2009) "What is the Contemporary." In: Agamben, *What is an Apparatus and Other Essays.* David Kishik and Stefan Pedatella, trans. Stanford: University of Stanford Press).
Alison, Archibald (1812) *Essays on Nature and Principles of Taste; from the Edinburgh edition of 1814.* Boston: Cummings and Hilliard.
Allison, David B. (2005) "Nietzsche's Aesthetic Taste for Moral Metacritique." *Symposium.* 9:2: 153–167.
Amann, Wilhelm (1999)*"Die stille Arbeit des Geschmacks": Die Kategorie des Geschmacks in der Aesthetik Schillers und in der Debatte der Aufklärung.* Würzburg: Königshausen und Neumann.
Aristotle (1941) *Nicomachean Ethics.* W. D. Ross, trans. In: Richard McKeon (Ed.), *The Basic Works of Aristotle.* New York: Random House.
Aristotle (1951) *Nicomachean Ethics.* Philip Wheelwright, trans. New York: Odyssey.
Arrowsmith, William. (2017) "Nietzsche on Classics and Classicists," *New Nietzsche Studies,* 10:3 and 4: 127–137.
Babich, Babette (2018) "Heidegger and Hölderlin on Aether and Life." *Études Phénoménologique, Phenomenological Studies.* 2. 111–133.
Babich, Babette (2017) "Nietzsche's Critique: Reading Kant's Critical Philosophy." In: Mark Conard (Ed.) *Nietzsche and the Philosophers.* Lanham: Rowman & Littlefield. 171–192.
Babich, Babette (2017) "Nietzsche's Influence and Meaning Today – With Weight on the Sameness of the Eternal Return." In: Ekaterina Polyakova and Yulia Sineokaya (Eds.), Фридрих Ницше: наследие и проект. М.: Культурная революция, / *Friedrich Nietzsche: Heritage and Prospects.* Moscow: LRC Publishing House. 391–406.
Babich, Babette (2017) "Nietzsches Lyrik. Archilochos, Musik, Metrik." In: Christian Benne and Claus Zittel (Eds.), *Nietzsche und die Lyrik. Ein Kompendium.* Frankfurt am Main: Springer/Metzler. 405–429.
Babich, Babette (2018) "Nietzsche's Archilochus." *New Nietzsche Studies.* Vol 10, Nos. 1/2 (2016): 133–170.
Babich, Babette (2015) "Friedrich Nietzsche." In: Niall Keane (Ed.) *Blackwell Companion to Hermeneutics.* Oxford: Wiley. 366–377.
Babich, Babette (2014) "Becoming and Purification: Empedocles, Zarathustra's *Übermensch*, and Lucian's Tyrant." In: Vanessa Lemm (Ed.) *Nietzsche and the Becoming of Life.* New York: Fordham University Press. 245–261; 359–368.
Babich, Babette (2013) "Nietzsche's Zarathustra, Nietzsche's Empedocles: The Time of Kings." In: Horst Hutter and Eli Friedlander (Eds.) *Nietzsche's Therapeutic Teaching: For Individuals and Culture.* London: Continuum. 157–174.
Babich, Babette (2012) "On Nietzsche's Judgment of Style and Hume's Quixotic Taste: On the Science of Aesthetics and 'Playing' the Satyr." *Journal of Nietzsche Studies.* 43:2: 240–259.

Babich, Babette (2012) "Nietzsche's Zarathustra and Parodic Style: On Lucian's *Hyperanthropos* and Nietzsche's *Übermensch*." *Diogenes*. 58:4: 58–74 [2013].

Babich, Babette (2011) "Le Zarathoustra de Nietzsche et le style parodique: A propos de l'hyperanthropos de Lucien et du surhomme de Nietzsche." *Diogène: Revue internationale des sciences humaines*. 232 (October): 70–93.

Babich, Babette (2011) "Sloterdijk's Cynicism: Diogenes in the Marketplace." In: Stuart Elden, (Ed.), *Sloterdijk Now*. Oxford: Polity. 17–36; 186–189.

Babich, Babette (2010) "Towards a Critical Philosophy of Science: Continental Beginnings and Bugbears, Whigs, and Waterbears." *International Studies in the Philosophy of Science*. 24/4: 343–391.

Babich, Babette (2010) "Das 'Problem der Wissenschaft' oder Nietzsches philosophische Kritik wissenschaftlicher Vernunft." In: Carlo Gentili and Cathrin Nielsen (Eds.) *Der Tod Gottes und die Wissenschaft: Zur Wissenschaftskritik Nietzsches*. Berlin: de Gruyter. 125–171.

Babich, Babette (1994) *Nietzsche's Philosophy of Science: Reflecting Science on the Ground of Art and Life*. Albany: State University of New York Press.

Baceski, Tina (2013) "Hume on Art Critics, Wise Men, and the Virtues of Taste." *Hume Studies*. 39:2: 233–256.

Baeumler, Alfred (1923) *Das Irrationalitätsproblem*. Tübingen: Max Niemeyer, [1923].

Baier, Annette C. (2006) "Hume's Deathbed Reading: A Tale of Three Letters." *Hume Studies*. 32:2: 347–356.

Baier, Annette C. (2008) *Death and Character: Further Reflections on Hume*. Cambridge: Harvard University Press.

Baier, Annette C. (1993) "Hume: The Reflective Women's Epistemologist?" In: Louise M. Anthony and Charlotte Witt (Ed.) *A Mind of One's Own*. Boulder, Colo.: Westview.

Baier, Annette C. (1987) "Hume, the Women's Moral Theorist?" In: Eva Feder Kittay and Diana T. Meyers (Eds.) *Women and Moral Theory*. Totowa, N.J.: Rowman and Littlefield.

Baier, Annette C. (1979) "Good Men's Women: Hume on Chastity and "Whist." *Hume Studies*. 5:1: 1–19.

Bahlman, Dudley W.R. (1957) *The Moral Revolution of 1688*. New Haven: Yale University Press.

Bahm, Archie J. (1972) "Is a Universal Science of Aesthetics Possible?" *Journal of Aesthetics and Art Criticism*. 31, 1: 3–7.

Balfour, James (1753) *A Delineation of the Nature and Obligation of Morality*. Edinburgh: Hamilton, Balfour and Neill.

Bambach, Charles. (2003) *Heidegger's Roots: Nietzsche, National Socialism and the Greeks*. Ithaca: University of Cornell Press.

Bambach, Charles and Theodore George (Eds.) (2018) *Philosophers and their Poets*. Albany: State University of New York Press.

Bamborough, John B. (1952) *The Little World of Man*. London: Longman, Green.

Battersby, Christine (1981) "An Enquiry Concerning the Humean Woman." *Philosophy*. 56:217 (July): 303–312.

Bayle, Pierre (1740) "Arcesilas," *Dictionnaire historique et critique*, 5th edition, 4 vols. Amsterdam-Leyde.

Beam, Craig (1996) "Hume and Nietzsche: Naturalists, Ethicists, Anti-Christians." *Hume Studies*. 22:2: 299–324.

Beare, John Isaac (1906) *Greek Theories of Elementary Cognition*. Oxford: Clarendon Press.

Bennholdt-Thomsen, Anke (1974) *Nietzsches Also Sprach Zarathustra als literarisches Phänomen*. Frankfurt am Main: Athenäum.
Berkeley, George (1713) *Three Dialogues Between Hylas and Philonous*. London: G. James for H. Clements.
Berry, Christopher J. (2018) *Essays on Hume, Smith and the Scottish Enlightenment*. Edinborough: Edinborough University Press.
Breazeale, Daniel (1975) *Toward a Nihilist Epistemology: Hume and Nietzsche*. Diss. Yale University.
Blumenbach, J. F. (1827) *A Manual of Comparative Anatomy*. William Lawrence, trans. 2nd edition William Coulson (Ed.) London: Printed for W. Simpkin and R. Marshall.
Boileau, Gilles (1700) *Epictetus his morals: with Simplicius his comment von Epictetus, Simplicius (of Cilicia)*. Made English from the Greek by George Stanhope. London: Printed for Richard Sare. 306–307.
Bornedal, Peter (2005) "A Silent World: Nietzsche's Radical Realism: World Sensation Language." *Nietzsche-Studien*. 34: 1–47.
Box, M. A. (1990) *The Suasive Art of David Hume*. Princeton: Princeton University Press.
Branham, R. Bracht (1989) *Unruly Eloquence: Lucian and the Comedy of Traditions* Cambridge: Cambridge University Press.
Breazeale, Daniel. 1971. *Toward a Nihilist Epistemology: Hume and Nietzsche*. New Haven: Yale University Press.
Brillat-Savarin, Jean Anthelme (1865) *The Handbook of Dining; or Corpulency and Leanness Scientifically Considered*, L. F. Simpson trans. New York: D. Appleton and Company.
Broadie, Alexander (2010) "Art and Aesthetic Theory." In: Broadie (Ed.), *The Cambridge Companion to The Scottish Enlightenment*. Cambridge: Cambridge University Press. 280–297.
Broisson, Ivan (2006) "*Ressentiment* und Wille zur Macht Nietzsche und Hume über Moral- und Religionskritik." In: Volker Gerhardt and Renate Reschke (Eds.) *Friedrich Nietzsche – Zwischen Musik, Philosophie und Ressentiment*. Berlin: Akademie. 117–128.
Brown, Stuart Gerry (1938) "Observations on Hume's Theory of Taste." *English Studies*. XX: 93–98.
Brunius, Teddy (1952) *David Hume on Criticism. Figura 2. Studies Edited by the Institute of Art History, University of Uppsala*. Stockholm: Almquist & Wiksell.
Budd, Malcolm (1991) "Hume's Tragic Emotions." *Hume Studies* 17:2 (November): 93–106.
Buffier, Claude (1732) *Géographie Universelle*. Paris: P.-F. Giffart. [1616]
Butler, Joseph (1729) "Preface" to *Fifteen Sermons Preached at the Rolls Chapel*, 2nd edition London: W. Botham for J. and J. Knapton.
Butler, Joseph (1736) *Of the Nature of Virtue*, in *The Analogy of Religion, Natural and Revealed to the Constitution and Course of Nature*. London: J. and P. Knapton.
Calder, Andy et al. (Eds.) (2011) *The Oxford Handbook of Face Perception*. Oxford: Oxford University Press.
Carroll, Noël (1984) "Hume's Standard of Taste." *Journal of Aesthetics and Art Criticism*. 43: 181–194.
Cassirer, Ernst (1932) *Die Philosophie der Aufklärung*. Tübingen: Mohr.
Caygill, Howard (1989) *The Art of Judgment*. Oxford: Blackwell.
Cervantes, Miguel de (1755) *The Adventures of Don Quixote de la Mancha*. Tobias Smollet, trans. London: Millar.

Christensen, Jerome (1987) *Practicing Enlightenment: Hume and the Formation of a Literary Career.* Madison: University of Wisconsin Press.
Cicero (1959) *The Verrine Orations*, Vol. 1. L. H. G. Greenwood, trans. Cambridge: Harvard University Press.
Cicero (1967) *De Oratore*, 2 vols. London: W. Heinemann.
Cicero (1979) *Academica.* In: *De Natura Deorum/Academica.* London: Harvard University Press.
Cicero (1928) *De officiis.* London: W. Heinemann.
Clark, Jonathan (1985) *English Society 1688–1832: Ideology, Social Structure and Political Practice during the Ancien Regime.* Cambridge: Cambridge University Press.
Cohen, Ted (1994) "Partial Enchantments of the *Quixote* Story in Hume's Essay on Taste." In: Robert J. Yanal (Ed.) *Institutions of Art: Reconsiderations of George Dickie's Philosophy.* University Park, Pennsylvania: The Pennsylvania State University Press. 145–156.
Conard, Mark T. (2017) "Nietzsche and Hume in the Genealogy and Psychology of Religion." In: Conard (Ed.), *Nietzsche and the Philosophers.* London: Routledge. 146–168.
Cooper, Andrew (2016) *The Tragedy of Philosophy: Kant's Critique of Judgment and the Project of Aesthetics.* State University of New York Press.
Cooper, John Gilbert (1951) *Letters Concerning Taste*, 3rd edition. Ralph Cohen, (Ed.) Los Angeles: University of California Press, [1757].
Costelloe, Timothy M. (2007) *Aesthetics and Morals in the Philosophy of David Hume.* New York: Routledge.
Costelloe, Timothy M. (2004) "Hume's Aesthetics: The Literature and Directions for Future Research." *Hume Studies.* 30:1: 87–126.
Costelloe, Timothy M. (2003) "Hume, Kant, and the 'Antinomy of Taste." *Journal of the History of Philosophy.* 41:2: 165–185.
Crombie, Alistair (1994) *Styles of Scientific Thinking in the European Tradition.* 3 vols. London: Duckworth.
Cullen William (1999) Letter to John Hunter, 17 September 1776. In: James Fieser, *Early Responses to Hume, Life, and Reputations.* London: Thoemes. Vol. 1. 292.
Curtius, Ernst Robert (1963) *European Literature and the Latin Middle Ages.* Willard R. Trask, trans. New York: Harper Torchbooks.
da Silva, Rafael Guimarães Tavares (2015) "The Laughter Within the Dialogues of the Dead." *Revele.* 8 (May): 232–246.
Dadějík, Ondřej (2017) "David Hume a logika soudů vkusu." *Filosofický časopis.* 2. 275–296.
Dadlez, Eva M. (2004) "Pleased and Afflicted: Hume on the Paradox of Tragic Pleasure." *Hume Studies*, 30:2: 213–236.
Danto, Arthur (1965) *Nietzsche as Philosopher.* New York: Columbia University Press.
Darwin, Erasmus (1794) *Zoonomia; or, the Laws of Organic Life.* 2 vols. London: J. Johnson.
Davidson, James (1997) *Courtesans and Fishcakes: The Consuming Passions of Classical Athens.* New York: Harper.
de La Mettrie, Julien Offray (1912) *Man a Machine.* Gertrude C. Bussey and M. W. Calkins, trans. Chicago: Open Court [1748].
Deleuze, Gilles (1993) *Empiricism and Subjectivity: An Essay on Hume's Theory of Human Nature.* New York: Columbia University Press.
de Martaelere, Patricia (1989) "A Taste for Hume." *Ratio* 2:2: 122–137.

Démuth, Andrej (2013) "David Hume a asociačné 'škandály' jeho myslenia." In: Démuth, A. et al. (Eds.), *Rozpravy o Humovej filozofii*. Pusté Úľany: Schola Philosophica. 9–23.
Démuth, Andrej (2009) Intuícia ako výpočet so zastretým algoritmom riešenia?" In: E. Krámsky (Ed.) *Kognitivní věda dnes a zítra*. Liberec: Nakladatelství Bor. 81–86.
Démuth, Andrej (2009) "Poznanie, vedenie alebo interpretácia?" *Pusté Úľany : Schola Philosophica:* 166–182.
Descartes, René (1996) *Meditationes de prima philosophia*. In: *Œuvres de Descartes*, 11 vols., C. Adam and P. Tannery (Eds.) Paris: Vrin.
Dickson, Peter George Muir (1967) *The Financial Revolution in England: A Study in the Development of Public Credit 1688–1756*. London: Macmillan.
Dickinson, Harry Thomas (1977) *Liberty and Property – Political Philosophy in Eighteenth Century Britain*. London: Weidenfeld and Nicolson.
Diels, Hermann (1903) *Die Fragmente der Vorsokratiker*. Berlin: Weidmannsche Buchhandlung.
Diels, Hermann (1879) *Doxographi Graeci*. Berlin: Weidmann.
Dryden, John (1970) "Defence of an Essay of Dramatic Poetry." In: *Selected Criticism*, James Kinsley & George Parfitt (Eds.) Oxford: Clarendon Press [1688].
Dubos, abbé Jean-Baptiste (1967) *Réflexions critiques sur le poésie et sur le peinture*. Geneva: Slatkine [1719].
Ebner, Martin Holger Gzella, Heinz-Günther Nesselrath, and Ernst Ribbat (Eds.) (2001) *Philopseudeis è Apiston. Die Lügenfreunde oder: Der Ungläubige*. Darmstadt: Wissenschaftliche Buchgesellschaft.
Elden, Stuart (Ed.), (2011) *Sloterdijk Now*. Oxford: Polity.
Emerson, Roger L. (2016) *Essays on David Hume, Medical Men and the Scottish Enlightenment: 'Industry, Knowledge and Humanity'*. London: Routledge.
Epictetus (1758) *Enchiridion*. http://classics.mit.edu/Epictetus/epicench.html. Also in: *All the Works of Epictetus, Which are Now Extant*. Elizabeth Carter, trans. London: Printed by S. Richardson.
Epictetus (1865) *The Works of Epictetus. Consisting of His Discourses, in Four Books, The Enchiridion, and Fragments. A Translation from the Greek based on that of Elizabeth Carter*. Thomas Wentworth Higginson, trans. Boston: Little, Brown, and Co.
Epictetus (1904) *Discourses of Epictetus*. George Long, trans. New York: D. Appleton and Company.
Epictetus (1928) *Discourses Books III–IV, The Encheiridion*, W. A. Oldfather, trans. Cambridge: Harvard University Press.
Epictetus 1998. *The Discourses as Reported by Arrian, Books I–II*. Cambridge: Harvard University Press.
Evans, Gareth (1973) "The Causal Theory of Names." *Proceedings of the Aristotelian Society: Supplementary* 47: 187–208.
Fieser, James (Ed.) (2005) *Early Responses to Hume's Writings on Religion*. Bristol: Thoemmes Press [2001].
Fénelon, François (1983) "Dialogues sur l'éloquence en général et sur celle de la chaire en particulier," in *Œuvres*, 2 Vols. J. Le Brun (Ed.) Paris: Gallimard, 1983–1997. vol. I, [1718].
Friday, Jonathan (1998) "Hume's Sceptical Standard of Taste." *Journal for the History of Philosophy*. 36:4 (October): 545–566.

Fordham, David. (2006) "Allan Ramsay's Enlightenment: Or, Hume and the Patronizing Portrait." *Art Bulletin.* 88: 3: 508–524.
Fogelin, Robert (1985) *Hume's Scepticism in the Treatise of Human Nature.* London: Routledge & Kegan Paul.
Fosl, Peter S. (1998) "The Bibliographic Bases of Hume's Understanding of Sextus Empiricus and Pyrrhonism." *Journal of the History of Philosophy.* 36:9 (April): 261–278.
Galgut, Elisa (2012) "Hume's Aesthetic Standard." *Hume Studies.* 38:2: 183–200.
Gallie Roger D. (1998) *Thomas Reid: Ethics, Aesthetics and the Anatomy of the Self.* Dordrecht: Kluwer.
Gerard, Alexander (1780) *An Essay on Taste: To which is now added Part Fourth, of the Standard of Taste*, 3rd edition. London: J. Bell and W. Creech; and T. Cadell.
Gigante, Denise (2008) "Purging Mist: On Hume, Humors, and Taste." In: *Taste: A Literary History.* New Haven: Yale University Press. 54–66.
Goldman, Alan H. (1995) *Aesthetic Value*, Boulder, CO: Westview Press.
Graham, Gordon (1997) *Philosophy of the Arts.* London: Routledge.
Goethe, Johann Wolfgang von (2012) *Faust, Volume 1 and 2.* Bayard Taylor, trans. New York: Modern Library.
Goldman, Alan H. (1995) *Aesthetic Value.* Boulder, CO: Westview Press.
Gibbon, Edward (1869) *Autobiography and correspondence of Edward Gibbon, the historian.* London: Alex. Murray [1794].
Gideion, Siegfried (1948) *Mechanization Takes Command: A Contribution to Anonymous History.* Oxford: Oxford University Press.
Gilmore, Jr., Thomas B. (Ed.) (1972) *Early 18th-Century Essays on Taste.* Delmar, NY: Scholars' Facsimiles and Reprints.
Gournay, M. le Jars de (1652) "Preface." In: Montaigne, *Les Essais.* Paris: I.B. Loyson.
Gracián y Morales, Baltasar (1953) *The Oracle: A Manual of the Art of Discretion.* L.B. Walton, trans. London: J.M. Dent & Sons [1647].
Gracián y Morales, Baltasar (1730) *The Compleat Gentleman.* London: T. Osborne.
Gracián y Morales, Baltasar (1728) *L'Homme du Cour.* Rotterdam: J. Hofhout.
Gracián y Morales, Baltasar (1714) *The Art of Prudence: or, A Companion for a Man of Sense.* London, D. Browne.
Gracián y Morales, Baltasar (1705) *L'Homme Detrompé, ou Le Criticon.* La Haye: J. van Ellinckhuysen.
Gracián y Morales, Baltasar (1681) *The Critick.* London: T.N. for H. Brome.
Gracyk, Theodore (2011) "Delicacy in Hume's Theory of Taste." *The Journal of Scottish Philosophy.* 9/1: 1–16.
Greene, Mott (1992) "Thales and the Halys." In: *Natural Knowledge and Preclassical Antiquity.* Baltimore: Johns Hopkins University Press.
Gunn, John Alexander Wilson (1983) *Beyond Liberty and Property: The Process of Self-Recognition in Eighteenth Century Political Thought.* Kingston/Montreal: McGill-Queen's University Press.
Gurstein, Rochelle (2000) "Taste and 'the Conversible World' in the Eighteenth Century." *Journal of the History of Ideas.* 61:2: 203–221.
Guthrie, William (1757) *An Essay Upon English Tragedy.* London: T. Waller.
Guyer, Paul (2013) *Knowledge, Reason, and Taste: Kant's Response to Hume.* Princeton: Princeton University Press.

Guyer, Paul (1993) "The Standard of Taste and the 'Most Ardent Desire of Society.'" In: Ted Cohen, Paul Guyer, and Hilary Putman (Eds.) *Pursuits of Reason: Essays in Honor of Stanley Cavell*. Lubbock, Texas: Texas Tech University Press, 1993, 37–66.

Guyer, Paul (2008) "Humean Critics, Imaginative Fluency, and Emotional Responsiveness: A Follow-up to Stephanie Ross." *British Journal of Aesthetics*. 48:4: 445–456.

Guyer, Paul (2014) *A History of Modern Aesthetics*. Vol. 1. Cambridge: Cambridge University Press.

Hadot, Pierre (1995) *Philosophy as a Way of Life*. Oxford: Blackwell.

Hall, Thomas S. (1969) *Ideas of Life and Matter: Studies in the History of General Physiology 600 B.C.–1900 AD*. 2 vols. Chicago: University of Chicago Press.

Hanslick, Eduard (1959) *On the Beautiful in Music*. Gustav Cohen, trans. Indianapolis: Bobbs-Merrill.

Hatab, Lawrence (2002) "Prospects for a Democratic Agon: Why We Can Still Be Nietzscheans." *Journal of Nietzsche Studies*. No. 24 (Fall): 132–147.

Hearn, Thomas K. (1970) "'General Rules' in Hume's *Treatise*." *Journal of the History of Philosophy*. 8:4: 405–422.

Heidegger, Martin (1975) "The Anaximander Fragment." In: Heidegger, *Early Greek Thinking*, David Krell and Frank Capuzzi, trans. New York: Harper & Row 13–58.

Helm, Bennett W. (1993) "Why We Believe in Induction: Standards of Taste and Hume's Two Definitions of Causation." *Hume Studies*. 19:1: 117–140.

Herdt, Jennifer A. (2008) *Putting On Virtue. The Legacy of the Splendid Vices*. Chicago: The University of Chicago Press.

Hester, Marcus (1979) "Hume on Principles and Perceptual Ability." *The Journal of Aesthetics and Art Criticism*. 37. 295–302.

Hill, Eric (1982) "Hume and the Delightful Tragedy Problem." *Philosophy*. 57:221 (July): 319–326.

Hipple, Walter J., Jr (1957) *The Beautiful, the Sublime, and the Picturesque in Eighteenth-Century British Aesthetic Theory*. Carbondale: Southern Illinois University Press.

Hirschmann, Alfred (1977) *The Passions and the Interests: Political Arguments for Capitalism Before its Triumph*. Princeton: Princeton University.

Hobbes, Thomas. (1996) *Leviathan*, J. C. A. Gaskin (Ed.), Oxford: Oxford University Press.

Hölderlin, Friedrich (1969) *Werke und Briefe*. Vol 1. Frankfurt am Main: Insel Verlag.

Home, Henry (Lord Kames) (1762) *Elements of Criticism*. Vol. 3. Edinburgh: A. Kincaid and J. Bell.

Home, Henry (1972) *Elements of Criticism*. New York: Garland.

Home, Henry (1751) *Essays in the Principles of Morality and Natural Religion*. Edinburgh: R. Fleming, for A. Kincaid and A. Donaldson.

Home, John (1969) *Douglas*, V.296. In: George H. Nettleton and Arthur E. Case (Eds.), *British Dramatists from Dryden to Sheridan*. Carbondale: Southern Illinois University Press. 643–668.

Horne, Thomas A. (1978) *The Social Thought of Bernard Mandeville: Virtue and Commerce in the Eighteenth Century*. London: MacMillan.

Hume, David (2014) *Further Letters of David Hume*. Felix Waldmann (Ed.) Edinburgh: Edinburgh Bibliographical Society.

Hume, David (2013) *Of the Standard of Taste: Post-Modern Times Aesthetic Classics*. Birmingham: The Birmingham Free Press.
Hume, David (2008) *Selected Essays*. Stephen Copley and Andrew Edgar (Eds.) Oxford: Oxford University Press.
Hume, David (2007) *A Dissertation on the Passions and The Natural History of Religion*. Tom L. Beauchamp (Ed.) Oxford: Clarendon Press.
Hume, David (2005) *On Suicide*. London: Penguin.
Hume, David (2000) *Four Dissertations and Essays on Suicide & the Immortality of the Soul*. South Bend Indiana: Saint Augustine.
Hume, David (2000) *A Treatise of Human Nature*. David Fate Norton and Mary Norton (Eds.) Oxford: Oxford University Press.
Hume, David (1999) *Enquiry Concerning Human Understanding*. Tom L. Beauchamp (Ed.) Oxford: Oxford University Press.
Hume, David (1998) *Enquiry Concerning the Principle of Morals*. (1998) Tom L. Beauchamp (Ed.) Oxford: Oxford University Press.
Hume, David (1993) Stephen Copley and Andrew Edgard (Eds.), *Selected Essays*. Oxford: Oxford University Press, 1993 [1993]).
Hume, David (1985) *Essays Moral, Political, and Literary*. Eugene F. Miller (Ed.) Indianapolis, IN: Liberty Fund.
Hume, David (1985) "On Essay Writing." In: *Essays Moral, Political and Literary*. E. F. Miller (Ed.) Indianapolis: Liberty Fund.
Hume, David (1985) "The Epicurean." In: Hume, *Essays Moral Political and Literary*, E. F. Millar (Ed.) Indianapolis: The Literary Fund. 138–145.
Hume, David (1983) *The History of England, From the Invasion of Julius Ceasar to the Revolution of 1688,* with the authors' last corrections and improvements, 6 vols. Indianapolis: Liberty Classic.
Hume, David (1981) *Treatise of Human Nature*. P.H. Nidditch (Ed.) Oxford: Oxford University Press [1739].
Hume, David (1978) *A Treatise of Human Nature*, L.A. Selby-Bigge (Ed.), P.H. Nidditch, (Ed.) Oxford: Clarendon Press.
Hume, David (1975) *Enquiries Concerning Human Understanding and Concerning the Principles of Morals*, L.A. Selby-Bigge (Ed.), P.H. Nidditch (Ed.) Oxford: Clarendon Press.
Hume, David (1965), John W. Lenz, Ed. *Of the Standard of Taste and Other Essays*. Upper Saddle River, New Jersey: Prentice Hall.
Hume, David (1965) *Hume's Ethical Writings*, Alasdair MacIntyre (Ed.), New York: Collier.
Hume, David (1954) Letter 104. In: Raymond Klibansky and Ernest Mossner (Ed.) *New Letters of David Hume*, Oxford: Clarendon Press.
Hume, David (1932) *The Letters of David Hume*, J. Y. T. Greig (Ed.) Oxford: Oxford University Press.
Hume, David (1903) "Of the Standard of Taste." *Essays*.
Hume, David (1903) "Of the Delicacy of Taste and Passion." *Essays*.
Hume, David (1903) "The Sceptic." In: *Essays*.
Hume, David (1875) *Essays Moral, Political, and Literary*. T.H. Green and T.H. Grose (Eds.) London: Longmans, Green, and Company.
Hume, David (1870) *Essays Literary, Moral, and Political* by David Hume, Esq., The Historian. London: Ward, Lock, and Tyler, Warwick House, Paternoster Row.

Hume, David (1824) *The History of England, from the Invasion of Julius Caesar to the Revolution in 1688.* Vol II. London: Thomas Kelly.
Hume, David (1770) *Essays and Treatises on Several Subjects*, 4 vols. London: T. Cadell, Edinburgh, A. Kincaid and A. Donaldson.
Hume, David (1766) *Exposé succinct de la contestation qui s'est élevéé entre M. Hume et M. Rousseau avec les pieces justificatives et la Lettre de M. de Voltaire à ce sujet. Il paraît à Paris au cours de l'automne 1766. Londres.* J. B. A. Sward, trans. Paris: Weller.
Hume, David (1764) *Essays and Treatises on several Subjects.* 2 vols. London: A. Millar.
Hume, David (1757) *The Natural History of Religion*, in: *Four Dissertations.* London: A. Millar.
Hume, David (1757) *Four Dissertations.* London: Millar, in the Strand.
Hume, David (1756) *Essays and Treatises on Several Subjects*, 2 vols. London: A. Millar.
Hume, David (1751) *An Enquiry Concerning the Principles of Morals.* London: A. Millar.
Hume, David (1748) *Philosophical Essays concerning Human Understanding.* London: A. Millar.
Hume, David (1741) "Advertisement" to *Essays, Moral and Political.* Edinburgh: R. Fleming and A. Alison for A. Kincaid.
Hume, David "Of the Origin of Government." In: *Essays*, Green and Grose (Eds.)
Hume, David "Of the Original Social Contract." In: *Essays*, Green and Grose (Eds.)
Hume, David "Of the Rise and Progress of the Arts and Sciences." In: *Essays*, Green and Grose (Eds.)
Hume, David "Of National Characters." In: *Essays*, Green and Grose (Eds.)
Hume, David "A Dissertation on the Passions." In: *Essays*, Green and Grose (Eds.)
Hume, David "On the Dignity or Meanness of Human Nature." In: *Essays*, Green and Grose (Eds.)
Hume, David "Of the Populousness of Ancient Nations." In: *Essays*, Green and Grose (Eds.)
Hume, David "Of Polygamy and Divorces." In: *Essays*, Green and Grose (Eds.)
Hume, David "Of Love and Marriage." In: *Essays*, Green and Grose (Eds.)
Hume, David "Of Eloquence." In: *Essays*, Green and Grose (Eds.)
Hume, David "Of Superstition and Enthusiasm," In: *Essays*, Green and Grose (Eds.)
Hume, David "Of Simplicity and Refinement," In: *Essays*, Green and Grose (Eds.)
Hume, David "The Epicurean." In: *Essays*, Green and Grose (Eds.)
Hume, David "Of Refinement in the Arts." In: *Essays*, Green and Grose (Eds.)
Hume, David "On My Own Life," in: *Essays Moral, Political, and Literary*, 1–8.
Hutcheson, Francis (1729) *An Inquiry into the Original of Our Ideas of Beauty and Virtue in Two Treatises*, 3rd edition, London: J. and J. Knapton.
Hutcheson, Francis (1990) *Opera Minora.* Hildesheim: G. Olms Verlag.
Hutcheson, Francis (2002) "The Preface" to the *An Essay on the Nature and Conduct of the Passions and Affections. With Illustrations on the Moral Sense.* A. Garrett (Ed.) Indianapolis: Liberty Fund.
Hutcheson, Francis (2004) *An Inquiry into the Original of Our Ideas of Beauty and Virtue in Two Treatises*, W. Leidhold (Ed.) Indianapolis: Liberty.
Hutter, Horst, and Eli Friedlander (Eds.) (2013) *Nietzsche's Therapeutic Teaching: For Individuals and Culture.* London: Continuum.
Immerwahr, John (1994) "Hume's Dissertation on the Passions." *Journal of the History of Philosophy.* 32:2 (April): 224–40.

Janko, Richard. (2006) "Review of *The Derveni Papyrus*, edited by Theokritos Kouremenos, George M. Parássoglou, and Kyriakos Tsantsanoglou." *Bryn Mawr Classical Review*. October 29.

Jensen, Henning (1978) "Comments on Peter Jones' "Hume on Art, Criticism and Language: Debts and Premises"', *Philosophical Studies*. 33: 135–40.

Jones, Peter (2011) "Hume on the Arts and 'The Standard of Taste': Texts and Contexts." In: David Fate Norton & Jacqueline Taylor (Eds.) *The Cambridge Companion to Hume*. 2nd edition. Cambridge: Cambridge University Press. 414–446.

Jones, Peter (1978) "Hume on Art, Criticism and Language: Debts and Premises." *Philosophical Studies*. 33: 109–134.

Jones, Peter (1976) "Hume's Aesthetics Reassessed." *Philosophical Quarterly*. 26: 48–62.

Jones, Peter (1970) "Another Look at Hume's Views of Aesthetic and Moral Judgments." *Philosophical Quarterly*. 20: 53–59.

Jost, Jacob Sider & John Immerwahr (2013) "Hume the Sociable Iconoclast: The Case of the Four Dissertations." *The European Legacy*. 18: 5: 603–618.

Kahn, Charles (1960) *Anaximander and the Origins of Greek Cosmology*. New York: Columbia University Press.

Kail, P. J. E. (2009) "Nietzsche and Hume: Naturalism and Explanation." *Journal of Nietzsche Studies*. 37: 5–22.

Kames, Lord. See: Henry Home.

Kant, Immanuel (2000) *The Critique of the Power of Judgment*. Paul Guyer and Eric Matthews, trans. Cambridge: Cambridge University Press [1790].

Kant, Immanuel (1996) *Critique of Pure Reason*. Indianapolis: Hackett.

Kant, Immanuel (1987) *Philosophical Correspondence 1759–99*. Arnulf Zweig, trans. Chicago: University of Chicago Press.

Kant, Immanuel (1956) *Kritik der reinen Vernunft. Nach der ersten und zweiten Original-Ausgabe*. Raymund Schmidt (Ed.) Hamburg: Meiner [1781].

Kant, Immanuel (1950) *Critique of Pure Reason*. Norman Kemp Smith, trans. New York: The Humanities Press [1929].

Kant, Immanuel (1929) *Critique of Pure Reason*, Norman Kemp Smith, trans. London: Macmillan and Co.

Kant, Immanuel (1911) *Critique of Aesthetic Judgement*. J. C. Meredith, trans. Oxford: Oxford University Press.

Kant, Immanuel (1902) *Kritik der Urteilskraft*. Königlich Preussischen Akademie der Wissenschaften, Berlin: Walter de Gruyter [and predecessors].

Kerrigan, William (1983) *The Sacred Complex: On the Psychogenesis of "Paradise Lost."* Cambridge: Harvard University Press.

Kieran, Matthew (2005) *Revealing Art*. London: Routledge.

Kirk, Geoffrey S., John E. Raven and Martin Schofield (1984) *The Presocratic Philosophers*. Cambridge: Cambridge University Press.

Kivy, Peter (1967) "Hume's Standard of Taste: Breaking the Circle." *British Journal of Aesthetics*. 7:1 (Jan.): 57–66.

Kivy, Peter (1975) "Aesthetics and Rationality." *Journal of Aesthetics and Art Criticism*. 34: 1: 51–57.

Kivy, Peter (1994) "Hume's "Sentiments" in the Essay on Taste." In: Lars-Olaf Ahlberg and Tommie Zaine (Eds.), Aesthetic Matters. Uppsala: The University Press.

Kivy, Peter (2003) *The Seventh Sense: Francis Hutcheson and Eighteenth-century British Aesthetics*. 2nd edition. Oxford: Oxford University Press.
Korsmeyer, Carolyn (1999) *Making Sense of Taste: Food and Philosophy*. Ithaca: Cornell University Press.
Korsmeyer, Carolyn (1976) "Hume and the Standard of Taste." *JAAC*. 35:2 (Winter): 201–215.
Krieger, Leonard (1970) *Kings and Philosophers 1689–1789*. Chicago: Chicago University Press.
Kripke, Saul (1972) "Naming and Necessity." In: D. Davidson and G. Harman (Eds.), *Semantics of Natural Language*. Boston: D. Reidel. 253–355.
Kulenkampff, Jens (1990) "The Objectivity of Taste: Kant and Hume." *Noûs* 24, 1: 93–110, 99–100.
Laird, John (1932) *Hume's Philosophy of Human Nature*. London: Methuen & Co.
Lang, Berel (2002) "Misinterpretation as the Author's Responsibility (Nietzsche's Fascism, For Instance)." In: Jacob Golomb and Robert S. Wistrich (Eds.), *Nietzsche, Godfather of Fascism? On the Uses and Abuses of a Philosophy*. Princeton, NJ: Princeton University Press. 47–65.
Langlois, Judith H. and Lori Roggman (1990) "Attractive Faces are only Average," *Psychological Science*. 1: 115–121.
La Rochefoucauld, François (1743) *Réflexions, Sentences et Maximes Morales*. Paris: Veuve Ganzeau.
La Rochefoucauld, François (1992) *Maximes*. J. Truchet (Ed.) Paris: Garnier.
Le Doeuff, Michele (1991) *Hypparchia's Choice*. Trista Selous, trans. Oxford: Blackwell.
Lehmann, William C. (1971) *Henry Home, Lord Kames, and the Scottish Enlightenment*. The Hague: Nijhoff.
Livingston, Donald W. (1984) *Hume's Philosophy of Common Life*. Chicago: University of Chicago Press.
Levinson, Jerrold (2002) "Hume's Standard of Taste: The Real Problem." *Journal of Aesthetics and Art Criticism*. 60: 227–238.
Locke, John (1977) *An Essay Concerning Human Understanding*. John W. Yolton (Ed.) London: J.M. Dent & Sons [1690].
Locke, John (1985) *An Essay Concerning Human Understanding*, P.H. Nidditch (Ed.) Oxford: Clarendon Press.
Longinus (1939) *On the Sublime*. W. Hamilton Fyfe, trans. London: Heinemann.
Lucian (1913–1967) A. M. Harmon, trans. Eight Vols. Cambridge, MA: Harvard University Press, Loeb Classical Library.
Lucian (1968) *Selected Satires of Lucian*, Lionel Casson, trans. New York: Norton.
Ludovici, Anthony (1911) *Nietzsche and Art*. London: Constable.
Mabille, Louise (2011) "Hume on the Use and Abuse of Skepticism for Life." In: Mabille, *Nietzsche and the Anglo-Saxon Tradition*. London: Continuum.
MacIntyre, Alasdair (1965). "Introduction," to: MacIntyre (Ed.), *Hume's Ethical Writings: Selections from David Hume*. Notre Dame: University of Notre Dame Press.
MacLachlan, Christopher (1986) "Hume and the Standard of Taste," *Hume Studies*. 12:1: 18–38.
MacMillan, Claude (1986) "Hume, Points of View and Aesthetic Judgments." *Journal of Value Inquiry*. 20: 1: 109–123.

Makkreel, Rudolf A. (2011) "Aesthetics." In: Knud Haakonssen (Ed.), *The Cambridge History of Eighteenth-Century Philosophy*. Vol. 1. Cambridge: Cambridge University Press. 516–556.

Malebranche, Nicolas (1991) *Recherche de la vérité*. 3rd edition, 3 vols., G. Rodis-Lewis (Ed.) Paris: Vrin.

Mandeville, Bernard (1924) *Fable of the Bees: or, Private Vices, Publick Benefits*, 2 vols., F.B. Kaye (Ed.) Oxford: Clarendon Press.

Mandeville, Bernard (1732) *A Letter to Dion*. London: J. Roberts.

Mandeville, Bernard (1732) *An Enquiry into the Origin of Honour, and The Usefulness of Christianity in War*. London: J. Brotherton.

Mandeville, Bernard (1761) *Anti-Shaftesbury oder die entlarvte Eitelkeit der Selbstliebe und Ruhmsucht in philosophische Gesprachen nach der Englandischen*. Frankfurt am Mayn: Garbe.

Mansfeld, Japp and David T. Runia (1997) *Aëtiana: The Method and Intellectual Context of a Doxographer. Volume I: The Sources, Philosophia Antiqua* 73. Leiden: E. J. Brill.

Margolis, Joseph (1965) *The Language of Art and Art Criticism*. Detroit: Wayne State University Press.

Marshall, David (1995) "Arguing by Analogy: Hume's Standard of Taste." *Eighteenth Century Studies*. 28: 3: 323–343.

Martin, Marie A. (1993) "The Rational Warrant for Hume's General Rules." *Journal of the History of Philosophy*, 31:2: 245–257.

Mazza, Emilio (2018) "The Eloquent *Enquiry*. Merit or Virtue in its Proper Colours." In: J. Taylor (Ed.) *Reading Hume on the Principles of Morals: Essays on "An Enquiry concerning the Principles of Morals."* Oxford: Oxford University Press.

Mazza, Emilio (2018) "Fluctuations. Manners, Tastes, and Religion in the Standard of Taste." In: Angela Coventry and Alexander Sager (Eds.) *The Humean Mind*. London: Routledge.

Mazza, Emilio (2007) and Emanuele Ronchetti (Eds.) *New Essays on David Hume*, Milan: Franco Angeli.

Merivale, Amyas. (2011) "Mixed Feelings, Mixed Metaphors: Hume on Tragic Pleasure." *British Journal of Aesthetics*. 51:3 (July): 259–269.

Miller, David (1981) *Philosophy and Ideology in Hume's Political Thought*. Oxford: Oxford University Press.

Miller, David (1999) "Being an Absolute Skeptic." *Science*, Vol. 284, no. 5420 (4 June): 1625–1626.

Montaigne, Michel de (1992) *Les Essais*, 3 vols., P. Villey (Ed.) Paris: PUF.

Montaigne, Michel de (1652) *Les Essais*. Paris: I.B. Loyson.

Morris, William Edward (2009) "David Hume." *Stanford Encyclopedia of Philosophy*. http://plato.stanford.edu/entries/hume/#Rel. Accessed 8 March 2018.

Mossner, Ernest Campbell (1940) "Hume and the Scottish Shakespeare." *Huntington Library Quarterly*, Vol. 3, No. 4 (Jul.): 419–441.

Mossner, Ernest Campbell (1948). "Hume's Early Memoranda, 1729–40: The Complete Text," *Journal of the History of Ideas*, 9/4 (October): 492–518.

Mossner, Ernest Campbell (1950) "Hume's 'Four Dissertations:' An Essay in Biography and Bibliography." *Modern Philology*. 48.1: 37–57.

Mossner, Ernest Campbell (1954) *The Life of David Hume*. Oxford: Oxford University Press.

Mothersill, Mary (1997) "In Defense of Hume and the Causal Theory of Taste." *The Journal of Aesthetics and Art Criticism*. Vol. 55, No. 3: 312–317.

Mothersill, Mary (1989) "Hume and the Paradox of Taste." In: George Dickie, Richard Scalfani, and Ronald Roblin (Eds.) *Aesthetics: A Critical Anthology*. New York: St. Martin's Press. 269–286 [1977].
Nehamas, Alexander (1985) *Life as Literature*. Cambridge: Harvard University Press.
Nehamas, Alexander (2007) *Only a Promise of Happiness: The Place of Beauty in a World of Art*. Princeton: Princeton University Press.
Nettleton, George H. and Arthur E. Case (Eds.) (1969) *British Dramatists from Dryden to Sheridan*. Carbondale: Southern Illinois University Press.
Neill, Alex (1999) "Hume's 'Singular Phenomenon.'" *British Journal of Aesthetics* 39.2 (April): 112–125.
Nietzsche, Friedrich (1996) *Human, All Too Human. A Book for Free Spirits*. R. J. Hollingdale, trans. Cambridge: Cambridge University Press.
Nietzsche, Friedrich (1995) Nietzsche, *Vorlesungsaufzeichnungen (WS 1871/72-WS 1874/75)*. KGW II$_4$. Fritz Bornamnn and Mario Carpitella (Eds.) Berlin: de Gruyter.
Nietzsche, Friedrich (1994) "Homer und die klassische Philologie." In: *Frühe Schriften*, Carl Koch and Carl Schlechta (Eds.) Munich: Beck.
Nietzsche, Friedrich (1983) "On the Uses and Disadvantages of History for Life." In: *Untimely Meditations*, R. J. Hollingdale, trans. Cambridge: Cambridge University Press. [1874]
Nietzsche, Friedrich (1980) *Kritische Studien-Ausgabe*. Mazzino Montinari and Giorgio Colli, (Eds.) Berlin: de Gruyter.
Nietzsche, Friedrich (1986) *Sämtliche Briefe. Kritische Studienausgabe*. Giorgio Colli and Mazzino Montinari (Eds.) Berlin: de Gruyter.
Nietzsche, Friedrich (1962) *Philosophy in the Tragic Age of the Greeks*. Chicago: Regnery [1903].
Nietzsche, Friedrich (1913) *Die vorplatonische Philosophen*. In: *Philologica*, Vol 3. Berlin: Kroner.
Nietzsche, Friedrich (1921) *Gesammelte Werke. Vierter Band, Vorträge, Schriften und Vorlesungen 1871–1876*. Munich: Musarion. 247–366.
Nietzsche, Friedrich (1903) *Nietzsche's Werke. Nachgelassene Werke. Von Friedrich Nietzsche. Aus den Jahren 1872/73–1875/76*. Vol 10. Leipzig: C. G. Naumann.
Nietzsche, Friedrich (1896) *Nietzsche's Werke*. 2. Abteilung, Vol X. Leipzig: C. G. Naumann.
Noxon, James (1961) "Hume's Opinion of Critics." *Journal of Aesthetics and Art Criticism*. 20, 2: 157–162.
Oakeshott, Michael (1991) *Rationalism in Politics and Other Essays*. Indianapolis, Indiana: Liberty Classics, [1962].
Oehler, Richard (1904) *Friedrich Nietzsche und die Vorsokratiker*. Leipzig: Verlag der Dürr'schen Buchhandlung.
Osborne, Catharine Rowan (1987) *Rethinking Early Greek Philosophy*. London: Duckworth.
Osborne, Harold (1978) "Some Theories of Aesthetic Judgment." *Journal of Aesthetics and Art Criticism*. 38: 2: 135–144.
Packer, Mark (1989) "Dissolving the Paradox of Tragedy." *The Journal of Aesthetics and Art Criticism*. 47.3 (Summer): 211–219.
Passmore, John (1952) *Hume's Intentions*. Cambridge: Cambridge University Press.
Perrett, David (2010) *In Your Face*. Palgrave: Macmillan.
Perricone, Christopher (1995) "The Body and Hume's Standard of Taste." *Journal of Aesthetics and Art Criticism*. 53:4 (Fall): 371–378.

Pocock, John G.A. (1999) *Barbarism and Religion, Volume Two: Narratives of Civil Government*. Cambridge: Cambridge University Press.

Pocock, John G.A. (1985) *Virtue, Commerce, and History*. Cambridge: Cambridge University Press.

Pocock, John G.A. (1975) *The Machiavellian Moment*. Princeton: Princeton University Press.

Poellner, Peter (1999) "Causation and Force in Nietzsche." In: Babette Babich and Robert Cohen (Eds.), *Nietzsche, Epistemology, and Philosophy of Science: Nietzsche and Science II*. Dordrecht: Kluwer. 287–297.

Polyakova, Ekaterina and Yulia Sineokaya (Eds.), (2017) *Фридрих Ницше: наследие и проект. М.: Культурная революция, / Friedrich Nietzsche: Heritage and Prospects*. Moscow, LRC Publishing House.

Price, John V. (1965) *The Ironic Hume*. Austin: University of Texas Press.

Pope, Alexander (1711) *Essay in Criticism*.

Pope, Alexander (1745) "The Design [1734]." In: *An Essay on Man [...]. With Notes by William Warburton*. London: J. and P. Knapton.

Price, John V. (1965) *The Ironic Hume*. Austin: University of Texas Press.

Rand, Benjamin (Ed.) (1900) *The Life, Unpublished Letters, and Philosophical Regimen of Anthony, Earl of Shaftesbury*. New York: Macmillan.

Rasmussen, Dennis C. (2017) *The Infidel and the Professor: David Hume, Adam Smith, and the Friendship That Shaped Modern Thought*. Princeton: Princeton University Press.

Rasmussen, Dennis C. (2013) *The Pragmatic Enlightenment: Recovering the Liberalism of Hume, Smith, Montesquieu, and Voltaire*. Cambridge: Cambridge University Press.

Reid, Thomas (1983) *Philosophical Works*. Sir William Hamilton (Ed.) 2 vols. Hildesheim: Georg Olms Verlag.

Reid, Thomas (1788) *Essays on the Active Powers of Man*. Edinburgh: J. Bell.

Reid, Thomas (1785) *Essays on the Intellectual Powers of Man*. Edinburgh: J. Bell.

Reid, Thomas (1764) *An Inquiry into the Human Mind, On the Principles of Common Sense*. Edinburgh: A. Millar *et alii*.

Reynolds, Sir Joshua (1776) *Discourses*.

Richardson, Samuel (1962) *Pamela*. New York: Everyman's Library.

Rhodes, Gillian, Fiona Proffitt, Jonathan M. Grady, & Alex Sumich, (1998) "Facial symmetry and perception of beauty." Psychonomic Bulletin & Review 5: 659–669.

Roelofs, Monique. (2014) *The Cultural Promise of the Aesthetic*. London: Bloomsbury.

Rose, Mary Carman (1976) "The Importance of Hume in the History of Western Aesthetics." British Journal of Aesthetics. 16: 218–229.

Rose, W. (1752) "Review of *Enquiry Concerning the Principles of Morals*." The Monthly Review, January.

Ross, Stephanie (2008) "Humean Critics: Real or Ideal?" British Journal of Aesthetics. 48:1: 20–28.

Ross, W. D. (1959) *Aristotle: A Complete Exposition of his Works and Thought*. New York: Meridian Books.

Saint-Réal, abbé de (César Vichard) (1757) *Les Œuvres de M. L'Abbé de Saint Réal*, 8 vols. Paris: Libraires Associés.

Saisselin, Remy G. (1970) *The Rule of Reason and the Ruses of the Heart: Philosophical Dictionary of Classical French Criticism, Critics, and Aesthetic Issues*. Cleveland: Press of Case Western Reserve University.

Sayre-McCord, Geoffrey (1994) "On Why Hume's 'General Point of View Isn't Ideal—And Shouldn't Be." In Ellen Frankel Paul, Fred D. Miller, Jr., and Jeffrey Paul (Eds.) *Cultural Pluralism and Moral Knowledge*. Cambridge: Cambridge University Press. 202–228.
Savile, Anthony (1993) *Kantian Ethics Pursued*. Edinburgh: Edinburgh University Press.
Schaeffer, Jean-Marie (2000) *Art of the Modern Age: Philosophy of Art from Kant to Heidegger*, trans. Steven Bendall. Princeton, NJ: Princeton University Press.
Schaper, Eva (1983) "The Pleasures of Taste." In: Eva Schaper (Ed.) *Pleasure, Preference and Value*. Cambridge: Cambridge University Press.
Schlaffer, Heinz (2007) *Das entfesselte Wort: Nietzsches Stil und seiner Folgen*. Munich: Hanser.
Schmidt, Claudia (2003), *David Hume: Reason in History*. University Park, Pennsylvania: The University of Pennsylvania Press.
Schulz, Sabine (Ed.) (2012) *"Leben Sie wohl für immer": Die Affäre Hume-Rousseau in Briefen und Zeitdokumenten*. Zürich: Diaphanes Verlag.
Scott, William R. (1900) *Francis Hutcheson: His Life, Teaching and Position in the History of Philosophy*, Cambridge: Cambridge University Press.
Scruton, Roger (2011) *Beauty: A Very Short Introduction*. Oxford: Oxford University Press. [2009].
Seddon, Keith (2008) *Epictetus' Handbook and the Tablet of Cebes: Guides to Stoic Living*. London: Routledge.
Sévigné, Mme de (1736) *Recueil des Lettres de Madame La Marquise de Sévigné*. Leide: Verbeel.
Shaftesbury (Anthony Ashley Cooper) (1914) *Second Characters: or, the Language of Forms*. Benjamin Rand (Ed.) Cambridge: Cambridge University Press.
Shaftesbury (1999) *Characteristics of Men, Manners, Opinions, Times*, L. E. Klein (Ed.) Cambridge: Cambridge University Press. (1964) [1711].
Shaftesbury (1977) *An Enquiry Concerning Virtue or Merit*. David Walford (Ed.), Manchester: Manchester University Press (1711) [1688].
Shapin, Steven (2016) "The Sciences of Subjectivity." In: Babette Babich (Ed.), *Hermeneutic Philosophies of Social Science*. Berlin: de Gruyter. 123–142.
Shelley, James (1994) "Hume's Double Standard of Taste." *Journal of Aesthetics and Art Criticism*. 52, 4 (Fall): 437–45.
Shelley, James (1998) "Hume and the Nature of Taste." *Journal of Aesthetics and Art Criticism*. 56, 1: 29–38.
Shelley, James (2007) "Aesthetics and the World at Large." *British Journal of Aesthetics* 47: 169–83.
Shelley, James (2013) "Hume and the Joint Verdict of True Judges." *Journal of Aesthetics and Art Criticism*. 71, 2: 145–153.
Shiner, Roger A. (1996) "Hume and the Causal Theory of Taste." *Journal of Aesthetics and Art Criticism*. 54:3: 237–249.
Shiner, Roger A. (1979) "Sense-Experience, Colours, and Tastes." *Mind*. 88: 161–178.
Shusterman, Richard (1989) "The Scandal of Taste: Social Privilege as Nature in the Aesthetic Theories of Hume and Kant." *The Philosophical Forum*. 20:3: 211–229.
Siemens, Herman and James Pearson (Eds.) (2018) *Conflict and Contest in Nietzsche's Philosophy*. London: Bloomsbury.

Singh, Devendra (1993) "Body Shape and Women's Attractiveness. The Critical Role of Waist-to-Hip Ratio." *Human Nature*. 4, (3): 297–321.
Smith, Adam LL.D. (1875). Letter to William Strahan, Esq. In: Hume. *Essays Moral, Political, and Literary*. London: Longmans, Green, and Company. 9–14.
Smith, Adam LL.D. (1982) *Essays on Philosophical Subjects*. W.P.D. Wightman and J.C. Bryce (Eds.) Indianapolis: Liberty Fund.
Smith, Norman Kemp (1941) *The Philosophy of David Hume*. London: Macmillan.
Steinrück, Martin (2008) *The Suitors in the Odyssey: The Clash Between Homer and Archilochus*. Oxford: Peter Lang.
Stevenson, Charles L. (1953) *Ethics and Language*. New Haven: Yale University Press.
Stewart, John B. (1963) *The Moral and Political Philosophy of David Hume*. New York: Columbia University Press.
Stolnitz, Jerome (1961) "On the Significance of Lord Shaftesbury in Modern Aesthetic Theory." *The Philosophical Quarterly*, Vol. 11: 97–113.
Stoutland, Frederick (1976) "The Causal Theory of Action." In: Juha Manninen and Raimo Tuomela (Eds.), *Essays on Explanation and Understanding: Studies in the Foundations of Humanities and Social Sciences*. Boston: D. Reidel.
Strong, Tracy Burr (2013) "In Defense of Rhetoric; or, How Hard it is to Take a Writer Seriously: The Case of Nietzsche." *Political Theory*. 41:4: 507–532.
Sverdlik, Steven (1986) "Hume's Key and Aesthetic Rationality." *Journal of Aesthetics and Art Criticism*. 45:1: 69–76.
Swift, Jonathan (1710) *A Tale of a Tub. Written for the Universal Improvement of Mankind*. London, J. Nutt.
Taminiaux, Jacques (1997) *The Thracian Maid and The Professional Thinker: Arendt and Heidegger*. Albany: State University of New York Press.
Taylor, William Leslie (1965) *Francis Hutcheson and David Hume as Predecessors of Adam Smith*. North Carolina: Duke University Press.
The Spectator. (1713) 8 vols. London: S. Buckley.
Tillyard, E. M. W. (1952) *The Elizabethan World Picture*. London: Chatto and Windus.
Townsend, Dabney (2001) *Hume's Aesthetic Theory: Sentiment and Taste in the History of Aesthetics*. New York: Routledge.
Tuncel, Yunus (2013) *Agon in Nietzsche*. Milwaukee: Marquette University Press, 2013.
Turco, Luigi (2007) "Hutcheson and Hume in a Recent Polemic." In E. Mazza and E. Ronchetti (Eds.) *New Essays on David Hume*, Milan: Franco Angeli. 193–198.
Turco, Luigi (1997) "La virilità perduta del *Trattato* di Hume." *I castelli di Yale*. 2: 227–252.
Ugolini, Gherardo (2003): "'*Philologus inter philologos*'. Friedrich Nietzsche, die Klassische Philologie und die griechische Tragödie. "*Zeitschrift für antike Literatur und ihre Rezeption. A Journal for Ancient Literature and its Reception*. 174:2: 316–342.
Van Cleve, James (2004): "Reid's Theory of Perception." In: T. Cuneo & R. v. Woudenberg (Eds.) *The Cambridge Companion to Thomas Reid*. Cambridge: Cambridge University Press. 101–133.
Vanterpool, Rudolph V. (1974) "Hume's Account of General Rules." *Southern Journal of Philosophy*. 12:4: 481–49.2.
Vickers, Brian (Ed.) (1995) *The Critical Heritage, Volume IV: 1753–1765*. London and New York.
Voltaire (1734) *Lettres philosophiques*. Amsterdam: E. Lucas.

Vopěnka, Petr (2000) *Úhelný kámen evropské vzdělanosti a moci*. Prague: Práh.
Wallen, Martin (2004) *City of Health, Fields of Disease: Revolutions in the Poetry, Medicine, and Philosophy of Romanticism*. Aldershot: Ashgate.
Warburton, William (1757) *Remarks on Mr. David Hume's Essay on The Natural History of Religion*. London: printed for M. Cooper.
Warnock, Mary (1976) *Imagination*. Berkeley: The University of California Press.
Waters, Edwin N. (1967) "Franz Liszt to Richard Pohl." *Studies in Romanticism*. 1:4: (Summer): 193–202.
Webb, Mark (1991) "The Argument of the Natural History." *Hume Studies*. 17:2 (November): 141–60.
Wenzel, Christian Helmut (2001) "Beauty, Genius, and Mathematics: Why Did Kant Change His Mind?" *History of Philosophy Quarterly*. 18/4: 415–432.
Wieand, Jeffrey (1984) "Hume's Two Standards of Taste." *The Philosophical Quarterly*. 34:135: 129–142.
Williams, Christopher (2007) "Some Questions in Hume's Aesthetics," *Philosophy Compass*. 2:2: 157–169.
Wilson, Glenn, David K. B. Nias, & Anthony H. Brazendale (1975) "Vital Statistics, Perceived Sexual Attractiveness, and Response to Risque Humor." *The Journal of Social Psychology*. 95 (2): 201–5.
Wollaston, William (1724) *The Religion of Nature Delineated*. London: S. Palmer. [1722]
Wollaston, William (1738) *The Religion of Nature Delineated* London: J. and P. Knapton [1722].
Wood, Paul B. (1986) "David Hume on Thomas Reid's *An Inquiry into the Human Mind, On the Principles of Common Sense:* A New Letter to Hugh Blair from July 1762." *Mind*. 95:380 (Oct): 411–416.
Woodmansee, Martha (1993) *The Author, Art and the Market*. New York: Columbia University Press.
Yanal, Robert J. (1991) "Hume and Others on the Paradox of Tragedy." *The Journal of Aesthetics and Art Criticism*. 49:1 (Winter): 75–76.
Youngquist, Paul (1999) "De Quincey's Crazy Body." *PMLA*. 114: 346–358.
Youngquist, Paul (2004) "Romantic Dietetics! or, Eating Your Way to a New You!" In: Timothy Morton, (Ed.), *Cultures of Taste: Eating Romanticism*. London: Palgrave. 237–255.
Zaretsky, Robert and John T Scott (2009) *The Philosophers' Quarrel: Rousseau, Hume, and the Limits of Human Understanding*. New Haven: Yale University Press.

Subject Index

aesthetic judgment   47, 214
– science   213
absolutism   168
aesthetics, aesthetic theory   44, 77, 148, 217
– applied   148
– German   235
– historical   220
– mathematization of, 140, 150, 249 ff
– science   218, 241
affect   253
affection   136, 144, 189, 251, 281
affectation   90
aging, ages of life, 37, 215, 229, 230, 232, 234, 274 f
agon or contest   217, 219
algorithm   258
alimentary, see gustatory
analogy   134 f, 162 f
analytic philosophy   3, 5 f, 9, 119, 214 f, 217, 222, 232
'analytic' vs 'continental' philosophy   6, 17, 19, 221 f
– and Brexit   17
anatomy   240, 281 ff, 291 f
ancient vs modern   58, 61 f
appetite   139, 191 ff, 196, 215, 288
appraisal   214, 274
archaeology   219, 240
architecture   15, 71, 74, 202, 217 f
– planning and design flourishes   67–68
argument   35, 44, 68 f, 71 f, 100, 138, 147 ff, 194 f, 217, 263
art, good   46 f, 49, 55
– as deception   217
– criticism   122
– hierarchy of   171
– history   240
– production and reception of   188
artist   142, 153, 188, 190, 214, 236 f,
artwork   66, 85 f, 119 ff, 126 ff, 274
attribution   209, 213 f, 216 ff, 218, 220, 240, 252

authority   29, 34, 50, 63, 65, 103, 130, 145, 167, 171, 217 f, 255, 260
autonomy   130, 163, 181 f

beauty   68 f, 72, 74 f, 78, 85, 87, 97, 128, 130, 134, 137, 138 f, 141, 144 f, 146, 150 ff, 157, 166, 169, 183, 187, 189, 192 f, 194, 201 f, 206
– productive of morality   202
beer   138 f, 227, 239, see also: Kulmbacher
belief   50 f, 59, 62, 64, 69, 134 f, 159, 224, 232, 266, 278
bigotry   56, 60
biology   126, 159
blame   25 ff, 32 ff, 38 f, 50 f, 154, 166, 207, 228, 255, 268, 282, 295
bread   226 f, 228, 230, 232. 234
British theory of taste   178 f, 235

canon, canonic   98, 160, 217
causal theory   118 ff, 121 f, 148, 221 f, 225 f, 297
causality, cause and effect   80, 81, 92, 134, 153, 221 f, 231, 235 f, 251, 293
– spiritual   232
Cartesian   207, 251
Catholicism   60
celebrity   264
chastity, as feminine virtue   101–2
character   140, 146
Christians   7, 59 f, 71, 276
– on becoming a   234 f
circle, circularity, 48 f, 149, 159 f, 163
– see also: regress
class, lower and higher   139, 235 ff
Classics, see philology
color   73, 142, 164, 296 f
commerce   183 ff, 191, 196
comic   28, 269
common sense   118, 120 f, 152, 198
– good   183
communal value   140

Subject Index

comparison   33, 35, 46f, 50, 55ff, 64f, 73, 85f, 107, 121, 141f, 145, 152, 166f, 170, 173, 218, , 268249ff, 254f, 269f, 292, 294
conflict   54, 57, 62, 120f, 192, 218f
conformity   27, 37, 74, 144, 177f, 198, 200, 206, 208ff, 252, 274
consensus   67, 170, 198
contemplation   32, 43, 47, 86, 127, 151, 205, 210, 250
contradiction   53, 55, 60, 78, 90f, 110, 224f, 275
contract   183, 187, 193, 195f, 199
convention   6f, 53, 55f, 60ff, 72, 99, 147, 220, 229, 230, 234, 236, 239, 278
conversion   36, 63f
conviction   31, 198f, 208f, 232, 258
cookery   80–81, 128
correlatives   105, 108
cosmology   217, 225
creativity   74, 82
criterial theory   120, 121, 126
criticism   45, 58, 156
cross-cultural   73
critic   47, 54, 56, 63, 65, 74, 77, 98, 99, 107, 130, 147f, 156f, 167
– ideal, or 'true judge' 61, 66, 74, 77, 87, 89, 90, 91, 214
– standard for critics   148
– vs bad (pretenders) 31, 54, 46, 63, 79, 157, 163
cross-cultural universals   72
culture, context   71, 146, 159
– democratic   67
– higher and lower   235
– national   171
custom   80, 106–107, 273
cyder/cider   138f

danger   202, 205
deception   191f, 217
deformity, defect   152, 201f, 206, 267
delicacy, delicate sentiment   47, 49, 50, 53f, 74, 84, 65–86, 99, 107, 121f, 123, 126, 134f, 140, 142, 147, 160f, 163, 165f, 170f, 196, 235f, 267f, 269, 278

delight   31, 182, 291, 214, 270
– instruction through   182, 201
desire   145, 67f, 71, 78, 104f, 110, 139, 142, 146, 183, 191f, 205ff, 214f, 231, 237, 253, 260, 274
difference, diversity   37, 51, 90, 98, 108, 111, 158, 171, 251, 253, 295
digital scholarship   223
discernment   32, 75, 107, 214, 235f, 239, 267f
discrimination   178, 189f, 195, 198f, 200ff, 209, 283
dissemblance, prudent   178
"disinterested spectator theory" 48f, 57, 157, 172 see observer, ideal
disputation   145, 157, 160, 171, 217, 265, 271
divine will   207ff
Don Quixote vignette   61, 122f, 144, 161f
doxography   183f, 216f

economics   9f, 15f, 17, 146, 180f, 193, 218, see commerce
eco-physiology   228f
ecstasy   279
effeminate   108
elegance   154
emotions   150, 253
Epicurean, Epicureanism   215, 288f, 297
epistemology   92, 144, 169f, 172, 216, 221, 264
error   240
evolution   240
excellence   254
experience,   265ff see also: practice
expert, see authority

fact, matters of   50–51, 90, 224f
faculty   177
fancy, see imagination
fashion   16, 68, 209
fantasy   180
feeling(s) 45, 198
feminine   97, 100f, 103f, 105f, 108f, 112
feminism   100
fine arts   196f, 199, 203, 205
food   139, 226f, 228ff, 265

force, see violence
freedom 72, 72f, 102, 177, 182f, 190, 223, 282
French Impressionism 268
French theory of taste 178f, 235f, 281f
friendship, between men and women 100
futures 16; see also economics, commerce, etc.

gallantry 102f
garden design 67, 71
gender 97f, 111f
genius 16, 27f, 29, 33ff, 39, 44, 63, 65, 78, 84, 132, 152f, 220f, 256f, 269, 272
– true 36, 63
geography of reason, mental 283f
good sense 26f, 34, 39, 46ff, 50ff, 55f, 65, 84, 92, 99, 107, 122, 135, 159, 168ff, 270
grammar 81f, 219, 221, 269
gratification 150
Greeks, ancient 59, 154; see pagan
gustatory (taste) 61, 122ff, 126, 129, 134, 139, 168, 213, 219, 240, 265

habit 28, 62, 80, 83, 106, 140, 155, 158, 160, 190, 198, 219, 223, 226, 230, 235f
harmony (musical) 72, 144
hermeneutics 12, 217, 221
history, 34, 85, 87, 92, 98, 143, 147, 178, 200, 209, 214ff, 220, 253, 265, 274
– of editions 3ff
Homer Question, the 216ff, 220, 239f
horses 160, 164f, 258
human nature 97, 111–112, 154f, 201
– universal, uniform 100, 169, 197f
– male and female 102f, 105, 107, 110–111, 230f, 234
– science of 200ff
humility 155

iconology, Christian 71, 201
ideas 28, 38, 43, 58, 80, 106f, 110f, 133ff, 139, 142, 146, 151f, 154ff, 158ff, 166ff 200, 2014, 224f, 266, 273, 286, 288f, 292
– (triangle) 151

ignorance 26, 79, 153, 170, 179, 209, 215, 263, 269, 273
illusion, see deception
imagination 80, 134, 139ff, 142, 144, 146, 161, 165, 169, 195, 258, 273f
imitation 33, 49, 68, 91, 108f, 178, 217, 277f, 289
impression 134, 140, 144, 150ff, 158, 165f, 291f
incommensurability 60
Indian classical music 71
inductive generalization 78f, 86, 88, 134
influence 26, 29ff, 34f, 46, 48f, 62f, 65ff, 79ff, 108f, 129, 134, 141, 148f, 153, 167, 173, 204, 222, 249, 256, 260, 294
interest, private/public 186f. 191
intuitive conception 119, 128f, 177, 198, 258
invisible hand 183, 193, 204
irony 57, 59–61, 235f, 240, 278, 297

jazz 72, 267f
je ne sais quoi 136, 141, 177f, 183ff, 200, 205
judging 86, 88, 98, 152, 165, 209, 213f
judge(ment), errors of 84
– faculty of 187, 209
– good 55, 77, 83, 89, 209
– internal 161
– reliable or true 170f, 270
– see good critic
jurisprudence 147
justice 146, 151, 183
justification, criterial 120

knowledge, propositional 81

language 25f, 29, 51, 56, 77f, 82, 92, 105, 119, 121, 130, 141, 151f, 154, 159, 169, 187, 214, 220, 222, 235, 255, 265ff, 297
law 28, 59, 67, 89, 128, 138, 160, 177, 181ff, 185f, 189ff, 193ff, 196ff, 200f, 206ff, 209f, 276, 285
legislation 187
and production 182f, 192f
legitimacy, structure of 181
lewd 'liberties' 288

love making, art of   128
logic   70, 83f, 90, 101, 110, 120f, 123f, 140, 158f, 200f, 206f, 223ff, 251, 285
luxury   191, 195f, 199

Machiavellian   196
males, adult (sexual dimorphism)   100
manners, cultural   102, 180f, 191
market, invisible hand of, see invisible hand
marriage   102, 109, 111
masculine   97, 105, 108, 155, 159
mathematics   140ff, 258
mechanics   129, 142, 151, 153
meta-aesthetics   148
metabolism   228f, 231, 233
metaphysics   232f, 291, 296
mocking, mockery   238
model   31f, 79, 89, 129, 105, 111, 131, 162f, 164f, 166f, 169f, 170ff, 178, 197, 259, 268
– wine   124
– cooking   128
modesty   26. 101ff, 108f
monstrous   153
morals   58, 62, 101, 141, 145, 148, 150, 154f, 172, 180f, 189–190, 197, 201, 216, 278, 285f, 290f, 296
– chemistry of   286
– science of   126, 128
morphology   219
musical (idea), musician's   141f, 144, 267, 271

nationality   58, 90. 100, 108, 110, 232, 274
nature   29, 30, 33, 36, 45, 52, 63, 71, 74, 79, 83, 99
natural law   181, 185, 193f
natural superiority of men over women, 102f
necessity   137f, 182, 186f, 202, 207, 224f, 292
normativity, normative discrimination   107, 110, 134, 249ff
nutrition, nutrition science   226f, 228, 230

objects, beautiful   97, 202, 253
objectivity   18, 56, 71, 72, 78, 117, 130, 173, 239f, 253, 273

obligation   110, 182, 187, 194f, 286f
observer, ideal, impartial, disinterested   60, 88, 144 , 167
olfactory sense, aroma   122, 240
opinion   7, 25, 27, 33, 36, 38f, 43, 54, 62ff, 85, 89f, 98, 102, 154, 156, 184f, 187, 198, 251f, 256f, 264, 282f, 287, 296
order   28, 33, 44, 65, 67f, 70, 72, 74, 90, 134, 138, 180, 182, 185ff, 190, 193, 196f, 207, 209, 291
originality   72, 74

pain   33, 48, 104, 120, 122, 126, 136, 140, 142, 144, 166, 195f, 201f, 205f, 208
painting, painter   16, 68, 70, 120, 129, 142f, 164f, 205, 218, 259, 264, 277, 282f, 287, 291
paradox   28, 44, 59, 208, 277, 281, 287ff, 290ff
particulars   25, 36, 56, 106, 147, 154, 208, 264
passions   28, 33f, 37, 48, 105f, 107, 118, 133ff, 142, 150f, 168f, 181, 197, 204f, 215, 272, 276, 282, 288, 290f
perception   29f, 36, 71, 84, 111, 118, 152, 154, 161, 190, 206ff, 229, 231, 249, 251f, 254f, 258f, 266, 278, 292
– disinterested   205
perfection   31f, 35, 74, 82, 84f, 87f, 143f, 163f, 188, 254, 259, 278
personality   49, 217f, 220
philology, classical   216ff, 219f, 221, 223
– text   219
physiology   226ff, 229f, 234f, 255
– national types   234
physics (natural philosophy) 153, 160, 232, 285, 292
Platonism   184, 187, 2??
play   29, 37, 70, 72f, 134, 208, 236, 268, 276
pleasure   139, 142, 145, 160, 177, 180, 190, 194, 210, 264, 267, 275
– and pain   136f, 194f, 201
– and utility   201ff
poetry   71, 85, 169, 271f
– epic   275

– folk   220f
– lyric   218
political activity   190
– economy   183, 193
Popery, see Catholicism
practice   85, 87–88, 127, 147, 165,
pragmatic   140f, 164
praise   25f, 32f, 43, 100, 108, 154, 166, 207, 238, 255, 264f, 268, 276, 282, 291, 294
predicates, aesthetic   123, 152f, 154, 162
prejudice   49, 57, 79, 129ff, 166f, 270f
– freedom from   61, 63, 166f, 169f, 173, 268
presocratics or preplatonics   219f
pride   105, 137, 145, 154f, 238, 281
production   192f, 200, 210
property   146f, 183, 193f, 195f
providence   178ff, 186, 193f, 195ff, 199, 203f, 210
psychology   149, 158, 252, 257f
public good   185f, 190, 214
– utility   61, 147, 190
– and private interest   186f, 190f

ragout   235f
rationality   72, 90, 188f, 193, 199, 250
reason, reasoning   45, 71, 199f, 207
reflection, ordinary and philosophical   83
regress, infinite, tendency to a   50, 148, 158f
regularity   201f, 206f, 209, 222
relation, relations of ideas   27f, 29, 32, 53f, 72, 105f, 120f, 128, 138, 151ff, 169, 183, 190, 195, 198, 200f, 202, 208f, 224
relativity, relativism   44, 62, 150, 172, 252, 265
religion   39–40, 56, 59–60, 62, 172
relish   33, 36, 38f, 44, 58, 63, 69, 134, 291
reputation   29, 64f, 123, 146, 161, 181, 282
resemblance   80, 106, 138, 142, 226
rhetoric   197, 214, 216
Ritterromane [Knightly tales] 236
romanticism   236

rule(s)   74, 77, 81, 86, 91, 125f, 140, 143f, 147, 152, 155f, 160, 162, 165f, 173, 178, 187f, 193, 199, 205, 208f, 253

satire   11, 37, 145, 237
scepticism see skeptic
science   16ff, 25f, 28, 72, 97, 126, 128, 154, 171, 206, 213f, 216ff, 219, 221f, 224f, 226f, 229ff, 241, 250f, 253, 265, 273, 287, 292
'science of man' see human nature, science of
Scottish letters   64–65
sculpture   16, 67, 71, 117, 119, 218
security   80, 101, 202
sense, good   26f, 34f, 39, 46f, 49, 50, 55, 65, 84, 92, 99, 107, 122, 135, 159, 168ff, 172f
sensus communis   49, 67, 186f, 282
sentiment(s)   25ff, 43, 50, 59, 78, 120, 129, 134f, 140f, 145, 147, 149, 151, 154, 157, 166, 173, 199f, 208f, 273, 294
– benevolent   185
– just   155, 158
– noble   194
sex and sexuality   101, 105, 110
skeptic, scepticism   3, 75, 98f, 121, 134, 148, 152, 178f, 214, 222, 183, 227f, 289f, 292, 295
slaves   103, 190, 277
social activity   255, 260
– contract theory   100
– privilege   78
– realm   190
– roles   105
spectator   37, 40, 45f, 58, 136, 187f, 190, 263, 266, 274, 276f
style (writerly)   55f, 214f, 217
– archaeological   219
– music   99
subjective, subjectivity   63, 73, 178, 208, 213, 217, 252, 264
succession, history of   216f
– protestant   185
suicide   3f, 228f
superstition   39, 60, 155, 172
symmetry   72, 259f, 282

sympathy   37, 57, 102, 139, 147, 204f, 274
– reflected   183

taste (wine) 53f, 65, 85–86
taste
– equality   28, 118, 289, 295
– multifariousness or variety of   25, 56, 65, 89f, 111, 155f, 210, 253
– superior   61, 108
taste (wine) 53f, 65, 85–86
– see also: good critic
teleology, telos   185f, 194, 197, 201, 205
time   36, 98, 142
touch, touching   140, 177, 293
tradition   61, 71, 74, 108, 136, 148, 170, 199, 201, 213, 219, 221, 241, 250f, 272, 289, 295
tragedy   34, 37, 59, 134, 171, 213, 218, 250, 276f
transgression   28, 74, 195

universality, universals   72, 98f, 106, 159, 183

utility   99, 101f, 108, 138, 147f, 165, 201ff
– formal   68, 205f
– immediate and reflected   205
– see also public

value judgments   45
vice   26, 38f, 43, 75, 138, 144, 154f, 186, 191, 195f, 201, 206, 265, 285, 288, 290, 292
violence   34, 57, 130, 167, 179, 184, 191f, 195, 199
virtue   147, 183f, 187, 189, 191f, 194ff, 199, 201, 296
virtue, monkish   101

weight gain   227, 229f
Whig Hellas   184ff, 196
wine   78, 85, 122f, 126ff, 134, 137, 144, 161f, 234ff, 239, 254–255, 267–268
– -pouring ritual   238
wit   135, 137, 144f, 284

Name Index

Acampora, C. D.   218
Addison, J.   16, 27, 44, 61, 84, 90, 98, 118, 143, 237, 250, 282, 292f, 297
Adorno, T.   16
Aeschylus   171
Agamben, G.   14
Alexander, C.   13, 62, 148, 215, 250, 256, 284
Alexandrian   219
Allison, D.   214f
Amman, W.   236
Aphrodite   276
Arain, F. A.   231
Arcesilaus   288
Archilochus   13, 218, 238
Arendt, H.   190
Aristophanes   110, 171
Aristotle   6, 13, 36, 52, 190, 217, 277, 297
Aron, R.   16
Arrowsmith, W.   221
Atropos   12
Austen, J.   16, 67

Babich, B.   3, 8, 12f., 17f., 213f., 216–218, 223, 228, 230, 236, 298
Baceski, C.   78
Bach, J. S. B.   67, 74
Bacon, F.   220
Baeumler, A.   236
Bahlman, D. W. R.   180
Baier, A.   6f., 9–11, 13, 100, 144
Balfour, J.   286
Bambi   71
Bastin-Hammou, M.   9
Bateman, C.   17
Battersby, C.   100
Bayle, P.   288
Beam, C.   214
Beattie, J.   168
Beaumarchais, P.-A. C de   73
Beethoven, L. von   124, 264
Bellini, G.   74
Bellow, Saul   265

Benn, G.   215
Berkeley, G.   149, 252, 296
Berry, D.   17
Bishop, Elizabeth   3
Blacklock, T.   64
Blake, W.   71
Bornedal, P.   222
Boscovich, R.   222
Box, M.A.   15, 123–125
Brahms, J.   68f, 271
Branham, R.B.   12
Breazeale, D.   214, 222
Brillat-Savarin, A.   226f, 234
Brobjer, T.   234
Broisson, I.   214
Brown, R.   230, 234
Brown, S.G.   46
Browning, R.   241
Bruce, L.   145
Brunius, T.   89
Budd, M.   91
Bunyan, J.   16, 27, 44, 84, 90, 98, 118, 143, 237
Burke, E.   74, 182, 186, 202, 210, 250
Burns, R.   65
Butler, J.   284, 290f, 294

Carlin, G.   145
Carroll, N.   149f, 159
Carter, E.   13, 269
Cassirer, E.   236
Caygill, H.   4, 17f, 177, 196, 210
Cervantes   14, 53, 123, 235–240, 275
Cezanne, P.   272
Charon   10, 12
Chikamatsu   73
Christensen, J.   103
Cicero   36, 277, 287f, 296
Clark, J.   181
Clotho   10, 12, 221
Cohen, T.   88
Coleman, O.   263, 269
Conard, M. T.   214

Cooper, Anthony Ashley see Shaftesbury
Copley, S. and A. Edgard   19
Cornaro, L.   215, 226, 230f, 233
Costelloe, T.   17f, 77, 91, 93, 268
Couvalis, G.   9f
Cullen, W.   6, 11
Cumberland, R.   181f, 185–187
Curtius, E.R.   139

da Silva, R.G.T.   11
da Vinci, L.   67, 264
Damon   215
Dante, A.   275
Danto, A.   222
de Beauvoir, S.   16, 234
de Gournay, M.   282f
de Martaelere, P.   148
de Saisselin, R.G.   178
Democritus   297
Démuth, A.   18, 252, 258
Démuthová, 18
Dennis, J.   17, 181f
Derrida, J.   215, 230
Derveni Krater, papyrus   219
Descartes, R.   36, 217, 282, 297
Desdemona   277
Dickinson, H.T.   181
Dickson, P.G.M.   180
Diderot, D.   184
Diogenes Laërtius   217, 240
Dionysus   276
Diotima   276
Don Quixote   14, 53, 61, 85. 123, 235f
Douglas   4, 65, 236
Du Bos, l'Abbé   143, 235f
Dulcinea   237
Dunbar, J.   17
Dürer, A.   8–10

Elsner, J.   8
Emerson, R.   5
Empedocles   8
Epictetus   13
Epicurus   36, 230, 233, 297
Erinyes   221
Evans, G.   119

Fable of the Bees   182, 184, 191f, 282, 284, 288
Favreau-Lindner, A.-M.   9
Fénelon L. A.   56, 281
Feuerbach, L. A.   234
Fieser, J.   4, 6, 18
Fogelin, R.   134
Fontenelle   104
Fordham, D.   17, 227
Fosl, P.S.   3
Friday, J.   18, 79

Gadamer, H.G.   3, 12, 215
Galgut, E.   89
George, S.   9, 145, 180, 273, 296
George III   196
Gerard, A.   62, 148, 250
Giedion, S.   232
Gigante, D.   18, 219
Gilmore, T.B.   148
Goethe, J. W. von   8, 13
Golding, W.   150
Goldman, A.H.   91
Gordon   147
Gracián, B.   282
Gracyk, T.   18, 148
Green, T.H. and T.H. Grose   4, 53, 69, 110
Grimm, R.   222
Gunn, J.A.W.   180
Gurstein, R.   87f, 90
Guyer, P.   18, 78, 89, 250, 256

Hamlet   73
Hanslick, E.   271
Harmon, A.M.   11
Hatab, L.   218
Hearn, T.   81
Hegel, G.W.F.   214, 233
Heidegger, M.   3, 8, 236, 273
Helm, B.   79, 88
Hemingway, E.   16
Henderson, J.   11
Heraclitus   234
Hercules, Herakles   8
Herdt, J.   283
Hermes   8–10, 221, 276
Hesiod   217, 219

Hirschman, A.   181
History of England   77, 146, 220
History of Scotland   146
Hobbes, T.   177, 182f, 185, 187f, 284f, 287, 296
Hokaibo   73
Hölderlin, F.   8, 218, 272f
Hollis, J. and Mattes, R.   228
Home, J.   4, 18, 64f, 68, 147, 193–195, 237
Homer   13, 26, 29, 38, 56, 59, 78, 154f, 157f, 160, 172, 213f, 216–221, 237–240, 264–266, 268, 275
Horace   37, 57
Horne, T.A.   192
Hume, J. (John Home, Lord of Ninewells)   105f.
Hunter, J.   6
Hutcheson, F.   17, 43, 151–153, 162, 173, 182, 184, 186, 192–195, 199, 201, 203, 210, 250, 284, 286, 290–295

Iliad   13, 157, 268
Irene   147

Janko, R.   219
Jarvis/Jarvas, C.   14, 53
Jewel   265
Johnson, S.   147, 165
Jones, P.   50, 53, 65, 148, 250, 253, 255, 257, 260
Jost, J. S. and J. Immerwahr,   4f, 18

Kahn, Ch.   219
Kail, P.   222
Kames, Lord, [Henry Home]   4, 62, 182, 185, 193–199, 203
Kandinsky, W.   272
Kant, I.   16, 18, 44, 49, 78, 91, 109, 154, 157, 177, 179, 184, 191, 193f, 199f, 214, 221–224, 233, 235f, 241, 249, 251, 256–259, 283
Keats, J.   272
Kieran, M.   91
King, S.   8, 37, 150, 181, 196
King Lear   74
Kittler, F.   230
Kivy, P.   17, 43, 52, 90, 149, 158f

Klee, P.   272
Koran   56, 155
Korsmeyer, C.   14, 18, 97, 99, 113, 148
Krieger, L.   9, 181
Kripke, S.   119
Kulenkampff, J.   18, 78
Kulmbacher   235

La Rochefoucauld, F.   281
Laird, J.   89
Lang, B.   9, 216, 235
Late Quartets   124–126
Laurentian Library   74–75
Le Doeuff, M.   100
Le Mariage de Figaro   73
Le Roux, F.   8
Lehmann, W. C.   193
Leibniz, G.   184, 250
Leiter, B.   216
Lenz, J. W.   19
Lingis, A.   230
Liszt, F.   271
Livingston, D. W.   98
Locke, J.   178f, 182, 184f, 187, 222, 282, 286, 293, 295–297
Löw, R.   222
Lucian of Samosata   5, 6, 7, 11, 12, 13, 17, 221, 238
Ludovici, A.   214
Lycidas   12

Mabille, L.   214
Mach, E.   224, 233
MacIntyre, A.   3, 19
MacLachlan, C.   17, 53, 66, 78
MacMillan, C.   88
Madame Bovary   71
Magic Flute, The   71
Malebranche, N.   294, 296f
Mandeville, B.   182–184, 191–193, 205, 282–284, 288, 291
Marshall, J.   87
Martin, M.A.   3, 7, 81, 219, 238, 273
Mauthner, F.   222
Mazza, E.   6f, 10, 18, 281, 283, 289
Megapenthes   10, 12
Mendelssohn, F.   271

Mensch, P.   234, 240
Michelangelo   74, 264
Mill, J.S.   100
Millar, A.   4, 14, 25
Miller, D.   77, 117, 201, 222, 240
Miller, J.   77, 117, 201, 222, 240
Milton, J.   12f, 16, 27, 44, 84, 90, 98, 118, 143, 152, 160, 164, 171, 213, 237, 275
Moleshott, J.   234
Montaigne, M. de   281f, 288
Moore, G.   230
Mossner, E.C.   3, 18, 64, 102, 291
Mothersill, M.   17, 78, 148
Motteux, P. A.   53
Mozart, W. A.   72, 264
Mucha, A.   67
Mycillus   10, 12

Nehamas, A.   215
Newton, I.   153, 251, 285
Nietzsche, F.   12, 213–225, 229–233, 235–237, 240f, 286
Noxon, J.   46

Oakeshott, M.   81f
Odysseus   154f, 157, 238
Odyssey   13, 238, 240, 275f
Ogilby, J.   13, 16, 27, 44, 84, 90, 118, 143, 152, 160, 171, 237
Ogmios,   8
Ortona, E.   231
Osborne, C. R. see Rowan, C.
Osborne, H.   88
Othello   276f
Ovid   37, 57, 108, 274

Paganini, N.   264
Palamedes   59, 289
Pamela   99, 106, 240
Parkes, G.   230
Parmenides   224
Parsifal   73
Parthenon   74
Passmore, J.   79
Patterson, J.   265
Philo   220, 289
Pindar   234

Pisistratus   219
Plato   13, 68, 110, 217, 220, 264f, 270f
Pocock, J.G.A.   180, 191
Poellner, P.   222
Pohl, R.   271f.
Pope, A.   160, 284
Popkin, R.   3
Price, J.V.   15, 100, 149, 182
Pride and Prejudice   103

Rand, B.   185
Raphael   164f
Rasmussen, D.C.   17
Reid, T.   168, 288, 293, 295–297
Relihan, J. C.   7
Rembrandt   90
Reynolds, Sir J.   62, 160
Richardson, S.   99
Richter, R.   222
Rickert, H.   3
Ritschl, F.   219, 221
Robertson, W.   146, 250
Robinson, C.   7
Roelofs, M.   14
Rose, M. C.   64
Rose, W.   71, 215, 287
Ross, S.   89
Rousseau, J.J.   17, 146, 216, 282
Rowan, C.   219
Rowling, J.K.   16

Salieri, A.   264
Sancho Panza   14, 53, 61, 79, 85, 88–89, 123, 125, 161, 162, 163, 236, 254–255, 267–268
Sartre, J.-P.   16
Savile, A.   156f
Sayre-McCord, G.   88
Schaeffer, J. S.   236
Schiller, F.   13, 235
Schiperges, H.   230
Schlaffer, H.   216
Schmidt, C.   87
Schopenhauer, A.   233
Schulz, S.   17
Scott, Sir W.   17, 65
Scruton, R.   14, 17, 67, 72, 75, 238

Seneca 234
Shaftesbury, A. A. C.   133, 135, 146, 149,
    173, 182, 184–193, 196, 199, 201, 203,
    205, 210, 282, 284
Shakespeare, W.   3, 13, 18, 220, 236 f, 252,
    264, 275–277
Shapin, S.   18, 219, 239
Shapiro, G.   230
Shelley, J.   87, 89, 91, 149, 156, 170
Shelton, T.   14
Shiner, R.   14, 17, 87, 117, 124, 148 f
Shusterman, R.   78, 109
Simoni, M. L. B. see Michelangelo
Sistine Chapel   73
Sloterdijk, P.   230
Smith, A.   4–8, 10–13, 17, 50, 183–185,
    191–194, 202–204, 206, 210, 228, 250,
    282
Smollett, T.   14
Socrates   230, 268, 270 f, 274–276
Sophocles   273
Steele, D.   67
Steinrück, M.   238
Sterne, L.   146
Stevenson, C.L.   50 f
Stewart, J. B.   89
Stolnitz, J.   188
Stoutland, F.   118
Strahan, W.   4, 10
Strauss, L.   3
Strong, T. B.   216
Stubbs horse paintings   164, 165
Sverdlik, S,   78, 88
Sweeney, K.   137
Swift, J.   11, 282 f
Symposium   66, 110, 276

Tacitus   57, 108
Taylor, W.L.   17, 174, 250
Tchaikovsky, P. I.   74
Telemachus   157
Teneriffe   27, 44, 98
Terence   36 f, 264

Tertullian   234
Thausing, M.   9
Theocles   189
Tiresias   275
Toland, J.   186
Townsend, D.   14, 18, 79, 123, 133, 174,
    264 f
Tuncel, Y.   218
Turco, L.   294

Vaihinger, H.   222
Van Gogh, V.   90, 272
Vanterpool, R. V.   81
Verlaine, P.   74
Verres   277
Vink, T.   15
Virgil   36, 264
Voltaire,   250, 282

Wagner, R.   220, 271
Wahl, W.   234
Warburton, N.   17
Warburton, W.   3, 18, 216, 220, 237, 241,
    284
Watson, R.   227–229
Whistler, J.   69 f
Wieand, J.   78, 87, 149, 155 f
Wilamowitz-Möllendorff, U. von   241
Wilkie, W.   64
William III   180
Williams, C.   79, 231
Wilson, E.   13, 240
Winckelmann, J. J.   235
Wittgenstein, L.   70, 152, 159
Wolf, F. A.   219, 250
Wollaston, W.   286, 288
Wollstonecraft, M.   100
Wood, Paul B.   295–297
Woodmansee, M.   146

Zaretsky, R. and J. T. Scott   17
Zeus   276

www.ingramcontent.com/pod-product-compliance
Lightning Source LLC
Chambersburg PA
CBHW071954220426
43662CB00009B/1131